# THE LETTER-JOURNAL OF
# GEORGE CANNING,
## 1793–1795

# THE LETTER-JOURNAL OF GEORGE CANNING, 1793–1795

edited by
PETER JUPP

CAMDEN FOURTH SERIES
VOLUME 41

LONDON
OFFICES OF THE ROYAL HISTORICAL
SOCIETY
UNIVERSITY COLLEGE LONDON
GOWER STREET WC1E 6BT
1991

**British Library Cataloguing in Publication Data**
Canning, George *1770–1827*
The letter-journal of George Canning, 1793–1795.
 1. Great Britain. Politics, history. Canning, George 1770–1827.
 I. Title   II. Jupp, Peter
 941.073092

 ISBN 0–86193–126–2

Printed and bound in Great Britain by
Butler & Tanner Ltd, Frome and London

# CONTENTS

# PREFACE

My first acknowledgement is to the Earl of Harewood for his generous permission to edit the letter-journal.

The staff of the Leeds District Archives, where the manuscript is kept as part of the George Canning papers, were very helpful in assisting me with its transcription and with other enquiries, particularly the District Archivist, W.J. Connor.

I would also like to thank those historians who have helped by answering awkward questions, particularly Mr. R.G. Thorne of the History of Parliament Trust; and to record a special debt of gratitude to my literary editors, Dr. Colin Matthew and Dr. John Ramsden for their encouragement and advice.

# EDITORIAL NOTE

The text has been transcribed from the original manuscript in the Canning collection in the Leeds District Archives, Chapeltown Road, Sheepscar, Leeds. The manuscript takes the form of sheets of paper of about $12\frac{1}{2}''$ by $7\frac{1}{2}''$ containing the text on both sides which were subsequently arranged and bound in date order, with the exception of the entries for 14–18 February 1794 which are inserted between 31 January and 2 February 1794. The journal has been known to specialists for some considerable time. The first historian to make extensive use of it, often in the form of long quotations, was Dorothy Marshall in her chapters on Canning's career between 1793–95 in *The Rise of George Canning* published in 1938. In addition, Professor Aspinall published short extracts of general political interest in two articles for the *New English Review* under the title 'George Canning as a Back Bencher' in 1946. However Marshall and Aspinall together published only a fifth of the journal which has meant that its full import as both a vivid record of parliamentary politics in the 1790s and a revealing portrait of Canning has been unavailable to the general reader. It is this lacuna that this edition is designed to remedy.

With regard to editorial policy, the main problem was that although Canning's handwriting is exceptionally clear and consistent, he rarely paragraphed entries for individual days and employed a form of grammar and abbreviation that could on occasion confuse the modern reader. Paragraphs have therefore been introduced and punctuation and capitalization have been modernised, although in the case of paragraphing and punctuation, this has been done in such a way as to retain as much of the pace of the original narrative as possible. In the case of Canning's abbreviations, these have been expanded where there might be any doubt as to their meaning.

In annotating the text the following rules have been applied: titled persons have generally not been given dates of birth and death or any career outline unless such information is essential to a full understanding of the text; non-titled persons have been given dates of birth and death where this was possible, together with any parliamentary seats or offices held during the period of the journal; a person identified in these ways once is not so identified again, unless such information amplifies the meaning of the text. With regard to Canning's numerous relations, the evidence that establishes their place in family trees can be found in the Canning and Patrick genealogies.

# ABBREVIATIONS

| | |
|---|---|
| Add. MSS | Additional Manuscripts in the British Library |
| *Bagot* | J. Bagot, *George Canning and his Friends*, (London, 2 vols. 1909) |
| Canning MSS and Canning MSS (Adnl) | Leeds District Archives, Chapeltown Road, Sheepscar, Leeds |
| *Dixon* | P. Dixon, *Canning* (London, 1976) |
| *Hinde* | W. Hinde, *George Canning*, (London, 1973) |
| *Marshall* | D. Marshall, *The Rise of George Canning*, (London, 1938) |
| *NER* | A. Aspinall, 'George Canning as a Back Bencher' pts. 1 and 2 in *New English Review*, vol. xii (1946), 452–59, 528–36 |
| *Parl. Hist.* | *The Parliamentary History of England from the earliest period to 1803* |
| *Parl. Reg.* | *The Parliamentary Register*, printed for J. Debrett 2nd series |
| P.R.O. | Public Record Office |
| *Thorne* | R.G. Thorne, *The House of Commons 1790–1820*, 5 vols. (London 1986) |
| *The Commons' Journal* | *The Journals of the House of Commons* |
| *The Senator* | *The Senator; or Clarendon's Parliamentary Chronicle*, printed for C. Cooke, 1st series |
| *Woodfall* | *An Impartial Report of the Debates . . .*, by W. Woodfall |

# INTRODUCTION

Canning began this letter-journal, principally to his uncle and aunt, the Rev. William and Elizabeth Leigh, when he was 23 and shortly before he took his seat as M.P. for Newtown in the Isle of Wight. Already highly regarded by such a diverse group of political leaders as Fox, Sheridan, the Duke of Portland, and Pitt, his parliamentary debut was eagerly awaited.[1] The injunction on the Leighs and the other intended recipients never to divulge any sensitive political comment in the journal suggests that Canning anticipated that in due course, he would be a politician of significance both to his contemporaries and to posterity.[2]

His early childhood had provided few grounds for such expectations. His father, George Canning, was the eldest son and heir of an Anglo-Irish country gentleman with an estate at Garvagh, co. Londonderry. In Ireland he earned his irascible father's disfavour by a combination of his politics and his female attachments and went to London under a cloud with an income of only £150 p.a. There, in the late 1750s and early '60s, he increased his father's ire by dabbling in writing and befriending Wilkes, and was eventually forced to alienate his inheritance in return for the payment of his debts, the estate at Garvagh passing eventually to his brother, Paul. In 1768 he married Mary Ann Costello, the penniless daughter of a Connaught squire but died in 1771, a year after Canning's birth. His mother subsequently embarked on a career as an actress and within a few years was living with a well known actor, singer and manager, Samuel Reddish, by whom she had five children – twins who died young, two boys, Samuel and Charles, and the latter's twin sister. Reddish's

---

[1] The outline of C.'s early life that follows is based on the following biographies: A.G. Stapleton, *The Political Life of the Rt. Hon. George Canning.* (3 vols., London, 1831); R. Bell, *The Life of the Rt. Hon. George Canning,* (London, 1846); A.G. Stapleton, *George Canning and His Times,* (London, 1859); H.W.V. Temperley, *George Canning,* (London, 1905); J. Bagot, *George Canning and his Friends,* (2 vols., London, 1909); Sir C. Petrie, *George Canning.* (London, 1930); D. Marshall, *The Rise of George Canning,* (London, 1938); P.J.V. Rolo, *George Canning,* (London, 1965); W. Hinde, *George Canning,* (London, 1973), P. Dixon, *Canning,* (London, 1976) and R.G. Thorne, *The House of Commons 1790–1820,* (5 vols., London, 1986), iii, 378–404. Amendments and additions to the facts presented there are indicated in the footnotes. For the expectations of his parliamentary debut see the leading article, 'Theatre de la Nation' in the *Morning Chronicle,* 20 Jan. 1794
[2] Letter-journal, 23

distinguished career came to an end in 1778 and he died in tragic circumstances in York Asylum in 1785. However, by that time Mrs Canning had left Reddish to marry Richard Hunn, a silk-mercer from Plymouth by whom she bore five more children, including a third set of twins. In keeping with his mother's misfortune this relationship also came to a sorry end, the two being virtually separated by the time that Canning began this journal.

These events cast a long shadow over Canning's childhood and his subsequent career. In particular, they were to lead to taunts of his social inferiority as the son of an actress and of therefore being unfit for the highest political offices. When writing this journal Canning was well aware of the threats to his standing in society and to his political career that his mother's past and continuing career on the stage posed. In 1791 he pointed out to his mother the low status of the stage and attributed Sheridan's 'want of success, and of popularity' to the connection; and on one occasion during the period of this journal declined to visit the west country for fear of her visiting him when he was in the company of the well-born.[3] On the other hand the journal provides abundant evidence that privately Canning treated all her connections – her sister and mother and her children by Reddish and by Hunn – as well as herself, to whom he wrote frequently, with considerable understanding and kindness.

His prospects were altered completely by the interventions of his uncle, Stratford Canning, and later, the Leighs. It was Stratford Canning, a partner with a fellow Irishman, Walter Borrowes, in a London firm of merchants, who became his guardian following his father's death and made arrangements for his education. He subsequently dispatched him to Hyde Abbey School in Winchester, to Eton, and with particular enthusiasm, to Christ Church, Oxford. In addition, he played a role in ensuring that the customs of inheritance were not completely overturned by the rift between his father and his brother. Canning, who went to Ireland for the first and only time in 1785, therefore inherited a life interest in a small estate of approximately 250 acres at Kilbraghan, co. Kilkenny worth £220 p.a.; and by the terms of his grandmother's will, some £3000 invested in the Irish funds when he came of age.[4]

The guardianship had other results. Stratford Canning and his wife, Mehitabel or 'Hetty', the daughter of Robert Patrick of Somerville, co. Dublin, were friends and partisans of several leading Rockingham whigs, including Fox and Sheridan and the redoubtable hostess, Mrs

[3] Canning MSS (2), Canning to his mother, 13 June 1791; Letter-Journal, 230–1
[4] Canning MSS (12), Canning to the Rev. William Leigh, 28 May 1791; (141), maps of the Kilbraghan estate, 1785, 1796

Crewe.[5] Canning therefore met them at an early age, and even after Stratford's guardianship ceased with his death in 1787, the connection was maintained through Hetty, a close friend of Sheridan and a fierce supporter of the Opposition Whig cause. Hetty's villa at Wanstead was a frequent port of call during the period covered by the journal and it was there that he kept in touch with Hetty's five children, and with her sister, Elizabeth, and her three brothers and their children – a grand total in 1794 of twenty-one Patricks. Given that all his aunts and uncles married Irish men or women, and that the Patricks were themselves Irish and introduced him to the Irish merchant community in London, the journal provides evidence of a more significant Irish dimension to Canning's early years than is sometimes realised.

Following Stratford's death in 1787, Walter Borrowes became his financial guardian but his care passed into the hands of a Norfolk parson, the Rev. William Leigh, who became the second husband of his aunt, Jane Elizabeth Canning, when Canning was at Eton. The Leighs appear to have been sociable and kindly and were able to provide a home that proved an acceptable substitute to that of his mother,[6] William Leigh in particular travelled regularly to London and to Bath and was known to as disparate a group of friends as the Bishop of Lincoln, the Lichfield set of Dr Erasmus Darwin and Richard Lovell Edgeworth, and Elizabeth Linley, the noted singer who became Sheridan's first wife.[7] In addition, they surrounded themselves with an extended family which in addition to their own daughters, Elizabeth or 'Bessy' and Frances Harriet or 'Fanny', included Elizabeth's sister, Frances or 'Fan', her son and daughter by her first marriage, Westby and Letitia Perceval or 'Tish', as well as Canning, who customarily passed his school and college vacations with them. They also seem to have been moderately wealthy, possibly as a result of Leigh's lime-kiln interests in his native county of Staffordshire.[8] He was certainly able to provide Canning with his electoral qualification in 1793[9] and was also able to foresake his clerical residence in Norwich and take a lease on Ashbourne Hall, near Derby, the substantial seat

---

[5] It is clear from the correspondence to be found in the Canning MSS (Adnl), (6) and (7) between Mehitabel Canning and her daughter, Elizabeth, that the Cannings and the Patricks were long-standing friends of the Crewes and Mrs Crewe's brother, Charles Greville. See also on this point Canning MSS (Adnl) (5), Canning to Frances Canning, 8 Aug. 1790

[6] For praise of the Leighs see Canning MSS (Adnl), (6), Mehitabel Canning to Elizabeth Canning, 7 June 1792

[7] C. Price (ed), *The Letters of Richard Brinsley Sheridan*, (3 vols., Oxford, 1966), i, 249, n. 4

[8] Canning MSS (Adnl), (6), Mehitabel Canning to Elizabeth Canning, 19 June [1792]

[9] Canning MSS (12), Canning to Rev. William Leigh, 22, 28 June 1793

of Sir Brooke Boothby. It was from Ashbourne that Canning travelled to London to prepare for the parliamentary season; and it was to Ashbourne that the letter-journal was sent.

It was Canning's education at Eton and Christ Church which initiated life-long friendships outside family circles and led to attainments that laid the basis of his success in later life. At Eton his closest, and most enduring, friends were John Hookham Frere, John 'Easly' Smith, Lord Henry Spencer, Thomas Wallace, Robert Percy 'Bobus' Smith, and Lord Morpeth, all mentioned frequently in the journal and all to have significant careers in public life. It was chiefly with Frere and the two Smiths that Canning produced between 1786–87, the *Microcosm*, a regular magazine containing humorous and satirical pieces on moral and literary subjects. Such was its quality that it attracted widespread notice outside the College. By the tenth number it was selling some 700 copies and buoyed up no doubt by Canning's subsequent political fame, passed through five editions by 1825. Later he crowned a distinguished academic career there by speaking last on Election Day. The prominent role that Eton possessed in the life of the elite was such that these activities and accomplishments laid the basis for his reputation within it. As Canning records in the journal, when he met the King and the Queen on the terrace at Windsor in 1794, they immediately remembered him by his association with Eton and the *Microcosm*.[9] In the following year Lord Porchester took a party of Etonians to meet him, presumably because he was one of the most promising 'old boys' and an ideal exemplar.[10]

At Christ Church he built on these foundations. There, under the watchful and admiring eye of the Dean, Dr Cyril Jackson, his conversation and intellect made him the centre of a circle of friends, many of whom were members of highly influential families and some of whom were to form the nucleus of Canning's personal political following in the early nineteenth-century. Chief amongst them, and frequently mentioned in the journal, were Robert Banks Jenkinson, the son of the President of the Board of Trade and the future prime minister, Lord Liverpool; Fox's nephew, Lord Holland; Lord Boringdon; Lord Granville Leveson Gower, a son of the Marquess of Stafford, the Lord Privy Seal; Edward Wilbraham Bootle; William Ralph Cartwright; Charles George Beauclerk; Charles Rose Ellis; John Henry Newbolt; William Sturges Bourne; Osborne Markham, a son of the Archbishop of York; and Charles Moore, a son of the Archbishop of Canterbury. In addition, he distinguished himself in the intellectual and academic life of the College. In the company of

[9] Letter-journal, 137
[10] Letter-journal, 209

five others, he instigated an exclusive debating club and at its meetings, which were dedicated ecumenically to the styles of Cicero, Demosthenes, Pitt and Fox, he established a reputation as a skilled debater. In his second year he won the Chancellor's Medal and a college prize for latin verses. In his third, in 1790, he was elected to a Studentship. On leaving Oxford Canning took up residence in London to study law at Lincoln's Inn where he had enrolled in 1787. His friends and accomplishments at Eton and Oxford had already led to introductions to circles beyond those provided by the Patricks and the Leighs, such as that of the powerful Gower family, supporters of Pitt; and in London he built on these foundations. Gradually his enthusiasm for the law was superseded by political ambitions. In view of his early contacts with Fox and Sheridan and his reputation for possessing anti-aristocratic and even republican sentiments, there was some expectation, particularly on the part of Hetty Canning, that he would enlist with the Opposition Whigs.[11] However, the bloody course taken by the French Revolution, the support given to popular radicalism by the Foxite section of that party and a degree of calculation, possibly, about the way the political wind was blowing, drew him in the opposite direction.[12] In the summer of 1792 he sought, and was granted, an interview with Pitt, the grounds for which were probably carefully laid by friends of both parties. At this Canning made it clear that he wished to enter Parliament as the prime minister's protégé; and Pitt volunteered to make a seat available at the first opportunity.[13] Following this agreement Canning became well known to some of Pitt's closest friends such as Pepper Arden and Lord Mornington[14] and having turned down a seat in the gift of the titular head of the Opposition Whigs, the Duke of Portland, in the Spring of 1793,[15] he was returned for Newtown at Pitt's instigation on 28 June of that year, a week after the close of the parliamentary session. He started his journal shortly after he had arrived in London to continue his studies at Lincoln's Inn and to prepare for taking his seat at the start of the new session.

   With hindsight the period covered by the journal, November 1793 to July 1795, was a watershed in the history of Pitt's first administration. The turning point was Britain's entry into the European

[11] Canning MSS (64), Lord Morpeth to Canning, n.d. but c.1793–94
[12] P.R.O. Chatham MSS, 30/8/120, f. 122, Canning to T. Wallace, 15 Mar. 1793
[13] *Thorne*, op. cit., iii, 379
[14] Letter-journal, 28–9; Canning MSS (Adnl), (5), C. to Frances Canning, 28 Sept. 1790
[15] P.R.O. Chatham MSS, 30/8/120, f. 122, Canning to T. Wallace, 15 Mar. 1793

war in February 1793. The government's initial hope was that the weight of the professional armies of Austria and Prussia, when combined with British naval and economic power, would soon overcome French republican forces. The reverse was the case. During 1793–95, the loosely allied forces of the First Coalition were forced to retreat from Toulon and Flanders; and were unable to prevent the occupation of the Austrian Netherlands and Holland. Moreover the Coalition was weakened fatally in the spring of 1795 when Prussia and France negotiated a separate peace at Basle. The only British success was in the West Indies where several French islands were captured. By the summer of 1795 the government's policy was directed more to the prospect of a long war which could only be won by an effective allied coalition acting principally on the European mainland. This, in essence, was the policy of all governments until success was achieved in 1815.

The war brought into sharper focus the questions of French revolutionary principles and the responses to them in Britain. Ministers had already taken measures to contain the growth of a more radical movement for Parliamentary reform, inspired by the Revolution and Thomas Paine's *Rights of Man*, but these were intensified with the onset of war and the resort to more challenging methods of radical propaganda such as the British Convention of radicals in Edinburgh in November 1793 and the mass meeting sponsored by the London Corresponding Society at Chalk Farm on 14 April 1794. In May 1794 the government responded by arresting radical leaders such as Hardy, Horne Tooke and Thelwall, by setting up parliamentary committees of secrecy to examine papers confiscated from the radical societies, and by suspending Habeas Corpus. Although the subsequent trials of radicals failed to convict, the progress of radicalism was slowed. Moreover in December of the following year it was halted by the passage of the Treasonable Practices Act and the Seditious Meetings Act, devised in response to continuing spasms of radical feeling such as the London Corresponding Society's meeting at St. George's Fields on 29 June 1795. The 'war of principles', as some branded the European conflict, had been extended to Britain and was maintained until Waterloo, and indeed beyond.

The war in its various guises also had an enduring impact on party politics. When the government entered the war, Pitt's position was weaker than his new responsibilities demanded because his personal following was numerically much smaller than the party of Opposition Whigs led by the Duke of Portland and Fox. This weakness was lessened, however, during 1793 and the early months of 1794 when the Opposition split on the government's case for Britain's participation in the war: the Duke of Portland, William Windham, and nearly 80 followers in the Commons supported it; whereas Fox and his near 70 or so followers opposed, demanding that the government negotiate a peace.[16] Furthermore the weakness was virtually eliminated when Pitt negotiated a junction with Portland's followers in July 1794. From then until Pitt's resignation in January 1801, Fox's Opposition party was unable to offer an effective challenge to the ministry.

Although Canning touches on all these developments in his journal, he does so with more emphasis on description than reflection or analysis. This is to be expected, perhaps, in a journal written to entertain relations at some distance from the glittering world he was entering. It is nevertheless the case that it is in its vivid descriptions of the leading persons and concerns of that world rather than in its speculative comment that the primary merit of the journal lies. In this regard it has few contemporary parallels.

For example, a particularly interesting portrait of Pitt emerges from these pages. The prime minister was anxious to recruit young men of talent and proven debating skill to strengthen his war time administration. Canning suited admirably, especially as he had rejected the advances of his family connections and admirers among the Opposition and made his devotion to Pitt crystal clear by accepting a seat in his gift. What is striking, however, are the lengths to which Pitt went to sponsor his new recruit's progress in politics. At the personal level, for example, the prime minister went out of his way to demonstrate his friendship. He was 'open, free, ready to answer questions without reserve' Canning recorded on one occasion;[17] and on another, that contrary to the image he sometimes presented to the world, he was 'a very hearty, *salutation-giving, shake-handy* sort of person',[18] As for guidance and encouragement on specific aspects of parliamentary life, Pitt could not have been more helpful. There are numerous examples of his inviting Canning to private dinners with senior members of the administration; of his conversing privately with him prior to debates and briefing him on his own opinions and those of the cabinet; and of providing him with special opportunities to shine, the most outstanding of which was to second the Address in December 1794. Finally, Pitt offered sage advice on how Canning's future career might be best developed: in particular, by encouraging him in his own wish to aspire to a post to which the Commons might feel him best suited.[19]

[16] *Thorne*, op. cit., i, 131–38
[17] Letter-journal, 150
[18] Letter-journal, 169
[19] Letter-journal, 272–73

Overall the journal provides one of the clearest insights we have of Pitt's private demeanour and of the ways he brought on his friends and his protégés. It also provides some justification for Frere's later judgement that 'Pitt's feeling for him was more that of a father than of a mere political leader. I am sure that from the first Pitt marked Canning out as his political heir, and had in addition the warmest personal regard for him'.[20] The journal also throws important light on Pitt's methods of doing business. Of particular significance are the details Canning provides of different kinds of dinner parties and of those who attended them. One such was the formal dinner for those privy councillors and office holders in the Commons prior to the debate on the Address.[21] Another, more regular, kind was for members of the administration most vitally concerned with topics of debate in Parliament.[22] Yet another was very informal and was open to any of Pitt's friends who happened to be available. Canning clearly felt that these occasions were very important to the morale of the upper reaches of the government. He was therefore critical of Pitt for apparently reducing the number of formal dinners for important members of the government during the first six months of 1795.[23] Taken in conjunction with other evidence here and elsewhere, the journal suggests a complex and informal method of doing business, with Pitt alone as the nerve-centre.

The journal also brings the House of Commons to life just at the time when Hickel was completing his famous picture of it. In fact in one respect Canning's version is a mirror of Hickel's; both convey the general impression of the Commons being a form of theatre dominated by a few great issues and a few great performers. He therefore records how the House filled to hear the tyros of debate on the subjects of war and peace but grew irritable and thin when they had said their pieces or when topics of lesser interest came on.[24] Canning himself recognised that on some occasions the House resembled more of a 'spectacle' than a deliberative assembly. Yet he was also aware that these mores made the House more, rather than less, difficult to master. He consequently put considerable preparation into the five major speeches which are recorded in the journal and although they were judged a success overall, he was initially found wanting in several respects: in his too energetic physical gestures; in the excessive speed of his delivery; in his predilection for wit and humour at the expense of more seasoned members; and when not actually speaking, his over-familiarity with

[20] Quoted in *Thorne*, op. cit., iii, 380
[21] Letter-journal, 46, 173
[22] Letter-journal, 194–195
[23] Letter-journal, 278
[24] Letter-journal, 278

members of the front bench.[25] Later he made efforts to reform in these respects. A form of theatre it may have been, but it was one in which reputations were not easily made.

Even more prominently portrayed than the House of Commons is the social life that accompanied the parliamentary season. As has been noted Canning was exceptionally well-endowed with overlapping circles of friends and acquaintances before he took his seat. What is revealed here in vivid detail are the practical effects of maintaining his position in those circles once they converged on London; and of establishing and maintaining a place in the other circles that sprang to life once the King's Speech had been read. His normal daily progress was therefore punctuated by a rich assortment of social engagements; breakfast with Frere or, on Saturdays, with a cast of many at Mrs Crewe's regular gatherings; frequent visits to either of the two principal Law Clubs, to White's or to the trial of Warren Hastings; dinner with the Markhams, the Moores, the Gowers, the Ellis's, or other members of the Christ Church set; evening gatherings at Lady Payne's or at Lady Jane Dundas's, where she was 'at home' on Mondays and Fridays; plays at Covent Garden or Drury Lane; and late suppers at a coffee house or a friend's abode. Such was Canning's normal daily routine in *addition* to his parliamentary activities. It was therefore with an almost audible sigh of relief that he retired to the Gowers' villa at Wimbledon for the odd weekend, or retreated to the quiet of Eton or Oxford for the recesses.

Above all the journal reveals a great deal about Canning – a politician who, apart from obtaining the highest offices, had an extraordinary impact on the politics of his own lifetime and well beyond. Perhaps the most striking conclusion to be drawn from these pages is that he was a man of strong emotions and preferences with regard to others. In the case of his family the writing of the journal is in itself an outstanding illustration of the affection he felt for the Leighs. Amongst its pages there are numerous indications of the warmth of his feelings for other relations and his generosity with regard to the time and attention he devoted to their needs. Notable examples are the steps he took to give financial and other assistance to his mother and some of her children by Reddish and Hunn; and his fondness for his cousins, especially Mrs Leigh's daughter, 'Bessy'.

Even more striking is the evidence of the warmth of Canning's feelings for his Eton and Christ Church friends. Strong individual friendships with school and college friends is, of course, not surprising: Canning was fatherless and separated from his mother; Eton and Christ Church encouraged close ties of friendship; and Canning

[25] Letter-journal, 168–69, 175; Canning MSS, (12), C. to Mrs Leigh, 4 Jan. 1795

himself was given to an almost romantic admiration for the directness of the young by comparison with the old.[26] What is striking, however, is the importance Canning placed on the continuing social and political harmony of the 'microcosmopolitans' and the Christ Church set. Notable examples are his attempts to mend relations with Jenkinson, broken temporarily by the latter's reaction to a practical joke at his expense; and the steps he took to convince Boringdon of the merits of Pitt's war policy.[27] Canning's propensity for a 'little senate' of his own seemed to have emotional as well as political roots.

In the case of women, the journal provides no clues of any serious romantic attachments but does underline that fact that he enjoyed their company. The warmth of his feelings for the female members of his family, all of whom he addressed with affectionate nick-names, has already been noted; and so too should be the evidence of his undisguised admiration for two slightly older married women, Lady Sutherland and Lady Elizabeth Monk.

On the other hand, there was a cooler, less tolerant, dimension to Canning's character. Thus although he mixed easily amongst all sorts and degrees, he confessed he cared little for those outside his immediate circle and positively disliked being in the company of strangers.[28] Moreover he nursed strong prejudices: for example, against balls and masquerades; against 'buckism' – the ethos of the duelling, hunting and riding brigade;[29] and against female politicians who, following Dr Johnson, he described as like dogs walking on hind legs.[30] This other aspect of his personality explains why, in addition to so much affection and loyalty, he engendered equal measures of dislike and mistrust within the political world.

With regard to Canning's politics, the journal is illuminating on several fronts. For example, it suggests that the figure he presented to the outside world was individualistic, precocious and spontaneous. Observers would therefore have noted that he made no secret of his friendly relations with Fox and Sheridan as well as with Pitt, and socialised with members of all parties[31]; that he treated Pitt and his front bench colleagues with open familiarity[32], on one occasion taking it upon himself to explain Pitt's absence to the House;[33] and that at a

[26] Letter-journal, 131
[27] Letter-journal, 168, 184–91
[28] Letter-journal, 117, 171
[29] Letter-journal, 51, 250; Canning MSS (64), Lord Morpeth to Canning, 14 Jan. 1789
[30] Letter-journal, 284
[31] Letter-journal, 82–3, 94, 104
[32] Letter-journal, 168–69
[33] Letter-journal, 102–3

later date he was to be seen lounging in the public gallery poking fun at a procession of rarely-heard speakers delivering set pieces on the Prince of Wales's debts.[34] Yet this aspect of his political style was not worn lightly. Below the surface Canning clearly found parliamentary life a considerable strain and on occasion sought solace in the company and political unanimity of his college friends. Thus he fell seriously ill with what appears to have been nervous exhaustion following his initial engagements in the House and later made it clear to his Christ Church friends – Jenkinson, Wallace, Boringdon, Morpeth, Ellis and Gower – that their acting together politically was essential to his peace of mind.[35]

In the case of his qualities as a debater – the role for which Pitt had returned him to Parliament – the journal is helpful but requires amplification from other sources. It certainly provides ample evidence that he took great pains to prepare himself thoroughly. In his maiden speech he surprised Pitt by the parallel he drew between the Anglo-Prussian subsidy of 1758 and that with Sardinia which was under discussion[36] and all his other major interventions were preceded by study, by briefings from Pitt and by conversations with friends and colleagues. It is an indication of the seriousness with which Canning approached the art of debate that he declined to speak on the Bill enlisting French and other continental emigrants into the Army on the ground that he was unfamiliar with the subject.[37]

With regard to the content of his speeches, the journal together with the various contemporary records demonstrate that all his major interventions were in defence of the government's war policy. Moreover they reveal a consistent, if conventional, line of argument: first, that the government was right to resist the aggressive aims of a destructive Republican ideology both abroad and at home; second, that it was correct in its policy of acting with allies until such time as a regime was established in France which could negotiate a secure and lasting peace; and third, that the war necessitated extraordinary measures at home, such as the suspension of Habeas Corpus. He therefore served Pitt well and in June 1795 received the prime minister's accolade that apart from the three ministers in the House responsible for war policy – Dundas, Windham and Pitt himself – he had shone more on that subject than any other on the government side.[38]

Another consistent feature of his speeches was that they combined substantive arguments such as those adumbrated above with debating points, the most effective of which was to turn the arguments of

[34] Letter-journal, 261
[35] Letter-journal, 187
[36] Letter-journal, 45, 55–6
[37] Letter-journal, 81
[38] Letter-journal, 270–71

opponents against them. Notable examples are his jibe that members of the Opposition were prepared to subscribe funds to deliver Poland from the Russian and German yoke but not to secure the freedom of their own country;[39] that the Opposition's case that precedents of 1722 and 1777 justified giving more time before suspending Habeas Corpus was not applicable;[40] that its case that the war was a cause of political convulsion in France was true but for the good, in that Jacobinism had collapsed;[41] and that Fox's argument that the government, like Spain, should place a war-tax on offices and pensions would simply play into the hands of the rich and disadvantage the poor man of talent who might render the country essential service in its hour of need.[42] It was in this combination of considered argument and instantaneous riposte that Canning's merit as a debater lay. Moreover it was one he clearly sought to achieve for as he records, his objective was to be a 'useful' debater and not just a purveyor of opinion.[43]

However, being 'useful' in debate was just the first stage in Canning's ultimate objective of office – an objective dictated, he recorded, by a combination of the expectations of his Eton and Oxford friends and his need of additional income.[44] In June 1795 he had a long conversation with Pitt on the subject. He felt that he had spoken well on the *general* topics of war and peace but that his next objective was to acquire 'a sort of right and property' in a specific subject and so qualify himself in the opinion of the House for employment in that area. He had no wish, he remarked, to be regarded in the next session as a generalist looking for any available place. He mentioned the posts of chief secretary in Ireland and under-secretary in the Home Office as ones which appealed.[45]

These thoughts indicate Canning's growing maturity as a politician and his sensitivity to parliamentary opinion, Pitt was delighted with them and although he held out no hopes of a post in Ireland, he promised to investigate the situation in the Home Office.[46] By the time the journal ends, however, no opening had been found. Instead Canning had to wait until the following year when Pitt was able to persuade Lord Grenville to agree to his appointment as under-secretary in the Foreign Office. In view of the subjects of Canning's initial performances in Parliament, it was the appropriate choice.

---

[39] *Parl. Reg.* 2nd series, vol. 38, 125
[40] *Parl. Hist.*, vol. 31, col. 535
[41] *Parl. Hist.*, vol. 31, col. 1015
[42] *Parl. Hist.*, vol. 31, col. 1405–06
[43] Letter-journal, 56, 83
[44] Letter-journal, 272–73
[45] Letter-journal, 271, 273–75
[46] Letter-journal, 274–76

# GENEALOGIES

# PATRICK GENEALOGY

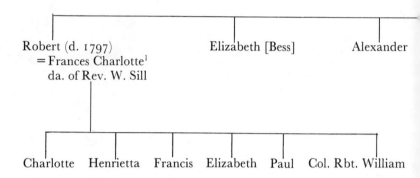

Robert (d. 1797)      Elizabeth [Bess]      Alexander
= Frances Charlotte[1]
da. of Rev. W. Sill

Charlotte  Henrietta  Francis  Elizabeth  Paul  Col. Rbt. William

[1] Canning MSS (Adnl), (15), a draft Patrick genealogy and a typescript memoir of
George Canning by the Rev. G.B. Hunt
[2] Canning MSS (Adnl), (7), Elizabeth Canning to her mother, Hetty, 9 May 1792
[3] *Letter-Journal*, 276
[4] For the names of Paul's children see Canning MSS (Adnl), (7), Elizabeth Canning
to her mother, Hetty, 9 May 1792

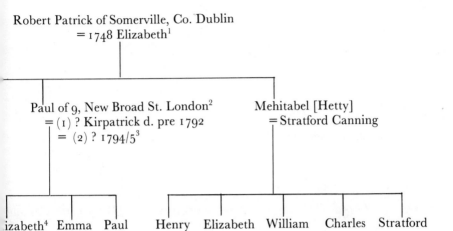

Robert Patrick of Somerville, Co. Dublin
= 1748 Elizabeth[1]

Paul of 9, New Broad St. London[2]     Mehitabel [Hetty]
= (1) ? Kirpatrick d. pre 1792          = Stratford Canning
= (2) ? 1794/5[3]

izabeth[4]  Emma  Paul     Henry  Elizabeth  William  Charles  Stratford

# CANNING GENEALOGY I

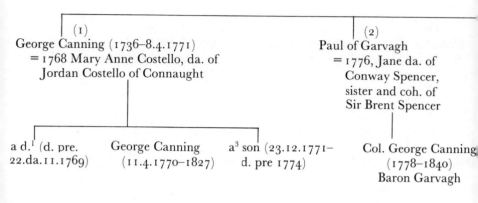

| (1) | (2) |
| George Canning (1736–8.4.1771)<br>= 1768 Mary Anne Costello, da. of<br>Jordan Costello of Connaught | Paul of Garvagh<br>= 1776, Jane da. of<br>Conway Spencer,<br>sister and coh. of<br>Sir Brent Spencer |

a d.[1] (d. pre.      George Canning      a[3] son (23.12.1771–            Col. George Canning
22.da.11.1769)        (11.4.1770–1827)    d. pre 1774)                    (1778–1840)
                                                                          Baron Garvagh

[1] For confirmation of the death of C.'s elder sister and the birth of a younger brother see Canning MSS (1), Stratford Canning to Mary Anne Canning, 22 Nov. 1769; and to John Beresford, 23 Dec. 1771
[2] For the approximate dates of birth of Stratford's children see Canning MSS (2), Canning to his mother, 15 Feb. 1784

ratford Canning of Garvagh, Co. Londonderry (1703–30.9.1775)
= Letitia, da. and sole h. of Obadiah Newburgh of Ballyhaise, Co. Cavan (d. 1786)

(3)
Stratford (d. May 1787)
= Mehitabel, da. of Robert Patrick [Hetty]
of Somerville, Co. Dublin

| enry[2] | Elizabeth | William | Charles Fox | Stratford |
|---|---|---|---|---|
| (8.7.74–) | (c. 1778– ) | (c. 1779– ) | (c. 1782– ) | (1786–1880) |
| | (b. c. 1778) | (b. c. 1779) | (b. c. 1782) | Viscount |
| | = M. G. H. | | | Stratford |
| | Barnett | | | de Redcliffe |
| Hal] | [Bessy] | [Willy] | | [Stratty] |
| r | or | | | |
| Harry] | [Bess] | | | |

# CANNING GENEALOGY II

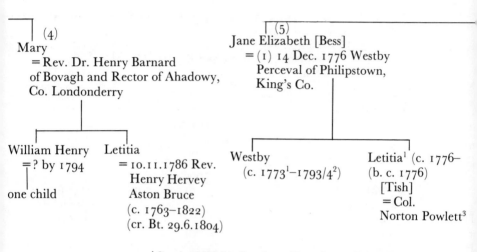

(4)
Mary
= Rev. Dr. Henry Barnard
of Bovagh and Rector of Ahadowy,
Co. Londonderry

(5)
Jane Elizabeth [Bess]
= (1) 14 Dec. 1776 Westby
Perceval of Philipstown,
King's Co.

William Henry
= ? by 1794
one child

Letitia
= 10.11.1786 Rev.
Henry Hervey
Aston Bruce
(c. 1763–1822)
(cr. Bt. 29.6.1804)

Westby
(c. 1773[1]–1793/4[2])

Letitia[1] (c. 1776–
(b. c. 1776)
[Tish]
= Col.
Norton Powlett[3]

[1] Canning MSS (2), Canning to his mother, 15 Feb. 1784
[2] Canning MSS (12), Canning to Rev. W. Leigh, 8, 28 Apr. 1794
[3] Canning MSS (13), Canning to Rev. W. Leigh, 20 Apr. 1795

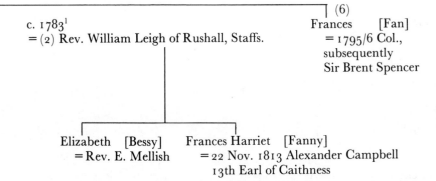

c. 1783[1]
= (2) Rev. William Leigh of Rushall, Staffs.

(6)
Frances     [Fan]
= 1795/6 Col.,
subsequently
Sir Brent Spencer

Elizabeth   [Bessy]
= Rev. E. Mellish

Frances Harriet   [Fanny]
= 22 Nov. 1813 Alexander Campbell
13th Earl of Caithness

# GEORGE CANNING'S LETTER-JOURNAL, 1793–1795

## GENERAL RULES

to be observed respecting this and other letters of a similar sort that may be sent to Ashborne[1] during the winter.

---

1st. That the *nature* and *intent* of the said letters be not talked of before any other than the family (that is to say, W[illiam] L[eigh] – E[lizabeth] L[eigh] – F[rances] [Canning] and L[etitia] P[erceval][2] – but if anything at all be said of a letter having come from George C[anning] (which must sometimes happen) before *strangers* – it must be said merely as of *a common ordinary* letter – not as of anything like a journal.

2nd. That they be never read *out* by or before any other persons than the four above-mentioned (Mrs. G. and the littler ones of course excepted)[3] – nor any part or parts of them read or quoted, without its being previously ascertained that the said letters, or the said part or parts of the said letters contain *only common ordinary* matters – not *names* or *characters* of *persons*, or anything relating to politicks (excepting of course the news of the day) – or to political plans and prospects.

[1] Ashbourne Hall, Ashbourne, Derbyshire, owned by Sir Brooke Boothby and rented at this time by C.'s guardian, the Rev. William Leigh, for whom see below n. 2

[2] 'W.L.' was the Rev. William Leigh (1752–1808), s. of John Burridge of Rushall Hall, Rushall, Staffs. Educ. Harrow, Trinity Coll. Camb., Corpus Christi, Oxf. Rector of Little Plumstead with Witton and Brundale annexed, Norfolk, 1779–1808 and installed dean of Hereford, Mar. 1808. He was the author of at least four published sermons, three being published in Bath. 'E.L.' and 'F.C.', sometimes referred to as 'Bess' and 'Fan' respectively, were his wife and sister in law, Jane Elizabeth and Frances Canning, das. of Stratford Canning (1703–75) and therefore C.'s aunts, 'L.P.', sometimes referred to as 'Tish', was Letitia Perceval, da. of Jane Elizabeth Leigh by her first husband, Westby Perceval of Philipstown, King's co.

[3] Mrs G. has not been identified but was probably the 'nanny' to the Leigh's children, Elizabeth or 'Bessy' and Frances Harriet or 'Fanny', both of whom were born in the 1780s

3$^{d.}$ That as – though they will, generally speaking, be pretty regular – it may often happen that they will be days or weeks behind-hand – it be not supposed therefore that there is any neglect or forgetfulness in the case – but only such pressure of accidents, or want of time, as must often in the course of the winter be unavoidable.

4th. That a little portfolio be assigned to them, in which they shall be laid orderly and smoothly, without crease or confusion, and preserved for the inspection of the writer of them, when he shall come to Ashborne in the summer.

# PAPER BUILDINGS,[4] MONDAY, NOVR.
## 25, 1793

You will have learned so much of my motions already from other quarters – that this first weekly account or bulletin will of necessity be less full than it otherwise would probably have been.

*15th [November]* I left Oxford on Friday the 15th – and arrived in town time enough to shew myself, for the keeping of the Term, in Lincolns Inn Hall. That day I dined at the Club,[5] where, in spite of the bad character which Bess and Leigh[6] heard of that Club when they were in London, I can assure you that we sat that day no longer than till $\frac{1}{2}$ past eleven o'clock – and that I then came home, and went to bed, as a sober man ought to do.

*16th [November]* On Saturday morning, rising early, I breakfasted alone, settled my accounts with Fleming,[7] and then proceeded to Westminster Hall, dressed as becomes a student of the Law, in professional black to shew to all whom it might concern my steady adherence to the profession. This measure I fould the more necessary, as I had heard from many quarters the most resolute assurances that I had resolved upon quitting the Law at once and altogether, and had even received some applications to know at what precise time my chambers would be to be let. From Westminster Hall, having displayed my person to the best advantage in the Court of King's Bench, I proceeded to Downing Street, left my name at Mr. Pitt's,[8] then went to the Public Offices[9] to enquire after news, and returned home making such calls as fell in my way; and dined quietly at my own chambers. Frere[10] dined with me, as did also Sturges.[11] The former you know – the latter you do not – but you may have heard me

---

[4] In Lincoln's Inn where C. had lived since 1790. His number was 13

[5] The Dining Club, The Crown and Anchor, the Strand, see below, 31

[6] Elizabeth and the Rev. William Leigh

[7] His Scottish valet

[8] William Pitt (1759–1806), prime minister 1783–1801, 1804–6. C. met Pitt for the first time in the summer of 1792 when he explained that he wished to owe his return to Parliament to him alone. Pitt accepted the commission and fulfilled it in June 1793, see *Thorne*, iii, 379–80

[9] In Whitehall (see below, 28)

[10] John Hookham Frere (1769–1846). C.'s contemporary at Eton and one of his closest friends; joint author of the *Microcosm*. A clerk in the Home Office

[11] William Sturges (afterwards Sturges Bourne, 1769–1845). C.'s contemporary at Christ Church

mention him as a Christ Church friend of mine, now studying the Law; very clever, and (what you cannot easily have heard of him) yesterday called to the Bar. By the bye, it may very often happen that a name of a person whom you do not know, may fall from me, without my remarking it, or giving you any description of the person. If the person be worth describing, I will, whenever I mention him for the first time, (and if I am aware that it *is* the first time) I will tell you who he is. If I should forget to do so, remind me of the omission, and I will correct it.

After dinner I went with Sturges to the Play; after the Play, with him and others to supper; and after supper, *by myself*, to bed.

*17th [November]* On Sunday morning I set out, accordng to my promise made in July last, and confirmed a few days before I left Ashborne, to pay a visit to Madame de Flahault,[12] at Lord Wycombe's[13] house at Wycombe. There I arrived by dinner-time, and found there the lady, Monsr. de Talleyrand[14] (ci-devant Bishop of Autun) and a Monsr. Beaumetz – or Bornet, an emigré lately come over from France after having been hidden in garrets and cellars, in daily danger of his life, ever since the affair of the 10th of Aug[t.15]; and my friend Smith – whom you know very well by description, and who, to distinguish him from others of his name, is called *Bobus* Smith.[16]

The evening passed here partly in French conversation, wherein I get on but lamely, and partly in English, which Mad. de F[lahaut] knows very tolerably but in which Beaumetz and Talleyrand hardly get on at all. Beaumetz and Talleyrand were members of the Constituent Assembly, and are both of them men of talents and information. Beaumetz is also, I believe, of unquestioned integrity. Talleyrand is said not to be so – but I think he is treated much more hardly than he deserves. Mad. de F[lahaut] is a very pleasing, sensible woman. Her *what-d'ye'callum* was not at home, having been sent, the

[12] Adélaide-Marie-Émilie Filleul, Comtesse de Flahaut and Talleyrand's mistress, see n. 14. She subsequently became Marquise de Souza

[13] Earl of Wycombe and subsequently the 2nd Mq. of Lansdowne, M.P. Wycombe 1786–1802

[14] Charles-Maurice de Talleyrand-Périgord (1754–1838); in exile in London but later French foreign minister

[15] Count de Beaumetz, a close friend of Talleyrand, who lived for a while with other French exiles at Juniper Hall, Surrey. On the morning of 10 August 1792, a combination of the Paris sans culottes and the provincial fédérés broke into the Tuileries, the royal residence in Paris, and killed 600 of the 900 Swiss guards. This led to the abolition of the French monarchy

[16] Robert Percy Smith (1770–1845). C.'s contemporary at Eton, one of his closest friends and known by him as 'Bobus'; a joint author of the *Microcosm*. Elder brother of the Rev. Sydney Smith

week before I arrived, to Windham[17] for his perusal. I shall have it when he restores it. It is a novel, in French; it will be published soon; it is written by her for her support, and when it comes out, you must subscribe to it.[18]

*18th [November]* Monday I passed at Wycombe, driving out Mad. de F[lahaut] in the morning, and taking French lessons of her in the afternoon.

*19th [November]* Tuesday I returned to town, and found Leigh there according to my expectation, and Bess with him to my great surprize. I dined with them, and when they went to the Play, trudged into the City, and supped with Harry and Paul Patrick.[19] I must not omit to say that I found an invitation from Mr. Pitt to dine with him on Friday.

*20th [November]* On Wednesday I called on the Leighs in the Morning; went to Westminster Hall and to the Public Offices – and dined and supped with the Leighs.

*21st [November]* On Thursday I had the honour of entertaining Leigh and Bess with a sumptuous breakfast at my apartments up three pair of stairs in Paper Buildings. I should have accompanied them to Wanstead,[20] whither they went this day, but that I had an engagement of long standing with Jenkinson,[21] to dine with him tête-à-tête in his new house – being the first dinner that he has yet given, though I do not by any means intend that it shall be the last.

This morning I went to Westmʳ· Hall and to the Public Offices, as usual, called on the Markhams,[22] and engaged to dine with them on

---

[17] William Windham (1750–1810). M.P. Norwich 1784–1802; the leading member in the Commons of the secessionist whigs led by the Duke of Portland. They supported the war and formed a coalition with Pitt in July 1794, Windham becoming sec. at war. He was an ardent supporter of French émigrés

[18] The Comtesse de Flahaut's novel, published in London in 1794, was *Adèle de Sénange ou lettres de Lord Sydenham*. It enjoyed 8 subsequent editions, 1794–1808, see Angus Martin et al, *Bibliographie du genre romanesque français 1751–1800*, (London, 1977), 376–77

[19] Paul Patrick was the brother of C.'s aunt, Mehitabel or 'Hetty' Canning, the widow of Stratford Canning, their father being Robert Patrick of Somerville, co. Dublin. The Patricks were of Irish merchant stock, there being a firm called Patrick & Co., wholesale merchants, of Bethseda Lane, Dublin. Paul Patrick, however, was based in London and was a partner in Patrick & Canning, merchants of New Broad St. 'Harry' was Henry, the son of 'Hetty'. He was working in the family firm at this time and was later sent to a counting house in Hamburg to gain further experience in trade, see below, 285

[20] Where his aunt, Mehitabel or 'Hetty' had lived since the death of her husband, Stratford Canning, in May 1787

[21] Robert Banks Jenkinson, 2nd Earl of Liverpool. C.'s contemporary at Christ Church; M.P. Rye, 1790–1803; commr. Board of Control, Apr. 1793–99

[22] He was a close friend of his Christ Church contemporary, Osborne Markham (1769–1827), s. of the Rev. William Markham, then archbishop of York

Saturday; on C. Greville and Ly. Charlotte[23] to apologize for not being able to dine with them, as they had desired, to-morrow; at Lord Stafford's,[24] where I found that the family were not yet come to town. I dined with Jenkinson according to my engagement; went with him about half-past nine for an hour to the Play; then returned with him to supper, and got home to bed about half-past two.

22[d.] [*November*] On Friday the Leighs returned from Wanstead. I saw them part of the morning, and passed the rest of it in my usual occupations; that is to say – partly busy at home, partly in Westminster Hall, and partly in collecting what news was to be collected at Whitehall (that is at the Public Offices).

The dinner[25] at Mr. Pitt's was pleasant, beyond any idea that I had formed of it. The company consisted of about a dozen people, three or four of whom I knew more or less intimately, but the rest I had never even seen before. And in this company (a circumstance which will give you a better notion of the comfortable way in which I found and felt myself than any other description could do) I had not been a quarter of an hour before I was as completely at my ease as I could have been at Wanstead or at Ashborne.

The persons who composed the company were – Mr. Pitt (1) – Lord Grenville (2) – Mr. Dundas (3) – the Master of the Rolls (Pepper Arden) (4) – Lord Bayham (5) – Lord Mornington (6) – Mr. Steele (7) – Mr. Villars (8) – Mr. Yorke (9) – 2 Mr. Eliotts (10, 11) – Jenkinson (12) and I (13) – See the annexed table.[26]

Lord Grenville has not the reputation of being a pleasant man – nor is he eminently so – but he has, at least he had this day, much less coldness and reserve in his manner than I had been taught to expect – and what little there was, appeared to me to proceed rather

[23] Charles Greville (1762–1832) and his wife, Lady Charlotte, da. of the 3rd Duke of Portland. Greville's sister, Mrs Crewe, w. of John, later 1st Baron Crewe, was a hostess to the Portland whigs and was a long standing friend of the Cannings. She had taken up C. during his time at Oxford, C. spending part of every summer vacation at Crewe Hall in Cheshire

[24] Granville Leveson Gower, 1st Mq. of Stafford. C.'s Christ Church contemporary was his 2nd s. Granville Leveson Gower, 1st Earl Granville

[25] 'The dinner ... Cock Robin' (p. 30), printed in *Marshall*, 46–49

[26] William Wyndham Grenville, 1st Baron Grenville, Foreign Secretary; Henry Dundas, 1st Visct. Melville, Home Secretary; Sir Richard Pepper Arden, 1st Baron Alvanley; John Jeffreys Pratt, Visct. Bayham and subsequently 2nd Earl (18 Apr. 1794) and 1st Mq. Camden, a ld. of Treasury; Richard Colley Wellesley, 2nd. Earl of Mornington and subsequently 1st Mq. Wellesley, a ld. of Treasury; Thomas Steele (1753–1823), commr. Board of Control and jnt. Paymaster Genl.; Hon. John Charles Villiers, 3rd Earl of Clarendon, chief justice in eyre North of Trent; Charles Philip Yorke (1764–1834), M.P. Cambs. and mover of the Address, 31. Jan. 1792; Hon. Edward James Eliot (1758–97), commr. Board of Control and his bro., Hon. John Eliot, 2nd Baron Eliot and subsequently 1st Earl of St. Germans

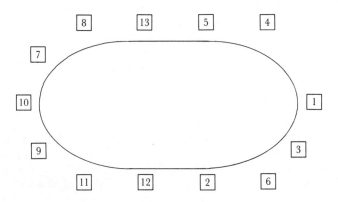

from shyness than haughtiness. But he is a man not to be judged-of by once seeing. Dundas is unaffected, frank and *jovial*. I did not sit near enough to him at dinner, *as you see*, to have much conversation with him, further than as we both mixed in the general talk that was going on – but after dinner, when we went into the other room, I made up to him, and we conversed a good deal, and I like him very much. What is best in him is that he invited us all to dine with him next Friday. The Master of the Rolls I believe you must have heard me mention often. I have known him a good while, and found him always very entertaining – but never so much so as at Mr. Pitt's table, where it was his business to-day, and is, I am told, most days, to laugh himself and make others do so too.

Ld. Bayham is son of Ld. Cambden (sic) – a Lord of the Treasury and an intimate friend of Pitt. He seems very pleasing and gentlemanly in his manners, and is very much liked and well spoken of. Lord Mornington I knew before – but like him better now than I ever did – both because he appears generally very sensible and pleasant, and was very good-naturedly attentive to me. He also is a Lord of the Treasury and one of Pitt's most intimate friends. Mr. Steele is Joint-Paymaster, and perhaps the most popular man in Administration. I have never heard him mentioned without praise. He is not a very forward man in company, but what little I did see of him seemed to justify his reputation.

Mr. Villars is a very intimate friend of Mr. Pitt, and has the place of one of the Chief Justices in Eyre. As I sat next to him I of course made acquaintance with him, and thought him a very gentlemanly, good-natured man. Mr. Yorke is brother of Lord Hardwicke, a barrister and in Parliament. The Mr. Eliotts are sons of Ld. Eliott – one of them married Mr. Pitt's sister, who died, and is in Parliament, and Joint Commissioner of the India Board with Jenkinson – the other in Parliament also, and a barrister, or studying the Law. Jenkinson you already know – and the other gentleman (No. 13) you may have heard mentioned. These five last, that is to say, Mr. Yorke – Mr. Eliotts – Jenkinson and No. 13 are all young men. So I say nothing yet of their characters.

Mr. Pitt is, at the head of his own table, exactly what hits my taste – attentive without being troublesome – mixing in the conversation without attempting to lead it – laughing often and easily – and boyish enough if it should fall in his way, to discuss the history of Cock Robin.

I like my first dinner with him, you see, exceedingly. We came away a little after 10, and I supped with the Leighs at Norris's.[27]

_23d._ [_November_] On Saturday I would have dined with the Leighs – but that I had engaged myself, and had named my own day too, to the Markhams. I dined there, nobody but the family – whom I like as much as ever. I supped with the Leighs at Lothians.

_24th_ [_November_] Sunday I should have gone to Wanstead – but that I received a message desiring me not to come owing to poor little Bessy's[28] illness. I dined at my own chambers and sent to Frere and Bobus Smith and Sturges to dine with me – which they did – and the evening concluded with the utmost harmony.

_25th_ [_November_] To-day I have been in the City and I hear from Harry [Canning] that Bessy is much better and in a fair progress towards her recovery. Adieu.

_25._ [_November_] On Monday I dined at Frere's, where besides the family were Bobus Smith and Sturges. And I supped at the Archbishop of York's, where besides the family (all of whom except Frederica Markham are at home – and she is in the country with her sister Mrs. Law) – I found our friend Miss Hotham,[29] in a tight red riding jacket, looking as though she were just alighted from a _dilly_ or slap-bang stage.

_26._ [_November_] Tuesday was a day of regularity. I was at home greater part of the morning; dined regularly at the Club, where was a large party. I supped at another Club, newly instituted, and which

[27] The home of Dr. William Norris, surgeon of Old Jewry, who ministered subsequently to the Rev. W. Leigh and to C.

[28] His cousin, Elizabeth, da. of Mehetibal or 'Hetty' Canning and C.'s closest family friend

[29] Probably one of the three das. of 2nd Baron Hotham

[30] 'The Dining Club ... without it', printed in _NER_, 452

must not be confounded with the dining Club, being of a different plan and construction.

The Dining Club,[30] which you have heard so much abused, is held at the Crown and Anchor in the Strand – meets every day during Term time, and as long after the expiration of Term as there are a sufficient number of members in town to make it an object – consists of about thirty members – out of whom, during the Term time, about from seven to fourteen, upon an average, dine there every day. The intention of this Club is dining *only*.

The other Club[31] is one which has been instituted within these six months, and is therefore yet it in its infancy. Its object is not confined to dining, or supping, or breakfasting, or *tea—ing*, but comprehends them all; and is in all respects (gaming excepted) exactly the same to us lawyers that White's and Brookes's[32] are to the people at the other end of the town. There are two large houses in Carey Street (a street hard by Lincoln's Inn which Mr. Leigh probably knows) thrown into one, and fitted up with private and publick rooms, for parties, or for stragglers, the private rooms for dinners etc., the public for coffee, newspapers etc. – open to subscribers – whose number amounts to about 140 at present – and will probably be about 200 in the course of six weeks – comprehending all the respectabil[it]y and eminence, and *fashion* of the Law. This place is open (to subscribers) at all hours from morning to midnight – and here at all hours one is sure of meeting informed and gentlemanly and often pleasant society. It is a thing that has so long been wanting to make a Law life comfortable – that now that it has once been established, everybody is wondering how they contrived to go on so long without it.

*27 [November]*. Wednesday was, like Tuesday, a regular day. I went to Westminster Hall in the morning, dined at the Club (Crown and Anchor) – and came home after dinner to my chambers, and to study, till bed-time.

*28 [November]*. Thursday I spent the morning in reading quietly at home. Dined at the Club (Cr. and Anch.) and supped at the Club in Carey Street.

*29 [November]* Friday morning was spent wholly in Westminster Hall. The evening was dedicated to more pleasant purposes – for I dined with Mr. Dundas at his house in Somerset Place. The company were Mr. Pitt, Lord Grenville, Lord Mornington, the Master of the Rolls, Mr. Villars, Mr, Eliott. Mr. Steele, Jenkinson (for all of whom I refer you to last week) and Lord Mulgrave, and a Mr. Graham,

---

[30] 'The Dining Club ... without it', printed in *NER*, 452
[31] The Carey Street Club
[32] The two main political clubs. C. was elected a member of White's in 1794

both just returned from Toulon.[33] Mr. Graham I do not know any farther than that he is a Scotchman, and has, I believe, been serving gallantly and usefully as a volunteer at Toulon. Lord Mulgrave, as you have seen in a hundred newspapers, has been there as Acting Brigadier-General. He is in some sort an old acquaintance of mine, as I met him very often last winter at Lord Abercorn's.[34] And I like him very well. He seems very good-humoured, and talks sensibly and abundantly. His conversation this day, as it turned upon the subject of Toulon, of which everybody was anxious to hear, and he was capable of giving information, was particularly entertaining. Unluckily Mr. Pitt was called away by business by nine o'clock. Our party consequently broke up soon after. I had time enough to see the last part of the Children in the Wood at the Haymarket – and afterwards supped at Carey Street.

*30 [November].* Saturday I was at Westminster Hall and at the Public Offices in the morning – at which last place all is anxiety about Lord Howe.[35] I called at Lambeth – where I found our friend Mrs. Lloyd[36] – who looked well and happy, and gave very good accounts of Mrs. Turner[37] and made a thousand kind enquiries and sent a thousand kind remembrances to you all.

I intended to have dined regularly at the Club, but meeting Sturges in my way home, and hearing from him that there was a fine *turtle* at the Piazza and a new Play at the Theatre in Covent Garden, I felt it to be a duty which I owed to myself to go with him, and assist at both these rarities. The turtle turned out to be excellent. I wish I could say as much for the Play, which was execrable.[38] At the Play we were joined by Osborne Markham, and with him went to supper in Carey Street.

[33] Lord Mulgrave was apptd. lt. gov. of Toulon following its capture in August 1793; Thomas Graham, 1st Baron Lynedoch, was his a.d.c. and a kinsman of Dundas. Mulgrave's return to London coincided with the loss of the port, for which he was criticised, see *Thorne*, iv, 799

[34] The 9th Earl and 1st Mq. of Abercorn, a long standing friend of Pitt whose soirées at his Middlesex home, The Priory, were important events in the political and social calendars. There is a strong possibility that Abercorn played an important part in introducing Pitt to C., see *Marshall*, 32–33

[35] Vice-admiral of England 1792–96. The government believed that the whole of the French fleet based at Brest had put to sea and that an engagement with Lord Howe's forces was imminent. On 18 Nov. six French sail of the line and two frigates were seen and pursued, but escaped. The news had clearly not reached Whitehall

[36] Mrs Rachel Lloyd, Housekeeper at Kensington Palace. Possibly the wife of Sampson Lloyd of Bordesley, Warwickshire who m. Rachel, da. of Samuel Barnes of London and d.1814. Sampson Lloyd d. 27 Dec. 1807

[37] Unidentified

[38] The play was 'The World in a Village', a new comedy of uncertain authorship. It was followed by the two-act comic opera 'The Flitch of Bacon'

I must not omit to tell you that this morning while I was dressing, Mr. Newbery[39] called on me, and after a good deal of general conversation, and after having obtained from me a promise to dine with him on Wednesday next, and after a thousand turnings and windings, proceeded to the subject of my poor mother's famous Collysium,[40] and with much profession and civility and good advice, concluded with *advising against* anything being attempted in its favour. He gave sundry wise reasons, which may be true enough for aught I know, but which did not put me at all in good humour with him, or his conduct in this business. For why so sanguine at first? And now all my poor mother's hopes are suddenly dashed, and with feelings the more painful to her, as she had been taught to promise herself very different success. Perhaps, however, if all he says be true, I have no reason justly to complain of him – but be that as it may, I'll be hanged if I dine with him on Wednesday.

*1 December.* Sunday I set out for Wanstead, and arrived there between one and two. I found little Bessy infinitely better – though far from having recovered her strength and looks. The family were divided into two dinner-parties. Harry and Paul and Bess Patrick were to dine at Sheridan's[41] – Hetty and Bessy and grandmother[42] at home. I joined the home party, and sat with them very comfortably after dinner till eight o'clock, discussing sundry innocent topicks but keeping pretty clear of politicks for poor Hetty's sake. Then I called at Sheridan's and had a long and amicable tête-à-tête conversation with him on politicks – then returned to town by eleven o'clock, and supped at Carey Street.

*2*[d.] *[December]* Monday I stayed at home reading and writing all the morning. Among others I wrote to my mother an account of my conversation with Mr. Newbery – and to Mr. N. an apology for not dining with him on Wednesday 'very sorry' – 'previous engagement which I did not recollect' &c., and to make my words almost good I received an invitation to dine on that day at Lambeth.

[39] Probably Francis Newbury of Heathfield, Surrey who m. 29 May 1770, Mary Raikes, a sister of Thomas Raikes who was a close friend of Stratford and Mehitabel Canning, see p. 77 below and n. 175

[40] An eye ointment invented by his mother and which she hoped would produce additional income, see *Marshall*, 116 where 'Colligium' is incorrectly given as the name

[41] Richard Brinsley Sheridan (1751–1816), M.P. Stafford 1780–1806, a close friend of C.'s uncle, Stratford Canning and who became a friend of the Leighs through Mehitabel Canning. Sheridan, in the company of Charles James Fox, had been impressed with C. when the latter was at Eton, and so close had become the relationship tht some believed C. was his ward. see *Hinde*, 22

[42] 'Bess' Patrick was the sister of Mehitabel and Paul. 'Bessy' was the da. of Mehitabel and the late Stratford Canning. The grandmother was probably Mehitabel Canning's mother, the wid. of Robert Patrick q.v.

I dined to-day with Mr. Lewis.[43] He is and has been for about two or three and twenty years past Under-Secretary-at-War; a man of very great sense, and very high character; a Christ Church man, and from his earliest years the most intimate friend of the Dean of Ch. Ch.[44] My first acquaintance with him was last winter through the Dean. Here I met no person, as I think, whom you are likely to know, or of whom I am likely to speak much again – except the Lord Chief Baron (Macdonald).[45] He married a daughter of Lord Stafford's (Lady Louisa) – and through his interest chiefly, has been raised to the situation which he holds, and which however he fills with very great credit and respectability. From Mr. Lewis's I went to sup at the Archbishop of York's, where were only one or two persons beside the family.[46]

*3ᵈ· [December]* Tuesday morning – Westminster Hall and the Public Offices – no news of Lord Howe. I dined this day at Lord Grenville's. Here were Mr. Pitt, Lord Mornington, the Master of the Rolls, Lord Mulgrave, Mr. Eliott, Jenkinson, *Arbuthnot*[47] (this is that friend of mine through whom my correspondence with Lord Abercorn was carried on. He is now in Lord Grenville's office, much in the same sort of situation in which Frere is in the Home Department, but with a better salary and more business, and in great favour with Lord Grenville) and Goddard,[48] who is, as you know, Lord Grenville's private secretary, and who, in a very proper secretarylike manner, sat at the bottom of the table and helped the soup and fish. In addition to those were what I have not before remarked in our *Cabinet-Dinners* (for so the newspapers constantly call them) two ladies, Lady Grenville, a pretty, little, quiet, timid, good-natured thing – and Lady Arden (the Master of the Rolls's wife) a bouncing jolly dame, but withal, very good-natured, and clever.

Before I left Lord Grenville's I contrived to have some private conversation with Mr. Pitt, as this was probably the last time that I should see him before I left town. (By the bye, I have not told you

[43] Matthew Lewis (b. c. 1750). Deputy sec. and 1st clerk at the W. O.

[44] Dr. Cyril Jackson (1746–1819); dean of Christ Church 1783–1809. A great friend of C. since the latter's Oxford days when he had successfully persuaded him to resign from the Christ Church Debating Club on the grounds that membership would be detrimental to his political career. See *Bagot*, i, 39n

[45] Sir Archibald MacDonald 1st Bt who was famous for his prosecution of Paine's *Rights of Man* in his earlier capacity of Attorney-General

[46] 'I dined ... and clever', printed in *NER*, 452–3

[47] Charles Arbuthnot (1767–1850), a contemporary of C. at Christ Church and nicknamed 'Gosh'. Précis-writer in the F.O.

[48] Charles Goddard (c. 1770–1845), a contemporary of C. at Christ Church. His mentor was Lord Grenville, the Foreign Secretary, to whom he was a private secretary. Later he took holy orders and was archdeacon of Lincoln 1817–44

before that I mean to leave town on Saturday for Christ Church, and to stay there studying and economizing – but so it is).

From Lord Grenville's I went to the Archbishop of York's to supper. Here was Frederica returned, and with her Mrs. Law (their sister) and her husband. Mr. Law is brother of the Law who is Mr. Hasting's counsel[49] – and is in Parliament, in a seat which it is supposed he will resign to his brother when Mr. Hasting's trial is at an end. The Markhams go to Bath this Christmas – and will probably be in the course of next week at Christ Church in their way. They usually take the opportunity of their journey to or from Bath to pay a visit to the Dean.

*4th. [December]* Wednesday. Westminster Hall and the Public Offices. No news of Lord Howe that can be believed. I[50] dined at Lambeth,[51] where besides the family were Mrs. Lloyd – and Lord and Lady Auckland[52] (whom I have not seen since I profited so much by their civilities at The Hague) – and the noted Mr. Rose of the Treasury,[53] whom I have never seen before, but with whom it is not easy to go on long in politicks without making some acquaintance and communication. Lord and Lady Auckland pressed me to go to Beckenham, their seat in Kent, on Friday – and held out as an inducement that Mr. Gibbon (the historian) is to be there. I should like to go of all things, but I have made up my mind to set out for Ch. Ch. on Saturday, and have written to say I shall do so – and so it is out of the question. I like Ld. and Ly. A. however very much indeed; and am very glad to have renewed my acquaintance with them.

From Lambeth I went to sup with Jenkinson, and there found Frederic North[54] just returned from Bath *after*, or rather *in* a severe fit of the gout, for he does not seem by any means to have gotten rid of it.

---

[49] Ewan Law (1747–1829), the brother of Edward, the 1st Baron Ellenborough and husband of Henrietta Sarah Markham. M.P. Westbury 1790–95. He was counsel to Warren Hastings, the former governor-general of India, whose trial was coming to a conclusion in Westminster Hall. C's prediction about Edward Law's return for Westbury proved inaccurate, see *Thorne*, iv, 392

[50] 'I dined ... with Jenkinson', printed in *NER*, 453

[51] Lambeth Palace, C. was a close friend and contemporary at Christ Church of Charles Moore (1771–1826), the 2nd s. of Rt. Rev. John Moore, archbishop of Canterbury 1783–1805. He and Moore had spent July and August 1791 in the Netherlands

[52] William Eden, 1st Baron Auckland, was British ambassador at the Hague. He was the brother of the archbishop of Canterbury's wife, Catherine

[53] George Rose (1744–1818). M.P. Christchurch 1790–1818; sec. to the Treasury

[54] Hon. Frederick North, 5th Earl of Guilford. M.P. Banbury 1792–94; chamberlain of the Exchequer

*5th [December]* Thursday. A bad cold kept me at home greatest part of the morning.

I dined with King[55] – one of the Under-Secretaries of State for the Home Department, and one of the worthiest and friendliest and best sort of men in the world. There were Jenkinson, and Fred. North, and Arbuthnot and Goddard. I had some talk with King upon the subject of that unlucky son of hers,[56] upon whose situation my mother wrote to me while I was at Ashborne. He is, you may recollect, a Serjeant in the corps that is going to Botany Bay. In this capacity, and of course in this only (without mentioning his relationship to me) I recommended him to King, in whose Department the Botany Bay establishment is; and he has promised me to procure for him such recommendations as may eventually be of service to him – and make his life in those parts as comfortable, and his rise as probable as could be expected or desired.

Having a very bad cold I returned home immediately and went to bed.

*6. [December]* Friday morning my cold was much worse, and I determined therefore to stay at home the whole day – and to keep Frere, who was to come to breakfast with me, to dine also, or at least not to let him go without a promise of returning. I was however obliged to go out myself for an hour or two to the Secretary of State's Office, for the purpose of renewing with King the conversation of last night, and giving him Samuel's address. I did so, and I wait the result in patience. I could not refrain from writing to my poor mother to say that I had seen King; but I took great care to raise her hopes as little as possible on the subject, and to caution her that she should not communicate anything about it to Samuel.

No news of Lord Howe.

On my return homewards, seeing the Staffords' house open as if the family were come to town, I called in, and found there Lady Georgina[57] – but her only. The rest of the family are to follow in a few days. I am sorry that I shall not see them before I go.

Frere dined with me – and Bobus (Smith) came in the evening. My cold was so very bad that I resolved to defer my setting out till Sunday – and at 1/2 past eleven I went to bed covered with flannel. Borrowes[58] called upon me in the course of the evening, and told me

[55] John King (1759–1830)

[56] Samuel Reddish, C.'s half-brother by Samuel Reddish, the actor, who d.1785

[57] Lady Georgiana Augusta Leveson Gower, 4th da. of the 1st Mq. of Stafford

[58] Walter Borrowes, probably the 2nd s. of Sir Kildare Dixon Borrowes 5th Bt. (I) and a partner in the City firm of merchants in which Stratford Canning, C.'s uncle, had had an interest. Following the latter's death in May 1787, Borrowes became Canning's guardian. In 1793 a Walter Borrows (sic) is recorded as being a merchant

among other things how he had heard on 'Change that I was to go to Ireland.[59] There is not a word of truth in it – but false as it is, it is the only piece of public news stirring this day.

7 *[December]* Saturday my cold is somewhat better though not much. I have taken some essence of coltsfoot (the *tussilago* of the Ancients, as the label informs me) and have sent for some pateroia lozenges. I hope my cold will get better as I want of all things to leave town to-morrow. Frere has breakfasted with me, and is now with me, but cannot stay to dine. Sturges is coming to partake of my sick dinner, and he will bring me the news, if there is any – and I would send it to you but that I must seal this, and send it to the post immediately, or Fleming, who has enough to do between packing up and preparing for dinner, will be outrageous.

I have received packets of letters from you to-day, to all of which I shall punctually attend. Adieu. 1/2 past 4 o'clock, Saturday, Decr. 7, 1793.


I concluded my last journal, I believe, on the day previous to my leaving town for Oxford, which was, if I recollect right, on Monday the eighth [in fact the ninth] of December 1793.

I stayed at Oxford from that day till Thursday the 26th – during which time I was pretty much and pretty uniformly employed in reading, in nursing a bad cold, which I had carried with me from London, and in living sometimes with old and sometimes with young; and sometimes, as was the case particularly for about the last week, in perfect silence and solitude.

On the 26th I set out for Charles Ellis's[60] house in Bedfordshire; a visit which I had long promised to pay, but which I certainly might have found less bitter cold weather for paying. I was two days upon the road, owing to the cold, partly, which made it impossible to travel in the evening, and partly to the badness of the roads, which made it difficult to get on in the day. The distance is not above 60 miles – but lies across a most miserable country.

I arrived to dinner on the 27th at Wootton, and found there nobody

of 10 Clement's Lane, London. He is later recorded as possessing a small villa in Banstead, Surrey and as being a supporter of Catholic relief in Ireland, (see below, pp. 229, 256)

[59] As chief secretary in the room of Hon. Robert Hobart, 4th Earl of Buckinghamshire, (styled Lord Hobart 1793–96), who had left Dublin on 2 Dec. The rumour suggests that C.'s wish to hold the office, which he revealed later to Pitt (see below, p. 273), was already formed

[60] Charles Rose Ellis, 1st Baron Seaford, C.'s contemporary at Christ Church; M.P. Heytesbury 1793–96. His seat was Wootton in Beds.

but C. Ellis, his elder brother J. Ellis and his wife,[61] and his cousin
Geo. Ellis, the co-author of the Rolliad,[62] &c. Here I stayed in peace
and quietness till Saturday the 4th of January – in a most comfortable
house, full of books, and billiards, and battledore and shuttlecock,
and good wine. The Ellises went fox-hunting now and then, and
would have tempted me to accompany them by offers of the finest
and safest horses, and assurances of the best sport in the world. But
as I think fox-hunting one of the many pleasures without which one
can very well contrive to pass through the world, I resisted their
solicitations (the more resolutely indeed after having gotten a fall a
day or two after my arrival in leaping a ditch) and confined myself
to the more domestic pleasures of the library and the dining-room.

On Saturday Jan[ry]. 4th I arrived in town after a very cold journey –
and being too late to dine with anybody else, I went to dine by myself
at the Piazza – and after dinner called on Jenkinson to hear news –
and not finding him left word that I would breakfast with him the
next morning. At my chambers I found a card from Mr. Pitt dated
some days back, and asking me to dinner for Thursay the 2[d.]. I wrote
to him as well to make my apologies as to let him know that I was
come to town, that he might ask me again when he was at leisure.

5th [January] Sunday – I breakfasted with Jenkinson – and we
croaked a little together over Wurmser's retreat[63] – but agreed that
Toulon was all as well as it could be, if it should appear that Lord
Hood had taken care before his departure to take proper account of
the shipping and arsenals.[64]

After breakfast I set out for Wanstead. There besides the usual
family I found Mr. and Mrs. Bruce.[65] I had never seen *her* before but
once, and him not at all. She seems very pleasing, and very good –
and to *him* I have taken a very great fancy. In the evening
Tom Sheridan[66] and Mr. Smyth[67] (whom I recognize for the same

---

[61] John Thomas Ellis (1756–1836) who m. 6 Jan. 1794 and not 1795 as recorded in
G.E. Cokayne, *The Complete Baronetage*, Antoinetta, da. of Sir Peter Parker, see n. 372

[62] George Ellis (1753–1815), a contributor to the *Rolliad*, a series of whig satires on
Pitt's administration which began to appear in 1784 and of which a complete edition
was published in 1791

[63] General Wurmser, commander of the Austrian forces which retreated across the
Rhine at the end of Dec.

[64] Vice-admiral of the fleet, commander in the Mediterranean since 1793, and responsible for the evacuation of Toulon

[65] Possibly Henry Hervey-Aston Bruce who m. 10 Nov. 1786, Letitia, da. of the Rev.
Dr. Henry Barnard of Bovagh, Co. Londonderry, C.'s uncle by marriage. Bruce was
cr. Bt. of Down Hill, co. Londonderry, 29 June 1804

[66] Thomas Sheridan (1775–1817), s. of Richard Brinsley Sheridan q.v.

[67] The only Smyth that might qualify is William Smyth (1764–1849) who is recorded
as being at Eton 1780–82

Smyth that I remember when first I went to Eton) – came to us – and we had a grand bout at Blind Man's Buff – running and sitting – and at eleven o'clock or near it – I set off, and returned to town.

*6th. [January]* Monday. I began making my different calls – and among others, calling upon King (the Under-Secretary of State) at his Office. He asked me to dine with him – which I did – and there met the poor old Bishop of St. Pol de Léon,[68] the patriarch and guardian of all the wretched French clergy in this country; and of whose venerable character and good conduct we have all heard so much for this last twelvemonth. He is a quiet, respectable old man in his appearance, and not the less so as he shews in his countenance strong traits of suffering and sorrow.

In my way from King's I called on Frere at his Office, and went with him to see the Pantomime at the Haymarket – which is shamefully stupid.

*7th. [January]* Tuesday. Frere breakfasted with me. Adderley[69] called upon me. You know who Adderley is, do you not? He is the eldest son of that Mrs. A. who is now Lady Hobart – and he is going, as you will have seen by the papers, as Secretary to Ld. Hobart to India. He was a very intimate acquaintance of mine at Christ Church, and one for whom I had, and have a very great value – and when Lord Hobart shall get to Bengal (for he goes first for a year or two to Madrass) – and when poor Westby[70] after all his calamities shall have settled there, as I trust he will do, at last – I look forward with great pleasure to the prospect of making him acquainted with Adderley, whose situation may perhaps enable him to be of some service to Westby, and I am sure his good-nature, and the footing on which he and I have lived together, will incline him to be so.

I walked to the other end of the town and continued my calls. No news worth hearing. I dined at Mr. Woodcock's in Bloomsbury Square. You know all about him, I am sure, and have heard me mention his son as a friend of mine.[71] At dinner there was nobody whom I am likely ever to mention again except Mr. Barker of Christ

[68] Jean-François de La Marche (1729–1806)

[69] Edward Hale Adderley (matric. Christ Church 4. Feb. 1790, aged 17), s. of Margaretta, wid. of Thomas Adderley of Innishannon, Co. Cork and w. of Hon. Robert Hobart, 4th Earl of Buckinghamshire

[70] Westby Perceval, the s. of Mrs. Leigh by her first husband of that name. He was drowned en route for India later in the year or early in 1795, Canning MSS, (12), C. to W. Leigh, 8, 28 Apr. 1794

[71] Elborough Woodcock of Bloomsbury Sq. and Mortlake, Surrey, an eminent solicitor. His son, Henry (c. 1770–1840) became a clergyman and was apptd. prebendary of Salisbury, 1818

Church,[72] a little clergyman, whom you saw last winter at Bath, and whom you will know better perhaps by his having been the author of those verses which I sent you upon a *hot day*.

In the evening I went by myself to enjoy the new Pantomime at Covent Garden.

*8th [ January]* Wednesday. I went into the City in the morning.

I[73] dined with Frederick North (I believe I forgot to say that I had called on him before, and found him laid up in great state with his legs in flannel, and receiving company like a lying-in-lady), where I met Mr. Ryder[74] (son of Lord Harrowby, and one of the Joint Paymasters of the army – Mr. Steele, whom I have had occasion to mention before, is the other) – two or three other persons, whose names you would not know, and whose qualities I know not enough to describe them – and – whom else do you think? – who but – Mahmoud Raif Effendi – The Turkish Secretary of Embassy, and Emanuel Persgani, the Dragoman or Interpreter.

The Secretary has the air and appearance of a very intelligent man, – and as much of what he said, as got to us through the interpreter, confirmed us our [sic] in our good opinion of him. He is a large fat figure, or rather perhaps his dress (which is in all its parts very much what you see on the stage for Turkish dresses) makes him look so. He has a long black bushy beard, and whiskers, and though he seems 40, is, in truth, only 28 years old. He professes himself very much pleased with an English dinner, at which he played his part to admiration. Wine is forbidden by his religion – but after a little discussion with the interpreter, we were informed by him that the Effendi was not *scrupulous* – and so it proved – at least, if Madeira, and port and claret be counted for wine in his creed.

The Interpreter is a Greek, and I believe a Christian. He does not wear a long beard, but contents himself with a huge pair of whiskers. In other respects his dress is much the same with the Turk's. They were altogether very entertaining – and our entertainment was heightened in the evening by the arrival (incog. for it seems he ought not to come out, not having yet been at the Drawing Room) of the Ambassador Yussuff Adijah Effendi himself. He is a well-looking dignified person, apparently about 60 – but in fact about 40 years of age. He brought his other Interpreter with him – so you may imagine that for an hour or two we had a fine jabbering among us. When I came away I left the Ambassador squatting upon a sofa, and playing at chess with Mr. Ryder.

[72] Probably the Rev. Charles Thomas Barker, matric. Christ Church 30 May 1777; B.A. 1781; M.A. 1784; Proctor, 1790
[73] 'I dined ... with Mr Ryder', printed in *NERT*, 453–54
[74] Hon. Dudley Ryder, 2nd Baron and 1st Earl of Harrowby

I supped with Jenkinson – who was to have been of the party at F. North's to-day, but that he was confined by a sore throat.

*9 [January]* Thursday. Bobus Smith called upon me, and with him I went to pay our respects to Dr. Heath,[75] our old tutor, and now master, of Eton. Afterwards I called at the Offices – on Arbuthnot and on Goddard, but could hear no news. I dined with Charles Greville and Lady Charlotte, a very comfortable trio. And in the evening went to Lady Malmesbury and her sister Lady Elliot[76] – who (as I had learned by a note from the former of them this morning) are just come to town; Lady M. to meet Lady E., and poor Lady E. herself, on her way, as she supposed, to *Toulon*. Sir Gilbert, however, will save her the trouble of so long a voyage by returning to join her in England – and so, poor soul, she has packed up her trunks and inoculated her children for nothing, and may begin to unpack and uninoculate when she pleases. I supped with them – and shall dine with them to-morrow.

*10 [January]* Friday. Newbolt called on me early by appointment, and I went with him to breakfast with his intended bride. But do you know who Newbolt is, and who his intended? Not you, I believe. Well then – Newbolt is a very particular friend of mine. We were together at Christ Church; and since, at the Temple. He is going to be married to Miss Julia Digby,[77] the Maid of Honour: and there is no objection to the match, nor any circumstance attending it, that does not promise the completest happiness, excepting only the grand want of all, the want of money. On this ground, when he consulted me in the summer upon his scheme of marriage (without mentioning the lady's name) and had, like most people who consult, already made up his mind upon the matter, I advised against it. This I rather feared might prejudice me in his *future's* opinion. And I was therefore very glad to receive an invitation from her, through him – as it proved that no such prejudice had arisen. I went with him then to breakfast at her apartments at St. James's: and I do not wonder, after seeing her (though she is not magnificently handsome, but as pleasing and interesting a countenance as you can conceive) and talking with her for an hour or two, that my advice, if it has been twenty times as sage as it was, should have been over-ruled by her charms.

We talked over their domestic economy, as it is to be established,

<hr>

[75] Rev. Dr. George Heath (1745–1822); assistant master at Eton, 1775–91; headmaster 1791–1801

[76] W. of Sir Gilbert Elliot Murray Kynynmound, 1st Earl of Minto, who was apptd. civil commr. of Toulon in Sept. 1793 but made his escape in Dec., see *Thorne*, iii, 695

[77] John Henry Newbolt (c. 1769–1823), m. 18 Feb. 1794, Elizabeth Juliana Rigby, 2nd. da. of Hon. Very Rev. William Digby, 3rd bro. of 1st Earl of Digby. She was maid of honour to Queen Charlotte

and I went with Newbolt, by her desire, to see their house, that is to be, and settle alterations and improvements.

I dined with Lady Elliot and Lady Malmesbury – and there dined nobody else but Mr. Windham. We had a comfortable long *coze* after dinner – and then Windham and I went to see F. North. We sat with him till it was time for him to go to bed, discussing politicks. Windham is most staunch and sturdy for the War. I set out on my way home – but passing by Jenkinson's door I could not refrain from going in – and going in I could not resist supping, though contrary to my rule; and supping, I could not easily prevent myself from staying till about two in the morning.

*11th. [January]* Saturday. I[78] called on Mr. Pitt – but he was at Council. Indeed I did not wish to see him, having nothing particular to say – but only to shew that I was in town, and that I had received the pressing circular letter which has been sent (as I believe is usual) to every member of Parliament, requesting their attendance on the 21st.[79]

Willy[80] [Canning] and I walked down to Wanstead together to dinner.

*12th. [January]* Sunday – I spent at Wanstead – where I saw the Bruces again, and liked them better and better. I slept at Sheridan's – but Sheridan was not there.

*13th. [January]* Monday. After breakfast I walked from Wanstead to town with Paul Patrick. I staid at home the whole morning – and received sundry visitors. I dined with Jenkinson – where dined also Frederic Hervey,[81] Lady Bristol's second son, with whom it has long been settled [by] Jenkinson and Wallace[82] and F. North, that I was to be acquainted. And so I am. And he brought a pressing sort of message from his mama, Lady B. (not the first that has come to me I would have you to know) desiring me to accompany him and Jenkinson there to-night. And so we went. There were Ly. B. and her eldest daughter Lady Erne, and her youngest daughter, Ly. Louisa Hervey[83] (her middle daughter, Ly. E[lizabeth]. Foster, is at Bath) – and there came Lady Ch[arlotte]. and C[harles]. Greville. Ly. B. and her family seem charming – and they are at home almost every night – and I think I shall do as they have desired me, and go there pretty often. Ly. B. talked about the Bruces – and so did Fr. Hervey very

[78]'I called ... the 21st', printed *NER*, 454. 'Council' probably means a cabinet [council]

[79]Parliament reassembled after the Christmas recess on 21 Jan. 1794

[80]William Canning, s. of Stratford and Mehitabel Canning and therefore C.'s cousin

[81]Frederick William Hervey, 5th Earl of Bristol

[82]Thomas Wallace, 1st Baron Wallace. C's contemporary at Eton and Christ Church

[83]Lady Theodosia Louisa Hervey

much. We (that is Jenk. and I) stayed there till rather late – but being my first night I was shy of staying supper – and so we went away – and I supped at Jenkinson's – and I am just this moment come home in Jenkinson's carriage – which saves me a hackney coach, or my legs – and it is past two o'clock – and so I must go to bed. Goodnight.

Tuesday – this day sennight, is the *important* day – for the nation I mean. *My* important day will not be till the day after, or probably the day after *that*.

Pray for *us*, that is for your country, and for *me*!

*14 [January]* Tuesday. I am afraid I lounged away the morning. I dined at Mr. Woodcock's – where besides the family were Mr. Barker – C. Moore and Adderley. I went with Adderley to the Opera, and from the Opera returned quietly to bed.

*15 [January]* Wednesday morning. I stayed at home – thinking over sundry matters – concerning the opening of Parliament. I dined with C. Greville and Lady Charlotte – where besides myself was only Frederick Hervey. In[84] the evening I should have gone with F. Hervey to his mother's – but that I was obliged to return home to entertain the *Irish Club* who were to sup with me. Do you know what the Irish Club is? It is a Club consisting chiefly of Irish merchants – such as Borrowes, Higginson (by the bye, do you know that Borrowes and Higginson are parted?) – P. Patrick &c. &c.[85] – to which, when first I came to settle in town, Mr. Borrowes proposed that I should belong. And I consented – and the rule of it is that they meet alternately at each other's houses to supper every second Wednesday – and play whist – and sup – and there is to be nothing *hot* but potatoes – and they break up at 12. It comes to each member's turn about twice a year. This was my night – and so I gave them a grand entertainment – and it is over.

*16 [January]* Thursday. I had received a note last night from Mr. Pitt – saying that he should be at home and glad to see me this morning at 10. So I went according to my appointment – and had a long conversation with him upon the state of public affairs. He gave me the King's Speech to read, and a copy of it to bring away with me – and desired me that if there were any questions that I wished to

[84] 'In the evening ... Beware of drinking.' (p. 45), printed *NER*, 454–55 and *Marshall*, 49

[85] The Borrowes and Higginson families were inter-related as a result of the m. of Sir Kildare Dixon Borrowes 5th Bt. (I) to his 2nd w. Jane, da. of Joseph Higginson of Mount Ophaly, co. Kildare. In the Directories for this date Philip and William Higginson are recorded as tea and wine merchants of various addresses in Dublin; and a firm of the name Higginson Barnard & Co., listed as merchants of New Court, Swithin's Lane, London.

ask or any papers to see, I should send to him, or call, whenever I pleased. I came home and set to work for the rest of the morning, and wrote to Mr. Pitt for several papers mentioned in the Speech, and others – which were all sent to me in the evening.

A party had been made last week for this day, for Lord Hobart, and Adderley and myself to dine together. I had a very great wish to be acquainted with Lord Hobart, and I had Adderley's word for his having the same wish with regard to me. We dined at Freemason's Tavern. The party were Ld. Hᵗ, Adderley, Mr. Corry (the Irish member),[86] Mr. Borough, [87] Ld. H.'s secretary in Ireland and now going with him to India, Mr. Marcus Beresford,[88] who is also going with him, and Mr. St. Leger[89] – and myself. We all seemed to like each other very well; and all agreed in shewing our attachment to the Madeira claret and excellent white Burgundy, so that by eleven o'clock I was perfectly unfit to go to the Dss. of Gordon's, but unluckily was incapacitated also from perceiving my own unfitness.

I had for this past week been receiving abundance of pressing messages from her Grace (whom by the way I never saw but once, that was last summer at Lord Abercorn's – but then we struck up a violent acquaintance) – and so tonight, finding that Ld. Hobart and Adderley were going there, I resolved to accompany them. What I said, or did then for *three* hours, the Lord knows, for I have only a very faint and dizzy recollection of it. I only know that I talked eternally – partly with the Duchess of Gordon, partly with my friends the *Turks*, partly with Lord Carlisle (who is a person that I never venture to talk to when I am sober), and that at two or three in the morning I found myself at home and in bed – and on waking about eight hours after, wondered what I had been doing.

*17 [January]* Friday morning. I felt sickish and uncomfortable – and had not courage to begin looking over the papers that Mr. Pitt had sent to me – but went to take a little quieting walk. I met Adderley coming to call upon me. It was a great satisfaction to me to find that I had not been the only person of the party upon whom the white Burgundy had operated – but that Adderley himself and Lord Hobart too had been as much unfitted for an assembly as I. Ld. H. indeed

---

[86] Isaac Corry (1752–1818). M.P. (I) Newry 1776–1800; commr. of Customs (I) 1789–97. He was in London to discuss Irish matters with the new chief secretary, Hon. Sylvester Douglas, 1st Baron Glenbervie, see F. Bickley (ed.), *The Diaries of Sylvester Douglas. Lord Glenbervie*, (London, 2 vols., 1928), i, 34

[87] Unidentified

[88] Marcus Beresford (1764–97). He had vacated his seat for St. Canice in the Irish Parliament to make way for the new chief secretary, see *The Diaries of Sylvester Douglas. Lord Glenbervie*, (London, 2 vols., 1928), i, 41. Lord Hobart was going to India as gov. of Madras

[89] Possibly John Hayes St. Leger (1756–1800), M.P., Okehampton, 1791–96.

had perceived the state in which he was, and cunningly withdrawn himself from the Dss. of Gordon's a quarter of an hour after he got there. And Adderley had not run the same risque of exposing himself that I did, for luckily he had sat down to a faro table the whole night, where, still more luckily he had won sixty guineas. Lord Hobart, before we parted last night, had asked me to dinner to-day – and, when you have been drunk once or twice, Fan, you will know that [it] is a great comfort to dine the following day with some of the persons who were the companions of your debauch, especially if they have had, as Lord Hobart had in this instance, the prudence to provide a sort of sick broth for your consolation. There were Ld. and Ly. Hobart, Adderley, his brother, his sister (all going to India) and a Mr. Hobart,[90] brother of Ld. H. I sat cozing with them great part of the evening – and then finding myself not stout enough to go anywhere else, I returned home, and perused papers till bed-time. I like Ld. Hobart very, very much. Beware of drinking.

*18 [January]* Saturday I was at home all the morning – reading, noting, composing, digesting and preparing – not with any view however of speaking the *first* day – *that* would be too forward and presumptuous. I asked Mr. Pitt if he did not think so – and he agreed with me.

I dined at Mr. Woodcock's – where was Mr. Barker and Bobus Smith – and I went in the evening to the Opera.

*19. [January]* Sunday – Frere breakfasted with me – and stayed in a comfortable lounge the whole morning – during which indeed I was obliged to leave him by himself for about two hours – while I went to call on Mr. Pitt. I had a pretty long conversation with him (Mr. Pitt) upon the same subjects as before – put to him all the questions which I wished to have answered, and got from him the remainder of the papers, treaties &c., which are to be laid before Parliament; and a corrected copy of the King's Speech, which is considerably altered in style, though not much in substance from the copy which I had before.

I dined at Lord Stafford's – where except myself there was none but the family – and their wives and husbands – that is to say Lady Worcester and her Lord[91] – Lord Gower and his Lady (Sutherland) – and the two unmarried Lady Levesons.[92] They are as pleasant in town as country, and live in a very comfortable quiet way. I stayed there the evening – and then went to sup with Jenkinson whom I found in the midst of papers, noting and preparing like me.

[90] Hon. George Vere Hobart (1761–1802)
[91] Henry Charles Somerset, styled Lord Worcester and subsequently, 6th Duke of Beaufort. M.P. Bristol 1790–96
[92] Lady Georgiana Augusta and Lady Susan Leveson-Gower

*20. [January]* Monday. I was at home all the morning. Leigh[93] is wrong in his conjecture that I dined at Mr. Pitt's to-day. It is the etiquette for the Minister to give a dinner the day before the meeting of Parliament, to all the ministerial members who are *Privy Counsellors*, or who hold *offices*, and to none others – and you are aware that I do not come immediately under either of these descriptions. From this dinner they proceed in a body to a place called the Cockpit (a large room in the Treasury) where *all* the members of Parlt. who mean to support Government meet at about nine o'clock – and there the Minister reads aloud the Speech, which the King is to make from the Throne the next day, and the Address which is to be moved in the House of Commons, and declares the names of the two persons who have undertaken to move and second the Address. (The same ceremony is gone through with regard to the House of Peers by Lord Grenville.) I dined at home alone – and at 9 set out for the Cockpit – where was such a crowd, and squeeze and heat, as was sufficient to give one a foretaste of the House of Commons. From the Cockpit, after hearing the Speech read etc. I went to the Play, and from the Play, with two or three people whom I met there, to sup at the Mount Coffee-house.

*21 [January]* This[94] was the important day. I got up with I know not how many odd feelings about me, and could not sit still for a moment till it was time to go down to the House. About three I went – and took my station under the Gallery (till I had been sworn-in I had no right in the *body* of the House) – then attended the Speaker to the House of Lords to hear the King's Speech – then returned to the House of Commons and took the oaths and my seat. I cannot describe [to] you with what emotions I felt myself walking about the floor which I had so often contemplated *in my youth* from the Gallery, and wondered when I should have a right to tread upon it. I sat down too upon the Treasury Bench, just to see how it felt – and from that situation met the grinning countenances of half of my acquaintances who were in the Gallery – I was all in a flutter for some minutes – but however I bowed to the Chair, and shook hands with the Speaker, and went through all the ceremonies, down to that of paying my fees, with the utmost decorum and propriety. – At 4 o'clock the debate began and lasted, as you will have seen by the papers, for thirteen hours, that is till 5 in the morning. It was to me one of the highest entertainments that can be conceived. I had no notion that there had been such a difference as I find there is, in the interest with which one hears a debate when merely a spectator in the Gallery, and that which

---

[93] 'Leigh is ... Coffee House', printed in *NER*, 456
[94] 'This was ... the decision' (p. 47), printed in *Marshall*, 50

one feels as a member, with the consciousness of having a right to join in it if one pleases, and to give one's vote upon the decision.

During[95] the dull parts of the debate I went out several times to dine, with C. Ellis and Lord Andover[96] and Tom Sheridan whom I found under the Gallery, to drink tea, to see what was going forward in the House of Lords. *There*, under the throne, I met the *Duchess of Gordon*, who had obtained the Chancellor's permission to stay to hear their debate. I had an opportunity of making my apologies for the character in which I had come to her house on Thursday. I found that she had perceived it pretty evidently, not in me only, but in Ld. Hobart and Adderley also. But she forgave it on condition that I would always come for the future to her parties, without waiting for the formality of invitation. And as a test of her good humour she asked me to partake of some beefsteak and oyster sauce, which she was just going to take by way of staying her stomach till the debate should end. I had dined, and therefore could not profit by her offer.

The division was, as you know, 277 to 59. I need hardly tell you in which of those numbers I was included. I got home about $\frac{1}{2}$ past six and slept soundly till about 1/2 past 12. What newspaper do you take in for the debates? *The Sun* is vile, *The Star*, tho' an Opposition paper, is better, but the *Morning Chronicle* better still.

*22 [January]* Wednesday morning I was waked by people coming to enquire after the debate – Bobus Smith and Sturges and Adderley – and desiring to know whether there was likely to be another debate this day, or no, and whether or no I meant to speak in it, that they might go and hear me. I told them, what was true, that Grey[97] had said after the division that he would give us another debate to-day, and that if there was one, and I found an opportunity that I liked, I fully intended speaking. They set off therefore for the Gallery, and I stayed at home ruminating, and plucking up resolution till 1/2 past three – then dressed and went down to the House – and walked up the House and made my bow, and took my seat just above Pitt, as bold as a lion. The House was very empty, and I found upon enquiry that the House had been too much tired the night before to have much expectation of a debate on this day. Not a single Opposition person appeared – till just as we were about to adjourn, Fox[98] and Grey

[95] 'During the dull ... better still', printed in *NER*, 456

[96] Charles Nevison Howard, e.s. of 15th Earl of Suffolk and styled Viscount Andover 1783–1800

[97] Charles Grey, 2nd Earl Grey. M.P. Northumberland 1786–1807 and a leading member of the Opposition

[98] Hon. Charles James Fox (1749–1806), the leader of the Opposition in the Commons. Fox and R.B. Sheridan q.v. had tried to engage C. for their party when the latter was at Eton, Fox evidently trying to teach him and Lord Holland 'political lessons' over dinner, see *Bagot*, i, 47n and *Marshall*, 8

entered, and Fox said something of what he meant to do whenever the
Sardinian Treaty[99] came before the House – but had nothing to offer
now – so that at a little after 5 o'clock, to the great mortification of
people who had been securing places in the Gallery, we adjourned.
Having no engagement for dinner, I poked out Sturges and Bobus
Smith among the crowd, and we went and dined together at a coffee
house.

In the evening I went to the Markhams – and in my way from
them called and supped at Mrs. Crewe's.

If you do resolve to take in the *Morning Chronicle* – do not *leave off*
your ministerial paper. Keep the *antidote* with the poison.

*23 [January]* Thursday. There was no business in the House except
the Speaker going up with the Address to the King – a ceremony
which I did not attend because I had no wish to deck myself out in a
dress coat – though I have got a very handsome one, I would have
you to know – dark brown with a white *sattin* lining – not to mention
a full suit of black for Court mournings or Lord Chancellor's Levées.

I dined at Mr. Pitt's – where were Lord Mornington, Lord Bayham,
Lord Apsley[100] (I do not believe you have heard his name before from
me – he is Lord Bathurst's son – a personal friend of Mr. Pitt – and
has a good deal of humour and pleasantness. I have some sort of
acquaintance with him, having met him at Lord Abercorn's), Lord
Worcester, Lord Euston (the Duke of Grafton's son and Mr. Pitt's
colleague for Cambridge) – Mr. Ryder (I do not much like Mr.
Ryder. He seems pert and self-sufficient, and I believe must at bottom
be foolish), Mr. Townshend[101] (Lord Sydney's son, a good-humoured,
stupidish sort of a young man), Mr. Eliott – Captn. Berkeley [102]
(something in the Ordnance and member of the House of Commons –
disagreeable enough at first sight, as I think) – Wallace and
Jenkinson – and Mr. C. Lenox, of whom you have often heard – and
against whom I had conceived a kind of prejudice – but he seems not
to deserve it – but to be a very gentlemanlike, pleasant man.[103] The

[99] A subsidy treaty between Britain and Sardinia which was criticised by Fox on 27 Jan. see *Parl. Hist.*, xxx, cols., 1310–1313
[100] Henry Bathurst, 3rd Earl Bathurst. M.P. Cirencester 1783–94; teller of Exchequer and commr. Board of Control
[101] Hon. John Thomas Townshend, 2nd Visct. Sydney. M.P. Whitchurch 1790–1800; ld. of Treasury 1793–1800
[102] Hon. George Cranfield Berkeley (1753–1818). M.P. Gloucestershire 1783–1810 and surveyor-gen. of Ordnance 1789–95
[103] Charles Lennox (1764–1819) later 4th Duke of Richmond; M.P. Sussex 1790–1806 and sec. to master-gen. of Ordnance 1784–1795. C.'s initial distaste may have been due to Lennox having fought at least two duels, one with the Duke of York, see *Thorne*, iv, 414

dinner was well enough – though not so well as the last which I had here.

From there I went to the Play – and meeting at the Play some young Christ Church people – Dawkins[104] – whom you have heard me mention – who spoke my verses so well – brother of the Dawkins whom you saw at Ashborne – and Stopford[105] – a son of Lord Courtown – whom I remember at Eton as well as at Oxford. I went with them, idly and foolishly, to sup at the Mount.

*24 [January]* Friday. I[106] was at home all the morning. I went down to the House at 4. There was no business, and we adjourned to Monday. I dined at Lord Courtown's – where was nobody but the family, Ld. & Ly. C., Ld. Stopford their eldest son, & his wife, Ly. Mary S[topford] – their other son, my acquaintance – & a Mr. Villiers,[107] brother of Mr. Villiers whom I have met at Mr. Pitt's. In the evening I went to the Play – and from the Play again, idly and foolishly as before, with Dawkins and Stopford and other *young ones*, to the Mount. I have been very idle lately of an evening. I ought to have gone to the Markhams. I ought to have gone to Mrs. Crewe's – to Lady Bristol's – to Lady Payne's – who has evening parties, & for the most part rather dull ones, & to the Dss. of Gordon's – & above all to the Staffords – where I have promised to go but have never been. And instead of this, here have I been gadding about to plays & operas every night – & supping afterwards just as I used when I was a youthful collegian, come up to London for the vacation. But all these young ones who *seduce* me, are going out of town to their studies – & then I shall reform & return to my sobriety & steadiness.

*25 [January]* Saturday. Frere breakfasted with me, and Bobus Smith called soon after – and being a woeful bad snowy day – we drew our chairs round the fire and sat cozing till between 4 and 5 in the afternoon.

I had letters from the Dean of Ch[rist] Ch[urch], full of good advice – from my poor mother, who had seen in the newspapers that I was to speak, and was wild to know when – and from her poor son, Samuel, who is under orders to embark with his company for Botany Bay. John King has promised me that something shall be done for him. I will remind him of his promise, and enforce the performance of it as much as I can. Poor Samuel, I am afraid, has much to go through, but he sets about it with a good spirit, and as I cannot

---

[104] Probably John Dawkins (1773–1844); matric. Christ Church, 4 Feb. 1791

[105] Hon. Richard Bruce Stopford (1774–1844), 4th s. of James, 2nd Earl of Courtown; Eton 1783–91; matric. Christ Church, 30 Apr. 1792

[106] 'I was … and steadiness', printed in *NER*, 456–57

[107] Hon. George Villiers (1759–1827) 3rd s. of Thomas Villiers, 1st Earl of Clarendon. M.P. Warwick 1792–1802; paymaster of marines 1792–1810 and a Household official

prevent his undergoing it, I have only to do what I can to soften the rigours of his situation.

There is a report that the Dean is to be the new Bishop. He says not a word of it – but I hope it may be true – and I think it not very unlikely – though Lord Courtown (a good authority, as he is always in attendance on the King)[108] told me yesterday that Dr. Courtney, a brother-in-law of Ld. Loughborough, was to have it.[109] That jobbing Scot, The Chancellor, gets everything.

I find that it is the opinion of all sober people that I was very ill-treated by that squib in the *Chronicle* [110] of Monday, of which I sent you a copy, and have kept one myself. I protest *I* do not think or feel it so – and to speak honestly, I would rather be abused a little, if I had my choice, than have nothing at all said about me. But I certainly have no reason to be sorry that *other* people see it in the *heinous* light in which I am told they do, if that circumstance produces, as I am told it has done, in many grave and respectable members of the House of Commons, a determination to hear and *chear* and *support* me, whenever I speak, in a very decided manner. There is no business expected in the House till Wednesday – when Mr. Pitt says he means to move for the Navy supplies. On that day he thinks there may be some skirmish, though probably not a very regular and serious debate. But on Friday when he moves for the Subsidies (Sardinian, Hessian, &c.) he thinks there will be *the* great debate of all – and if so for that day I shall prepare myself. On the Monday following he has given notice of the Army supplies – and on the Wednesday he intends to open the Budget. This is all that is yet fixed or known, for Opposition have given notice of nothing. I cannot think – nor can anybody with whom I have talked about it – what it is that makes them so tardy.

[108] He was treasurer of the Household

[109] Lord Courtown was correct. Dr. Henry R. Courtney became bishop of Bristol in 1794. Lord Loughborough, subsequently the 1st Earl of Rosslyn, was Lord Chancellor 1793–1801

[110] In a leader in the *Morning Chronicle* of 20 Jan. 1794 under the title 'Theatre de la Nation', it was pointed out that 'The Manager' (Pitt) had taken on several new performers for the new season (session) and that 'great expectations indeed are entertained of a young performer, who has as yet never appeared upon any stage. What salary has been promised him has not yet transpired, but it is certain that the utmost industry was employed by THE MANAGER to secure him to his Company. It was said indeed, that he was bound apprentice to another Manager, that the lad had been prevailed upon to run away from his articles, and that the business was not unlikely to come to be the subject of a law-suit. This turns out however to be not true; he was we are assured, under no obligation to the gentleman who brought him up, but that of gratitude; and as strictness of morals is no more looked for in this Theatre than any other, if he acquits himself ably as an Actor, it is all the public have any right, or reason to expect from him.' The allusions to the stage and to Sheridan were very pointed given C.'s sensitivities on those points.

The Duke of Portland, you know, has at length taken a decided part with Government.[111] There was some danger, as I apprehended, at the beginning of the Session, that the middle party (Mr. Burke,[112] Windham &c. &c.) might take the line of supporting the *war*, but impeaching the *conduct* of it – a line which would have been almost as embarrassing to Ministry as an actual opposition. But this apprehension is at an end. They have spoken out fairly and honourably – and avowed their intention to support Ministry, in the same manner, and with the same zeal, with the friends of Ministry themselves – not only voting for the carrying on of the war – but resisting all *factious* motions of *enquiry*, which might weaken the hands of Gov. and throw impediments in their way. This is good – and makes a campaign – in and out of doors, plain and easy, which might otherwise have been perplexed and difficult, and even hazardous.

I dined with C. Greville and Lady Charlotte – nobody but Lord Sackville. He is a very worthy and pleasant young man, but attached to nothing but *hunting* and such-like sports and pastimes – without, however, having a grain of the black-guardedness which sometimes accompanies such a taste, in his disposition. We had never met before – though we had known each other a long time through many common friends – John Sneyd,[113] Arbuthnot, Edw. Legge,[114] &c. They all speak of him very highly.

I went to the Opera – and there was all the world. From the Opera I went home with Jenkinson to supper. The Dean is to be the Bishop.

*26 [January]* Sunday. I[115] dedicated the morning to paying visits (*after* Divine service). I dined at Sir R. Payne's.[116] The company were Sir R. and Ly. P[ayne], Lord Sheffield, Mr. Metcalfe (a M.P.),[117]

---

[111] Portland was leader of the Opposition in the House of Lords and on 20 Jan. had called a meeting at Burlington House of those members of his party who wished, like him, to support the government's war policy. This divided the Opposition, Portland and his followers coalescing with the Government in July 1794. C. had first been introduced to Portland by the Duchess, a close friend of Mrs Crewe. In March 1793 he declined to be returned to Parliament by Portland on the grounds that the Opposition party contained parliamentary reformers, see *Marshall*, 43–44; *Thorne*, iii, 380

[112] Edmund Burke (1729–97)

[113] John Sneyd (1760–1835), 5th s. of Ralph Sneyd of Keele Hall, Staffs.; rector of Elford, Staffs, 1792-d. Sneyd left Eton as C. arrived; and then went to Cambridge. They therefore became friends through a medium other than school or university – possibly that of Mrs Crewe

[114] Hon. Edward Legge (c. 1767–1827), 4th s. of 2nd Earl of Dartmouth; matric. Christ Church, 14 June 1784; B.A. 1788; fellow of All Souls, 1789; bishop of Oxford 1815-d.

[115] 'I dedicated ... Mrs Crewe's' (p. 52), printed in *NER*, 457

[116] A recent convert to the cause of Pitt and cr. Baron Lavington in 1795, see *Thorne*, iv, 737–38

[117] Philip Metcalfe (1733–1818). M.P. Plympton Erle 1790–96

Wallace and myself. Ld. Sheffield and I renewed an old acquaintance that had subsisted between us 8 or 10 years ago when I was at Eton. He gave us a long description of Gibbon's death,[118] whom he had attended almost in his last moments. He died *without* recanting (tho' he was said to have done so) and what may perhaps explain that circumstance, without having entertained the least apprehension that his death was approaching. It seems he had expressed great desire to be acquainted with *me* – and we were to have been brought together by Lord S. this winter. I wish he had lived that I might have seen him.

In the ev^g. I went to Lady Stafford's – and aft^ds. supp'd with Wallace and Fred. North at Mrs. Crewe's.

*27 [January]* Monday. The day on which I sent off to you my last journal and within an hour after I had sent it came Samuel Reddish – poor fellow – in his serjeant's accoutrements, to take leave of me on his being about to set out for Botany Bay in command of a guard of 12 men with the first convict ship that sails. He is a bold, wild fellow, apparently, and seems to have spirits and health that will carry him through the undertaking. He expressed great thankfulness for the small assistance that he had received from me – and which Bess and Fan were kind enough to enable me to give to him – and for inter-ference which I have promised and in which I hope to succeed, for his advantage with the Secretary of State's Office. He had no books, I found, to amuse himself during his long voyage – so I rummaged out a quantity of Spectators, Adventures, Worlds &c., and packed them up for him in my travelling bag – with which over his shoulder he trudged away as merrily as though he had been just setting out on a party of pleasure. With him came his brother, Charles – the one who, as I have before told you, had been so generously taken by the coachmaker. Generosity, however, is but a precarious dependence, at least in a coachmaker, for the poor boy complains now that Mr. Morton uses him ill, and frequently expressed very loudly a wish that he had never taken, or could now get rid of him. I could only counsel the poor little fellow to bear it as well as he can, and give him a guinea to keep my counsel in mind. But I must look out for something else for him, and as he writes admirably and is an excellent accountant I hope I may find it not impracticable to get him into some trades-men's or merchant's countinghouse. But of that – more, when I am able.

I went down to the House – where there was no business for the day – but some notices given by Opposition – though none upon the war. That is the subject which I want to have brought forward, but

[118] Edward Gibbon, the historian, who d. 16 Jan. 1794

the Opposition are cruelly tardy and guarded. Mr. Adam[119] gave notice of a motion that he intends to make to assimilate the law of Scotland in criminal cases with that of England – in the course of which he means also to consider Mr. Muir's and Mr. Palmer's trials.[120] Mr. Sheridan made some enquiries respecting the jobs and appointments of the summer – and promised a motion upon it soon.

I was engaged provisionally to dine with Mr. Maxwell[121] – to meet Harry and Paul Patrick and Norris – but as the House sat till 6 – and it was then too late (I was not sorry to find it so) to set off for Camomile Street, I dined upstairs at Bellamy's with Wallace and Jenkinson – and went in the evening – and supped with the Markhams.

*28 [January]* Tuesday – I spent the morning partly at home – and partly in making sundry visits – which had long been lying heavy on my hands – Ld. and Ly. Hobart, Ld. and Ly. Auckland, the Chief Baron and Ly. Louisa Mcdonald, &c.

The House – nothing done.

I dined by old appointment with Bobus Smith and his father and Frere – at a tavern. In the evening I went to Covent Garden to see the Pantomime and met the Markhams there. In my way home I called at our Carey Street Club – and read newspapers – and drank a glass of negus, and came quietly home to bed.

*29 [January]* Wednesday. Bobus[122] called on me before I was up, and told me a story of an emigré,[123] a friend of his, who had yesterday received notice, under the Alien Bill, from Mr. Dundas, to quit England in five days – begging me, if I could do it, to apply to Mr. Pitt to endeavour to get a reversal, or at least a suspension, of the sentence. I dressed myself immediately, and went to Downing Street – stated my business to Mr. Pitt, but found that the resolution concerning the person in question, had been too decidedly taken by Ministers to allow of alteration. It was, however, gratifying to me that he received my application with the utmost kindness and attention, and that, when I attempted to apologize for the presumption &c. of having interfered, he stopped me short with a thousand assurances of his willingness and wish to see me, hear me, and do for me, whatever was in his power.

[119] William Adam (1751–1839), M.P. Ross-shire 1790–94 and the leading manager of the Opposition in the Commons
[120] Thomas Fyshe Palmer (1747–1802) and Thomas Muir (1765–98) were convicted by Scottish courts of sedition in 1793. On 4 Feb. 1794 William Adam q.v. introduced a motion, one of whose objects was to enable those convicted in Scotland to appeal to the House of Lords. The motion was defeated 126 v 31, see *Thorne*, iii, 30.
[121] William Maxwell (1768–1833) of Carriden, Linlithgow; C.'s contemporary at Christ Church
[122] 'Bobus … power', printed in *NER*, 457
[123] Charles-Maurice de Talleyrand Périgord

House – The Navy Estimates voted with little or no discussion. I dined upstairs with C. Ellis – Mr. Mundy[124] (of Derbyshire) and Lord Mornington. Went with C. Ellis to the Play, and from the Play returned quietly home.

*30 [January]* Thursday. Being the 30th of Janry. there was no parliamentary business – but a sermon to be preached by the Chaplain – which I did not feel myself much called upon to attend. I stayed at home the whole morning – turning over in my mind the Sardinian Treaty which is to be discussed tomorrow. I dined with Jenkinson. There were Edw^d. Legge, Arbuthnot and Charles Ellis – a very, very pleasant dinner. In the ev^g I went w[i]th Jenkinson to Lady Bristol's – and there stayed, and supped very comfortably with Ly. B[ristol], Lady Louisa Hervey and Ly. Eliz^th. Foster.[125]

*31 Friday–Jan^ry. 31st, 1794.* Perhaps the most important day of my life. I[126] really tremble when I look back and consider what I undertook on this day. When I recollect that *on three quarters of an hour* in this day depended perhaps the whole colour and character of my future fortune, condition and reputation – that if I had many people who were anxious that I should do well, there were not wanting some to whom my failure would have been matter of triumph – and that the chances of my doing well, or of my failure, on whatever other circumstances they might depend, were rendered not a little more precarious by the circumstance of the public expectation having been raised *so high* not only by the solicitous *puffings* of my friends, but by the designing and feigned ardour of those who wished to prejudice me, that it was no *improbable* thing, but rather the most likely in the world, that *they* would find opportunity of saying with apparent *candour* and fairness, but with a more fatal effect to my reputation than could arise from downright abuse, 'that it was *pretty well, to be sure*; but nothing like what they had been taught to *expect*, &c. &c.' There is but *one* man who *has* said this. I will tell you *who*, by and by. Let me now begin by telling you, dear Leigh and dear Fan, and dear Bess and dear Tish, that my success has been equal to – nay beyond my most sanguine expectations. When I proceed to explain this to you I feel that this will be so *vain* a sheet that when I have written it I shall be inclined to burn it. But I am sure your delight in hearing particulars will be so much more, in proportion, than the backwardness which I *ought* to feel in relating them (if I were properly modest) that I will

---

[124] Edward Miller Mundy (1750–1822). M.P. Derbyshire 1784–1822
[125] Lady Bristol's da. in law and da. respectively
[126] 'I really tremble ... could have been' (p. 60), printed in *Marshall*, 52–60

get the better of all my feelings and go through the task manfully from beginning to end.

On Friday morning then I was scarcely up when Frere and Sturges and Bobus Smith came to tell me that they were setting off to get places in the Gallery – Frere and Sturges succeeded, and placed themselves just opposite to the situation from which I spoke. Bobus, to his great regret, and mine also, was detained by his good-natured attentions to his poor emigré,[127] till he was too late to get in. As soon as they were gone, I walked up and down in my room, in an agitation something like what I should suppose a man to feel who is going to be hanged, but why dying *innocent* has hopes of salvation. I argued the Sardinian Treaty over with great success in my own mind – and was going on very satisfactorily to myself – when Charles Ellis called by appointment to tell me that it was time to dress and go down to the House – I dressed therefore and sent for a bit of cold meat and a glass of white wine – for Jenkinson and all wise people had told me that it was necessary to have some support to prevent a sensation of *sinking* and emptiness. Then off I set with Ch. Ellis – got to the House in a sort of aguish fever – took a place immediately behind Pitt and Dundas on the second bench (for I did not think it decorous to speak from the floor the first time) and sat myself down to wait the beginning of the debate. In the Gallery, besides Sturges and Frere, before-mentioned, I spied the two Legges, Edwd. and Aug<sup>s</sup>.,[128] Adderley and two or three Christ Church faces, who might have come there by chance, but looked shrewdly as if they had smelt out the probability of my speaking, and were come to hear me. I whispered to Pitt – 'If there comes on a debate I have thoughts of speaking'. P., 'You cannot chuse a better time'. C., 'If Fox opens, I think I will not speak immediately after him, but wait for Grey or some other young one'.

P. 'I think you judge very rightly – and I think I can augur from Grey's looks that he will probably give you an opportunity'.

C. 'Pray have you the dates and minutes of all the old Sardinian Treaties about you? I want to look at them again'.

P. 'No, really I have not – but here comes Ryder[129] – he has them, I know, and he shall let you see them'.

C. 'I have another Treaty, which strikes me as being much more completely analagous than even any of the former Sardinian ones. It is the Prussian Subsidy of 1758 – what do you think of it?'

[127] Charles-Maurice de Talleyrand Périgord
[128] Hon. Rev. Augustus George Legge (1773–1828), 5th s. of 2nd Earl of Dartmouth. C.'s contemporary at Christ Church
[129] Dudley Ryder had served as under-sec. of state for Foreign affairs, 1789–90

P. 'Good God – aye – it is exactly in point – it will do admirably. £670,000 if I recollect right[130] – I am glad of it – it is the very thing'.

The Order of the Day – Fox began and spoke for about 20 minutes or half an hour. At this time the House was not very full. I was afraid it would not fill – but was glad to see people come flocking.

I took no notes, being resolved not to get a habit of using them – but I committed to my memory as many of Fox's arguments as I could, and was lucky enough to retain them – when I came to speak. I had always determined that my first speech should be in reply – that it might not be said 'Aye, this will do as a speech, but it does not promise a *debater*', and it is my business, you know, if I would get forward, to be useful. After Mr. Fox – rose Mr. Powys[131] – and very luckily for me – took up the question in the point of view in which I had resolved to consider it – as connected with the subject of the *whole war* – very luckily, I say, because he is not the sort of speaker to anticipate ones *arguments* – but is the sort of man, of weight and consequence in the House, to justify any man who follows him, in taking up the *subject* in a point of view different from other people, which but for such an *authority*, might have looked like *lugging* foreign matter into discussion. After Powys – Ryder spoke and confined himself solely to the consideration of the Treaty and to the justification of it by the other *Sardinian* Treaties. After Ryder, *Grey*, in answer to him, and on precisely the same grounds of the Treaty and its precedents. Oh! what I felt while Grey was speaking! What I felt when I saw him retreating towards his seat! What I felt when I found myself, standing bolt upright, and saw the Speaker pull off his hat towards me, and heard him cry and the House echo 'Mr. Canning!' It was not fear – it was tumult. I began – shall I tell you how I began? It must have been nearly as follows –

'Mr Speaker'. A long interruption of Hear – Hear – Order – Places – during which I adjusted myself and pulled out my handkerchief and put it in my hat, which Lord Bayham who sat by me, held – Pitt and Dundas sat immediately below me, and next to them Ryder – and Jenkinson – Wallace stood a good way to my left hand, near the Speaker's chair – Lord Hobart was immediately behind me, and Ch.

---

[130] Pitt's memory was sound, his father having negotiated a subsidy to Prussia of this sum in the second Convention of Westminster, signed on 11 April 1758. C.'s choice of this treaty was judicious on two grounds: first, because Pitt's father had been its architect; and second, because Pitt himself was in pursuit of another Anglo-Prussian subsidy treaty despite the misgivings of his Foreign Secretary, Lord Grenville, see P. Jupp, *Lord Grenville 1759–1834*, (Oxford, 1985), 163–173

[131] Thomas Powys (1743–1800). M.P. Northamptonshire 1774–1797 and an independent country gentleman

Ellis behind me – but a good way to the left. I began, somehow in this manner.

'If, Sir, I could consider this question in the same point of view in which it has been considered by the Hon. gent. (Grey) who spoke last – as a single, insulated and independent question, standing on its own narrow grounds, and to be argued solely on its own limited and appropriate principles – I should have sat contented by, while gentlemen possessed of more official information, and every way of better ability than myself for such a purpose, had given the proper answers to such objections as have been urged against this Treaty. I should [have] sat by contented, with the answer which an Hon. gent below me (Ryder) has already given to every objection of that kind, in a most ample and able and, to my mind, satisfactory manner.

'But, Sir, as I do much rather agree with the Hon. gent. who spoke second in this debate (Powys) in viewing this question as a question of much wider references, connexions and dependencies – in viewing it not as a matter of mere mercantile bargain and sale, not as an investigation of the quid pro quo which we may or may not have gained by this Treaty, not as a tradesmanlike prudential enquiry whether or no we may have been extravagant or overreached – but as an extensive important political question, growing out of, and inseparable from, a great, connected and comprehensive system – Sir – as upon this system, I have found little difficulty, nor can I conceive how any gent. can have found much in *forming* an opinion – so – Sir – I trust, that I shall stand excused from the charge of presumption if I attempt to *deliver mine*.'

I then went on to argue the Treaty itself – and to defend it against Fox's objections – I did intend to have fought against Grey *rather* – but he disappointed my intention by wholly omitting anything like an argument that was worth consideration. In answering Fox, I trumphantly produced my Prussian Treaty – which being new to the House had great effect – and put me in spirits. Finding after a certain time, that I had been attacking Fox *only* and *continually* – I thought it decent, even if I had not known him or liked or admired him, or his connections as I do, yet simply as a young man, commenting on what a great and established character had said – to make some little apology for what I *modestly* stiled my presumption, and to assure him that if I treated his arguments, as I found them in my way, it was not from any want of admiration for his talents, or of respect and esteem for his person. While I was doing this, I necessarily looked, where I had not much looked before to the Opposition Bench, and saw how they were situated – Sheridan was behaving perfectly well – sitting quiet and attentive, looking neither to the right nor to the left. Fox was, as [is] his usual custom, turning round and talking over what I said, as I was going on – this was a little embarrassing but he meant nothing uncivil. But there was one person who did mean and did show much incivility – if I forgive him till I have revenged myself I say – but I will not swear – this person was *Grey*. Agitated as I was, it did not require much to put me in still greater agitation. Once – for half a minute or a minute I was nearly overcome. But I summoned all my resolution. The thoughts of the great game that I was playing, that I had staked my *all*, and must win or lose through life, by the event of this night – anger too, and indignation against the person who was playing his anticks to perplex me – all conspired at once. I made one effort, regained my breath – drew myself up as undauntedly as I could. The House supported me nobly – and I got triumphantly to the end. During the latter part of my speech – I know no pleasure (*sensual* pleasure I had almost said) equal to that which I experienced. I had complete possession of all that I meant to say, and of myself, and I saw my way clear before me. The House was with me to a degree that was most comfortably assuring and delightful. I ventured to look boldly round me and before me and on each side, and met good-natured, chearing countenances – and there were Pitt and Dundas – as I was afterwards informed by those who saw them in front, with their countenances smirking and glittering, rubbing their hands and beating time to the sentences and nodding to each other – and it was during this period that Dundas exclaimed in the way that I told you yesterday. 'By God, this will do'. All this, as you may suppose, was rapture to me – should [you] like to see some of my concluding topics?

'Sir, we are told this is a war of *passion*. If by a war of passion gent[n.] mean that we have been hurried into a war contrary to justice, to humanity and to sound policy, by the indulgence of some blameable propensity in our dispositions – if they mean to prove this, Sir, they appear to have undertaken a very difficult task indeed. They must arraign nature and confute instinct – for they must prove that self-*preservation* is a passion which it is criminal to indulge. But if by a war of passion they intend no more than that in addition to all the acknowledged and legitimate causes of war, for which we contend we have been forced into *this* – in addition to the necessity of repelling unprovoked aggression, of extending our assistance to our allies, of preserving Europe, of saving ourselves – that in addition to all this, Sir, it is a war in which the best feelings and instincts of our nature are engaged, Sir, we are proud to own that in *this* sense it may be called a war of passion – and if ever from this dignified character it should be degraded to [a] war of interest and aggrandisement, I, Sir, for one should cease to be its warm defender.

'But when our feelings cannot be convinced, they attack our

prudence. They ask us – what are we to get by the war? Sir, in the first place, *I* would ask to what species of war such a question fairly applies – to a war, which I contend this *not* to be of aggradisement and speculation – or to *one* which I contend this to be – of self-defence and self-preservation? Sir, if Ministry had come down to this House, and said, we have an opportunity of gaining from the French some accession of commerce, some enlargement of territory, if you will but support us in a war for that purpose; and if upon these grounds this House had agreed to support them in that *war* – then I admit this question might fairly have been put – then I admit that it would have been conclusive and the issue of the whole debate between Ministers in this House would be – Well, what are we, after all, to get by this War? But in a war forced upon us by necessity, &c. no such issue is fair. We are proud to say – it was not the first question we asked – I should be ashamed to be an advocate for a war in which it was the only question that could be answered. And yet, Sir, I would not have it supposed that we have gained nothing – Sir – that we have a [sic] still a Government and Constitution – Sir, that when we are now assembled there is not assembled in our room a Corresponding Society or a Scotch Convention[132] – Sir – that instead of sitting to debate here whether or no we shall subsidize the King of Sardinia – we are not rather discussing the means of raising a forced loan to satisfy the rapaciousness of some proconsular deputy whom the banditti of Paris might have sent to receive our contributions – Sir, that we *sit here at all*, these are the fruits of the war'.

Then came my French madness – and my strumpets and Calendar, all of which *took* amazingly.[133] The *strumpets* indeed tickled everybody, and I assure you I have had very pretty and very chaste mouths beginning to say to me since, 'Oh, but what you said about the str----, I mean about the women in oak leaves'.

Well, I sat down at last in an agitation great indeed, but of a very different kind from that in which I had risen. Must I tell you all that was said to me? No, that I cannot do – you must guess – I will only say that everybody – whom I did know – and many whom I did not, came up and shook hands, and thanked and complimented, and so on – and – what Jenkinson had long ago warned me to consider as a sure test of a speech having succeeded, and made an impression – there was a general buz and stir and changing of places and going

[132] References to the radical London Corresponding Society and the British Convention of radicals held in Edinburgh in November 1793

[133] C. is reported to have said that if the 'madness' of the French republicans had been limited to 'dressing up strumpets in oak-leaves, and inventing nick-names for the kalendar' he would not have thought it worth while going to war with them, *Parl. Hist.*, xxx, col. 1325

out, and no disposition to hear the person who got up after – by which – by the bye I lost a very fine compliment which Mr. Stanley,[134] if they had heard him, was about to pay me. Burke came across the House and said, 'I lament that the debate upon this subject is at an end – I want to say *aloud* to all the House what I think of you – I would get up on purpose to do so – but that I think that would look as if I thought you *wanted* help. It is more dignified to let you *go alone*'.

As soon as it was decent to go down the House I withdrew, and Jenkinson and Wallace and Ch. Ellis from the House, and Edw. Legge and Aug[s.] from the Gallery came and we dined upstairs – and the bumpers of port wine that I swallowed – and the mutton chops that I devoured – and the sensations that I felt, are not to be described.

I find I was about 3 qrs. of an hour upon my legs – and my faults are – that I speak too rapidly, so much so as to run myself entirely out of breath – and louder than is necessary for filling the House – of which however I could not judge the first time – and that I use too violent and theatrical action, insomuch that people about me are apprehensive of some mischief from me. Lord Bayham I did once hit a plaguey hard blow on the shoulder – Pitt who was beneath me, sidled a little out of the way, and Dundas was obliged to *bob* to save his *wig* from confusion. All this was told me as well by friends as by some utter strangers among the members – who very goodnaturedly came up to me for the purpose, and whose interference in this manner I looked upon as an instance of as much kindness as the most flummery compliments could have been.

Another debate followed the same night. I sat it out – and for the first time, since I have been a member of the House, sat boldly, as a supporter of Ministry, on the Treasury bench among them. After this was over I went home with Jenkinson to supper – as did Wallace and C. Ellis and Ed. Legge. I supped *chearily*. I came home and went to bed – but sleep was out of the question.

*Feby. 1.* Saturday morning – I got up early after a tossing and tumbling night (By the way, Tish, your night-ribbon *is* come into wear) – and passed the morning in receiving visits – notes, &c. I ought to have written a line to Ashborne – but I could do nothing.

I dined at Lord Stafford's – where was Ed. Legge, Ld. and Ly. Worcester – Lady S. took me aside to tell me how long a letter abt. it at all [sic] she was writing to Granville.

I went to the Opera. There I saw Mrs. Crewe – the Dss. of Portland – the Dss. of Gordon, and God knows who. Adderley[135] told

---

[134] Thomas Stanley (1749–1816). M.P. Lancashire 1780–1812 and a recent convert to the government's war policy.
[135] 'Adderley ... of all' (p. 61), printed in *Marshall*, 60

me that he had seen a letter, all so fine, that Ld. Hobart had been writing to Ireland, to Ld. Westmorland; Ld. Ossory[136] – he had been writing to Holland. Ld. Carlisle was sure how happy Morpeth[137] would be. Jenkinson had written to the Dean [of Christ Church]. Mr. Pitt had said this, Mr. Burke that, and Mr. Windham t'other – and the Speaker – and Hatsell,[138] the Clerk – perhaps the best testimony of all.

Jenkinson and I went and supped with Mrs. Crewe.

I determined not to shew you fine things – but I cannot resist the letter which I enclose. Read it – and return it sacredly to me. You have read one from the same hand once before. Do you know it?

*2ᵈ· [February]* Sunday. Adderley and Frere breakfasted with me, and Sturges called – and they all brought their different accounts of the manner in which they had heard the speech talked of – and all very comfortable. I dined at the Bootles. I think you must have heard me mention them. They are a Mr. and Mrs. Wilbraham Bootle, a rich old Lancashire couple – two sons of whom, one named Bootle, the other Wilbraham,[139] I knew very intimately, and lived very much with them at Christ Church. These two sons are now abroad. The humour of the old people is that they give a great dinner every Sunday to about a dozen of their acquaintance, and I usually dine there two or three times in the course of the winter. There are two daughters unmarried, who are great friends and flirts of mine. Here was a large party – and here I had a quantity of fine things to hear about the speech. From there – in the evening I went to the Markhams. They were all of them, as you may suppose, all goodness and congratulations. I supped there very comfortably, as you may also suppose.

*3 [February]* Monday – I wrote to my mother – enclosing her the best newspaper copies that I could find of my speech. Debrett the bookseller sent me a copy of it, requesting me to correct it for his Parliamentary Register – which I shall do.[140]

---

[136] The future 1st Mq. of Ormonde, C.'s contemporary at Eton
[137] The future 6th Earl of Carlisle. C.'s contemporary at Christ Church but not ret. to Plt. until the following year
[138] John Hatsell (1743–1820); clerk of the House of Commons 1768–97
[139] The two sons of Richard and Mary Wilbraham Bootle of Latham House, Lancs were Edward Wilbraham–Bootle, (afterwards Bootle Wilbraham), 1st Baron Skelmersdale; and Randle Wilbraham-Bootle (1773–1861)
[140] The version of the speech in J. Debrett's *Parl. Reg.*, 2nd series, vol. 37, p. 216 et. seq., conforms very closely with C.'s own and this suggests that he had committed a fair proportion to memory in advance. Later, he wrote of Debrett's version as 'tolerably correct', Canning MSS (12), to Rev. William Leigh, 16 May 1794. The *Parl. Hist.* version, vol. xxx, cols. 1317–29, is almost identical to that in *Parl. Reg.*, except that certain words and phrases ae underlined in the latter, presumably at C.'s request.

House of Commons – the Army Estimates voted. No debate – the House up at 7. I dined upstairs with Wallace – then went to the Play – and from the Play to a great ball and assembly at the Duchess of Gordon's.

*4 [February]* Tuesday. I was at home all the morning very busy – among other things sending off to Ashborne my journal up to Saturday last.

At the House of Commons there was [William] Adam's motion for giving an appeal to the House of Lords from the Court of Justiciary in Scotland. I ought to have staid to hear the debate – but knowing very little about Scotch law, and being determined to vote *in confidence* with Ministry, I was tempted to spare myself the trouble of hearing the discussion, and set off to keep an engagement which I had to dine with the Chief Baron and Lady Louisa Macdonald – who live not a hundred yards off in Parliament Street – leaving word with the doorkeeper where I was, that I might be sent for in case of a division.

At dinner I met Mr Villiers and Lord Gower, who, like me, ought to have been attending to the debate, but like me preferred dining first and voting aft[erwar]ds, and their wives, Mrs. Villiers and Lady Sutherland – and in addition to these – *Wilkes*[141] – whom I was glad to meet once in my life, having never yet seen him, though I find he knew my father, and my uncle very well, and seemed disposed to be violently civil to me – Miss Wilkes – and Mr. Erskine[142] – not *the Erskine*[143] – but the person whose name you have seen in the papers as having come over here from the Pope. The party was a curious mixture – and not unentertaining. I like Lady Sutherland mightily. She is very handsome – and very pleasant – and clever – and ATTENTIVE.

About nine o'clock we were summoned to the House of Commons: Ld. G[ower]. and Mr. V[illiers]. and I, and arrived just in time to divide against Mr. Adam's motion 126 to 31. From the House I went

Digests of the speech are printed in *Woodfall*. vol. 1, 204–206 and in *The Senator*, 1st series, vol. 8, pp. 148–152. The first referred to it as 'a very masterly maiden speech'; the latter, that it 'displayed much talent and information, combined with a flow of elocution, which contained considerable promise.' C. reported that of the newspapers the *True Briton*, *Sun* and *Morning Herald* gave the best accounts but the *Morning Chronicle* 'treats me ill on purpose', Canning MSS (12), Canning to Rev. William Leigh, Monday, 3 Feb. 1794. A selection of contemporary reactions can be found in *Marshall*, 61–62

[141] John Wilkes (1727–97)
[142] Monsignor Charles Erskine (1739–1811), later (1801), Cardinal. He was sent by the Pope to establish closer relations with Britain in view of the French threat to Italy
[143] Hon. Thomas Erskine (1750–1823), 1st Baron Erskine, the brilliant whig lawyer who defended successfully Hardy, Horne Tooke and Thelwall in the treason trials of 1794

to the Opera – and after the Opera Wallace and I supped with Mrs. Crewe.

5 [*February*] Wednesday – At home all the morning. Mr. Archdeacon Travis called to canvass me for the Rochdale Canal.[144] I have been canvassed against it also – by the Dean of Christ Church. I shall write to him to know what he thinks about it at present. It seems clear to me that it *ought not* to be *thrown out*. Lord Sheffield called – and we are become very intimate.

House of Commons – The Budget – and such a Budget – and such a manly impressive speech from Pitt – never was anything like it. Harry Bruce was in the Gallery. Pitt asked me to go home to dinner with him – but I was engaged to Mr. Villiers – and so with Mr. Villiers I went – and there were Lord Gower and Ly. Sutherland and Mr. G. Villiers[145] – and the Master of the Rolls and Mr. Lindsay[146] (half-brother of Geo. Ellis – and who has been employed as Foreign Minister at different times – at Petersburgh, Paris &c. &c.) In the evg. I called & [sic] Ly. Payne's – and from thence went to supper with Mrs. Crewe.

6 [*February*] Thursday. At home all the morning. Began correcting a copy of my speech for Debrett. House of Commons – No particular debate, but variety of business wch. lasted till past 6 – so that I was too late to dine where I was engaged, with Frere, and went home to dinner with Charles Ellis. So did Jenkinson – and we found Geo. Ellis and Mr. Pelham.[147] Pelham you know was in Ireland once. He is the particular friend of Windham, Burke, &c., and is looked upon as one of the best and most leading characters in the middle party. He is also very pleasant. We dined so comfortably – and sat so long that it was necessary to sup before we parted. And then I came home to bed.

7 [*February*] – At home all morning – till it was time to go down to the House. Wilberforce's motion for the abolition of the *foreign* slave trade[148] I was engaged to dine with Sir R. Payne, if the House should be up in time – and as the motion seemed to be of no great

[144] The Rochdale Canal Bill was a private bill to construct a canal from Sowerby Bridge Wharf in Yorkshire to connect with the Calder and Hebble Canal and so enable goods to be transported from Hull to Liverpool and from there, by canal, down to London. Leave was given for the bill to be introduced on 28 Jan. 1794 and despite some objections by mill owners on the rivers Roach, Irwell and Irk, was passed on 4 April, see *The Commons' Journal*, vol. 20, 63, 65, 126, 145, 153, 156, 162. George Travis was archdeacon of Chester
[145] Hon. George Villiers (1759–1827) q.v.
[146] William Lindsay, sec. of Legation, St Petersburg 1789–91; chargé d'Affaires, Berlin, 1791
[147] Hon. Thomas Pelham, 2nd Earl of Chichester; chief sec. (I) 1783–84
[148] William Wilberforce (1759–1833), 'Wilberforce's motion ... dined with him' (p. 64), printed in *NER*, 457–58

consequence, I was hesitating whether I should lose my dinner by staying to vote upon it or no – when seeing Charles Ellis – who is, you must know, in property a West Indian, and as such violently against the abolition of any part of the slave trade – and being very much pressed by him to go home with him to dinner after the debate – I gave him his choice very fairly thus: 'If I stay the debate out I shall *vote against you* – but then I will dine with you. If I go away now I shall not be in the House to vote at all. So take you choice'. He chose that I should vote against his property, so that I would but partake of his dinner – and so I stayed, divided *for* the motion, consequently agt. him and the W[es]*t*. Indians [149] (63 to 40) – and then went home and dined with him. Jenkinson went with us and so did Mr. Mundy (of Shipley) [150] and we found Geo. Ellis there – and had a very pleasant dinner – but we did not sit so long as last night – for Jenkinson and I had an old engagement, he to take me and I to be taken, to Lady Jane Dundas's (Mr. D.'s wife) who is at home on Monday and Friday evenings. It seems a pretty good sort of thing – the rather perhaps to *me*, as being at Somerset Place it is in my way home from the other end of the town. What made it better tonight than it would otherwise have been, was that I sat next Ly. Sutherland at supper.

*8 [February]* Saturday morning, just as I was getting up, Leigh presented himself before my eyes, newly arrived in town, and panting for news and breakfast. I gave him as much of both as he could conveniently swallow at that time, and then we set about our several vocations. I called on Mr. Pitt and had a pretty long and satisfactory conversation about politicks in general. He[151] said nothing personally *to me* about the speech – which perhaps was the more delicate part to take – but happening to call on Arbuthnot at the Secretary of State's Office, just after I had left Pitt, I learned that he had been there the morning before, and meeting Arbuthnot by chance, and said such things to him, probably meaning that I should hear them again – as would make you hair stand on end to hear them – *'power of argument, wit, eloquence'* – in short the Lord above knows what. I had talked to P. Patrick some days ago about the poor little boy of my mother's that is with the coachmaker, who, as I told you, did not use him very well – and had been wishing that I could get him into any tradesman's shop or counting-house. I received a note from him this morning, very good-natured and friendly, telling me that he hopes to be able to do something of the kind for me in the course of next month.

[149] M.P.s with interests in the West Indies of whom there were between 20 and 30 in 1794
[150] Edward Miller Mundy who lived at Shipley Hall, Derbys., see n. 124
[151] 'He said ... knows what', printed in *Marshall*, 60

I dined with John King (the Under-Secretary) – rather a dullish party. After dinner I went to the Opera – and from the Opera returned quietly home.

C. Ellis is gone out of town to Brookwood – but has left absolute power with me to call him up when I think his attendance proper.

*9. [February]* Sunday. Mr. Leigh went to Wanstead, and I should have gone with him but that I was obliged to go this night to the Speaker's[152] – in my grand full dress, bag and sword &c. I was at home all the morning. Bobus[153] came to me, and brought with him M. Talleyrand (the Bp. of Autun) to take leave, and to thank me &c. for having interfered in his behalf with Mr. Pitt. He and his friend M. Beaumetz set out immediately for America. While they were with me Lord Auckland called – but by great good luck was not let in. The meeting between him and Talleyrand would have been curious. He, I believe, looks upon Talleyrand, as one degree worse than the devil – and Talleyrand must feel some abhorrence against the man, who, in a manifesto published at the Hague, recommended the bringing all the ex-Constitutionalists of France under *the sword* of the law.

I dined with C. Greville – where I met Arbuthnot and Lord Lorne.[154] In the evening I went, all so grand, to the Speaker's – and from thence to supper at the Abp. of York's – where Leigh also came on his return from Wanstead.

*10. [February]* Monday I stayed at home all the morning and finished the correcting of my speech and sent it to Debrett. Leigh came and wrote his letters here – and stayed with me till it was time to go down to the House. I took him down and got him into the Gallery, where he had a very comfortable place and heard a very entertaining debate upon Grey's motion respecting the landing of Hessian troops. I felt once or twice a very strong disposition to speak, which I certainly should have indulged had I not known that Wallace intended to speak, and that I ought not to be in his way. He did speak – and after he had done there was no longer any opening that I liked. The division for the Previous Question agt. Grey's motion 184 to 35. After the division Dundas asked me and Jenkinson and Wallace to go home to dinner at his house with him and Mr. Pitt – which, as I had eat [sic] nothing since breakfast, and it was now 11 o'clock was no unacceptable proposal. We went – stept for a quarter of an hour while dinner was getting on [the] table, into Lady Jane Dundas's assembly – then sat down to a comfortable dinner – and chatted very

---

[152] Henry Addington, 1st Visct. Sidmouth. Speaker of the House of Commons 1789–1801

[153] 'Bobus ... of the law', printed in *NER*, 48

[154] George William Campbell, styled Mq. of Lorne and subsequently the 6th Duke of Argyll. M.P. St. Germans 1790–96

pleasantly till past 2 in the morning. I forgot to say that I had received a message this morning through Arbuthnot from Lady Sutherland and Mrs. Villiers, desiring me to meet them at the Play, which of course I could not do.

*11 [February]* Tuesday. At home all the morning. House of Commons up before I got down. I dined upstairs with Windham and Jenkinson, who I met there – then called at Lady Payne's – then went to the Opera – and from the Opera, with Mr. Leigh and Wallace, to sup at Mrs. Crewe's.

*12 [February]* Wednesday. At home all the morning. I had a letter from the Dean which shewed me that he did not care much about the Rochdale Canal. I determined therefore to vote with my conscience to-day for the *second reading* of it. I went down to the House and voted accordingly. Leigh and Harry Bruce and I dined with Paul Patrick and H[?arry]. Canning, where was a Mr. Waggitt,[155] a young Irish lawyer and a great democrat – and somewhat foolish. In the evening I went to Mrs. Villiers's and supped there. There were the Dss. of Devonshire – and Ld. and Ly. Jersey and their beautiful daughter, and Lord Carlisle – and God knows what fine people besides – so as to be upon the whole rather a dullish aristocratic meeting – and had I not been relieved in some degree by sitting at supper next to Lady Sutherland and Mrs. Villiers, I should have been most exceedingly bored. It was past 3 when I got to bed.

*13. [February]* Leigh called here with his eye all on fire – and after bathing it for an hour in rose water, went home to wait for Norris and have it cooked. This day had been appointed for Mr. Hastings's trial.[156] I set out about one o'clock for Westmr. Hall – and found all the people just coming away – and so I came home again. The trial is put off that Mr. H.'s counsel may examine Ld. Cornwallis.

I[157] dined at Mr. Crewe's – where was nobody but Miss Fox, Ld. Holland's sister. She is a very charming girl – and if she had teeth would be very pretty. She is very comfortable to me for I always hear from her her brother's sentiments,[158] and find how impossible it is that politics shoould ever set us at variance.

I called at Lothian's – and heard that Leigh was gone to bed, and I would not disturb him. I went to the Markhams – and spent a quiet

[155] Probably William Waggett (1771–1840); adm. Trinity, Dublin 25 Jan. 1788 aged 17; cld. Irish Bar 1795; subsequently recorder of Cork 1808–d.

[156] Warren Hastings (1732–1818). Gov. genl. of India 1773–85. His impeachment for corruption and cruelty in India began in 1788, and concluded with his acquittal in 1795

[157] 'I dined ... variance', printed in *NER*, 458

[158] Henry Fox, 3rd Baron Holland, C.'s contemporary at Christ Church, and his sister, Hon. Caroline Fox

evening and supped there, and meant to come home quietly to bed –
but passing by Jenkinson's door at abt. 12 o'clock I enquired if he
was at home – and finding him by himself, and not having had a
long tête-à-tête conversation upon all possible matters, personal and
political, for some time, we set to – and it was near 3 before I got
home.

*14.* [*February*] Friday. At home all the morning. Frere breakfasted
with me. Mr. Fox's motion respecting convoys[159] which stood for to-
day was put off – so that when I went down I found nothing to keep
me from dining at Mr. Crewe's, where Wallace and Leigh and I were
engaged to dine, if there should be no House to detain us. Wallace
and I called on Leigh – but found his eye still too bad to suffer him
to go with us to dinner. At dinner there was nobody but old Lady
Clermont. In the evening I went to the Markhams and spent another
comfortable evening – but from them I went to Mrs. Villiers's, where
I had promised on Wednesday evg. that I would come again to-day –
and where I expected to find a smaller party – but there was as much
aristocracy as before – and it was duller because I did not sit next Ly.
Sutherland – and I was not very well, and was glad to get home.

*15.* [*February*] Saturday morning. I felt not at all well. Leigh came,
looking much better for his discipline of yesterday, and brought with
him Mr. Porson and another man about *his* canal.[160] By the way – I
have made up my mind to have nothing to do one way or other
with any more canals (unless it be Leigh's) for I have found by the
experience of the Rochdale that there is so much tricking and so much
ill-blood that it is not worth while to risk the disobliging of many
people – for so foolish a matter as a vote upon what one does not
understand – and so with all canals, and the Rochdale among them –
and with all private business I have done.

This morning I took a pretty long walk, thinking it might do me
good. I took the opportunity of making many calls which in my hurry
of these last weeks I had omitted.

The House – nothing material. I dined at Lord Stafford's – none
but the family – and not all of them – for Lord Gower and my friend
Lady Sutherland were gone out of town. I went with the Levesons to
the Opera. In my way home I supped at the Club in Carey Street.

*16.* [*February*] Sunday morning – after a very uncomfortable night
I felt myself more and more unwell, and determined to apply to Norris

---

[159] Fox had raised the issue of alleged inadequate convoying of British fleets in the
debate on naval supplies on 27 Jan and promised a motion which was put on 18 Feb.
1794

[160] The Rev. William Leigh had an interest in Staffordshire lime kilns and this was
probably the reason behind his sponsorship of a canal bill. The identity of Mr Porson
has not been established

for some remedy. I called by appointment on Lord Stafford, to talk
with him abt. Mr. L[eigh]'s canal – which as far as I can judge from
him, seems to be in no state of forwardness. I found Norris – and he
recommended an emetick. Calling on Leigh I found him somewhat
better but still confined. I came home to dress and found myself so
little disposed to go out that I would gladly have taken my emetick
at once and gone to bed – but it was an engagement of long standing
that I could not decently break – and so I went and dined with the
Master of the Rolls. There were Mr. and Mrs. Villiers, and the Chief
Baron and Lady Louisa – and a few other people. As early as I could
I came away – found my ipecacuanha and camomile ready – had
every reason to be satisfied with their operation – and went to bed in
hopes of enjoying a sound sleep and waking wonderfully refreshed in
the morning.

*17 [February]* On Monday morning however I did not wake near
so well as I had expected, but on the contrary found myself oppressed
with so dreadful a headache as to be obliged to lie in bed till between
two and three – before which time however I had sundry visitors at
my bedside – who kept me from getting quite so much sleep as I
wanted. When I got up I sent to enquire after Leigh in hopes he might
be well enough to come and eat part of my sick dinner – but it was a
day of discipline with him. I went to Frere, and he came. I had long
letters to write to a knot of people, Boringdon,[161] Leveson, Morpeth,
Holland &c who are all at Naples[162] – which if they were ready by
tonight Lady Stafford had engaged to send for me by a messenger so
there was no delay – and I found my head rather better for writing.

Frere dined with me as I said before, and Bobus called in the
evening; and they staid with me till about 1/2 past 9 – when I sent
them off and went to bed.

*18. [February]* I had a very good night's rest – and waked Tuesday
morning much better. Leigh called on me, quite well. A letter from
Tish – foolish Tish! If you had read or heard the last journal accurately
you would have found (in a parenthesis) that your night-ribbon was
duely brought into service.

At[163] three I set out for the House of Commons – called at Jenkinson's in my way and eat some cold meat, and drank a few glasses
of strong wine to support myself during the sitting – and then we went

---

[161] The 2nd Baron Boringdon, subsequently 1st Earl of Morley. C.'s contemporary at
Christ Church
[162] Lady Webster, the future Lady Holland, recorded: 'Reached Naples on the 26th
February ... A numerous band of young Englishmen from college; gambling and
gallantry filled up the evenings and mornings.' The Earl of Ilchester (ed.), *The Journal
of Elizabeth Lady Holland*, (London, 2 vols. 1908), i, 120–21
[163] 'At three ... my bed' (p. 69), printed in *NER*, 458

down together. The debate was on Mr. Fox's motion respecting convoys – and by much the dullest debate that I have heard. It lasted from a little after 4 till near 2 in the morning. I sat it out though most grievously tired – till the division, which was 202 to 48 – and after the division, being perfectly exhausted, I went home with Jenkinson to a comfortable hot *fowl and rice soup* and some good heartening port wine – and sat chatting and cheering myself by the fire till about 4 – when finding myself stout and restored – I set off for my chambers and my bed.

How long it seems since I wrote to you on a long sheet of paper! Wednesday Febry. the 19th – as I find by my pocket-book – was the day on which I sent you the last number of my journal – and since that day – long as the interval appears – little has happened that you would be glad to see detailed or to have recalled and fixed in your remembrance.

Rather, however, than there shall be an absolute chasm in the series, I will fill up the time between the day on which I laid down my pen, and this present hour that I resume it, with a cursory narrative of what has passed; and then start afresh upon a more particular account of what may pass hereafter.

*19th [February]* Wednesday the 19th Mr. Leigh you know was still in town. He thought I looked ill – I knew I felt so – but not being able to determine what was the matter I determined if possible to bully my complaint rather than yield to it and lock myself up to be disciplined by physic which might not do me any essential service. I lay in bed till one o'clock. Leigh called; then I got up and walked to the other end of the town in hopes of shaking off the heaviness that hung upon me, but in vain. I dined at Mr. Ryder's (Paymaster) where was a party which would have been very pleasant had I been in spirits to enjoy it – which I was not till I had taken a little wine – and I was afraid to take as much of that as would exhilarate me. The persons present were Mr. Wilberforce, Mr. Smith (a Lord of the Admiralty, a very pleasant, gentlemanly man),[164] F. North, Jenkinson and 4 or 5 more. From thence early in the evening I went to the Bruces, where were Leigh, Hetty and Bess Canning – and as soon as I could I came home and went to bed.

*20. [February]* Thursday. I was at home all the morning. I dined – much against my inclination – not because I did not like the place – but because I was too unwell to dine chearfully anywhere – at John Ellis's (Charles's brother, who married Miss Parker). There were Dr. Brocklesby, an old physician, and King (the Under-Secretary) and

---

[164]John Smyth (1748–1811) of Heath Hall, nr. Wakefield, Yorks. M.P. Pontefract 1783–1807; ld. of Admiralty 1791–May 1794

Mrs. King. I came away early – went to the Markhams to spend the evg. quietly – supped – and came home early to bed.

*21. [February]* I stayed at home all the morning – and thought I found myself well enough to go down to the House where Sheridan's motion upon the defence of Halifax was to come on.[165] I called in my way and eat a sandwich at the Bruces. I felt very shivery and unwell during the whole night in the House of Commons – and had a thousand times a mind to come away – but I wanted something to eat and preferred going home comfortably with Jenkinson to dinner after the debate – to eating a strong mutton-chop (indeed I could *not* have eaten one) upstairs. Luckily the House did not sit very late. Jenkinson and I got to dinner tête-à-tête by 1/2 pt. 11. I felt myself better after dining, and sat chatting till abt. 1.

*22. [February]* Saturday morning I found myself very uncomfortable I had symptoms of a violent and encreasing headache and a general unfitness for doing anything of any kind. I resolved therefore to stay at home – and discipling myself, hoping that one or two days confinement would set me right. I sent an excuse to the Archbp. of York, where I was engaged, and dined at home. Leigh dined with me, being to leave town the next day. I went early to bed, and

*23 [February]* Sunday morning I waked not a bit better than I had found myself yesterday, but my headache rather encreased. Norris came and ordered my sundry matters of physic and regimen. Frere came to me in the morning, and I made him stay and dine with me – and we had as comfortable an evening as my state of head would permit.

*24 [February]* Monday – my headache encreased, and so did my languor and general uneasiness. Norris called and ordered me to go on with my bark. He did not seem to apprehend anything serious. I stayed at home all day – dined alone and went to bed early.

*25. [February]* I was worse, but my illness had taken no shape by which it could be distinctly known. A great many people called on me, and all joined in pressing me to send for a physician, and even threatened to send one to me if I did not do so. I consulted with Norris and we resolved that if I was not better *to-morrow* he should bring Turton[166] next day. He advised me to try cupping for my head. I stayed at home – alone – in bed early.

*26 [February]* Wednesday – I was worse – particularly as to my head. The cupping-man came – and I underwent the operation, but

[165] On 21 Feb. 1794 Sheridan moved for all despatches and statements of trade about Halifax to be laid before the House, *Parl. Reg.*, 2nd series, vol. 37, 398–407

[166] Probably Dr. J. Turton (1735–1806); fellow of the R.C. of Physicians and physician extraordinary to the King

it gave me no manner of relief. Norris called, and we agreed that he should bring Turton next day.

*27 [February]* Thursday morning Turton came and did not seem to know what to make of me. It would turn, he thought, either to an intermittent or a low fever. He prescribed – and ordered me, above all things, to be kept quite and free from any exertion or agitation of mind. I felt worse and worse.

*28. [February]* On Friday Turton called again. He thought me somewhat better. Hetty came to me and sat with me the whole morning, which circumstance alarmed me very much and I therefore tried to persuade her that I was much better than I really felt myself – and this exertion did me no good.

*1 March.* On Saturday Turton evidently thought me worse. Hetty came and sat with me. She told me however that she was going out of town next day, and I promised her that I would have a nurse to attend me. Norris was commissioned to procure one.

*2 March.* Sunday morning. Hetty came and took leave of me. Turton came and seemed delighted [to] hear that I had a nurse coming, and that if I did not find myself better, I should lie in bed the next day. This was what he had wanted all along, but he had been afraid of proposing it lest he should alarm me. I went to bed early, and from the time of my going to bed on that night, to the time of my getting up again about a week after – that is all the days – 3d, 4th, 5th, 6th, 7th of March are but one indistinct mass in my recollection. I remember only my general feelings – but not at all the particular periods at which each of them was most strong upon me. It never once occurred to me that my life was absolutely in danger – though from what I have since learned there was one period of 24 hours during which some doubt was entertained – and several of my friends at the other end of the town – whether it was that they received exaggerated accounts from their servants whom they sent to enquire after me – or from Fleming, in answer to the enquiries which they made after me in person – or from Turton perhaps to prevent their coming to call upon me which was what he most dreaded – however it happened, it is certain that for two days they thought this next account might probably be that I was gone. Jenkinson and Wallace, when first I saw them after my recovery, addressed me in a manner that quite affected me, as a person whom they had never expected to see again – and you will be pleased to hear of C. Moore – what the Archbp. [of Canterbury] and his mother both told me yesterday: 'There was one day that we feared the worst for you – for when we asked Charles as usual upon his coming to dinner, how you were, he could not answer us – but was obliged to get up and leave the room'. Indeed, when I consider all the kindness and solicitude of which my illness made me the object – I am almost persuaded that it is worth while to have been ill to experience it. Poor Hetty is quite smitten with the 'pretty young men' who were her constant visitors or correspondents – among whom, however, I think Fred. North (though by no means the *prettiest*) and Frere, seem to have obtained the greatest share of her affection. As to females – when I saw the Markhams, the Levesons, Mrs. Crewe, Lady M[almesbur]y for the first time after my recovery, and received their congratulations, I began to doubt which occasioned the pleasantest sensations – the having made a speech – or the having had a swinging fit of sickness. I must not omit that Lady Louisa Hervey told me the other night that I should [have] been much comforted under my indisposition, if not *absolutely* glad of it, had I overheard a conversation which she had with Mr. Pitt about me at Wimbledon. 'And you know (added she) he is not in *general* a great *praiser*.' Among all these fine things I should be most thankful indeed if I did not mention with the highest praise and pleasure, as I shall ever remember with the warmest gratitude, poor Hetty's kind and unremitting attention. You have probably heard from her how little satisfaction I expressed at the time in her constant attendance, and how often I endeavoured by open advice as well as by other little ways and means to persuade her to return to Wanstead. This may appear very odd and unaccountable at first – but I am confident that were I again in the same situation I should again experience pretty nearly the same feelings. I do not know whether you will exactly understand them – nor can I exactly define them. They were not peevishness I am sure, nor insensibility to her good offices, nor want of pleasure in her society – but a sort of fanciful delicacy and fastidiousness which could not bear to have anything about me that looked like controul and management; and that really made me shudder at the notion of anything, especially of the female kind, higher than my nurse, being witness to all the indelicacies and uncomfortablenesses with which a sick room necessarily abounds. I hope she understood me at the time – but since, I have been at great pains to explain myself to her, and she is convinced how little a desire to get rid of her company had to do with the wish I so often expressed that she should return home, and how sensible I am and always shall be to the tenderness of the care with which she watched me, and the advantages which I derived from it.

Another thing which I remember particularly during my confinement to my bed is – that I had a most painful and constant apprehension of becoming *delirious*. And my usual employment when I was not asleep was to examine myself by questions and long reasonsings upon God knows what subjects, whether I was actually in my senses or no. Do you remember in Boswell's Life of Johnson that the same thing is related of him? It was that circumstance which put it into my head, and I derived great comfort and satisfaction from the practice. Perhaps it prevented what I so much dreaded. People in putrid fevers usually are delirious. I do not think that I was ever so for a moment. It was a source also of great comfort to me that I *had* spoken in the House of Commons. I thought and dreamt of it night and day – and had the weight of anxiety which oppressed me for some time *before* I had spoken, not been off my mind, I am convinced it would much have retarded my recovery. My recovery now came on rapidly, so rapidly as to occasion much surprize to Turton, who seemed to have apprehended that it might be at least as gradual as the coming on of my illness had been.

*8th Saturday – the 8th March –* I was able to get up at abt. 2 o'clock – eat some chicken for my dinner and sat up till 9.

*9th [March]* Sunday – Turton called 'for the last time as a physician' – as he told me. This day it was – or yesterday, I am not sure which – that I happened to ask if there were any letters or notes for me – and Fleming brought me in a heap, which I could not easily conceive to have come in *one* day – and upon enquiry I found that for several days past I had not been allowed to receive any letter – lest it might contain anything to *agitate* me. This was the first circumstance that occasioned me to suspect that I had been seriously ill. I do not know that they need to have been so very circumspect – as none of the letters happened to be of a very nervous import – except indeed *one*, which informed me that my Lottery ticket was drawn a *blank*. To-day I read comfortably enough in bed till 1 – then got up. Hetty and Frere dined with me – and she set off for Wanstead in the evening.

*10th – 11th – 12th – 13th – 14th – 15th – 16th – [March]* During this week I continued gradually mending and strengthening – and was well enough to enjoy the company of people who called on me, and the novels, romances and fairy tales and parliamentary debates, which I read, when I was alone, not to mention how much I relished my dinner, especially when Frere or F. North, or some one other person that I liked, partook of it – which was generally the case. F. North called when the day was fine enough to take me out airing. The gruel which my nurse made, was in such request that she had to feed four or five persons with it almost every morning. Some day this week I had a letter from Samuel Reddish, informing me of his being actually on board the ship bound for Botany Bay and ready to sail. I sent to Mr King for the letters of recommendation which he had promised me to the Governor and Deputy Govr. of the Settlement. He sent me one for the Dy. Govr. who is now there, which I forwarded to Samuel, and he promised to speak again, having once already spoken to the Govr. himself who is now in Engld., in Samuel's behalf, so I hope the poor fellow may do well. It was a great amusement to me this week writing notes of thanks for enquiry, and receiving answers of congratulation.

*17 [March]* – I had intended to go to Wanstead on Saturday but deferred my journey on hearing that certain Philistines were to dine there on Sunday. This day, Monday 17th I set out and arrived at about 3 o'clock – where I found everything prepared in the most comfortable manner, for my reception. Bess Patrick had insisted upon resigning her bed to me – and I was put in possession of the little drawing-room opposite – for my breakfasting room and study – and had a great arm chair with a tall back and soft cushions, and got my books and papers about me, and felt myself settled very much to my satisfaction. [R.B.] Sheridan was there on the day of my arrival and offered me the use of his house[167] if I should find Hetty's too noisy from Paul's children, and of his horses, if I chose to ride. He promised too to come down to Wanstead again before I left it.

*18, 19, 20, 21, 22, 23, 24, 25, 26, 27, 28, 29, 30, 31, [March]* This fortnight passed in great comfort and tranquillity. I did at first intend to have returned to town before the end of it, but was easily persuaded to prolong my stay, and certainly found the benefits of it. The first week did a great deal for me – but by the end of the second I was quite another thing. And so

*1st April* – on Tuesday the first of April, I ordered the chaise to be at the door at 10 o'clock, and set out for this bustling metropolis. I had gotten so reconciled to a quiet life that though absence from London and Parliament had dwelt upon my mind a good deal, I did not however leave Wanstead without much regret. My employments there had not indeed been very various or very active – but there is a fund of disposition to idleness in man, at least in me, which if it were indulged, would I am sure very soon grow to a surprising height and overwhelm all other dispositions (however powerful at times) to activity and ambition. The most serious occupation that I had during my stay at Wanstead was making Mrs. Patrick's will.

I set Willy down at Hackney[168] in my way – having sent for him home the day before that I might see him and ascertain a fact which Hetty mentioned to me with glowing indignation – namely that he was a most determined *bad politician*. I found she had told me true. He had quite *proper* notions – insomuch that I promised to send for him to town the first day that I was sure there would be a good debate or thought there was any chance of my speaking.

---

[167] Sheridan leased a house in Wanstead, see Walter Sichel, *Sheridan*, (London, 2 vols. 1909) i, 537

[168] William Canning attended Mr Newcome's Academy in Upper Clapton, Mdx.

My first business on getting to town was to call upon my poor aunt
(my mother's sister) and grandmother[169] – who heard of my illness
some way or other – and had been cruelly agitated about it – and so
it was a great comfort to them to see me alive. My next was to come
home to my chambers – where I found Frere waiting for me. I found
also a letter from Lady Malmesbury insisting that I should dine with
her the very first day of my coming to town, and I set off to obey her
injunctions. Lord Malmesbury, you know, is abroad on an Embassy
to the King of Prussia, and Lady Malmesbury is living therefore
*en veuve* with another (real) widow – Mrs. Robinson,[170] an aunt of
Boringdon's, and a very pleasant comfortable menage they have.
I dined there – and there was nobody but themselves – and Ly.
Malmesbury's children – two very pretty girls – one about Tish's age,
and the other about Bessy's (your Bessy's) – or a little bigger. She has
a son too, of which I was not aware, a great boy at Eton. But what
have you to do with her family?

After dinner, being so near the House of Commons (in Privy Garden
Mrs. R.'s house is) I could not refrain from going down just to take
a peep at the inside of it and see if anything was doing. I persuaded
Lady Malmesbury to carry me there – tho' it was only upon condition
that I should not stay five minutes in the House – but come out
again, and be carried away immediately. This condition proved
unnecessary – for the House was up so I did not go in at all, but after
making one call – on Jenkinson – came home, and was in bed before
12.

2 *[April]* Wednesday morning – I got up early and took a whole-
some walk in the Temple Garden before breakfast – a practice which
I resolved to repeat every morning. Frere breakfasted with me and
after breakfast I set out to begin the round of visits which I had to
pay in consequence of long absence and kind enquiries. I called on
Mr. Pitt but did not get admitted – or he was out – on the Staffords,
the Markhams &c. &c. – and on Lord Abercorn who, I believe I
have not told you before, is in England for a few weeks, and called
on me during my illness – and we renewed our acquaintance, and are
greater friends than ever. I dined at the Archbishop of York's – and
stayed there all the evening – and came home time enough to be in
bed by 12.

3 *[April]* Thursday – the morning being wet I could not continue
my rounds but was obliged to remain at home till it was time to go

[169] Miss Costello and Mrs Costello of Connaught
[170] Lord Malmesbury, the most distinguished diplomat of his day, was on a special
mission to conclude subsidy treaties with Prussia and the United Provinces – a mission
accomplished on 19 Apr. 1794. Mrs Robinson was his sister, Catherine Gertrude, the
widow of Hon. Frederick Robinson who had d. 28 Dec. 1792

down to the House. A motion by Major Maitland[171] on the conduct of the War in Europe during the last campaign was fixed for to-day – but he only moved for papers relating to the subject, and put off the motion itself to this day sen'night. The House was up by about 6 – so I went and dined with Sir Ralph and Lady Payne, to whom I had a conditional engagement. There was nobody but Lady Malmesbury. In the evening I went and sat quietly with Jenkinson and supped with him, and returned home to bed by 12.

*4 [April]* – Friday – I continued my calls – in the course of which I found Lady Charlotte Greville delivered of a fine boy. I was to have dined with Lady Malmesbury – but the House sat – upon the India Budget till about 7 – and so I dined upstairs with Lord Mornington and Wallace and Jenkinson – and then went with Jenkinson to Lady Bristol's – where for some time were several people – but all went away in time except F. North and Jenkinson and I, who stayed and supped very pleasantly with Lady Bristol and Lady Louisa.

*5 [April]* Saturday – I still continued my round of visits and therein called at Lambeth, where I heard the trait which I have already mentioned, of C. Moore. I dined at Frere's – where was only the family – and Mr. Maltby,[172], whom you remember, and I remember at Norwich, a boy. He is now a clergyman and chaplain, I believe, to the Bp. of Lincoln. Frere became acquainted with him at Cambridge and speaks very highly of him as to scholarship and good nature. I went to the Opera – and from the Opera with Wallace to supper at Mrs. Crewe's.

*6. [April]* Sunday also was devoted to calls, as far as the badness of the weather would allow. Among others I called with Ed[d.] Legge on the Birches. They are to give a grand ball on Easter Monday to which I shall go, if I am (which is not likely) in town. I called also on Newbolt, whom I have before mentioned to you – and his wife – for he is now married to the Miss Julia Digby (the Maid of Honour that was) with whom I told you he was in love, and she with him. And they appear still as much in love as ever – and are settled in a small house and want nothing but money to make them quite comfortable – but alas they have only £400 a year.

I dined at Lord Stafford's – nobody but Arbuthnot and an old Mrs. Howe. I supped, as usual on Sundays, with the Markhams.

*7 [April]* Monday – I was at home greater part of the morning – then went to Hasting's trial and thence to the House – where was a long debate on the Bill for raising corps &c. for internal defence. After

---

[171]Hon. Thomas Maitland (1760–1824). M.P. Haddington Burghs 1790–96 and a critic of the war
[172]The Rev. Edward Maltby (1770–1859)

the debate at about 1/2 pt. 12 Jenkinson and I went home with Mr. Pitt to supper. There was besides us only Eliott[173] (Pitt's brother-in-law, who lives in his house) – and we supped *chearily* and had a good deal of pleasant talk.

I have forgot to tell you till now – that since my illness I have, in obedience to Dr. Turton, left off a bad custom which I hd of going down to the House *fasting*. I[174] find it is a practice with which everybody fancies himself stout enough to begin, but soon experiences the inconvenience of it. Pitt always eats at least a fowl and drinks I know not how much Madeira before he goes down. Jenkinson does so too. I held them very cheap at first – but Turton has converted me – and now I either feed myself before I go out at about 3 o'clock – or call at Jenkinson's and get fed in my way – taking care however not to drink enough to puzzle one's self – nor to eat so much but that one may be prepared for a dinner or supper after the debate whenever it may happen to be over. On days when nothing is expected in the House of Coms. I do not take anything.

*8 [April]* – Tuesday was dedicated to City visits – Paul and Borrowes and William Maxwell – and Mr. Newbery and Mr. T. Raikes[175] and Mr. Van Hartals.[176] These two last are great friends of Hetty's as they were of my uncle's – and I knew I should gratify her by calling on them.

In[177] the House was the debate on Sinecure Places and Pensions which a foolish Mr. Harrison[178] would fain have abolished or applied to the purposes of the War. The division was 117 to 48. I should have liked to speak to-day but that I thought it was as well for a *young man* to let alone anything that might look like a *defence of corruption* – for so, in spite of truth and common sense, some stupid country gentlemen might construe it. After the debate I went home and supped with Jenkinson – and I am afraid I was not in bed before 3 or 4 o'clock.

*9 [April]* Wednesday morning I was not up very soon but almost as I was up I went down to Hasting's trial to hear Lord Cornwallis examined. All the world was there upon the same errand – and among them Edwd. Legge, who had been commissioned by Lady Sutherland to send me, from her, a card for Mrs. Scott's great ball to-night. I do not often go to balls nor do I know Mrs. Scott – but a card so sent

[173] Hon. Edward James Eliot (1758–97), see above p. 28 n. 26
[174] 'I find ... be over', printed in *Marshall*, 62
[175] Thomas Raikes (1741–1848) of Freelands, Kent and Duntsbourne, Gloucestershire. An eminent London merchant and gov. of the Bank of England 1797–99. His sister, Mary, had m. Francis Newbury of Heathfield, Surrey, q.v. in 1770
[176] Probably Edward Van Hartals, a merchant of 6 Copthall St, London
[177] 'In the House ... construe it', printed in *NER*, 458–89
[178] John Harrison (1738–1811). M.P. Gt. Grimsby 1793–96

almost commands one's attendance. I shall see about it – thought I –
and if I have time I will go.

There was nothing in the House of Commons but private business –
for which Wednesday is usually set apart. I dined with Lady Malmesbury and Mrs. Robinson and met Mr. Pelham (I must have had
occasion to mention him before, I think. He is one of the *alarmist* Party
and one of the most respectable of them – the great friend of Windham,
the Duke of Portland, Burke &c) and Miss Parker, Boringdon's sister.

In the evening I called on Mrs. Crewe – and meeting Wallace
there, got him to carry me to Mrs. Scott's – where for the second time
to-day I saw all the world – and for the first time since my illness –
Lady Sutherland. I did not stay very long – just long enough to make
an engagement to spend part of the Easter holydays at Wimbledon.[179]
Then returned to supper at Mrs. Crewe's – and then home to
bed.

*10. [April]* Thursday I was at home all the morning. I had sent for
Willy from Hackney in pursuance of a promise which I had made to
him and to his mother, that I would take him to the House of
Commons the first day on which there was a certainty of a good
debate and a chance of my speaking. He came to me about three –
and I gave him some dinner – and we set out. The debate was on
Major [Thomas] Maitland's motion for an enquiry into the conduct
of the War last campaign. Jenkinson spoke first on our side of the
question and made a very admirable speech – of which I was most
exceedingly glad both for his own sake and because I had never before
heard him – indeed he had not before had any good opportunity of
speaking this Session.

The[180] debate went on with great variety of speakers and for some
time I saw no opening that I liked. At length after Jekyll[181] I jumped
up – but a Major Mcleod[182] caught the Speaker's eye – and so I was
obliged to lose that turn – and that beast kept speaking on and on for
half an hour, while I was sitting in hot water. When he finished I
rose. The *professional* part of the subject had been already quite exhausted, first by Jenkinson generally (who was quite master of it) and
then, in detail by Lord Mulgrave[183] and Sir J. Murray,[184] one of whom
had *served* at Toulon – and the latter at Dunkirk. I passed by the
military part therefore, and confined myself to the objections which

---

[179] Where Lord Gower and Lady Sutherland had a villa
[180] 'The debate … late in the morning' (p. 81), printed in *Marshall*, 63–65
[181] Joseph Jekyll (1754–1837). M.P. Calne 1787–1816
[182] Norman Macleod (1754–1801). M.P. Inverness-shire 1790–96
[183] Brig. gen. and lt.-gov. Toulon
[184] Sir James Murray, 7th Bt. M.P. Melcombe Regis 1790–1811. He had been adj.-
gen. to the Duke of York in the Flanders campaign

had been made to the Declaration published at Toulon[185] – to replying
to the straggling observations which had fallen from Jekyll and other
speakers, and concluded with a comparison between our situation,
such as it was now, and such as it would have been, if *gentlemen on the
other side* had held the government of the country for the last twelvemonth. All went off as well as could be.[186] The *gentlemen on the other
side*, indeed, were a little *disorderly*, and the Speaker called to them.
But I felt as bold as a lion about it – so much so as to say to the
Speaker – in a sort of parenthesis – 'It is no matter, Sir, the gentlemen
could disconcert me *once* – but they cannot do so again!' Sheridan,
who is as good-natured as it is possible for a man to be, came to me
after the debate and commended me very much for doing so. I had
no sooner sat down than Mr. Courtenay[187] started up opposite to me.
But he too was unlucky enough to miss the Speaker's eye and was
obliged to keep his venom till somebody else had finished speaking.

During this interval you would have laughed to see the two opposite
sides of the House – on the one Grey and Mcleod and Whitbread[188] –
and all the minor Oppositionists *figging-up* Mr. Courtenay, and sug-
gesting matter for his observation – on ours – Pitt and Mornington
and Jenkinson – getting about me – and telling me that I must expect
a violent attack – but that I must not mind it from such a blackguard,
and above all things that I must not think of condescending to take
the smallest notice of him by reply. Well – up he got – and honoured
me with his particular attention for about a quarter of an hour – in
a strain of the stupidest abuse of my speech and myself that can easily
be conceived.[189] You cannot think what an odd feeling it is to sit and
hear one's self abused before 3 or 400 people. I found however that I
could bear it without any unpleasant feeling – and that it was not
wholly without satisfaction that I saw the eyes and attention of all
persons turned to me. Once or twice in the course of his speech I could
not but feel a desire to give vent to the answers which occurred to
me – and accordingly said to those about me – 'Don't you think *this*

---

[185] A reference to the Declaration published by Lord Hood and others at Toulon, 20
Nov. 1793, which set out British war aims.

[186] Similar versions of this speech can be found in *Parl. Hist.*, vol. xxxi, cols. 254–55;
*Parl. Reg.*, 2nd series, vol. 38, 120–22; *Woodfall*, vol. 2, 197–99; and *The Senator*, 1st
series, vol. 9, 969–71. The version in *Parl. Reg.* has C. quoting from *Henry IV, pt. 1*, and
concluding 'with an animated description of the cruelty, barbarity, and atheism of the
French'

[187] John Courtenay (1738–1816). M.P. Tamworth 1780–1796

[188] Samuel Whitbread (1764–1815). M.P. Bedford 1790–1815

[189] Courtenay is reported to have said of C.'s speech: '... he had endeavoured to catch
the spirit of it, but as soon as it was poured out, it evaporated. He strove then to
condense the thin floating vapours, and make them palatable, but all his endeavours
were in vain.' *Parl. Hist.*, xxxi, col. 255

requires that I should speak?' – No no – no such thing, was the
constant answer – and Pitt in particular was very earnest with me
that I should treat it with contemptuous silence. 'Nobody *ever* answers
Courtenay (says he) and why would you break through so good a
rule?' As soon as Mr. Courtenay turned his attention from me to the
question – I went down to Willy who was sitting under the Gallery –
to send him home to bed – for it was late – and then returned to my
place thinking my troubles for the night over. Willy had been highly
edified and delighted during the whole evening, and had a mouth
expanded to a size hardly human, gaping with attention. I wish I had
not dismissed him so soon for he might have heard more abuse of his
cousin. After Mr. Courtenay, rose Mr. Francis[190] in one of the most
violent passions that I had ever witnessed. I was not at first aware –
why – but it seems I had mentioned, as he thought disrespectfully,
the subscription for Poland, of which he had been a great promoter –
and so he set out to complete Mr. Courtenay's panegyric – and went
on volubly enough with the coarsest Billingsgate invective – till he
was called to order by the united voice of the House – when ludicrously
enough he declared that he meant no personal reflection. 'I may say
one word in *explanation* to this, may I not? for he has misrepresented
what I said'. 'Yes, yes', said Pitt and two or three others, 'there will
be no harm in that – but take care not to be angry – and not a word
of Courtenay, I beg of you'. When Francis had done therefore I
claimed a minute's explanation. 'I did *not* mean to speak disrespectfully, nor *did* I, of the subscription for Poland, separately and
by itself considered. Perhaps I might be rather inclined to approve it.
But that is no matter. What I *did* mean was to express my admiration
of that *delicate refinement*, that *patriotic sensibility* – which could so distinguish as to approve subscriptions for the service of a *foreign* country,
and disapprove them for the service of *its own*'. Here was an end of
my scuffle. The debate continued pretty late. The division was 35 to
168. I must not forget to tell you that Mr. Pitt spoke of me in his
speech in the handsomest terms possible – at least in terms which
appear to *me* more satisfactory than any general praise which he could
have bestowed – as a person 'who had now for the second time &c. –
and of whom, *in his own presence*, I will *not* say how much *I* think – but
I am confident that the whole House is sensible of the value of the
acquisition which it has made', and there's for you.[191] After the debate
I went home and supped tête-a-tête with Jenkinson, and we talked

[190] Philip Francis (1740–1818). M.P. Bletchingly 1790–96. Francis upbraided C. for
his 'unprovoked and uncalled for' attack, especially when it came from 'younger minds,
fresh from the study of the classes and supposed to be animated by the recent impression
of virtuous examples', *Parl. Reg.*, 2nd series vol. 38, 124–25
[191] The second intervention by C. can be found in *Parl. Reg.*, 2nd series, vol. 38, 125

over our speeches and the events of the night, till pretty late in the morning.

*11 [April]* Friday morning I was obliged to get up rather earlier than I was inclined to do, because I had an engagement to breakfast with Lord Abercorn – to take leave of him previous to his departure for Ireland. We parted with great professions of friendship – which we shall have an opportunity of renewing early next winter – as at that time he is to return to England for good.

Once out in a morning there is no returning home to do anything – and so I spent the whole of this morning in calls and lounging. I called at Lady Malmesbury's and got a nice little dinner or luncheon in my way to the House. There was a short debate – on the Second Reading of Mr. Pitt's bill for embodying the emigrants – in which I felt much inclination to take part but not much power – not having yet turned my attention to the subject. I resolved however to be master of it by the time that the great day of its discussion should come – and for that purpose made an appointment with Mr. Pitt to call upon him and talk it over tomorrow. I dined upstairs (for as yet I had only *lunched* you know) with Jenkinson, Wallace, Steele, Ryder, Mornington, and Lord Titchfield[192] – then went with Jenkinson to the Oratorio at Drury Lane (the first time that I had seen the house – which is beautiful) – and then with him to supper at Mrs. Crewe's.

*12. [April]* Saturday morning. I called on Mr. Pitt – and had a long conversation about the emigrants. *Once out*, as I said before, there is no returning to any purpose, and so I loitered away this morning also with more pleasure than profit. I dined at the Master of the Rolls'. The company were, Mr. Pitt, the Attorney Genl.,[193] the Solicitor Genl.,[194] the Lord Advocate of Scotland,[195] Sir William Scott,[196] two Dundas's[197] (a son and a nephew of Dundas), Wallace, and Jenkinson. The dinner was very pleasant. From thence I went to the Opera – and from the Opera to sup very pleasantly at Mrs. Crewe's with Jenkinson and Wallace and *Sheridan*.

*13. [April]* Sunday morning. Frere breakfasted with me – and I was at home till dinner-time. I dined at Sir Ralph Payne's with some people whom I did not know – except one of them a Mr. Craufurd – whom I do not know how to describe to you further than by saying

[192] Subsequently the 4th Duke of Portland. M.P. Buckinghamshire 1791–1809. He had followed his father in supporting the govt.'s war policy
[193] Sir John Scott, 1st Earl of Eldon
[194] Sir John Mitford, 1st Baron Redesdale
[195] Robert Dundas (1758–1819). M.P. Edinburghshire 1790–1801. Ld. advocate 1789–1801
[196] Subsequently 1st Baron Stowell. King's advocate 1788–98
[197] Robert Dundas, 2nd Visct. Melville and probably William Dundas (1762–1845)

he is Mr. Craufurd[198] – a rich old bachelor who lives about and gives dinners. In the evening I went with Sir Ralph to the Chancellor's Levée in my full dress – wherein I would have you to understand I am not a *quiz* – but on the contrary look very striking. This was my first introduction to the Chancellor. He was all civility and attention – and a day is to be fixed after the holydays for me to eat a bit of mutton with him – for we must be better acquainted. He is a great *rogue* I believe – but that is none of my business – and so I will go with all my heart, and eat his bit of mutton, when he pleases.

I supped with Lady Malmesbury. There was Mrs. Robinson and Ly. M.'s sister Lady Elliot – and Mr. Elliot[199] (Sir Gilbert's cousin) and George and Charles Ellis. John Ellis, Charles's elder brother, is very seriously ill – and Turton attending him.

*14. [April]* Monday. I was at home all the morning. In the House there was the Committee on Mr. Pitt's Emigrant Bill – but it was agreed, by a negotiation which I carried on between Pitt and Fox and Sheridan – that the *debate* on the Bill should be on Wednesday, and that tonight they would not fight it at all. So far from keeping their bargain however – they did fight it inch by inch – and Pitt would have revenged this infraction of the treaty by bringing on the Bill to-morrow – but that he recollected that he was engaged to dine at Ryder's, and thought it would be pleasanter to put off the debate than to lose his dinner. I, who had exactly the same engagement, liked his decision very much – and promised not to betray to Sheridan the *cause* of it – as he would certainly for the joke's sake contrive to spoil our dinner. To-night's *sparring* in the Committee lasted till past 12 – and there were two divisions in the course of it. I came home immediately, eat a cold fowl, being ravenous, and went to bed.

*15. [April]* Tuesday morning I called on Mr. Pitt – and had more conversation with him respecting the Emigrant Bill – on which I fully intended to speak whenever the *debate* came on. It is the best subject that has occurred this Session. The rest of the morning was consumed I know not how. I dined at Ryder's – where were Mr. Pitt, Lord Titchfield, Steele, Jenkinson, Wallace, Mornington, Mr. Smith[200] (of the Admiralty) and Mr. Montague (a nephew of the famous Mrs. Montague's, and a frequent and tolerable good speaker in Parliament).[201] We sat some time and then I went to sup with Lady Malmesbury – the Ellises,&c

---

[198] John Crauford (?1742–1814). A former M.P. and a crony of C.J. Fox
[199] William Elliot (1766–1818). M.P. 1801–1818
[200] John Smyth (1748–1811), see above p. 69, n. 164
[201] Matthew Montagu, 4th Baron Rokeby. Heir to the estates in Yorks. and Northumb. of his aunt, Mrs. Elizabeth Montagu (1720–1800), whose fame arose from her having made her house in Portman Sq. for more than thirty years 'the central point of union,

*16 [April]* Wednesday. I was at home till it was time to go to the House. I dined – first – and then set out.

This[202] was to have been the great debate of all, upon the Emigrant Bill [203] – but it was soon evident from their manner of conducting themselves that Opposition were not prepared to make it so. Their Treaty therefore is quite broken – for they stipulated that they would bring it on to-day and have done with it. Instead of this they began fighting over again the points and clauses which had been fought on Monday in the Committee. – *Speaking* therefore was out of the question as to making a regular speech. But in the course of the skirmishing sort of battle, which was kept up, I had an opportunity, of which I was glad to avail myself, to speak for a short time in answer to some objections which fell from Sheridan.[204] I took occasion in the conclusion of this little speech to express myself, as I felt, about Sheridan and he was very civil and friendly in reply – and we called each other *honble. friends* – and shewed to each other and to the House that our political differences had not altered our private sentiments of regard. It is astonishing, by the way, how many people are per-suaded that S. was my guardian. I have had to set right a thousand upon this head. I was glad to have spoken in this little way to-night for other reasons – first as *usefulness* is the character which it is most my interest to attain – and that character depends much upon the speaking on any unexpected point or sudden emergency, and the not seeming to care too much about picking nice occasions as who should say, 'I will not throw myself away – give me a good subject and I will work upon it, but do your piddling work in Committees and skirmishing debates yourself!' This is the language or at least the sentiment that ruins or at least lessens the value of most youngling speakers – and which I wish to avoid and to have the shew and reputation of avoiding – and this I think Pitt seems to understand. I was glad for another reason, that I accidentally spoke *from the floor* where perhaps, had I been predetermined to make a speech, I should not have thought it right to place myself – but it is twice as pleasant as any other place and more particularly for me, since the having the table before me corrects in some measure the fault which they lay to me, and of which I am certainly guilty, though I hope to conquer it.

---

for all those persons who already were known, or who emulated to become known, by their talents and productions.', Sir N.W. Wraxall, *Historical Memoirs of My Own Time*, (London, 1904), 84

[202] 'This was ... exceedingly animating' (p. 84), printed in *Marshall*, 66–67

[203] To enable subjects of France to enlist as soldiers in the British Army

[204] *Parl. Reg.*, 2nd series, vol. 38, 171. He defended the duration of the Bill, arguing that the Mutiny Bill was not annual for troops serving in India, nor for the Volunteer Corps embodied for internal defence

I mean making use of too *violent action*. They tell me I was quite *a lamb* to-night – indeed the subject was not exceedingly animating. After the debate I went home and supped and talked all these and such-like matters over, with Jenkinson.

*17. [April]* Thursday. Frere breakfasted with me – and stayed with me great part of the morning and then set out to get a place in the Gallery of the House of Commons, for the debate on the Emigrant Bill was certainly to come on to-day, and I fully intended speaking.

Fox[205] had given notice yesterday that he should make his opposition to the Bill this day – indeed he could not defer it longer – as this is the last reading and we adjourn to-day till after the holydays. Such a notice as this a year ago from Fox would have filled the House at 4 o'clock. I was therefore not a little surprized on going down at 5 – to find not 50 persons come. This is a melancholy proof for poor Fox of the disrepute into which he is fallen – and it really was quite pitiable to see him sitting almost alone on his Bench, with none of the principal people of his party about him, for even they did not attend in time. It has been evident indeed throughout the Session that Opposition have not drawn well together – and that there must be some little differences of opinion amongst them which unhinge all their plans and operations. On the days when Grey is in the humour to debate, Fox is not – when they are, Sheridan is away. No instance could be more strong to this point than the negotiation which I have before told you I carried on between Sheridan and Pitt for arranging the day on which this same debate was to come on. Sheridan made I know not how many stipulations, by not one of which Fox has been persuaded to abide. The principal was that we should have the question debated once for all yesterday – and so far from it – Fox had purposely reserved himself for to-day. Well – the House was thus *thin* – as I before said – and Fox seemed very much out of spirits and very unwilling to begin his speech before so few people. And to save him this mortification his friends resorted to one of the shabbiest tricks that ever was played in the House of Commons, but in vain.

There is, it seems, a Standing Order of the House that any member may at any time insist upon the House being *counted*, and if there shall appear to be fewer than *forty* members present, the House is ispo facto *adjourned* and no business can go on till their next meeting. Now this being the last day of business before the holydays (to-morrow being Good Friday) if they could have succeeded in procuring an adjourn-ment *now*, the Bill, which it is of the utmost consequence to pass immediately if at all – would have been put off till the House met again – this is for *ten days*. To effect this – all the Opposition members

[205] 'Fox had given ... their sentiments' (p. 86), printed in *Marshall*, 67–70

who were present, about 8 or 10 – in number – left the House one by
one, thinking to reduce the number of members below 40 – and
leaving only Fox himself – in whom it would have been too indecent
to withdraw (it was bad enough countenancing such a paltry proceeding) and Mr. Church,[206] who was to be the instrument for putting
the trick in practice. And as soon as the House appeared thin enough,
up jumped Mr. Church accordingly, and moved *that the House be
counted*. I never saw fright and anger in Pitt's countenance before. The
appearance was such that we had no hopes of 40 persons being present,
and then the Bill, which he had pushed so vigorously and on the
passing of which before the holydays he had set his heart and laid his
plans, was gone for God knows how long. Messengers were despatched
to scour the eating-rooms and Committee-rooms, and bring down all
stray members. The Speaker began the counting – *1 – 2 – 3* – our
hearts failed us – *38 – 39 – 40 – 41 – 42*. Huzza, the thing was saved
by a hair's breadth, and the salvation of it was accomplished by a
burst of laughter from our side of the House at the failure of this
miserable contrivance. Presently after came dropping in, one by one,
as they had gone out, the Oppositionists who had gone away to make
the deficiency – and we enjoyed, as you may suppose, their looks of
dismay and disappointment. Now then there was no help – but poor
Fox must get up and begin – which he did, at first in a very mournful
and melancholy strain. But he warmed by degrees, and made as good
a speech as I have heard from him this Session. The House too filled
gradually, and everything began to look gay and to promise a long
and lively debate – and I looked forward to speaking with great
satisfaction. Fox spoke about two hours – and then Dundas rose – and
spoke for about two hours more. During his speech Burke, who sat
next to me, said he meant to speak after Dundas. There was no
interfering with so old and venerable a performer. And so he did
speak – and for at least two hours. Immediately after him it was
impossible to speak – as there had already been two speeches running
on our side – and so Sheridan rose in reply to Burke – and *he* too
spoke for about two hours, and by the time he had about half done,
the House was thoroughly tired and wornout, some sleeping, some
yawning, and all showing evident marks of disinclination to hear
anything more upon the subject.[207] You must observe that 4 *long*
speeches tire out an audience ten times more than a *dozen* shorter ones
which may take up a good deal more time all together – and you
must understand that there is nothing which offends more, or tends
to make a speaker, particularly a young one, unpopular with the

---

[206] John Barker Church (1748–1818). M.P. Wendover 1790–96
[207] The bill was then read a third time and passed

House, than pressing himself upon their attention when they are tired, and more disposed to sleep or to divide. Of all this I had some notion before – and this night confirmed me in it – for Pitt, who knew that I was ready and willing to speak, if I saw occasion, told me at once that he thought there was no good opportunity, and that it would be foolish to throw myself away upon the drowsiness and inattention of that night. I was sorry to lose this subject for I had thought much upon it, and pleased myself with the way in which I had thought it might be treated – and so I wished all long speeches at the Devil – and made a sort of vow never to exceed *an hour* except on very particular occasions. Jenkinson like me was ready to have raised a speech for the service of Government, but like me was told that it would be better to let it alone. And so the debate ended, and Jenkinson and I went home together to supper at his house, grumbling against long-winded speakers who prevent young folks from delivering their sentiments.

The House adjourned to Monday sen'night, April 28 – when the Prussian Treaty will be ready – and *that* is thought to be the only business likely to remain for discussion.

*18. [April]* Friday I stayed at home all the morning till about 4 o'clock – when I set out with Wallace to dine at Mrs. Crewe's villa at Hampton. Jenkinson came there also – and there was Jane Linley[208] – and Fitzpatrick[209] and Lady Caroline Price (of whom you have heard before now) and her husband Mr. Price.[210] Fitzpatrick you know was the author, and Ly. Caroline the circulator of the epigram upon me.[211] We were not a bit the less pleasant together for that. On the contrary Ly. Caroline and I somehow or other struck a great intimacy, insomuch that she asked me to dine, not with *her* but with the Mr. Craufurd, the old bachelor whom I have before mentioned to you as having met him at Sir Ralph Payne's, at a dinner

[208] Jane Nash Linley (d.1806), 4th da. of Thomas Linley, a noted singer, and sister in law of R.B. Sheridan. She was also a singer

[209] Hon. Richard Fitzpatrick (1748–1813). M.P. Tavistock 1774–1807 and a Foxite whig

[210] Sir Uvedale Price 1st Bt., (cr. 1828), who m. 28 Apr. 1774, Lady Caroline Carpenter, da. of 1st Earl of Tyrconnel. Price was a noted gardener, his *Essay on the Picturesque* being published in 1794

[211] C. Informed John Sneyd on 31 Aug. 1794 that Fitzpatrick's and Mrs. Price's epigram went as follows:

'*Men's* turning their coats such a practice is grown
   That with satire 'tis vain to attack it
  But sure till this time no example was shown
   Of a *Child* ever turning his jacket'
see, *Bagot*, i, 48

which he is to give soon, and to which she is commissioned to invite good company. And I have willingly accepted the invitation. She and her swains went away after dinner. But Jenkinson and Wallace and I stayd supper – and made Jenny Linley sing and play to us – and passed a very pleasant evening, and then returned together to London. We are promised a grand breakfast and other gaieties at Hampstead in the course of a week or two.

*19. [April]* Saturday morning Frere breakfasted with me. Adderley called to tell me that Lord Hobart was to set out for Portsmouth to-morrow, and he with him. I settled to breakfast with him to-morrow morning before his departure. I had received a note from Lord Gower and Lady Sutherland to put me in mind of my engagement to spend part of the Easter holydays with them at Wimbledon – and to desire that I would set out for them to-day. This I could not do – having promised to dine with Fred. North – but to-morrow I have engaged to go, and I intend it. Fred. North sent to put me off on account of his sister-in-law's illness – and so I had to get a dinner where I could. This turned out to be at Mr. Woodcock's, where Bobus Smith dined also. In the evening I went to Lady Malmesbury's and supped there – and there were the two Ellis[e]s, Charles and George – and they told me that John Ellis, Charles's elder brother, was somewhat better.

*20. [April]* Sunday morning I breakfasted with Adderley according to my appointment – and took leave of him with all good wishes on both sides – and agreed to correspond during his absence. At two o'clock I set out for Wimbledon – and arrived there in due time. Lord Gower and Lady Sutherland were out walking and Lady Worcester arriving within a few minutes after me, we set out together to find them. Lady Worcester, you know, is Lord Stafford's daughter, and consequently Lord Gower's sister. You have seen her at Litchfield and therefore know how pretty she is, if not how pleasant. But you have not seen Lady Sutherland – and so you cannot know how very pretty she is, and how very pleasant, and how very clever, and how much I like and admire her. On our return from our walk we found Lord Worcester arrived – and Mr. Steele,[212] brother of Steele of the Pay Office. We dined – and in the evening read – played cassino – supped – and went to bed, much like other people.

*21. [April]* Monday – Lord and Lady Worcester and Mr. Steele went to town, and Lady Sutherland rode with them – but she of course to return to dinner, till which time Lord Gower and I were left to amuse ourselves together. We heard the guns firing, and went across the Common to Dundas's house to enquire the cause, which

[212] Probably Robert Steele (1757–1817) of Westhampnett, nr. Chichester, Sussex. Recorder of Chichester 1787-d

proved to be the taking of Martinico. (Observe, always say Martin*ico* not Martini*que* – as little trace of French as can be helped in these times). The rest of the morning we consumed in walking and reading. This place[213] is exceedingly beautiful – singularly so – considering its small distance from London – with hills, vales, wood, water &c. – of all which you are aware however that I am no very enthusiastic judge or admirer for their *own sakes*. They must be *well-tenanted* to make me look at them with delight. The house is excellent. It was formerly M. de Calonne's,[214] who had made it almost all that was necessary for convenience or pleasure. But there wanted, I should think, what Lord Gower has added, and without which no house is complete – a room of *all hours*, I mean one in which you may live morning, noon and night, full of books and maps and easy chairs, and *sofas to sit by those one likes*. Lord Gower himself I think a very sensible, good-natured, well-informed man and having seen a great deal of the world both here and abroad, capable of affording one very considerable instruction and entertainment. He is not however a popular man, I find – and my liking of him has added one to the many jokes which Jenkinson has against me, 'for always (as he says) taking mightily, to unpleasant people'. This charge, at least this instance of it, I wholly deny – for the reasons which I have already given in giving you my opinion of his character – and because he seems to like *me* – which I am not ashamed to confess has its weight *always* in my estimation, and because he is Leveson's brother, and perhaps I might add, Ly. Sutherland's husband. Ly. Sutherland returned time enough to walk with us before dinner and about the same time also came Arbuthnot – whom I have often had occasion to name to you as one of those with whom though I have never lived in very strict habits of intimacy, yet I am very fond of him, and like of all things to meet him. Indeed I have real obligations to him for the use of which he was to me in my transactions with Lord Abercorn, and he is pleasant, quick, gentlemanly and universally a favourite. He is very intimate here, and a very comfortable inmate. I do not recollect to have passed a more delightful evening for some time than we four (for there was no other person) did this day – not at cassino – for we did not find it necessary to resort to cards though we were *just a set*, but with books and conversation in the library.

*22 [April]* Tuesday morning – Arbuthnot had intended to set off for town – but I persuaded him to stay – as no other person was expected here, and yesterday had given me hopes that to-day might pass as pleasantly. The morning went I know not how. We dined at

---

[213] Lord Gower's villa in Wimbledon

[214] Charles-Alexandre de Calonne (1734–1802). Controller General of Finance in France 1783–87

Mr. Dundas's[215] – where besides *our family* were Ly. Jane Dundas (of course – being Dundas's lady) – the Lord Advocate of Scotland (Dundas's nephew) and Major, or rather Colonel Grey,[216] who had brought the news of the surrender of Martinico. The dinner[217] was quite as it should be – for nobody has pleasanter conversation and better wine than Dundas – and he was not the less disposed to be liberal of both, from having at his table the messenger of good news from Martinico, while he had in his pocket the letter of the Duke of York, announcing the victory near Landrecy. I did rather envy him the power, as much as I admired in him his manner, of informing Grey of his promotion to a Lieut. Colonelcy. Everybody else of course called him, as we thought him to be, *Major* Grey – Dundas in drinking to him – said carelessly, 'Col.[1] Grey, your health.! Grey seemed not aware of the truth of the title. 'The Gazette will be here in five minutes', said Dundas, 'and you will then see that I do not mistake in calling you so'. These are not things to *abate* the *thirst of power* in those who are witnesses of them. We returned *home* across the Common about nine or ten o'clock – and as much of the evening as was left, and the supper with which it ended, were as completely to my satisfaction as the preceding day had been.

*23 [April]* Wednesday morning. Arbuthnot went away. I began to think of going too – or at least of offering to go, as I did not know who, or how many people might be coming – and I knew the house was not so large but that one person's staying longer than had been calculated, might put them to inconvenience. I had no sooner begun to intimate my intention of departing, at breakfast, than I found abundant reason to retract it – and *un*ordered my chaise with all the willingness imaginable. The morning passed partly in a walk which we took all together – and partly in reading, which we took each by ourselves. To dinner came the Bishop of Carlisle[218] and Lady Anne Vernon (his wife). The Bishop, who is a son of Lord Vernon, married a daughter of Lord Stafford's, and through his interest, at the age of two or three and thirty, arrived at the Bench. He is a very good sort of man, though not guilty of having invented gunpowder. He was before his bishopric, and indeed is still, a Canon of Christ Church – and *there* I had known him and Ly. Anne, and they had been very civil to me.

[215] Dundas had a villa at Wimbledon at which he dispensed generous hospitality. Pitt had a room reserved for him there, see C. Matheson, *Life of Henry Dundas*, (London, 1933), 120–21
[216] Sir Henry George Grey (1766–1845), 2nd s. of Charles, 1st Earl Grey who was responsible, with Admiral Sir John Jervis, for the capture of Martinique
[217] 'The dinner ... witnesses of them', printed in *NER*, 459
[218] Edward Vernon (subsequently Harcourt, 1757–1847). Bishop of Carlisle 1791–1807; archbishop of York 1807–d

*24 [April]* Thursday came to dinner Lord and Lady Carlisle. She too is a daughter of Lord Stafford's – so that every person at the table or in the house called each other brother and sister – except myself. I do not dislike this – I know there are many people who think it an exceeding *bore* to be of a family party – but I confess I am of another mind – and when it happens to me, as it does perpetually with the Markhams, and frequently with the Levesons, and elsewhere, to be the only person not related to every other in the company, I am so far from feeling awkward, that I am not sure but it gives me additional ease and comfort and satisfaction, for they soon forget that one is a stranger. This day and the preceding past much alike – with walks and books in the morning, and books and conversation in the evening. Lord and Lady Carlisle did not stay all night but returned to town – and the Bp. of Carlisle and Lady Anne followed them on Friday morning, so that.

*25 [April]* On Friday I was left alone with Lord Gower and Lady Sutherland, and I was not sorry to find that nobody else was expected. (Mind '*left alone*' *with two* people is *not* a blunder, its meaning and true intent being no other than '*I alone* of all who had been here was left' – nor would it have been a blunder if I had said left tête-à-tête with *these* particular *two* – man and wife being *one* person – though upon the whole *a trio* is the properer expression). I need hardly tell you that this day passed at least as much to my taste as any of the former, though I do not know that it had any particular incident to mark it. O – yes – one – a slight one indeed – but somewhat ludicrous. It had happened a few days ago that I had at Lady S.'s request written out for her my Oxford verses – that in consequence of the sort of compliments, &c. which follow duely on such occasions – the conversation had turned for some time on poetry in general, and that upon my opinion, and that of others in the company, being asked about different English poets, I had given mine, as I always do, very warmly in favour of Dryden, and of Dryden's Works had particularly commended that volume which contains his Fables, as comprehending the finest system of versification that I knew. 'I wonder', said Lady S., 'if that is the same book which I was tempted to buy the other day at Edwards' – and which was called, I think, Dryden's *Miscellanies*'. Now I ought to have known better than to answer in the affirmative to this – for I ought to have recollected that Dryden was employed by the booksellers to publish a miscellaneous collection of poems by different authors – and that *these* and not *his own Fables*, were probably the book in question.[219] I did not happen to think of this at the time,

[219] Dryden's *Miscellany Poems* was pub. 1692. His *Fables Ancient and Modern* was pub. 1700. The bookseller was probably James Edwards (1757–1816)

and indeed, not much apprehending any consequence that might follow from what I said, I thought very little about it, and carelessly answered, 'I dare say it was – and if so – you ought to have yielded to the temptation and bought the book'. Of this conversation I never took any farther notice or had any remembrance of it till today – when, as we were sitting after dinner, Ld. G., Ly. S., and I – a parcel was delivered to Ly. S., and upon Ld. G.'s enquiring what it contained – the answer was 'Something that I am sure Mr. C. will approve'. The parcel was accordingly opened, and out came six little volumes, lettered *'Dryden's Miscellanies'* containing *not* his *fables* – nor anything *half so decent*, but a collection of all the *grossest*, *filthiest* and *most improper* poems of the *worst authors* of Charles the Second's time. We each of us took a volume – and each opened at once upon a piece which in decency we ought never to have seen, at least in company. 'Upon my word,' said I, 'this is a pretty recommendation of mine, as it turns out.' 'Yes, the books seem to be well chosen,' said Ld. G. 'I am afraid they must be locked up, Ld. G.' said Ly. S. (for there was one part of the library under lock and key, which, it had been a joke among us to agree was filled wholly with books not fit to be inspected – or why lock it?). In short, the poor Miscellanies were condemned to perpetual banishment – and I made a resolution never to recommend a book again, into which I had not looked myself – and Ly. S. never again to buy one, till she understood the grounds of its recommendation.

I must endeavour to atone for my blunder, which, by the way, was not wholly MINE either. And so since I came to town I have given Mr. Edwards a good scolding for having been the first to suggest a purchase to a lady, and have ordered a set of the Fables to be bound, that I may convince Ly. D. that I was not *quite* so bent upon misleading her judgement and corrupting her taste as she may have had reason to imagine. It is fortunate that the castastrophe happened before I left Wimbledon, or I should perhaps never have had an opportunity of exculpation.

*26 – [April]* Saturday morning I left Wimbledon and went across the country to Addiscombe. I found Lord Hawkesbury at home.[220] Jenkinson was not yet returned from the Cinque Ports, where he had been with Mr. Pitt visiting his (Jenkinson's) constituents.[221] But he came to dinner. There was none but the family – that is – Ld. and Ly. H., Jenkinson, and his sister. Jenkinson is to be Colonel of a Regiment of Fencible Cavalry raised for the internal defence of the country – and he would have me take *a troop* in it as *Captain*. It

[220] At Coombe Wood, nr. Kingston, Surrey
[221] He was M.P. Rye 1790–1803

would be good fun enough. But I do not find the military disposition
sufficiently strong within me – and so I have only bargained *not* to
*laugh* at *him* about it.

*27. [April]* Sunday we went regularly decently to church, all the
family. Ld. Hawkesbury is remarkably accurate in his responses and
has a sort of a knack at Pslam-singing. Before dinner Jenkinson and
I rode over to Beckenham to call on Lord and Lady Auckland. At
dinner – none but the family.

To-morrow Parliament meets again – and Jenkinson and I set off
together early for London. News of 3 French frigates being taken.

*28 – [April]* Monday morning I came to town with Jenkinson. I
passed the morning partly in going about to hear the news, and partly
at Hasting's trial, till it was time to go to the House of Commons.
There the Prussian Treaty was laid upon the table – a good round
sum we pay his Majesty – £1,400,000 or thereabouts.[222] There was
no debate upon it to-day. The House was up at 6 – and as I had no
engagement and had not dined, I walked quietly to Covent Garden,
dined at the Piazza Coffee House, and then went to see the Play
(Macbeth) at Drury Lane. In my way home from the Play I supped
at our Law Coffee House in Carey Street.

*29. [April]* Tuesday I called on Mr. Pitt, and had a long talk with
him about the Prussian Treaty, the discussion of which was expected
to-day or to-morrow.

Hasting's trial. In the House of Commons – a Motion was made
by Opposition for a Call of the House – that there might be a full
attendance (as was pretended) at the discussion of the Treaty but (in
truth) that *that* discussion might be deferred a fortnight or three
weeks – by which means the marching of the Prussian troops, now
fixed for the 24th May, would be delayed God knows how long, and
the plan of the campaign perhaps very materially deranged. It was
agreed on our side of the House that as the Motion was obviously
captious and absurd, and as the debate on the Treaty was to come
on next day, and it was as well not to have *two* debates instead of *one* –
nobody should answer Opposition. This silence on our part produced
the most ludicrous effect that you can imagine. Mr Curwen[223] spoke
violently. Nobody answered – Mr. Taylor[224] vehemently – All silence –
Mr. Sheridan in a great passion. Our only answer – a call for the
Question. Mr. Whitbread like mad – on our part a laugh and a
repeated cry of 'Question' – till at length about 8 o'clock they grew

---

[222] A subsidy of c. £1,350,000 was to be paid to the King of Prussia in return for an
army of 62,400 men
[223] John Christian Curwen (1756–1828). M.P. Carlisle 1791–1812
[224] Michael Angelo Taylor (?1757–1834). M.P. Poole 1791–96

tired of exerting themselves to no purpose – and suffered the Question to be put and negatived without a division. I dined upstairs with a multitude of people – then went to the Opera – and from the Opera to sup with Mrs. Crewe, where also was Windham.

*30. [April]* Wednesday I staid at home all the morning – and eat something before I went down expecting a violent debate on the Prussian Treaty, and intending to speak, if I found occasion. But whether it was that the good news of victories in Flanders which came to-day damped Opposition, or whatever else was the cause, none of them spoke but Mr. Fox – and of course nobody on our side but Pitt and Windham – and the House was up at 8.[225] Jenkinson as well as I, were ready to speak, if provoked – and we agreed it was very unfair in Opposition not to provoke us. From the House I went to a Child's Ball at Mrs. Robinson's (Privy Garden) and from thence to sup at the Abp. of York's – which I did most heartily, having had no regular dinner, nothing but the little which I eat before going down to the House – upon confessing which circumstance I had mutton chops prepared for me to a great amount.

*1st May* Thursday – Frere breakfasted with me. And the morning went I know not how. There was no House. I dined with Mr. Craufurd (the old bachelor whom I have mentioned to you before) – a grand dinner, to which I was invited not so much by Craufurd himself as by Ly. Caroline Price. There were Ly. Caroline and Mr. Price, Mrs. Crewe, Fitzpatrick, Lord Clermont, Sir Ralph and Ly. Payne – Mr. Fawkener[226] &c. &c. In the evg. I went to the Play – and from the Play to the Dss. of Gordon's – and from the Dss. of Gordon's, after sweltering there for a little time in such a crowd, as never was seen – straight home.

*2. [May]* Friday – I was at home all the morning till I went down to the House – where the Prussian Treaty was to be *Reported* – and as it had passed the first day with so little discussion – and as the reason of its passing so had been supposed to be the good news from Flanders, I apprehended that the bad news which came to-day, of Pichegru having beaten Clairfait[227] might have given them spirits to rally and debate to-day. There was but little said, however, and we were up before 7, so that I thought myself in time to go and dine with the Bp. of Carlisle, wth. whom I had a conditional engagement. In my way from the House of C. to dinner, I saw in a post-chaise, just driving into two, two faces which I thought I knew, and which upon nearer

[225] Fox's motion against the Treaty was defeated 134 v.33
[226] Probably William Augustus Fawkener (d.1811), clerk of the Privy Council and one of the secs. of the Board of Trade. A s. of Sir Everard Fawkener.
[227] On 29 April General Pichegru defeated the Austrian and Hanoverian forces of General Clairfait which were occupying the post of Moucron, near Courtrai

inspection, proved to be those of Boringdon and Leveson, just returned from their travels. I found dinner over at the Bp. of Carlisle's – but they had kept something hot for me – so I dined – and then went with the Bp. to Whitehall as I had promised Leveson I would do – and there I found him with all his family – brothers – sisters – brothers-in-law, and sisters-in-law, welcoming his arrival. I stayed there till late – and then went to sup with Lady Malmesbury, where as usual were Charles and George Ellis.

*3 [May]* Saturday. Frere breakfasted with me. Charles Reddish came to me according to an appointment, made when last I saw him – and I fitted him out with shirts, stockings, and coats, waistcoats, and breeches, made out of some of my old ones – and sent him away smart and happy. Paul continues to give me hopes of providing for him, by placing him wth Mr. Styan and – I forget who also – eminent grocers and tea-dealers &c. I called on Leveson and with him on Boringdon – and heard the stories of their travels, and of those whom they have left behind them in Italy (Holland, Morpeth, &c.) – and satisfied their curiosity with respect to transactions at home. I dined with Mr. Rose (Secretary of the Treasury) – where was a very grand entertainment and a very large party, male and female – amongst them Mrs. Montague (the famous letter'd lady) – Wallace – Ryder &c. – I went to the Opera – and from the Opera with Boringdon and the Ellises to sup with Mrs. Robinson (Boringdon's aunt, as I have before told you) and Lady Malmesbury.

*4. [May]* Sunday. I[228] went with Wallace to Mrs. Crewe's at Hampstead. A large party dined there, and all except ourselves, Opposition – Mr. Whitbread and his wife (who is Grey's sister), Mr. M.A. Taylor and Mrs. T., our old friend Richardson,[229] and Col. Grey (Grey's brother, who brought the news from Martinico.) It was a very pleasant dinner indeed. Whitbread, though violent in debate, and vulgarish in his manner, is very pleasant and good-humoured. Mrs. W. is very well. Mrs. Taylor charming  – and M.A. Taylor himself by far the most ridiculous man in the world. He is quite a treasure to his friends, the Opposition, giving them dinners, and affording them diversion, without end. I have long had a street and House of Coms. acquaintance with him – but never met him at dinner before, and to-day, with the help of Richardson, who sat opposite to me, I laughed so immoderately, that I feared Mrs. Taylor, who sat next to me, would think me the rudest beast that had ever come near her, and that Michael himself would challenge me. But it seems she

---

[228] 'I went with ... in London' (p. 95), printed in *NER*, 528
[229] Probably Joseph Richardson (1755–1803), a staunch Foxite whig and R. B. Sheridan's closest friend after the death of Richard Tickell in 1793, see *Thorne*, v. 14–15

must be a woman of most admirable sense and discretion, for though she is too quick and clever not to find out at once that her husband is the jest of the company, and indeed if she were as dull as a post, his friends would force her to see it – yet she never once appears to have the smallest suspicion of what is going on, and behaves to him, and talks of him, as if she thought him the perfectest of human beings – and as to Michael, he has no more suspicion in *fact*, than she *appears* to have, how laughable an animal he is, so little that when he took Richardson and Wallace and myself aside in the evening, instead of calling us to account, it was only to desire us to fix a day, which we did most gladly, for dining with him, and of course laughing at him, at his own house in London. Tuesday is fixed for that purpose. In the evening I returned to town – and supped with C. and G. Ellis at Lady Malmesbury's.

*5th [May]* Monday I was at home greatest part of the morning – went down to Hasting's trial, and from there to the House, where there was no business – dined, by appointment, with Bobus, Frere and a Cambridge friend of theirs, at the Bedford Coffee House. Went afterwards with Frere to the Play, and from the Play to supper at the Abp. of York's.

*6th [May]* Tuesday – was like yesterday till dinner-time. Then came Michael Angelo. Our company at dinner was Wallace, Jenkinson, Richardson and Col. Grey. Grey himself and Sheridan had promised to meet us – but there was a Whig Club which detained them. Michael's ridicules are not a bit less entertaining in his own house than abroad. On the contrary, it is here he shines in his full glory. I have seldom laughed more – and the best of the joke is, that he has taken to us young ministerialists so mightily that he promises us many good dinners next year in conjunction with his Opposition friends – and Sheridan, with whom I was talking about him, promises us that we shall see good sport when we meet there.

In the evening I went to the Opera and supped afterwards at Mrs. Crewe's with Windham, the Lady Norths, and Mr. Secretary Douglas.

*7. [May]* Wednesday. I was at home all the morning. In the House was nothing material. I dined with Mr. Legge[230] of Grosvenor Square – a very pleasant gentlemanly man – of good fortune and with a learned wife. There were C. and Geo. Ellis – and Arbuthnot. In the evening I went to Whitehall – and from thence to Privy Gardens to supper with Ly. Malmesbury and Mrs. Robinson – where were the Ellises, Boringdon and Legge.

[230] Heneage Legge (1747–1827), a cousin of the 2nd Earl of Dartmouth, lived at 35 Grosvenor Sq. with his wife, Elizabeth. The other 'H. Legge' that C. mentions later in the text is Hon. Henry Legge (1765–1844), 2nd s. of the 2nd Earl of Dartmouth

*8 [May]* Thursday. I went to Hasting's trial to hear Grey begin his summing-up. Here all the world were talking of Mr. Stone's taking-up, and of the examinations of Sheridan, Ld. Lauderdale, Majr. Maitland, Mr. Vaughan and W. Smith before the Cabinet.[231] In the House – nothing. I dined with Jenkinson – as did C. and G. Ellis, and Leveson. In the evening I went with Jenkinson to Lady Bristol's but could not stay supper there – having engaged to meet Leveson and the Ellises again at Lady Malmesbury's.

*9. [May]* Friday I was at home the whole morning. There was nothing in the House – at least nothing that I felt any disposition to attend. I dined at Mrs. Robinson's – where were Lady Malmesbury, C. and G. Ellis – Boringdon, Jenkinson and Lord Malmesbury, who is just returned from negotiating with the King of Prussia the Subsidy Treaty – and is to return to his Mission as soon as it has passed the House of Coms. and House of Lords, carrying with him the first advanced payment to his Majesty, about £400,000.

I went with Jenkinson to Lady Bristol's, where were a good number of people, but he and I only stayed supper.

*10 [May]* Saturday – Frere breakfasted with me.

Leveson called by appointment to have a long tête-à-tête talk-over of all that has happened, and is to happen, politically and personally, since our last meeting, and till we shall meet again – which will not be till next year – as he is going out of town in a few days to join his militia at Plymouth. He is to come into Parliament before the next meeting – probably for Litchfield – if so he will be obliged perhaps to attend his election – and then we may meet in Staffordshire this summer. Morpeth also is to come in, as soon as he is of age, which will, I believe, be in September.

Mrs. Crewe had a breakfast this day at Hampstead and I intended to have gone to it – but it rained desperately – and I am not so fond of rural promenades as to get wet to the skin for the sake of them. I dined at Sir Ralph Payne's. A grand party – Lord and Lady Carlisle, Lord and Lady Hawkesbury – Jenkinson, Wallace and Mr. Fawkener. I went to the Opera and from thence with C. Ellis to super at Ly. Malmesbury's.

*11. [May]* Sunday morning was occupied by various visitations which had long been owing – and by an appointment with Boringdon,

---

[231] William Stone (1763–1818) had been arrested and charged with high treason on grounds of being an agent of the French Republic. R.B. Sheridan, Lord Lauderdale, Hon. T. Maitland q.v., Benjamin Vaughan (1751–1835), M.P. Calne 1792–96, and William Smith (1756–1835), M.P. Camelford 1791–96, were examined at the Sec. of State's Office on conversations they had had with Stone on the prospects of a French invasion. Stone was tried and acquitted in 1796, see C. Price (ed.,) *The Letters of Richard Brinsley Sheridan*, (Oxford, 3 vols. 1966), ii, 5–8, 10

similar to that with Leveson yesterday – for he too is going out of town in a few days, but to return again – and I had a great deal of good advice to give him upon many topics public and private, and a great many of his opinions to hear. I dined at Whitehall – the family, and Leveson among them, who goes to-morrow, and the Duke of Dorset. This latter gentleman I had never seen before. There seems nothing very remarkable in him one way or other. In the evening came a crowd of people – for they have their Sunday evenings as well as other people – but I stayed only a little while, and then went for the rest of the evening and for supper, to the Abp. of York's.

*12 [May]* Monday morning, as soon as I had breakfasted I set out to call on Mr. Pitt. I had found a note from him on my return home last night, requesting that I would call upon him any time that was convenient to me this morning – as he wished to speak with me on the subject of Mr. Sheridan's motion, which was to come on to-day. Mr. Sheridan's motion, as he had given notice of it, was to relate to something about relieving the Roman Catholics and Dissenters.[232]

You[233] may remember to have heard from me that about the Test Act I am rather inclined to differ in opinion with Mr. Pitt (not that I have by any means made up my mind upon it – but such is *rather* the *bent* of my present *inclination*, perhaps upon studying the subject more deeply than I can pretend ever to have done, I may some day or other see occasion to correct my opinion) and that at the very first interview that we had, I stated this circumstance to him, and he received it with the utmost fairness and candour. Now this motion of Sheridan's, the exact nature and tendency of which I did not know, had occasioned me a little embarrassment – for on the one hand I was not disposed to countenance or support any measure, taken at *these* times, and under such *circumstances* as the present, for the repeal of the Test, however upon the whole I might think it prudent and proper, and on the other hand I was by no means prepared to resist it altogether, and so I had determined either to *stay away* and so have nothing to do with the debate, or if I did go down, to *vote against* Sheridan's motion, on the ground of its being, as I clearly think it, ill-timed and mischievous in the highest degree – but to *speak* at the same time, and in my *speech* to reserve to myself my opinion on the *general* question whenever it might be brought on in a proper shape, – distinctly stating that I *voted against* it now, *only* on account of its being introduced improperly. These alternatives I meant myself to propose

---

[232] Sheridan's motion was to repeal the qualifications under the Test Act which prevented Roman Catholics and dissenters from being appointed to posts in the Army and Navy; it was presented on 26 May 1794. A similar proposal made by Lord Grenville's government in March 1807 led to its downfall

[233] 'You may ... exactly tallied' (p. 100), printed in *Marshall*, 71–74

to Pitt, and to adopt that which should seem to him the more advise-able, preferring, however, in my own mind, the former, the staying away, as much the more simple, and liable to the fewest mis-representations. When I received his note requesting a conversation on the subject, which I should have asked if he had not, I was a little curious to know what he intended to say to me. What he did say gave me a higher opinion of his liberality, and a more confident reliance on his goodwill towards me than I had till this time ever entertained. He told me that recollecting, as he well did, the conversation which had passed between us on the subject of the Test Act the first time, that he had had the pleasure &c. of seeing me, he had thought that he should not act the part of a friend towards me, or keep up to that unreserved communication which had hitherto subsisted between us on political subjects, if he were not to take an opportunity of men-tioning what had suggested itself to him on the present occasion – that he begged me to be assured that in what he should say he had no reference whatever to *himself* but to me, and my interest solely – that he did not know how far I might feel myself *pledged* upon the subject of the Test, or how far obliged therefore to take a part in the debate of that day – but that if I were not pledged so far as to make *that* necessary, I should, in *his* opinion, do well to reflect how very large a part of England the Church of England party were, how great a value they attached to this particular question (which he would confess *he* thought comparatively speaking of very little importance) – and how rash it would be in a young man, just entering into political life, and likely to become and to continue a public character – to do anything, *unnecessarily*, that might prejudice so large a party of the people against him – he intreated me to believe that he did not mean or wish in the remotest degree to influence my opinion – but that he would only have me consider whether or no that opinion was so firmly rooted, and so publically pledged, as that I could not help acting upon it *now*, when it was by no means *called for*, and as that I should be sure of never hereafter repenting that I had done so. If my opinion *were* so *pledged* – God forbid that he should counsel me to shrink from it, – if it were *not*, he thought he had done no more than his duty and his good wishes demanded, in endeavouring to point out to me, which his experience in public life enabled him to do, the risque which I should run, and as he thought, without any apparent necessity – he wished very much to know how this matter had struck me and what I had determined upon it. I answered – that I felt myself infinitely obliged to him, as well for his fair recollection of what had formerly passed between us, as for his kindness in cautioning me, in a case where perhaps without such a caution I might have acted less guardedly than I ought to do – that what he said in this case, however, had partly occurred to me already, & I did intend to have sought an opportunity of communicating it to him if he had not voluntarily afforded me one – that as to *pledge* or *publicity* of my opinion upon the subject of the Test Act, there was nothing of that sort to bind me to act where any other consideration might interfere to restrain me – that I was very far from pretending to have sifted the subject so thoroughly as to have made up an unalterable opinion upon it – but that, having undoubtedly a *bias* in my mind to one side of the question, and that side being opposite to the side on which I knew *his* opinion to be, I had thought it but *fair*, at the time when I had first the honour to become known to him, to state that difference of sentiment, and to state it, if anything, rather *stronger* than I really felt it – for I should have reproached myself with something like *deceit* had I omitted to make him acquainted with it, at that time – that as to Mr. Sheridan's motion, I was so far from considering *that* as coming under the description of questions which I should wish to support, that on the contrary, for many extraneous and temporary reasons, if I voted *at all*, I should *vote against* it, that I should not however like to do *that*, without at the same time reserving the main question to myself, and *speaking* to that effect – but that, as in such a mode of proceeding there might be some little trouble and perplexity, I had thought that the most eligible mode of all would be to *stay away* – that when the main question should come fairly before the House, if ever it should do so, *then* would be time enough to determine and deliver my opinion upon it – but that when it was brought on thus distinctly and collaterally, and connected with other measures and circumstances foreign to its real meaning, I was so far from feeling myself called upon to give it any support, that I should very much prefer giving no opinion upon it at all. He replied that he was delighted beyond measure at finding my mode of thinking so exactly coincide with his own – that the very measure which he had meant to suggest to me was that which I had myself adopted, of keeping myself wholly out of the way – but that he had felt some little delicacy about being the first to mention it, and indeed should not perhaps have mentioned it directly had I shewn any marked disposition to take a different line of conduct. He again repeated that he hoped I would believe him to have been actuated by no other motive but a desire to guard me, for my own sake against anything which might prejudice me, as a public man, in the opinions of any body of men whatever – that the declaration which I had made of my opinions the first time I saw him, he had considered as a mark of great frankness &c. – and that he should have repaid it very ill if he had omitted to suggest to me what had occurred to him as so material a consideration for my service.

You will readily believe that I was not a little satisfied with this conduct – and what made it the more pleasing to me, and the more convinced me of its sincerity is, that the conversation on his part was almost word for word the same with one which I had heard from the Dean of Christ Church on the same subject. I have had an opportunity of repeating it to the Dean since – and *he* is mightily pleased that his advice and Mr. Pitt's should have so exactly tallied.

Sheridan's motion did not come on to-day, and there was nothing at all in the House.

I dined at Mr. Lewis's (the Dean's friend – of the War Office). There were Jenkinson – Garthshore[234] (a great friend of the Dean's also – whom I remember some time ago at Christ Church, and who for these last three years had been travelling with Lord Dalkeith – son of the Duke of Buccleugh – and is now returned, and going to be married to a great fortune) – Lord Digby (a contemporary of mine at Christ Church – but somewhat younger – just returned from his travels, and by the death of his father come into a large fortune and a peerage, and having just taken his seat in the House of Lords – a very good sort of young man) – and sundry other persons. After dinner I went with Jenkinson to the Play, where we found Lady Bristol and Lady Louisa Hervey. After the Play I came home, supping at the Law Coffee-house in Carey Street, in my way.

*13. [May]* Tuesday I was at home all the morning. In the House of Commons Dundas laid upon the table the papers which had been seized from the different treasonous Societies[235] – and moved for a Secret Committee for which we are to ballot tomorrow. I dined upstairs with Wallace and others, and went in the evening to the Markhams and supped there. In my home after supper (for the Markhams you know are early people) I called in and chatted for an hour with Mrs. Crewe.

*14. [May]* Wednesday. I[236] went to the trial [of Hastings] to hear Mr. Sheridan's reply, which was by far the most brilliant and entertaining speech that I ever heard from him or any other person. At the House of Commons was the ballot for the Secret Committee[237] – the members of which were chosen pretty unanimously – a circumstance which will not surprize you when you hear that a list is made out at the Treasury and sent round in the morning to all friends of Government – and the Opposition for the most part save themselves the trouble of balloting.

[234] William Garthshore (1764–1806). Christ Church, Oxf. 1782–86. M.P. 1795–1806
[235] Chiefly the Society for Constitutional Information and the London Corresponding Society
[236] 'I went ... balloting' printed in *NER*, 528
[237] This was established to investigate seditious practices. Its report was first debated in the Commons on 16 May

A party had been fixed for to-day to go to Sadler's Wells – Lady Malmesbury and her children, the Ellises, Edwd. Legge, Windham and I. I had to dress after the House of Coms., so that when I came to C. Ellis's, which was our place of rendezvous, and where we were to dine before we set out, I found the party set off. I found however a very good dinner left for me to eat, and a carriage to carry me – and so I dined quietly by myself – and arrived afterwards at Sadler's Wells time enough for the rope dancing and the Pantomime. From *the Wells* we returned to C. Ellis's to supper.

This day poor little Charles Reddish went to P. Patrick according to appointment, and with him to Mr. Popplewell and Styan,[238] the merchants, who are to take him. He gives me a good account of his reception and I trust they will take him – and then he is settled and may do well. This day brought me another on my hands – for I received a letter by this post from a clergyman and schoolmaster in Yorkshire, a Mr. Milner, informing me that my mother's children had been with him Lord knows how long, that *one* (his name *William*)[239] was still with him, that they were taught, boarded and cloathed for about £18 a year – and finally that my mother was indebted to him £28-3-2- and he in great distress. God helps him! and her! and me! and all of us! I cannot yet send him an answer. One circumstance amidst all the sadness of his letter which almost makes me laugh, is that she has been sending him cart-loads of *Collysium* (her eye-ointment) for payment, which the poor man complains bitterly nobody will buy.

*15. [May]* Thursday I was at home all the morning. There was nothing in the House of Commons. I[240] dined at the Chief Baron's (Sir. A. M'donald – you know all about him) – with Lord Gower and Lady Sutherland. Mr. Hawkins Browne[241] (a member of Parlt, and of the Secret Committee – a very sensible man, though queer in his manners – and a respectable though somewhat tiresome speaker) – Mr. Jackson[242] (a Ch. Ch. man, brother of the Dean – but as unlike to him as a most disagreeable man must be to a most pleasant one) – and the Bishop of Durham[243] – the most perfect clerical coxcomb that I ever had the satisfaction of beholding. The first thing I heard him say was 'that when last he had been at Lambeth (the Abp. of

[238] Popplewell and Styan are recorded as tea-brokers of 5 Scot's Yard, Birch Lane, London

[239] William Hunn who was one of his mother's children by Richard Hunn

[240] 'I dined – lived well' (p. 102), printed in *NER*, 528–29

[241] Isaac Hawkins Browne (1745–1818). M.P. Bridgnorth 1784–1812

[242] William Jackson (1751–1815). Professor of Greek at Oxford, 1783 and subsequently bishop of Oxford 1812–d.

[243] Hon. Shute Barrington (1734–1826). Bishop of Durham 1791–d.

Canterbury's) he was *astonished*'. It was a matter of general curiosity how an Archbishop could astonish a Bishop – and so we all enquired eagerly. 'I was astonished at the asparagus', said he, 'which was the largest I had ever seen'. I caught Ly. Sutherland's eye – we laughed – and I am afraid he saw us. He put us in mind, as we agreed afterwards, of that passage in Shakespear where Richard the 3d – addressing the Bishop of Ely at the Council Board says

My Lord of Ely, when I was last in Holborn
I saw good *strawberries* in your garden there.

The Church has always lived well.

In the evening I went to Whitehall – having first settled with Lord Gower and Lady Sutherland to go to Wimbledon on Saturday – and stay till Monday. From Whitehall to Privy Garden – to sup with Ly. Malmesb[ur]y – the Ellises.

*16 [May]* Friday – I was at home all the morning.

Going down to the House I met Mr. Pitt, who informed me of his intention to move for a suspension of the Habeas Corpus Act immediately after the reading of the Report of the Secret Committee. I returned home to dress – for I had gone down with no idea of the House lasting a quarter of an hour, and meaning to return afterwards, and dress, and dine with C. Greville. Had I been provident, I should have dined too, while I was dressing – but I was in a hurry, afraid of losing any part of the Report, and so I went down fasting, and was kept so till one o'clock for my pains – which, together with the harrassing work of dividing 16 times,[244] so completely wore me by 1/2 past 3, that I know not when in my life I have been more tired.

*17. [May]* Saturday morning. I lay in bed till it was within a few hours' time of going down to the House.

When I came into the House I found Mr. Pitt not come, and Sheridan moving to adjourn on account of his absence. I knew nothing of the cause of his delay, nor could I find anybody near who could inform me – so I thought it best to *dart* that my Rt. Honble. friend had been called away by some very important business, which however would not detain him long – that considering how long we often waited for other gent. I thought it would be hard to deny five minutes to my R.H.F. who had so many *superior* engagements – and finally that if they persisted in their motion, I should divide the House upon it (which would at least have taken 20 minutes or half an hour, and so give Pitt time to come down)[245].

Sheridan in answer pretended to understand *superior* engagements as meaning engagements *superior* to the business of the House – which

[244] On the Habeas Corpus Suspension Bill which passed with substantial majorities
[245] 'When ... before experienced' (p. 103), printed in *NER*, 529–30

I in explanation asserted to mean no more than *superior* to the engagements of most of those gent. for whom we were most in the habit *of
waiting* (meaning principally S. himself, who is never in time, when
he has a motion to make). While this was going on Pitt came in, and
I found upon enquiry that his *superior engagements* this time, had been
to eat a very hearty dinner. I wished I had been with him at that
ceremony instead of *lying* for him in the House.

After dividing upon the question of adjournment, came on the third
Reading of the Habeas Corpus Bill. I had come down without the
smallest intention of speaking. But I took notes of some of the Opposition speeches, and particularly Grey's – and feeling myself bold
enough, and Pitt, next to whom I was sitting, appearing very desirous
that I should speak – up I got, as soon as Grey sat down, and travelled
along through a very pretty speech, with as much success, I believe,
and with more ease, and satisfaction to myself, than I had ever before
experienced.[246]

I had occasion in the course of my speech to defend Pitt, whom
Grey had been attacking most violently, on the subject of parliamentary reform. I took occasion at the end of it to attack Grey on
account of a declaration which he had volunteered, ten days ago,
about his secession from Parliament. These two topics furnished
occasion – the first to Mr. Courtenay for a most blackguard invective
against me and Mr. Pitt jointly[247] Mr. Pitt, who on the former day
when Mr. Courtenay attacked me, had cautioned me so earnestly, as
I told you, against being provoked to answer him, was no sooner
touched by him *himself*, than up he jumped to express his resentment
Oh! ho!, thought I. People can give good advice to others, which they
do not follow themselves – but I will be hanged if I will be persuaded
out of my little repartees this time, and so, when Courtenay sat down,
having called me, in the course of his speech, a sort of '*politico-poetical
character*', I rose in explanation and said 'that it had not been my
intention to say anything in answer to what might fall from that gent.,
as I had understood from my hon. friends near me, that *nobody ever
did* take notice of *him*; and I would not willingly break through an old
rule. But that as my Rt. hon. fd. had set me the example in *this*, as in
*other* points, I would follow him. That the hon. gent. had called me a
politico-poetical character. I did not exactly know what he might
mean by that – at all events I would not retort the charge upon him –

[246] These interventions and a subsequent speech in the debate are recorded in *Parl.
Hist.*, xxxi, cols. 526, 535–37. Virtually identical reports are to be found in *Parl. Reg.*,
*Woodfall*, and *The Senator*
[247] Courtenay began by complimenting 'Mr Canning on the brilliant display of
abilities he had again exhibited, and congratulated the chancellor of the Exchequer
on having procured such an able and honourable apologist.', *Parl. Hist.*, xxxi, col. 537

those who attended to his speeches, I would leave to judge of his politicks, and those who read his works, I was sure would acquit him of poetry'.

The other topic, that of Grey's retirement, Sheridan mistook, or pretended to mistake, for an attack upon Fox – who it seems had said – but I did not know it – something to the same purpose. I should have been very unwilling that Fox should have continued to think that I had made a personal attack upon *him* – both because I personally respect him very much, and feel that he has been very civil to me – and because I think it always indecorous in a young man to *begin* a warfare with one so much his elder in age, and of so superior and confirmed a name and station. He did think so for a time, and Sheridan had told him so (for he was not himself in the House when I spoke) for in this speech he adverted to what he supposed me to have said, and defended himself. Having once already risen to explain, and knowing how much the House dislike a man's rising often, I did not publicly undeceive Fox in this particular – but as soon as the debate was over, I went across to him and Sheridan, and assured them that I had no manner of intention of saying anything pointed to Fox – that it was against Grey, whom I had heard make the declaration alluded to, that all which I had said was directed – that I did not even know that Fox had said the same thing – if I had – I would have abstained from the topic altogether. He received my explanation with the utmost good humour – and Sheridan professed himself very sorry for having misunderstood me. Windham, as you know, said very handsome things in my behalf, in his speech. The debate lasted till 3 o'clock. I got no supper, or rather dinner, till 1, and came home to bed rather fatigued.

*18 [May]* Sunday morning I refreshed myself with as long a sleep as was compatible with my setting out in good time for Wimbledon. I had settled to be there yesterday, as I said – but the debate prevented both me and them from going. I arrived about 3 – and had taken a long walk with Lord Gower and Ly. Sutherland – when on coming in to dress we found Lord and Lady Stafford and Lady Worcester – and the Lady Levesons come.

There was nobody else here to-day except Mr. Huskisson[248] (Lord Gower's Secretary who was with him at Paris – and who was therefore no impediment to its being almost entirely what you know I like, a family party). The dinner, the evening, the supper were all very pleasant, insomuch that when I went to bed I was sorry to reflect that I was to get up next morning, not to lounge away the whole day at Wimbledon – but to return to the swelter and fatigue of London.

[248] William Huskisson (1770–1830)

*19 [May]* Monday morning I returned to town from Wimbledon. I stayed at home till it was time to go down to the House – and then went down, not so much expecting anything in our own House, as that the Lords would receive our Report, and proceed to a debate on the Suspension of the Habeas Corpus. But to my great disappointment I found the slow Lords had chosen to appoint a Committee of their own, instead of adopting the Report of ours, and had adjourned their debate till Thursday, a proceeding which, by delaying so long the passing of a Bill, the very essence of which *we* had contended to be immediate and quick effect, throws a degree of ridicule upon the precipitancy with which the Bill was pushed through the House of Commons. What made me feel this the more angrily at the time was that I had calculated upon passing the evening under the Throne at their Lordships' debate; it was now six o'clock – and I had provided no engagement for dinner. I set off in mighty ill-humour – but arriving at Mrs. Crewe's just as they were going to sit down to dinner, I resumed the natural serenity of temper, dined pleasantly with Mr. and Mrs. C. and her brother – went in the evening to S. Audley Street, played whist with the Abp. [of York] and supped – and came home quietly to bed.

*20. [May]* Tuesday morning. Frere breakfasted with me. I was at home busy the greater part of the morning – went down about four o'clock to the trial, [of Hastings] where Fox was speaking, and found nothing to be done in either House. I dined at C. Ellis's with Geo. Ellis, Edwd. Legge and Newbolt (you have heard of him before – he that married Miss Digby, the Maid of Honour). From a very snug dinner we adjourned to the Opera – and from the Opera I went with Wallace to sup at Mrs. Crewe's.

*21 [May]* Wednesday I was at home all the morning till I went down about four o'clock to hear Fox conclude his reply at the trial, and to satisfy myself that there was nothing in the House of Commons.

I dined with the Clives.[249] There was C. Moore, Wallace, Lord Sheffield and a large party besides. They have a very comfortable house – but it is a plaguy way off, to be sure. In the evening I went to Whitehall and stayed with them till it was time to go a hundred yards off to sup with Ly. Malmesbury, and to meet there the Ellises and T. Pelham.

*22 [May]* Thursday morning was spent partly at home, and partly in City visits – Borrowes – P. Patrick &c.

[249] The Clives have not been identified. The most obvious candidate is the Hon. Robert Clive (1769–1833), 2nd surv. s. of the 1st Baron Clive and an exact contemporary of C.'s at Eton and Christ Church. However C. later refers to Mrs. Clive (p. 255) and the Hon. Robert did not marry

I[250] had engaged myself to dine early and go to the Play with Ly. M[almesbur]y and the Ellises, and I almost wished I had not done so, as the debate in the Lords was fixed for to-day. However the play was *The Gamester*[251] – and Mrs. Siddons in it – and I thought she would speak better than most of the Lords, whom I should hear – and that I should be in time for the flower of the debate, when the play was over. We dined accordingly at 1/2 pt. 4 in Privy Garden, and then packed off, the Ellises, Ly. M. and I to the Play.

I am not exceedingly fond of such expeditions. They jumble one's dinner, and make one feverish. As soon as the Tragedy was over, I set out towards the House of Lords, for the entertainment. The first thing I heard, upon coming in, was the *Boringdon* had spoken for his first time, and very well. I was marvellously provoked at having missed him. Had he given me the least hint of his intention, I would have given up my Play, and my dinner, to be at hand to hear him. The debate lasted till past 2 o'clock – and all that time did I stand stewing under the Throne, like a fool, for I heard but little that rewarded my perseverance. Trust me, these nobles of the land have but a tame notion of debates. By the time of the division, I was so exhausted, what with my long attendance and my early dinner, that I could not go homewards till I had replenished myself at a Coffee house hard by, with about 3 pounds of cold roast beef and 2 pots of porter.

*23 [May]* Friday morning I was at home till 4. I then went down to the trial where I found M.A. Taylor speaking upon the *Opium Contract*,[252] in a manner very congenial with the subject – and from thence to the House of Commons where I found nothing to be done. I dined at C. Greville's – where, beside himself and Ly. Charlotte were Arbuthnot and Lord Dungannon – an Irishman whom perhaps Fan or some of you know – a very good-humoured man. We sat till it was just time for me to go and sup at Mrs. Crewe's, which I accordingly did, and met there Windham.

*24 [May]* Saturday – I was at home great part of the morning. I wrote to the poor Yorkshire clergyman, from whom I have told you I had a letter some days ago about my mother's arrears to him, and sent him a £10 note.

I dined at Ld. Digby's with Adml. Digby (his uncle) and Boringdon. In the evening I called at the Markhams – and hearing they were

[250]'I had ... of porter' (p. 106), printed in *NER*, 530

[251]A comedy by James Shirley acted in 1633 and printed in 1637

[252]One of the charges against Hastings was that he had awarded contracts for the management of the East India Company's opium monopoly without due regard to the Company's best interests, see P.J. Marshall, *The Impeachment of Warren Hastings*, (Oxford, 1965), 168–71

gone to the Play, followed them thither – found them, returned with
them to supper – and afterwards in my way home, finding myself not
late, I called at Lady Malmesbury's, not to sup again but to see her
and C. Ellis and Jenkinson, who were supping there.

I have been intending, dear Fan and dear Leigh too, ever since I
came to town, to sit for my picture, large and little, according to your
respective directions and my promise. The first month or six weeks
that I was in town I would not sit to Lawrence[253] or to anybody else –
because, thought I, I will be *known* first, and then they will take more
trouble about me. Miss Folkstone (sic),[254] whom Fan would like best,
paints no more – and so I was at a loss what miniature painter to
chuse. At all events I determined to wait till Parliament was up, that
I might have had time to make my choice, and that I might have
leisure to sit day after day till I was finished. Parliament however did
not rise – and what with my illness – which took up eight weeks in its
rise, progress and consequences, and what with my ill looks, which
unfitted me, for some time afterwards, and what with the business
which has occupied me ever since, I began to think it hopeless to sit
this year, and had determined to put it off altogether to next winter.
So far however I have got, as to resolve that Lawrence should be the
painter of the large picture. About a miniature painter I could resolve
nothing, knowing none – till yesterday Lady Malmesbury began
telling a long story how she wanted to fit up a little *boudoir* with little
sketches of portraits, and how C. Ellis and Geo. Ellis had promised
her theirs – and how there was a man, a Mr. Edridge,[255] who drew
in a particular style of his own, which was the prettiest in the world,
and how I and Jenky must let him draw us to compleat her group –
and finally how she should put me into the coach and lug me there
this very morning. Remonstrance was vain – where the plot had been
so happily laid – and so I was actually forced into the coach – consoling
myself with the idea, 'Well, this picture of Ly. M's then shall be an
*experiment* – and if I like Mr. Edridge's way of doing it, *then* he shall
have the honour of painting me next winter (or this summer if I stay
long enough in town to give him ample time) for my Fan. If not, I
will seek a better'. So with this determination I have suffered him to
begin tracing my physionomy, cautioning him only that two *styes* (for
alas! I have my styes yet, and I know not how to get rid of them) are
not a natural and necessary part of my person – but visitors only,
who, I trust, will take their leave some day or other, and who are

[253] Sir Thomas Lawrence (1769–1830), kt., 1815. Apptd. principal portrait-painter in
ordinary to George III, 1792
[254] Miss Anne Foldsone (c. 1770/75–1851). A pupil of Romney and patronised by the
Prince of Wales, 1790–91
[255] Henry Edridge (1769–1821)

not therefore to be expressed, like more permanent features, in my portrait.

Mr. Edridge's style of drawing is certainly a very pretty and singular one – and I wish I could anyhow contrive that you should see some of his performances, Fan, that you might chuse between one of them, and a miniature. His are in black and white only, small whole-lengths or three-quarters at least, and in the nicest taste imaginable. But then they only do for framing and hanging-up, and cannot be *worn*, as a miniature is. In short, I will tell you how I settle the business in my own mind. *Fan's* shall be a regular miniature, as all miniatures are, *wearable* and *puttable* into bracelet &c. or *fausse montre* or what not – and *besides* that (if I like Mr. Edridge as much at the end as I do at the beginning) he shall do one of *his own style* to be framed and hung up in some pretty little corner of a room at Ashborne, which shall be *common* property to *Bess* and *Fan* and *Leigh*. I hope I shall have time for *this* before I leave town – but I know not till I hear about Parliament.

*25 [May]* Sunday I was at home all the morning. Boringdon called on me by appointment to have a long discussion of politicks and of his first oratorical entry into political life. I dined at Lord Stafford's with Boringdon, Hamilton[256] (a Christ Church contemporary of ours, son of Ld. Archibald Hamilton) and Miss Hamilton (his sister, a very pretty girl, and great friend of the Lady Levesons) and Mrs. Howe (and old lady, sister of Lord Howe – who lives a great deal with the Staffords – and who, whenever I meet her there, has a puzzle ready for me). She gave me a puzzle to-day which she said she had kept in her pocket for me this month, and we all set about guessing it – but nobody could find it out. It is as follows. Set Tish about it.

Plant *nine* trees in *ten* rows

*Three* trees in *each* row – and

In *each* row the *three* trees at *equal distances* from each other.

N.B. the *rows* need *not* be of *equal lengths*.[257]

I stayed at Whitehall till late and then went to supper at the Markhams. There was the Dean of Christ Church – who is come up to town (as he always does at this time of year) to the election at Westminster College, of boys upon the Foundation, for Christ Church – and Trinity Coll., Cambridge. There were so many people at supper that I had no opportunity of much conversation with the Dean – but we settled that he should call on me on Thursday

---

[256] Archibald Hamilton (1770–1827); styled Lord Archibald Hamilton from 1799 when his father succ. as 9th Duke of Hamilton

[257] Lord Howe's sister Caroline (c. 1722–1814) who m. John Howe of Hanslop, Bucks. For the solution to the puzzle see p. 117

morning – and have our talk out, upon matters of various kinds. I
have not seen him, you know, since the meeting of Parliament.

*26. [May]* Monday. Frere breakfasted with me. I was at home
greater part of the morning. In the House of Commons was Sheridan's
Motion respecting Dissenters &c. – from which, as you may suppose,
I staid away. It produced little debate and no division.

I dined at Sir. R. Payne's. There was Lady Malmesbury, C. and
Geo. Ellis. Wallace and Arbuthnot – and two or three other people.
From dinner I went to Whitehall – spent the evening there – and then
went to supper at Privy Garden – and there after supper, at the
suggestion and with the assistance of Ly. M. and the Ellises, I turned
*Jenkinson's hand-bill* into verse. You remember, do you not? – that
Jenkinson is raising a Regiment of Fencible Cavalry – of which he is
Colonel. Since the beginning of this business he thinks and talks and
cares about nothing else in the world – and he has of course great
handbills stuck up in every part of the streets of London, inviting *all
aspiring young heroes* to enlist with him. This handbill I had often
threatened him with converting into doggrell – and so tonight they
put me in mind of my threat – and we set about it – and if you will
take my word for the verses (for as the thing has unluckily turned out,
you must never see them) they were excellent. It was agreed that on
Wednesday, when Jenkinson dines at C. Ellis's, and when none but
friends are to be present – a packet should be brought in to him after
dinner as from a printer, containing the verses – and a picture of a
Fencible Sergeant, which Geo. Ellis, who draws remarkably well,
undertook to provide – with a note from the supposed printer, to the
following effect –

'Rickaby's respects to the Honble. Col. Jenkinson – has struck off
the No. ordered (500) of the enclosed handbill, and returns the
original, as desired. Rickaby has procured an etching to be made,
according to order, from the enclosed drawing of a Fencible Serjt.
chacing sans-culottes into the water – which makes a handsome
appearance – and hopes will meet approbation. N.B. Unless
further orders – bill-stickers will be about with the bills at six this
evening'.

From this, you see, Jenkinson was to be led to apprehend that
somebody having sent the verses to a printer, the bills were actually
printed off, and (as he would not receive the packet till between 7
and 8) that by the time of his receiving it, they were actually pasted-
up in several parts of the metropolis. The Ellises wanted to have one
or two *printed* really, by a printer on whom they could depend, to
make poor Jenkinson the more sure of his fate – but I would not suffer
that, lest perchance copies of them should get about – which would
be by no means justifiable, as the joke was not intended to pass a

select number of particular friends. The making the verses and the laughing, as we went on, kept us till about 4 o'clock in the morning.

*27. [May]* Tuesday morning – as soon as I was up I went to the trial [of Hastings] – calling in my way at Privy Garden to see if the Serjeant's picture was in forwardness. At the trial Michael Angelo Taylor was speaking – and in the House there was nothing to be done – so I came back to dress. I dined at C. Greville's – with Frederick Hervey – went to the Opera – and from the Opera, for five minutes to Privy Garden – and from Privy Garden early to bed.

*28 [May]* Wednesday Frere breakfasted with me. I went to the trial where Burke began his reply. In the House, nothing. I should have liked to dine at C. Ellis's – where Jenkinson and the verses were to be – but I had an engagement of long standing to Woodcock – and so I dined with him, and there was a numerous Christ Church party – Ld. Digby – C. Moore – Sturges – &c. &c. &c. It was very *young* and very pleasant. We sat till it was time for me to go and sup with Mrs. Crewe.


*29. [May]* Thursday. I had promised to stay at home for the Dean, who was to call in the course of the morning. I expected to hear from C. Ellis of the event of the joke yesterday – but how was I surprized and astonished at receiving a note to the following purport:
'My dear C. – Jenky is exceedingly hurt at the verses – we did all we could to soothe him, and to convince him that no ridicule was intended to be cast on him personally – but without much effect – I will call on you as soon as I possibly can in the morning and talk with you about it. Yrs. – C. Ellis'.

What possible quirk and nonsense can Jenkinson have got into his head now?, thought I – how can he have imagined that I could mean anything towards him, but in playfulness and good humour? In a little time Charles Ellis came and gave me a distinct account of all that had passed. 'The company at dinner were Ly. M[almesbury], Geo. Ellis, Ed.ᵈ Legge and Sir Harry Englefield'[258] (I daresay I have had occasion to mention him before – a quiet, clever, literary, goodhumoured man – who lives a great deal with the Malmesburys, and with all sorts of people, and goes his own way, and interrupts nobody). 'After dinner the packet was brought in – Jenkinson opened it, enquired who brought it, read it through, and put it in his pocket – 'What is that?' said everybody at once – 'A picture? Nay then we have a right to look – Verses? – then I protest we will read them' And so they got possession of the papers, and Edw.ᵈ Legge was appointed

---

[258] Sir Henry Charles Englefield 7th Bt. An antiquary and scientific writer. FRS 1778; FSA 1779

reader – and read them through. Before they were quite finished Lady M. whispered me – 'I am sure, Jenkinson does not like it' – I thought this impossible – but observing his countenance narrowly I began to be of her opinion, and by the time Edwd. Legge had done, it was evident that the thing had a very different effect from what had been intended, and from what anybody in their senses could possibly have calculated that it would have.' 'Was he *angry* then?' interrupted I. 'No' said C. Ellis, 'but he seemed very *sorry*. We did not sit very long, as you may suppose – and as soon as I could take him aside, I did so – and remonstrated with him upon the unaccountable manner in which he seemed inclined to take so pleasant and so innocent a joke. I told him the whole detail and all the circumstances of the making of the verses, and put it to him whether he could possibly suppose that a person who loved him, as you do, could mean to hurt his feelings in the smallest degree – and whether he could not distinguish between the ideas of *personal* ridicule, which this was *not*, and a little harmless ridicule of the *thing* and *system* altogether, in which *he* was no more involved than any other individual concerned in the present military preparations.' 'In short', continued C. Ellis, 'I said everything that I could think of to bring him to his senses, or at least to induce him to tell me how and why he felt so perversely upon the occasion – but without success, and so I thought it best to deliver him over to Lady Malmesbury – and she took him into the next room – and they sat down on a sofa together – *he* with *her* hand in *his* and *she muching* him and coaxing him for about two hours, and putting the folly of his conduct in every possible light, and saying of your good intentions and affection for him – everything that she could devise – but she could get no answer from him but tears (for he cried like a child) and that he was not *angry* with anybody – but that in Canning it was *so unkind*. We hoped that you would have called in the evening – for we felt persuaded that if you had been by at the time, or had come in afterwards at any moment before his feelings had got to such a pitch as to have lost all command – that the thing in the first instance would never have taken such a turn at all – for he would have *understood you* – or that it would have been set to rights in a minute.' I do not recollect that I was ever in my life more seriously vexed and affected than by this narrative. That he should have supposed me capable of intentional unkindness towards him – that he should have seen so perfectly childish and harmless a joke in any other light than that in which it was meant to be presented to him, did so surprize, and the manner in which he had expressed his feelings, so affect me – that before Charles had done speaking, I had begun to do as foolishly as Jenkinson, and was even crying like a child too – 'Nay in God's name', said C.E. – 'do not *you* make yourself a fool too. Here's a piece of work –

Nonsense – I am sure he will have come to his right mind, and be ashamed of his absurdity by this time – do let me go and bring him to you – or write if you will, and I will carry your note, and bring back either himself or an answer. I shall find him at the Committee of Secrecy in half an hour – and if he cannot come away – he shall send some message to you.' I wrote, therefore, and shewed what I had written to C.E. – and had just sealed it – and given it to him to carry, and had not yet composed myself sufficiently to look like a quiet Christian person, when the door opened, and in stalked the Dean. Charles staid about ten minutes to talk to him (*he* was a great favourite with the Dean at Christ Church) and to give me time to look a little more rationally, and then set off on his embassy. It was impossible that the Dean should not observe something extraordinary in our manners – and so, as he is the man of all others, notwithstanding his great wig and short cassock, to whom a matter of feeling may be confided with perfect security of his entering into and understanding it, I told him at once what the matter was. 'Upon my word, for three members of Parliament as foolish a business as ever I heard – and so Ellis is gone to negotiate between Jenkinson and you an affair about some doggrell verses. Why, child, this is more nonsensical than you used to be at Christ Church, where you were quarrelling and making-up again all day long – pretty people to govern a nation truly – I see what work you all make of it as soon as you get from under my government. But come – I suppose it will all be well again – and I have a thousand things to talk to you about – and so let us sit down'. We did so – and had a long, long talk which lasted till it was time for him to go to dress, and to leave me to do the same, that we might be ready to meet at dinner at his friend Mr. Lewis's – where he always lives mostly when he comes to town, and where all his young Christ Church flock, whom he happens to see in London, are asked to meet him. Charles Ellis returned to tell me that he had seen Jenkinson, who was so busy at the Committee that he could not write at that time but had sent word that *he* should dine at Mr. Lewis's, that we should meet there and have an opportunity of talking together afterwards. I must not omit to tell you that Fleming would fain have had the Dean swallow a mess of chocolate which he had prepared for him, and which he was sure he must want after his walk.

I went to dinner at Mr. Lewis's. There was, as I have mentioned, the Dean and his party – that is – Garthshore (whom I have before named to you) and Moss[259] (son of the Bishop of Bath and Wells) friends and élèves of the Dean some few years before *our* time – and *of our time*, Wallace and Jenkinson and Boringdon, and I.

---

[259] Charles Moss (1763–1811). Bishop of Oxford 1807–11

The dinner was very pleasant, except that Jenkinson and I had a sort of weight upon our minds which I looked for an opportunity of shaking off. An opportunity did not occur till we were going away – when I told him that I would go in his carriage. As soon as we were alone I began to repeat in substance what I had already written to him in the morning, for there was nothing else that could be said upon the occasion, beside expressing my sorrow that he should for a moment have so far misconceived my intentions, and imagined that I could possibly mean to give him pain, and my hope that he had by this time reconsidered the matter, and was prepared to atone for the injustice that he had then done me, by acknowledging that he did not continue to believe me guilty of unkindness. To this he began to answer with less acknowledgement than I thought myself entitled to – for whatever might have been his *first* feelings – I had determined with myself that, after so ample a reparation as I conceived my letter, and my eagerness to exculpate myself to be, he ought not to have hesitated a moment – and so (perhaps somewhat too briskly) I interrupted him with saying, 'If this be not enough, I know not what more can be said and so perhaps the affair had best end here', and stopping the carriage, I got out and left him.

I went to supper at the Markhams – the Dean supped there too. I did *not* tell him how my interview with Jenkinson had ended – I took leave of him for he goes back to Christ Church tomorrow.

*30. [May]* Friday. Frere breakfasted with me. I went down to the trial [of Hastings], where Burke was speaking – and from thence to the House of Commons – where came on Fox's motion for peace. Jenkinson spoke in answer to Fox – and spoke very well – after him Sheridan – and then Pitt. The debate lasted till $\frac{1}{2}$ pt. 12. The division was 208 to 55. The Opposition had summoned all their forces. After the debate was over I supped upstairs with C. Ellis – and then came home to bed.

*31. [May]* Saturday – I was at home – and C. Ellis with me [the] greater part of the morning. Then I went to Mr. Hickel,[260] a German painter, to sit for my picture. This is odd enough, say you – sitting again – and not for us. It *is* odd – but this is the meaning of it. I had made, as I told you, about a fortnight ago two resolutions. 1st – that I would not sit this year for a little picture. 2$^{d.}$ – that I would not sit this year for a large one. The first resolution I was *bullied* and made to break through in the manner that I have already described. The second could not hold out against this Mr. Hickel the German. He came to me one day with recommendations from F. North, Burke,

---

[260] Karl Anton Hickel (1745–98)

Windham, the Master of the Rolls, and God knows how many more members of Parliament that he named, and proceeded to inform me that his design was to paint a picture of the House of Commons,[261] from which in due time was to be taken a print, of the size of that of the Death of Lord Chatham – which would be a most pleasing and interesting thing for the present age and for posterity – and that he was anxious to rank me among those distinguished members of the House, who had condescended &c. to give him the length, breadth and expression of their phyzzes. There was no resisting the attainment of immortality at so easy a rate, especially when he added that he took his likeness in half-an-hour – and asked nothing for taking it. I went accordingly – sat my half hour in the morning, and half an hour more for the finishing, as I returned from my morning walk to the Temple – and the business is done. He has taken 40 or 50 already of all parties and complexions – Fox, Sheridan, Burke, Windham, Ryder, Mornington &c. &c. and is to have Pitt and a thousand others, as soon as the rising of Parliament gives them leisure to sit. The *painting* of course is a *daub* – but the likeness is most formidable and astonishing. It certainly will be an interesting print – and I would advise you by all means to subscribe for it. Next winter will be time enough.

I dined at Charles Ellis's – a quartetto – that is – Charles, George, Ly. Malmesbury and I – and we had Jenkinson's business upon the tapis.

You will have seen enough of Charles Ellis in this and former journals to like him very much. I will tell you something that passed this morning which will make you love him. It had happened a few days ago, that I had been talking of this Mr. Hickel and his picture – and saying that he had taken care to get some of all parties – that he had ministerialists – Oppositionists – and a few *Alarmists* – but not enough – and so, Charles, said I, you must go and sit for an Alarmist. (The Alarmists, it is hardly necessary to tell you, is a name given to Windham and those who follow him, and who, though they give their whole support to Ministry at this time, yet are not considered, and do not give themselves, as *ministerial* men, but as a distinct party acting, for this juncture, in co-operation with Mr. Pitt)[262]. He took no notice of what I said at that time – further than saying 'I'll be damned if I do', or some such slight expression of refusal. But this morning, when he was with me, happening to mention Mr. Hickel again – 'Pray', said Charles, 'what did you mean the other day by desiring

---

[261] The famous picture is called 'The House of Commons in 1793'

[262] It was approximately at this time that Windham and the Duke of Portland agreed that their two sets of supporters should coalesce with Pitt's government. See *Thorne*, v, 615

me to sit for an Alarmist?' – 'Nay – nothing very particular – but that I do not know that I could call you a ministerial man fairly, and I thank God you are not in opposition – and so you see there is nothing else left for you.' 'Yes, but you did me great injustice. I am not indeed a *ministerial* man in the *sense* in which *you* or *Jenkinson* are said to be so – that is, I do not *now*, nor do I mean *ever* to take an *active part* in the politicks of any party. But I give my whole support to Ministry, and that, not only from conviction at the present juncture of affairs – but from party *attachment* also – attachment *not* indeed to *Ministers*, but to *people whom I love*, and *whose interests are connected with Ministry*. I would not indeed be introduced to Pitt, as Jenkinson thought of persuading me at one time – because I want nothing, would never take anything, and do not see any particular reason for pledging myself, and in some measure giving up my independence. And in this I remember you thought me right'. 'Perfectly – and Jenkinson thinks so too at present'. 'Well, but though I do not know Pitt, I know others to whom I am attached – and in short – I should think it strange indeed, and I should be sorry if *you* thought it *possible* – that – *little* interested as *I* am *myself* in politicks, and *greatly* as *you* as well as *Jenkinson* and others – are interested – I could ever fail to support *that* party, with which *you* are connected. Though I do not like politicks particularly, I like Parliament – because it is an occupation – because it gives one a sort of situation and countenance – but for nothing so much as because it may enable me to be of service and support to those that I love. For these reasons I think it likely that I shall always wish, and I suppose I shall always be able, to procure a seat in Parliament – and I think I can venture to say, that, so long as I have one, there are few circumstances under which it could *possibly happen* that *you* should vote with *one* party, and *I* with *another*'. Is not this noble?

To return to our dinner. The conversation went upon the subject of Jenkinson. I told them what had passed between us – and they were inclined to be angry with him – but I explained to them fairly what I felt, and intend. Perhaps I had been a little too hasty in quitting him when he might be upon the eve of coming to a reconciliation. At all events – though I do think he ought to have come about at *once*, and though I am a little angry with him for continuing in a mistake after my letter and explanation – yet I think also that he may do it from a thousand motives and feelings, with which I have no right to be *permanently* offended. I shall wait some time to give him opportunity of getting into proper temper of mind. His Secret Committee occupies him now night and day, so that his mind perhaps may not be quite so much at leisure as it ought to be – and as the same cause keeps us very much out of each other's way, there is none of that awkwardness which might arise from our meeting frequently in society. Under these circumstances there can be no harm in letting him take his swing for a little time longer. But I love him too well, and too well know his regard for me, to feel at all scrupulous about forms and ceremonies with him – and so after having held out some time to plague him a little (which I have a right to do) for his present sturdiness – I certainly shall not leave town without having settled everything as it ought to be.

After dinner they went to the Opera – and I to spend the evening and sup with the Markhams.

There is another history of Charles Ellis which I do not know whether I have yet told you or not. I think I must, and yet I am not sure that I knew it myself when last I wrote to you. If I did not – it is one that you ought to hear. If I did, you will not mind hearing so good a thing twice. It is shortly this. He sent the other day to a Dr. King,[263] who had been his private tutor, a present of £5,000 – and lest from delicacy he (Dr. K.) should refuse it, he contrived to make that impossible by settling it upon his wife and children. What is better – he told nobody of this (unless perhaps Ly. M[almesbury] – and her with a strict charge not to mention it again). I heard it by mere accident – and *taxed* him with it. Is not *this*, too, noble? Adieu.

June 1st – Sunday – I was at home quietly all the morning – till it was time to set out with Wallace to dine at Mrs. Crewe's at Hampstead. There we met Bobus Smith (for Mrs. Crewe is lately acquainted with *him*) – and a person with whom I had never before been in company, though from his character and reputation I was very anxious to see him – Mr. Erskine.[264] I had been taught to expect in him a very great *bore*, one, who talked on no subject but himself, and on that all day long. He does talk of himself, to be sure, and I can easily conceive that to meet him often might be tiresome – but for once I liked him much more than I had been prepared to do – and thought him entertaining, and exceedingly good-humoured. There were his wife and daughter too – but they are *stickish*.

In the ev<sup>g.</sup> we returned to town. I went to Whitehall – and found a number of people there – and from Whitehall to Privy Garden – where I supped with Lady Malmesbury and Elliott.

*2<sup>d.</sup> [June]* Monday morning Frere breakfasted with me. Little C. Reddish called – but I had received no farther information from Paul Patrick resp<sup>g.</sup> Mr. Popplewell and Styan – and therefore could give

[263] Rev. Dr. Thomas King (d.1801). Prebendary of Canterbury; chancellor of Lincoln and rector of Bladon in Woodstock. A bro. of John King q.v.
[264] Hon. Thomas Erskine q.v., see above p. 62, n.143

him none. I was at home all the morning. I dined at Lord Stafford's. There were Boringdon, and my friend Mrs. Howe – whose puzzle I sent you in my last packet. I wonder if you have made it out – if not, here it is.

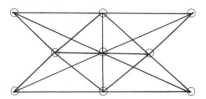

I found it out my own self, to the great admiration of the family, and shewed it this day to Mrs. H. in triumph. By the way Mrs. Howe always goes with us by the name of The Archbishop – owing to a likeness which I discovered the first day that I saw her, between her and his Grace of Canterbury and which they all acknowledge to be most striking. There was also Mrs. Lloyd – whose breakfasts at Kensington you see mentioned in the papers. She did me the honour of a card for her last, through the Levesons – and I quite forgot to go. In the ev.ᵍ I called at Mrs. Legge's (of Grosvenor Square) who is in the habit of being at home and seeing all who will come to her. I stayed a little while there – for as I never play cards – and do not talk much to people whom I do not particularly care about, I find very little in an assembly to detain me long.

I then called at F. North's, who is confined with the gout – and found him at supper with half a dozen of his friends the Turks about him.[265] I stayed there just long enough to hear the Interpreter sing a Greek song, and then, finding the *smell* of these his guests grow so powerful as to over-balance the charms of their heathen conversation, I made my retreat, and went to sup with Mrs. Crewe.

*3. [June]* Tuesday – Frere breakfasted with me. I went to the trial where Burke was speaking. There was no House. I dined with C. Ellis. There were Ly. Malm.ʸ, Sir R. and Ly. Payne, Sir H. Englefield, Geo. Ellis, and Jenky. From this said Jenky I had heard nothing, good,

---

[265] North was an enthusiastic philhellene and was received into the Orthodox church in Corfu in 1791. His ambition was to be ambassador at Constantinople, see *Thorne*, iv, 676

bad or indifferent – and so I was very angry in my own mind with him. But I hold it to be very *bad taste* to disturb society in general with an appearance of disagreement, with which nobody but the parties have anything to do. And so my behaviour to him, and his consequently to me was just such as if nothing unpleasant had taken place between us. So much so – that Ly. M^y. was persuaded that some explanation must have been had, and all our differences reconciled – and for this conduct she gave us both, and I give Jenkinson and myself too, great credit. I had no private conversation with him. After dinner we all went to the Opera. And after the Opera I supped, as did Ly. M^y. and Geo. Ellis at Charles's.

*4. [June]* Wednesday morning. The first thing that I heard to my great astonishment was the death of the Dss. of Portland. I had heard of her illness indeed on Sunday – but Mrs. Crewe had told me on Monday night, and she had appeared firmly to believe that the danger was over. Poor woman! She was a good and almost a *great character*. I say *almost* because I do not know whether a woman in private life can fairly have that epithet attached to her. I do not know indeed that it would become them if they could. It is rather from *male* virtues that such an attribute arises – and such virtues she had in as great a degree as perhaps she could have them without detracting from the *feminineness* of her character. Mrs. Crewe must be seriously afflicted, and most lastingly, by her loss, for she valued the Dss. of P., I think, beyond any person of her own sex in the world.

This was the King's birthday, and I spent it as idly and foolishly as a day can be spent in walking about and seeing people go to Court. Sturges was with me. As we passed along Piccadilly we had the entertainment of seeing a coach apparently quite full of people, suddenly and violently overturned. We ran among the crowd to give what assistance we could to the sufferers. I *fished* and brought out a very pretty girl – terrified almost to death, but luckily unhurt, and thinking only of her mother, who, she said, was at the bottom of the carriage. This was not strictly true, though she thought so – for the mother had bustled up with wonderful alertness and presented at this moment out of the coach window (as the coach lay flat on one side) the most formidable head-dress and bust, as to size and decoration, that had been seen for some time by the rabble, who were regaling themselves with the sight – at the same time that they were very good-naturedly busy in devising means to haul the exhibitress of it out of the window. This labour – and it was really no small one – as the good lady weighed at least as much as all the rest of the party in the coach (and there were 5 of them) put together – it fell to Sturges's lot to accomplish. And upon my return from lodging my fair charge in a shop at her request to look after her mama, I found Sturges (who is a very little man) sweating under the load of this most enormous good woman, who hobbled along, tho' unhurt, screaming and bellowing, and protesting among other things that she had *no legs*, though with Sturges's assistance she was displaying such a pair as were not ill-suited to support the body under which they dangled. Had I been disposed for an adventure, here was an opportunity – but I contented myself with ascertaining that there was no serious hurt in the case, and seeing the carriage reinstated in a position for proceeding – and then mingled again in the crowd, with Sturges, who felt no violent inclination to examine what other deficiency of limb his fair and fat burden might most unjustly charge upon herself.

I dined with Newbolt and his wife in their new house in Bedford Street, Bedford Square. I was delighted to see them settled so comfortably. She is a charming woman, and calculated admirably by her good sense, and by the proper sort of influence which she appears to have acquired over him, to remedy the only defect which Newbolt has, and which alone prevents him from being an useful and respectable, as well as he is a most amiable and sufficiently clever, man – a certain unsteadiness and imprudence. If she cures this, as I have little doubt she will – and if I see them as happy this time twelvemonth as they appear to be now, I shall almost give up my opinion, hitherto steadily maintained, that a marriage cannot be but miserable without something more than a *competence* of fortune.

There was nobody at dinner but his father and his sister, who are come to town upon a visit to him. In the evening I went to the Play – then walked about looking at illuminations – called at Whitehall where I found nobody at home but Lord Stafford himself – and supped in Privy Garden, where were Geo. and Charles Ellis.

5 [*June*] Thursday. Frere breakfasted with me. I sat to Edridge for half an hour – went to Hastings' trial – and to the House – where there was nothing. I went into the City to P. Patrick's, meaning to surprise him at dinner – but was surprized myself by finding that he was out, and that Hal [Henry Canning] had just dined. I returned – and dined by myself at the Carey Street Coffee House – went to the Play – then to the Abp. of York's – where I found them all dancing – and not being inclined to mingle in that amusement I came away as soon as I could slip out of the room – called at Mrs. Crewe's, who, I found, was too unwell to see anybody – and so returned back again to Carey Street, supped sulkily and went early to bed. I found on my table a letter from my mother, informing me of her arrival in town – for what? I wonder.

6. [*June*] Friday morning – as soon as I had breakfasted I set off to see my mother – who has taken up her abode at my grandmother and aunt's lodgings at a place called Somers Town, just beyond Gray's

Inn Lane, in the way to Hampstead, I mean. She is come up on a thousand little matters – and seemed so happy to see me, and looked in so much better health and spirits than I had expected to see her – that I could not find in my heart to represent to her as I had intended, the folly of jigging about up and down from place to place – when God knows how she contrives to the able to live at any place.

I[266] dined at the Crown and Anchor Law Club – where I have not been, this long time – not since the very beginning of the winter. Perhaps I should not have gone to-day had I not happened to hear that they have just passed a law, inflicting upon ever member, who is in town, and who fails attending for a whole week, a fine of 5 shillings. So I went and dined at my own expence out of pure economy to save the fine.

I went from dinner with Sturges, to the Play – and from the Play to the Opera – for to-morrow being Whitsun Eve the Opera was to-night instead. After the Opera I supped in Privy Garden with the Ellises and Lord Cole.[267] Do you know Lord Cole, Fan? – a young Irishman – a very good sort of young man – but very Irish.

7. [June] Saturday – I was at home greatest part of the morning till it was time to go to the House of Commons. There the Second Report of the Secret Committee had been brought up yesterday – and the Appendix was received to-day. The Second Report of the Lords was brought up to-day.

I dined at Sir R. Payne's. There were Mr. and Ly. Caroline Price – a Mr. Graham (a Scotchman whom I met early in the year at Mr. Dundas's – then just returned from Toulon – where he had done great service as a Volunteer) – and Wallace. In the ev^g. I went to the Abp. of York's – supped with them – and took leave of them – for they go out of town on Monday. They made me promise that if I possibly could I would visit them at Bishop Thorpe [sic] in the course of the summer. In my way home I called on Mrs. Crewe – and was admitted to see her. She has been much afflicted indeed – but she is getting better.

8. [June] Sunday morning – I set out for Wanstead – found them all well; saw Sheridan (who was setting off to town) and had a good deal of conversation with him (we are upon the best terms imaginable) – dined – walked out – supped – and returned to town about 12 o'clock at night.

9th [June] Monday morning – Frere breakfasted with me and Bobus

---

[266] 'I dined ... the fine', printed in *NER*, 530

[267] John Willoughby Cole, styled Viscount Cole 1768–1803, when he succ. as 2nd Earl of Enniskillen

called – and they both went with me to see my pictures at Mr. Hickel's and Mr. Edridge's. I[268] dined at White's for the first time since I have been a member of that Club (by the way I am not sure that I ever told you of my being a member. I was elected during my illness – and had formal notification of my election while I was at Wanstead – Hetty glowed crimson on hearing it). There was nobody but Boringdon and Wallace. We talked about making a dinner there once a week next winter – of young men – I think it may do very well – but it is a plan that requires some consideration. I went to the Play – and in my [way] home from thence supped soberly at out *Law White's* in Carey Street.

   *10 [June]* Tuesday morning I called on my mother. I sat to Edridge for the finishing of my picture – and the rest of the morning I passed in walking about the streets – partly from laziness and partly to fix on a pleasant place for dining. In my walk I met Elliot, who told me he was to dine in Privy Garden – so I called and left word that I would dine there. There were the Ellises and Elliot. In the evening we went to the Opera. We had not been there above half an hour when we perceived a degree of bustle and hurry in the lower boxes – presently the Opera stopped – people stood up, some knowing, but the greater part wondering, for what reason – and Boringdon came prancing into the box where I was with the news of Lord Howe's victory.[269] I never saw a finer or more affecting spectacle than the almost electric and universal sensation that seemed to pervade every part of the House – the transport and triumph which burst forth as soon as their astonishment had a little subsided. The effect to an impartial observer was not a little heightened by the contrast between the feeling *generally* apparent, and that which was discoverable in one or two boxes – the *Bouverie*[270] box (to which I sat nearly opposite) in particular. Not a breath appeared to be stirring there – no tumult, no anxiety – and when the Opera was permitted to proceed, the attention which they paid to the stage (rather than look about them to see rejoicing faces) was highly entertaining. Lady Chatham, who brought the news from the Admiralty to the Opera, dispatched gentlemen with it to both the Playhouses – and the reception of it there was equally satisfactory.

   I supped at C. Ellis's – with Ly. M[almesbur]y, Ed[d.] Legge and

---

[268] 'I dined … consideration, (p. 121), printed in *NER*, 530–31

[269] The naval victory known as 'the glorious first of June' which took place near Ushant, an island off the coast of Finisterre

[270] The Hon. Edward Bouverie (1738–1810), s. of 1st Vsct. Folkestone and M.P. Northampton 1790–1810, and the Bouverie brothers, Hon. Edward and Hon. William Henry, sons of the 1st Earl of Radnor, the last being M.P. for Salisbury 1776–1802, were all Foxite whigs and hostile to the war

Geo. Ellis. There was a great supper at White's on the occasion, to which I intended going, but when the time came I did not find myself in the humour.

*11 [June]* Wednesday. The first thing I did was to set out with Bobus to call on Easley Smith's (the other Microcosm Smith) mother, and his uncle Judge Grose,[271] to enquire whether or no they had any tidings of him. He is in the army, as you have heard me say, having, after three years study of the law, suddenly taken a military turn last year, and his Regiment was on board Sir Alexander Hood's ship in the late action. No news of him was come, but I trust he is safe.

I went to the trial – and afterwards to the House. The Report of the Committee was printed and delivered. The debate on it to come on next Monday. I dined at Mr. Legge's (Grosvenor Square). There were the Ellises – Wallace – Newbolt and his father. In the evening I called at Whitehall – but found nobody at home except Lord Stafford. I supped at Privy Garden. – The Ellises.

*12. [June]* Thursday – Frere breakfasted with me. I was at home greater part of the morning – then went to Hastings's trial – and to the House – nothing. I dined at Charles Ellis's – with Geo. Ellis – Mr. Legge – and Ed. Legge. Staid there all the evening (except walking out to see the illuminations) – and supped – and to supper came Lord Cole, Lindsay[272] and Lady Malmesbury.

*13. [June]* Friday morning I called on Mr. Pitt wishing to know from him about the rising of Parliament – that I might be the better able to determine upon the time of my going to Oxford – whither I must go to take my Degree. He was in the country – so I came home as wise as I went.

In the House of Com$^s$ there was nothing. In the House of Lords there was a debate on the $2^d$ Report of their Secret Committee – which I attended till it was time to go to dinner at C. Ellis's – where I met Geo. Ellis and Newbolt. In the ev$^g$ I went down again to the H. of Lds. – but found the debate over – so I contented myself with going to the Play instead – and supped at Carey St. in my way home.

*14. [June]* Saturday morning, while I was at breakfast Sir Nash Grose called, and brought with him a letter which he had received from Easly Smith, giving an account of the action, and what was of more consequence to us, of his own safety. As soon as S$^r$ N. was gone I set out to call on – Jenkinson. You will remember that my

[271] John Smith (1767–1827). A contemporary of C. at Eton and a joint-author of the *Microcosm*. He was known as 'Easley' because this is the way he pronounced 'aisle' on first encountering the word, see *Thorne*, v, 194. His mother was Mary, sis, of Sir Nash Grose (1740–1814), judge of King's Bench 1787–1813

[272] William Lindsay q.v.

determination with respect to him had been that I would let the thing take its own course for a certain time – but that, right or wrong, I would not leave town without having seen him and made all well.

Now as I had resolved upon leaving town for Oxford on Tuesday morning next – conceiving that Monday's debate would be the last thing to require my attendance – and as he always goes out of town to Addiscombe on Saturdays and Sundays, I found that unless I saw him this morning I should have no other opportunity before I went, and that as he could not *know* this, I thought myself bound to communicate it to him. I wrote him a little note therefore last night, from Charles Ellis's, saying that as I wished we should understand each other before we separated for so long a time as would probably intervene between my leaving London (as I intended) for the summer and our meeting next winter – I would call upon him any time that he might have 10 minutes leisure before the House of Coms.' time on Monday. In his answer he appointed this morning – and accordingly I set out for his house. I found him waiting for me. Our conversation began upon indifferent subjects and lasted in that strain for some time – politicks, news, changes &c. – in short anything but the business upon which we had met. At length, taking up my hat as if to go away – 'Jenkinson' said I, 'I could not resolve to leave town without explaining myself shortly, but fully, upon circumstances as they now stand between us – and I say therefore all that I have to say in these few words, I think no more of it.' I wish you had seen his face upon hearing these words. After gazing some little while in astonishment, he had well nigh burst out into a violent laugh, and I perhaps, but that I had predetermined to be very grave, might possibly have accompanied him. 'Well, after all this is the oddest and most unreasonable thing,' says he, 'that I am to be made out to be in the wrong, and to have need of forgiveness.' – 'Nay but so it is upon my word (and I gave my serious opinion in saying so) – the offence, what-ever it might be, that the verses gave, was, or ought to have been completely done away by my expression of sorrow for having offended. Having made that apology, no more remained for me to do, and it was your business either to have accepted it as a full and complete satisfaction – or at least to have stated *new* reasons (if you had any) for your still continuing to be dissatisfied. Now this you have not done, either the one or the other. And so, had I not felt how foolish it would be to suffer any little nonsensical pique or waywardness to get the better of an old friendship like ours – and had I not known that this must necessarily be your feeling as well as my own, and been very little anxious, therefore, whether you or myself were the *first* to express it, I might very justifiably have preserved a perfect silence and left you to form your own conclusions and make up your mind without interruption. But this would have been very absurd – as indeed the whole business has been – so, pray let us think no more of it.'

We shook hands – and all was over – and being so, we talked the business over again from the beginning as laughingly as if it had been the affair of two other persons and not ourselves. And then we had so much to say after a fortnight's embargo, or more, on our communication, that we presently talked the morning away, and found it time to go down and see if anything was doing in the House of Coms. Burke was still speaking in Westminster Hall – and in the House nothing was expected. I went home and dined with Wallace tête-à-tête. Having made up a quarrel of my own in the morning I was employed this evening in devising the means of making up another between two other people. Did I ever tell you before that Wallace and Charles Ellis had quarrelled? They travelled together – and at setting out were dear friends – though I never thought their tempers exactly such as were likely to suit each other long. Abroad – a thousand things happened not necessary, and indeed which I am not at liberty, to detail – and at their return to England, I heard from each of them that they had broken entirely and for ever. Wallace returned indeed six months before Charles Ellis – and told me what had happened – and *that* so fairly that from his account alone I ventured to form an opinion that *he* was wrong – which opinion I declared to him, adding at the same time that 'even if he had not given me so clear an account, I should have *presumed* Charles Ellis to be right, for so convinced was I of C. Ellis's goodness of temper, that if ever *he* (C. Ellis) and *I* differed, I would give Wallace leave to form the same conclusion against *me* that I did against *him* in this instance'. About six months after, that is about the beginning of last year C. Ellis returned – and from him I heard the *fact* of their having disagreed, but with much less detail of circumstances. He was satisfied with knowing himself to be in the right without wishing to prejudice me against Wallace by shewing how far *he* had been wrong. The question which I put to him at once was simply this – 'Tell me fairly and openly, is it a quarrel of such a nature, in your mind, as that explanation and apology may set it right again, and seeing you together, as you were before? Or has it arisen from so many little, trivial, undescribable provocations that a renewal of your former friendship and habit of intercourse is out of the question? If it be the former, command my services in any way to mediate between you. If, as I rather think from all that I have heard, it be the latter – then my advice is to both of you, that you should endeavour to put as good a face upon it to the world as possible – and as you will probably meet not very often, contrive when you do meet to behave (to the eyes of other people) as if nothing particular had happened'. He answered that he certainly did feel that the difference had arisen from causes not likely to be removed, and that it was impossible that Wallace and he should ever be together as they had been, and that he thought, for their own comfort, for that of their common friends, and for the sake of not making themselves fools in the eyes of society, it would be advisable to act exactly as if nothing had happened when they did accidentally meet in public – and that if W. was ready to do so, he was willing to do his part.

I communicated to Wallace what had passed. He saw the propriety of the conduct proposed, and agreed to adopt it – and so the most *amicable hostility* was arranged between them – and was carried on with the utmost propriety. There were not a great many places where they met – but one or two there were, where they met often (Sir R. Payne's and Mr. Legge's for instance). When they did meet they exchanged their How d'ye do's – and no person who was not aware of the circumstances would have concluded that they were enemies, any more than that they had been dear friends. This lasted all last year and all this, during which their accidental meetings became rather more frequent – and in all this time it is to the credit of both of them that I never heard either speak ill of the other – Ellis of W. *never* – W. of Ellis but *once*, and *that* triflingly – and for that I reproached him bitterly, and he acknowledged himself wrong, and never repeated the offence. Perfectly satisfied with this line of conduct, I did not attempt any formal plan of reconciliation, but talking the matter over with Jenkinson, agreed that it was better to let the thing work its own way, and that, with common friends, common pursuits, and the respect which they had remaining for each other, it was likely that they would some day or other come to a nearer communication. In the meantime it was our business not to relax our attention, or liking to either, in favour of either – but to take care that we did not put them in any awkward situation with respect to one another. This plan, as we foresaw, has answered. For some time past I had observed with pleasure that Wallace had done even more than bare civility required towards Ellis – that he not only had not seemed to think Ellis's being with me, or with Jenkinson, an objection to joining either of us – but that often, at Hastings's trial, when Ellis was sitting on one side of me, he had come and posted himself on the other – and particularly that the other day at Sir Ralph Payne's when we three and a large party of other people dined there – and Charles Ellis had sat next me at dinner, and Wallace on the opposite side of the table – as soon as the ladies were withdrawn Wallace had come round from his place to take a chair – which was left vacant by me – and he and I and C. Ellis had a long talk together.

These sound *little* things – but they mark a great deal – and in a man of Wallace's temper, which though very good and very amiable,

is rather *stern* and decided, I thought they marked a very visible
change and improvement. I was not mistaken. This day, after dinner,
the conversation turning on my difference and reconcilement with
Jenkinson – and that introducing the subject of C. Ellis – Wallace
said that he had for some time wished for an opportunity of saying to
me how much he felt his mind softened with regard to *him* – that he
had found, though but lately, from some circumstances which had
come to his knowledge, that he had formerly been much misled upon
the subject of their differences, that he had been misled into thinking
Ellis culpable when he certainly was *not* so – and that upon the whole
he was now convinced that he had been *himself* throughout and
entirely in the wrong.' I asked him whether or no he had any objection
to my stating this as what I had heard from him to Ellis. He said,
none in the world – that it would rather be an ease to his conscience
to think that he had made the only reparation in his power by such
an acknowledgement – that he did not indeed expect that they could
ever again be upon quite the same footing that they had been – but
that I must have observed that for some time past (that is to say ever
since he had come to know that he had been so much in the wrong)
he had rather made up to Ellis more than formerly. This you see was
manly, handsome and candid as could be – and I very cheerfully
undertook the commission to Ellis.

In the evening we went to the Opera. From the Opera I went home
to sup with Ly. Malmesbury – where were Geo. and Ch. Ellis – but
I had no opportunity of talking to Ch. alone. Lady M. leaves town
to-morrow for the summer.

*15. [June]* Sunday. C. Ellis and I had determined to spend at Bushy
with Fred. North – but several things I know not what conspired to
put it off – and so I sent to Lady Stafford, whose invitation I had
before refused, to say I would dine at Whitehall. I did so. There were
Mrs. Howe – and in fine spirits the Archbishop was as you may
suppose after her brother's victory. Sir Wm. Gordon[273] – an old
Knight of the Bath, of whom I know nothing but that he eats more
than any other two persons – and Lord Fincastle[274] – a son of Lord I
forget who – but some way or other a nephew of Ly. Stafford's. I
stayed at Whitehall all the evg. and supped in my way home at the
Club in Carey Street.

*16. [June]* Monday – Frere breakfasted with me. I went to Hasting's
trial – where Burke concluded his reply, having spoken nine days. At

[273] Sir William Gordon cr. KB. 3 Feb. 1775 for diplomatic services. M.P. Portsmouth
1777–83
[274] George Murray, styled Vsct. Fincastle 1762–1809 when he succ. as 5th Earl of
Dunmore

the trial I found C. Ellis – and taking him aside – I told him all that had passed between Wallace and me on Saturday. He received it as I had expected. 'Nothing', he said, could give him greater pleasure than to find that W. acquitted him of having acted wrongly towards him – and that nothing could be more candid and manly then the frankness with which Wallace had made the acknowledgement – that for it he felt much obliged to W. – and whatever disposition he (W.) might shew towards a more near communication, he would certainly meet him half way. I asked him whether he did not think that, as things stood, any formal explanation or enquiry into circumstances would do more harm than good – inasmuch as it could only produce a recollection of unpleasant events and feelings – and everything seemed to bid fair for a perfect good understanding without it. He agreed with me – and it was settled that when next they met, it should be with more cordiality than hitherto, but without any investigation of the causes which produced the change. I had no opportunity immediately of reporting my success to Wallace.

There was a debate on the 2$^d$ Report of the Secret Committee – in which I felt no inclination and saw no opportunity to take part. There was no division. The House was up at 11 – and I was going away to sup with C. Ellis – as was Jenkinson – when Wallace, joining me accidentally and asking me to sup with him – 'Yes', said I, 'if you will sup where I do' – and brought him vis-à-vis to C. Ellis. I then got into W.'s carriage – explained to him as we went along what had passed between Ellis and me that morning. We arrived at Ellis's house, and we four had one of the pleasantest suppers that I have enjoyed since I came to town.

*17. [June]* Tuesday morning I employed in City visits previous to my going out of town. I called on P. Patrick – Maxwell – Borrowes – and had with the last a conversation which gives me a very different opinion, and one much more favourable to him, concerning his separation from Higginson, than I had before entertained.

At the House of Commons Pitt was to have made his motion for thanks to the Managers of the Impeachment [of Hastings] – but the House was so thin – and of the members present so large a proportion were Indians,[275] that he saw it would fail if made, and so put it off to Thursday.

I dined at Charles Ellis's with Geo. Ellis – Jenkinson – and King. In the evening I went to the Opera – and from the Opera to sup with Jenkinson tête-à-tête.

*18. [June]* Wednesday morning Frere breakfasted with me. I called

---

[275] M.P.s with interests in, or special connections with, British India of whom there were about 60 in any Parliament at this time, see *Thorne*, i, 325

on Mr. Pitt – enquired of him respecting the Prorogation, which he told me was not yet settled – and informed him of my being about to go out of town to Oxford – but that if anything material should occur in the House of Commons I should be obliged to him if he would have the goodness to let me know – and I would come up to town immediately – that I should not go till after Thursday's debate.

Very very bad news to-day from Flanders. Ypres must fall – and the whole of West Flanders must follow it unless some better fortune attends our arms and those of our allies, than we have lately experienced. The only good news that I can hear is from Edwd. Legge whom I met this morning – and that is – that the Bishop of Winchester has given him the living of Witney, worth £800 or £1,000 a year – to hold for his (the B.'s son) – who will be of age to hold it himself indeed in 3 or 4 years – but by that time Ed. Legge may get more certain provision, and in the meantime it is a handsome sum of money in his pocket.

This day the two Houses of Parliament went up with the Address to the King upon the Reports of the Committees promising to stand by him &c. I did not attend. I went with Wallace to dine at Mrs. Crewe's at Hampstead. There were only ourselves – and we had a very snug dinner and a rural walk afterwards. When we returned to town I went to call at Whitehall – and found nobody at home. They were all at the Play – whither I went too and found them. I was too lazy to go with them after the Play to the Dss. of Gordon's – so I came home, supping in my way at Carey Street.

*19 [June]* Thursday morning I called on my mother and took leave of her, my aunt and grandmother, upon my going out of town. I dressed and went down to the House expecting the debate, which had been fixed for to-day – but in my way down I met everybody coming away – there not having been 40 members present at 4 o'clock, to make a House – which operates of course as an adjournment. What should I do? – left on the pavè (sic) at 1/2 pt. 4 o'clock, without an engagement, and dressed too?

I was very angry – and swearing internally at the folly of people for not attending, and at the punctuality of the Speaker – when I met Geo. Ellis – and enquiring of him whether or no Charles dined at home, and finding that he did *not*, but that he and George were going to dine at Mr. Mundy's (your neighbour at Shipley) I resolved to dine there too – and went to Mundy's house to give warning. I met Mundy by the way, which cut the matter still shorter. We dined there with a *largish* party. He has a daughter who sits at the head of his table, and is very pretty. In the evening I went to Whitehall – where I found them all at home, and Lady Sutherland with them – and I staid there till about 12 o'clock when it was time to go and sup with Charles Ellis.

*20. [June]* Friday. Frere breakfasted with me. I was at home till it was time to go to the House of Commons. Then came on the debate on the Thanks to the Managers,[276] which were carried by 55 to 21. Afterwards came the Thanks to Lord Hood for the capture of Bastia, which were much debated[277] – but carried at last without a division. I was to have dined to-day, as were 10 or 12 other people, with Mr. Smyth of the Treasury[278] (he was of the Admiralty when last I had occasion to mention him to you – but he has lately been removed). The debate prevented it. I got something to eat in the course of the debate upstairs – and when it was over at 11 o'clock I went home with C. Ellis to supper. Charles goes out of town to-morrow.

*21. [June]* Saturday. Frere breakfasted with me. Bobus called and told me he had got a prize at Cambridge for a Latin Essay. I called on Jenkinson and sundry other people – and had a mind to set out to-day for Oxford, but that I found a hundred things to do – which kept me.

One thing which might have kept me but did not was a note from Ly. Sutherland asking me to Wimbledon to-morrow. I forgot to say that I had sent her yesterday a *Dryden's Fables* (finely bound) with a letter apologizing for having been so late in atoning for that unlucky recommendation at Wimbledon – and assuring her that *this* book and not those which Mr. Edwards had substituted in its place, was what I designed to recommend to her perusal – though even for *this* I would not venture to assert that it was just the book that she would put into Ly. Charlotte's ( her little daughter's) hands immediately after her *Gay's* Fables[279] – but that it was at least a book of such character as that she might get safely through it with a very little *skipping* – and by no means such as Lord Gower would be justified in locking up from human inspection among the naughty books in the little room. Her note of invitation this morning was in acknowlegement of the book and my letter – and if I had not been very firmly settled in my determination about going to Oxford, I should have felt very strongly tempted to set off for Wimbledon without delay. I did not. Finding myself kept in town to-day I dined with Mr. Smyth of the Treasury, who had put off his party of yesterday to this day – but his party

[276] The managers of the impeachment of Warren Hastings
[277] The Vote of Thanks to Lord Hood was 'much debated' because Bastia but not Corsica had been captured. The Opposition alleged that ministers were attempting to obscure a failed expedition, see *Parl. Hist.*, xxxi, cols. 954–7
[278] John Smyth q.v.
[279] John Gay (1685–1732). The first series of his '*Fables*' was pub. in 1727; the second in 1738

was so diminished by people hurrying out of town to Portsmouth,[280] whither every man who can hire post-horses, or procure a lodging within five miles of the place is gone – that there were only three persons besides myself – Mr. Burke and his son[281] – and Mr. Metcalfe[282] (a friend of Burke's and M.P., &c.) – but a company in which Burke is one, cannot be otherwise than amusing. After dinner I came straight home, having still much to do before my setting-out.

*22 [June]* Sunday morning – as soon as I had breakfasted I set out on my journey to Oxford – where I arrived without accident at about six o'clock – eat a bit of dinner at the Star Inn – and then sallied out to look about me.

I do not think that it is worth while to give you a detailed account day by day of my life at Oxford. One day passes for the most part like another – and not unpleasantly in a quiet lounging way – and (*this* time) in perfect idleness – interrupted only by the task of going through certain forms and ceremonies in preparing for, and taking my Degree – and by reading – not Sciences, Classics, poets or philosophers – but the new novel of the Mysteries of Udolpho[283] – this and the newspapers form the whole of my studies there. The persons whom I know, and with whom I live alternately at Oxford, are of two sorts. The first consists of the Masters and Tutors – amongst whom are some very pleasant people – as for instance Pett[284], who was my Tutor when I was at Ch. Ch. a younker – and [Rev. Charles Thomas] Barker, of whom you have heard me speak more than once – who was at Bath – and Leigh saw him there – who perhaps will call at Ashborne this summer, as he is going into the north, and who is the author of the Verses upon a hot day. Their way of life is – that they dine every day in the Hall, at a table of their own – and after dinner retire all together to a large room called the Common Room – to drink their wine – and in this room they also sup at 10 o'clock. Of this room, being now myself an A.M., I am a rightful member – but before I was so I could frequent it almost as much as if I were, going there whenever I pleased, as the guest of Pett or Barker, or any other person among them. The

---

[280] Where the King was to reward the Admirals of Lord Howe's fleet with gold chains and launch a 98-gun ship. He ordered for Sunday 29 June in the Chapel of Portsmouth Dock 'that a proper Sermon may be preached on the late victory, wherein may with great propriety be made some remark on a nation attached to religion, good government and obedience to law, in opposition to those hurried on by anarchy, irreligion and every horrid excess.', see A. Aspinall, *The Later Correspondence of George III* (Cambridge, 5 vols., 1962–70), ii, 1089

[281] Richard Burke (1758–94)

[282] Philip Metcalfe q.v.

[283] Mrs. Radcliffe's novel had just been published

[284] Phineas Pett (c. 1758–1830). Rector of Wentnor, Salop, 1794 and Chilbottom, Hants 1795–1830. Archdeacon of Oxford 1797–d.

other sort are the young ones – none of whom as you may suppose I recollect from having known them personally when I was myself at Ch. Ch. – but I have been so much there at times, since I ceased to be a constant resident, that I am not a stranger among them, and have acquaintance enough to make my day pass very pleasantly.

And then I like *young* people, as you have often heard me say. There is an ingenuousness, a glow, a heart, as it were, in a young man, that a few years – aye, a very few years' rubbing and tumbling about in the world, does away – insomuch that *I* who *think* myself virtuous enough as things go, feel very often that I am a SCOUNDREL compared with a boy of 18 or 19. One gets hard and wise and odious – undeceived – or rather (which is the only good word to express what I mean, and a word for which we have no adequate translation) *desabusè* (sic), as to a thousand sentiments and feelings, which one was the *better* for entertaining. And so, as I said before, I very much like young people. Among the present generation at Ch. Ch. – those whom I principally know are [John] Dawkins – who was indeed there in my time but I did not then know him. I first became acquainted with him last year – and what brought us nearer to each other was his speaking my verses – and speaking them so well, with such *heart* – that I have quite loved him ever since. He has now almost done with Ch. Ch., and is going to be a candidate next year for a Fellowship of All Souls – in which I trust he will succeed – and he then comes to town to study the law, and I do not mean to lose sight of him. Next to him, I think, is [Hon. Richard Bruce] Stopford, a younger son of Ld. Courtown's, whom I remember at Eton, when I was at the head of the School, a little, scurvy, red-headed boy – and now he is a pleasant, gentlemanlike man. He is the great friend of Dawkins, and like him a great favourite of mine. Then comes Lord Andover, son of Ld. Suffolk – who also was at Eton – but I do not remember him – a very amiable and sensible sort of person, and I like him much. Then there is just come from Westminster, and younger than any of them, Ld. Stormont (Lord Mansfield's son) whom I knew now for the first time. I think he promises well both as to talents and disposition – and let me tell you it is of no small consequence that persons who five or six years hence are likely from their situation in life, their talents, or what other cause soever, to occupy a conspicuous place in the public eye, should be of good promise. This or any country, in such times as the present, depends upon *men*, perhaps, more than upon *events*, for its safety.

I took to this young Ld. S. the rather as his tutor is a contemporary of mine – almost the only one of my contemporaries that I knew, who is still resident at Christ Church. His name is Carey[285] – a great friend

---

[285] William Carey (c. 1770–1846). B.A. Oxf. 1793; M.A. 1796; B.D. 1804; bishop of Exeter 1820–30; of St. Asaph 1830–d.

of the Dean – with whom he has been in the habit of travelling about
England during the Vacations. This summer he travels about with
his pupil Ld. S. and I have made him promise that if he passes through
Ashborne in the course of their tour (which I believe they will) he
will bring himself and his charge to see Ashborne Hall. He (Carey) is
the person who would have accompanied the Dean last year, if he
had paid his promised visit at Ashborne.

The life of this younger part of the College is much as follows. They
get up to prayers at seven o'clock every morning (in summer) except
on Sundays and Saints' days, then at eight. From that time they are,
or supposed to be, at their studies, some reading a good deal many a
little, and most of them nothing, till three. At three they dine in
the Hall, and from dinner adjourn to each other's rooms to drink
wine till 6, 7, or as late as they please. In the evening those who
like it, read again – and at 10 o'clock they sup at each other's
rooms – and that supper is their pleasantest and principal meal of the
day.

Between these two sets of young and old, and the Dean, who is a
*species* of himself, and of whom I saw as much as I could (though,
owing to the employment which he cuts out for himself during the
last weeks of a Term, that was but little) – my life was usually on this
plan. I rose tolerably early, on Saint's Day or Sunday to prayers, on
other days time enough to get a walk in Christ Church Meadow
before breakfast. I breakfasted invariably at Dawkins's rooms – and
lounged there and elsewhere the whole of the morning except such
portion of it as I was obliged to spend in the Schools (the place where
exercises are performed for the taking of a Degree). I dined sometimes
in Hall, with the Masters, and went with them to the Common
Room – sometimes at other tables there, and went to drink wine
afterwards with the young ones – now and then at my lodgings, and
Dawkins and other young with me – and now and then at my lodgings
alone when I found it too hot to dress in time, or had an interesting
part of the 'Mysteries of Udolopho' to read. I must not forget that I
dined once with William Barnard[286] and his wife, upon whom I called
soon after my arrival in Oxford, and found them very comfortably
settled – and I should have repeated my dinner there, as I did more
than once my visit, had it not happened that they were thrown into
some confusion by the inoculation of their little child, who, however,
is now perfectly recovered. The evening commenced by a tea drinking
at my lodgings, which was attended by all the idle persons that were

[286] William Henry Barnard. Matric. Pembroke, Camb. 22 June 1790 aged 23; BCL,
1797. He was the s. of the Rev. Dr Henry Barnard by Mary Canning, da. of Stratford
and Letitia Canning. He was therefore C.'s cousin

straggling about the High Street (Christ Church itself was so full that I could not, as heretofore, borrow rooms there during my stay – and so I took lodgings in the most indolent and dissipated part of the town). After this came a walk – which lasted till supper-time – and during the last half hour of which, while it was dark – recourse was had to several appropriate and classical pastimes – such as the attaching a string to the knockers of two doors, neighbouring to each other, and rapping at one, which, opening, by means of the connection so formed, rapped at the other – *that* again, by the same means, returned the compliment – and *this* repeated it – till by dint of frequent summonses the two doors came to be opened at once, and an éclaircissement took place in which the openers mutually accused each other. N.B. This must be done to two doors opening *from*, not *towards* each other, or the connection is immediately evident. Nor is it unpleasing to watch the setting-off of a stage coach, and to observe the ostler bringing out his lanthorn to light the passengers in – which he has no sooner done than he places his lanthorn on the ground. One end of a packthread may be very conveniently slipped through the ring at the top of the lanthorn, the other end having been previously fastened to a wheel of the coach. The coach drives on – and the lanthorn, to the great surprize of its owner, manifests a very strong inclination to follow it – and unless rescued in very good time, hops after it down the street with remarkable celerity and perseverance. Some good also hath been found to result from sending one person unobserved into a room on the ground floor at the Bear Inn, where a table was laid for supper, and the party not yet come in – which person ties a string to one of the candlesticks, or both, if time serves, and conducts the string along the floor and out of the window (left open at this time of the year for air) into the street. You may then walk about at your leisure till you imagine the gentlefolks quietly seated at their meal – and the next time you pass, seizing the loop which you have left dangling out at window, you may with one twitch remove the candlesticks from the table to the ground with more quickness and dexterity than fifty waiters could have shewn in taking them away.

From these and suchlike pursuits, most of which I shared, and some I suggested to the inexperienced youth of my companions (and I flatter myself you will allow them to be rational and necessary relaxations from the fatigues of publick business and political research) I went to supper, generally with some of those who had been engaged in the adventure whatever it might be – often with the masters in the Common Room – and sometimes with the Dean, at neither of which two last places, however, I thought it expedient to mention how the half hour immediately preceding had been employed. And from supper I retired home to bed with the conscious satisfaction that if I had done nothing that day, I should probably do as little on the day succeeding.

After leading the life which I have described to you at Oxford for about a fortnight, on

*Saturday, July 5th* I took my Degree of M.A and became possessed of a vote in the University and a right to wear a gown with a sleeve

shaped thus

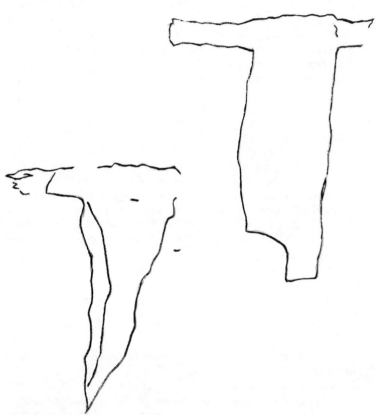

instead of one in this shape

which you see is not half so pretty as the former, with sundry other invaluable privileges – and then after having a long conversation with the Dean upon the state of things private and political, I left Oxford –

and made the best of my way to Eton – where I had long promised
a visit to my old Tutor, now Head Master of the School, Dr. Heath –
and where I arrived just as the Dr. and his family were sitting down
to dinner.

By the way the word Dr. puts me in mind to tell you that the great
Dr. Parr[287] was at Oxford during the time that I was there. A pupil
of his, and friend of mine (his name Bartlam)[288] had won the Bachelor's
Prize in the University by an essay on Liberty – and the Dr. came to
hear him recite it in the Theatre. We met but once during the whole
week – and that was accidentally at Bartlam's rooms – when I found
him very profoundly but distantly civil. I heard afterwards that one
of his chief amusements every night, after supper, while he was
smoking his pipe, was to abuse *me*.

I arrived at Eton, as I said, and after dinner went to explore my
former haunts in Eton and Windsor: the playing fields, the Terrace
and above all the bookseller's shop where Microcosm was published –
which this time indeed I had an additional reason for visiting – which
was *this*. For some time past there had been paragraphs in several
papers, stating *me* to have written and published a *History of Invasions*[289]
of which God knows I am as innocent as the child unborn. Day after
day 'Young C____'s *History of Invasions* was mentioned – sometimes
as just coming out, sometimes as selling well, and at last as having
attained a second edition. For a good while I thought it altogether a
joke, though for aught I could see, a very dull one – and did not even
believe the existence of any such book – till one day at Christ Church
I was shewn a formal advertisement of it – not with my name – but
as published by C. Knight,[290] Windsor, '*where also may be had the
Microcosm*'. This explained to me why I was supposed to be its author –
and I called upon Mr. Knight to find out why he had chosen to play
this trick – for it was evidently such, and upon what authority. I had
no sooner entered his shop than he began to mutter apologies for a
little inadvertency into which he had fallen, really without any intention – but from which the newspapers had taken occasion &c &c. The
*Oracle* in particular, he said, had done so, and he believed he could
tell why. The editor of that paper was a great personal friend of the

[287] Dr. Samuel Parr (1747–1825). Former Headmaster of Colchester and Norwich
Grammar Schools and private tutor at his residence at Hatton in Warwickshire from
1785. Since 1787 he had become known as a political writer in the Foxite whig cause

[288] John Bartlam (d. 1823). He won the Chancellor's Prize for an English Essay and
became Fellow and Bursar of Merton. He subsequently became Parr's closest friend.
See W. Derry, *Dr. Parr*, (Oxford, 1966), 63–4, 348

[289] The pamphlet, *History of Invasions*, has not been traced

[290] Charles Knight was a Windsor bookseller and the publisher of the *Microcosm*. He
was the father of the more famous publisher (1791–1873) of the same name

author of the pamphlet in question, and thought perhaps he might *puff* it, and produce a larger sale by ascribing it &c &c. Finally Mr. Knight offered to put any paragraph that I should please, into the papers, to clear me of the imputation of having written a very dull performance (as it appeared to be) – and one which with all its puffing, it seems did not go off very rapidly. But I thought that would be making more fuss about the thing than it was worth – especially as the sale being very small few people seemed to think about it, and as the book is very stupid I hoped any friends of mine who might happen to see it, would acquit me of having a hand in the composition.

I returned to supper at Dr. Heath's.

5. *[July]* Sunday morning – I went first to Eton Chapel – and then up to Windsor. In my way there I met Stopford and Andover – the former of whom pressed me to dine at his father's (Ld. Courtown) who has apartments in the Round Tower at Windsor.[291] This I could not do, being necessarily engaged to my host Dr. Heath – but I called on Ld. and Ly. C. in the morning – and promised to come up to Windsor immediately after dinner to walk with Ld. C. and Stopford and Andover on the Terrace.

I dined[292] at Eton accordingly. Poor Dr. Heath seems oppressed, I think, with the weight of his present office and dignity, and has not half the spirits and facetiousness that he had when I was at school, and when he was only an Assistant. Indeed I found every face at Eton clouded with melancholy in consequence of the fatal accident which happened a few days ago, in the drowning of a litle boy, Ld. Walde-grave.[293] Yesterday was his funeral, attended by the whole school – and as I have heard it described, it must have been one of the most affecting sights in the world – four or five hundred boys assembled round the grave – not a word – nor a look – nor a thought but what was intent upon the solemn scene passing before them. One boy particularly was pointed out to me – who had indeed behaved most gallantly. He was at some distance from the spot where the accident happened – but on hearing it, tho' without any knowledge of the poor little fellow who was lost, he jumped into the water in search of him, and repeated this so often that he was *himself* taken out senseless, and carried home and put to bed, with some doubts of his recovery. His name is Stewart,[294] a son of Ld. Londonderry. Ld. Waldegrave was not taken out for many hours after.

[291] He had been treasurer of the Household 1784–93

[292] 'I dined ... hours after', printed in *NER*, 531

[293] George, the 5th Earl Waldegrave was drowned in the Thames shortly before his 10th birthday

[294] Hon. Charles William Stewart, the 3rd Mq. of Londonderry. His more famous brother, Viscount Castlereagh, had also made a brave attempt to save a boy from

In the evening I went to Ld. Courtown's according to my appointment – and we went to the Terrace. We soon fell in with the K. and Q. – and their Maj$^s$ were graciously pleased to recognise me, not having seen me since I left Eton – and to honour me with many kind and sensible observations – such as 'that I was much grown' – 'that I must be very happy in revisiting Eton now and then' – that they hoped I had not forgotten our old friend the Microcosm – for they had not' to all which matters I replied with that politeness and perspicuity which becomes a dutiful subject in these times.

I returned to Eton to supper.

7 [*July*] Monday morning – after paying two or three visits – one to my dame[295] – and another to Mr. Pote's (the bookseller's) shop[296] – upon whom I had some time ago written an Epithalamium – containing prophecies of '*little Potes*' which he had great pleasure in shewing me, he has verified (the Provost Dr. Davies, who was Head Master when I was at Eton, was absent – or I should have visited him too) – I set off for London. I had no sooner arrived than I set out upon a round of visits in quest of news, particularly respecting the new arrangements. I find them all settled – least nearly so – the D. of P.[ortland] Secretary of State for the Home Department – but not taking the correspondence of the War – that is to remain with Dundas – Mr. Windham Secretary at War and in the Cabinet – Ld. Fitzwilliam Pres$^t$ of the Council. Of these new arrangements, and the system which will result from them, I hardly know how to form an opinion. Pitt[297] certainly must think them very desireable or he would never have taken so much pains about them – and of the D. of P. and Mr. W. I can never entertain any other opinion than that they are convinced in their own minds that the step which they are taking is best adapted to the dignity of their own characters, to the effectual support of the Government, and to the safety and happiness of the country. But it may be doubted, perhaps, whether or no their characters might not have stood higher with the people, had they continued to give their support to Administration without taking office, which, however pure their motives may be (and they cannot be purer than I believe them) is easily misconstrued and misrepresented. It may be doubted too whether or no such an accession as the present does in reality confer strength and stability upon an Administration, when we recollect that there is not an instance in the history of the country

---

drowning in Strangford Lough in 1787– in his case successfully, see M. Hyde, *The Rise of Castlereagh* (London, 1933), 42

[295] Mrs. Hannington who d. 27 Dec. 1807 aged 88

[296] Probably the son of Joseph Pote (?1703–87) who was a well known bookseller and publisher in Eton and kept a boarding house for collegers

[297] 'Pitt ... been done' (p. 138), printed in *Marshall*, 74–5

of a Ministry composed of two distinct parties, uniting, coalescing (or whatever it may be called) which has not split and fallen within a very short time after its establishment. All this however remains to be proved – what is certain at present is that a few people, a very few, talk of it as the grandest and most secure work that ever was undertaken – while many, very many, and amongst them some of Pitt's friends in particular, either *grumble* pretty audibly at the distribution of so great a part of the power among the new comers, or at best, shake their heads and wish that it may answer in the end. For my own part it is to me individually of less consequence than to almost any other person in Pitt's Party. If this arrangement had *not* taken place, a *move* would have been made among his immediate connections. I have no reason to believe, from anything that I had ever heard, that such a *move* could have reached to me, when I know there are persons who have been in Parliament since the beginning of this Parl.ᵗ, who yet have nothing, and for whom something must in justice first have been done. So that in that respect I stand just as I should have done – and there is this circumstance peculiarly pleasant to me, that if the D. of P[ortland] ever entertained the smallest doubt of the perfect propriety of *my* conduct, the principles on which he has now shaped his own must long ago have convinced him that I acted rightly.²⁹⁸ Indeed it does seem to have struck him in that light – for the very first thing that I heard form Mrs. Crewe was that the D. of P. had been sending to ask me to dinner while I was out of town – a thing which had never happened before in London, though I had visited at Welbeck, as you know, several times.

At the House of Commons there was nothing particular, except that Windham's writ was moved – and for the acceptance of the Chiltern Hundreds – which looked as if the thing was not yet quite settled, at least that it was not yet to be publicly declared, what post he was to have.

I dined at the Bedford Coffee House with Frere, Bobus and Easley Smith. The last is just came to town after his bloody fight on board Ld. Howe's fleet – sound wind and limb, and giving a very entertaining account of the whole transaction. I went to the Play to see the Glorious First of June – one of the stupidest businesses that I ever beheld – and I supped at Carey Street in my way home.

*8 [July]* Tuesday. Frere and Easley and Bobus breakfasted with me. Easley is returning to his station. I called at Edridge's, the miniature-painter, and settled to sit to him for the picture – for you, dear Fan, on Friday. I dined at the Club – at the Crown and Anchor –

---

²⁹⁸ A reference to C.'s having declined to be returned to Parliament by the Duke, see above p. 51, n. 111

and in the evening having a good deal to do, came home and was busy till 10 o'clock – and then went to sup at Mrs. Crewe's with Wallace and F. North. F. North has raked out an old promise of mine, made I suppose, if at all, when I was ill, and he nursing me, that we should travel together into Derbyshire. I don't like that same travelling together. But if I promised, it must be so.

9. *[July]* Wednesday morning Leveson and Morpeth called upon me. Morpeth has been returned from Italy about a fortnight. He wrote to announce his arrival to me while I was at Oxford – and I meant to have called upon him as soon as I came to town. There are to be great doings at Castle Howard in September on his coming of age – and I must be there, he says, as Boringdon and Leveson will be. I had rather be there, or anywhere, at any other time than when grand doings are going on – but I could not refuse. It in some sort tallies with my plan of visiting the Markhams, which I think I must do – but September is a long way off – and it is time enough to think of it when it arrives – sufficient to the month is the pleasure thereof, and my first pleasure is Ashborne.

With Morpeth I went to call on *Marsh*[299] – of whom I am sure you have heard me speak. He was my contemporary at Ch. Ch., an admirable scholar, and very good sort of man – and partly at my instigation became private tutor to Morpeth and Holland when they came to Ch. Ch. Since that, he has been travelling with Morpeth.

I dined at Sir R. Payne's – with Mrs. Crewe, Wallace, and Mr. Cholmondeley[300] (a Comr. of Excise and famous as a pleasant man – I think him *rather* so than otherwise). In the evening I went with Wallace for an hour or two to White's, where we met Leveson and Morpeth – and afterwards to sup at Mrs. Crewe's. Mrs. Crewe leaves town to-morrow.

10. *[July]* Thursday. Frere breakfasted with me. Edwd. Legge called. I am afraid he will not be in Staff[ord]shire much this summer. His new living will take him up so entirely.

In the House of Coms. was a *factious* motion of Sheridan's to address the King to prorogue the Parlt. &c. No division – but the debate lasted till past 7 o'clock whereby I lost my dinner at the Lord Chancellor's, on a turtle. Wallace, who was to dine there too, was wiser than to lose his dinner – and so he set off as soon as Pitt had done speaking – while I like a ninny sat out Grey's speech, thinking there might be something to answer in it (Jenkinson staid too – but he had previously dined)

[299] Probably Matthew Marsh (1770–1840). Matric. Christ Church, 28 Jan. 1788, aged 18; B.A. 1791; M.A. 1794; canon of Salisbury 1825–d.
[300] George James Cholmondeley (1752–1830), a nephew of the 1st Mq. of Cholmondeley

and so, as I said before, lost my turtle and had to send the Chancellor an apology. I might have repaired my loss by dining at Whitehall – where I was asked – but, foolishly enough, I had omitted to dress before the House, and I could not go in all *sweaty* and dirty to dinner. I came home therefore and cleaned myself and dined alone, and was very busy till near 10 – and then went to Whitehall – where I found them all at home and Ly. Sutherland with them. She put me in mind of my promise to come to Wimbledon before I left town, to examine her touching her progress in *Dryden's Fables* – and so I will. I went to supper at Jenkinson's – there was Wallace. I find he is going into the north, and Barker his quondam tutor, and my friend at Ch. Ch. – with him. So we have agreed to go all together – and a jolly party we shall be (for though I dislike travelling parties in general, yet as I find I *must* have *one* companion, F. North – I care not how many more) and they will all come to Ashborne next week.

*11 [July]* Friday morning. I went to call on my mother and took leave of her and my aunt and grandmother. My mother is to leave town in a few days. She has accomplished all the object of her coming-up, she says – and has established her Collysium with I know not how many respectable venders.

I was to have sat to-day to Edridge, Fan – but your good-natured letter, and a wise one too – for I fear I should not have had time to sit properly – relieved me from anxiety on that head – and it is adjourned to next year – when it shall be done, without doubt or delay.

I went to the House of Coms. ([Edmund] Burke's writ was moved *yesterday* so he is out of Parlt. I wonder what provision he will have – he ought to have some. Thirty years of public service, with such talents, ought to be acknowledged handsomely for the credit of the country). The King came down and prorogued the Parliament – at last – the Speech most *warlike*. I came home and dined alone, very busy. In the evg. I went to Whitehall. It is true that Lord Stafford has resigned.[301] I am sorry for it. Though he has done it cheerfully I am afraid he will miss his occupations, to which has been accustomed all his life – Councils, Cabinets, dinners, red tape and green boxes. But he seems mighty happy. In my way home I met Bobus, and went with him to his lodgings – and chatted and picked a bit of supper.

*12 [July]* Saturday morning. William Barnard breakfasted with me. He had agreed at Oxford that when he came to town we would go down together to Wanstead – and meeting yesterday in the street we renewed our appointment. We got to Wanstead by 2 o'clock, that

[301] As Lord Privy Seal

we might give poor Hetty time to add a bacon and egg to her family dinner. She and W.B. had not met for an age – and were delighted to see each other. He returned to town at night, promising to come again next day, and bring Mrs. B (whom by the bye I thought he had left at Oxford – so he intended doing) with him. I staid at Wanstead. Paul and Harry came. I had some talk with Paul abt. my little Charles Reddish, and Paul gives me hopes that the business will be settled very shortly. I hope so, for the coachmaker begins to be a-weary of waiting.

*13. [July]* Sunday morning. It was most profligately agreed to be too hot for Church-going. I sat at home – and read – and wrote letters – till W.B. and Mrs. B. came. After dinner we walked and enjoyed the cool of the evg. and at night after taking my leave of all the family I returned with W.B. and Mrs. B. to town. I went to eat a bit of bread and cheese and drink spruce beer at Carey Street – and then to bed.

*14. [July]* Monday morning Frere breakfasted with me – and Bobus called – and I took leave of them in case I should not see them again before I leave town. I wish I could prevail upon either of them to visit Ashborne. But they have both engagements which they cannot quit – Frere his office and his family – and Bobus his family, who live in Dorsetshire – all the way in a direction diametrically contrary to Ashborne. C. Reddish came and I sent him to P. Patrick – and it is settled that he is to leave the coachmaker, who wants him gone, and proceed to my mother's room, on her leaving town – where, under the inspection of his aunt and grandmother, I hope he will be kept out of harm's way till Mr. Popplewell is ready to send for him.

Calling on Jenkinson, Wallace, Fred. North and Morpeth in my way – I made sail for Wimbledon – and arrived there about an hour before dinner time. All the Stafford family were there (not including Leveson, who is returned to his regiment) – and Mr. and Mrs. Villiers. The evening passed very comfortably with Cassino for the elderly and grave ones – and for the rest, moonlight walks and reading poetry aloud – to which labour they kept *me* till – supper-time.

*15 [July]* Tuesday morning. Everybody went after their own inventions. Mine was to call on Lady Bristol and her family – who have taken a house upon the Common here, within a hundred yards of Lord Gower's – a very pleasant, comfortable habitation – in which they talk of being settled for good – that is for the winter as well as the summer. I hope not – for theirs is a house that one should miss in town. The Archbishop (that is, Mrs. Howe) came to dinner, which circumstance confirmed the Levesons in an opinion which they profess to entertain of a tender attachment between me and the old lady – especially (as I suggested to them) now that by the death of *their old*

*aunt* the Dss. of Bedford, I am a *widower*. In the evg. Ly. Sutherland,
Mrs. Villiers and I walked to Lady Bristol's. At night, after supper,
the whole party except Ld. G., Ly. Sutherland and me, set out for
London. We shall all meet at Trentham – except perhaps my flame,
the Archbishop.

*16 [July]* Wednesday morning – I set out very early and got to
town to breakfast with Wallace. We had fixed this day for our setting
out – but I find Wallace with a swelled face – to which it is but charity
to allow one night's fomentation – and I have a good deal to do before
I set out – and so we have put off our departure till to-morrow
morning. Pretty work it seems at Windham's election.[302] I hope Leigh
canvassed strenuously. I was at home all the morning, very busy in
settling books and papers &c. – and now after all I shall go out of
town leaving half, or more than half, of what I had to do, undone. I
dined at Frere's with Bobus – and we had a long walk and talk
together in the evening. Then I called on Wallace and found him
steeping his swollen cheek in bread and milk. I hope it will subside
before to-morrow or it will be out of the chaise window as he goes
along and what with his face and Fred. North's gout in his stomach
you will think I am bringing you an hospital. I supped in my way
home at Carey Street. Went to bed early, and now this.

*17 – day of July – Thursday.* I am up early bustling and preparing
for my journey, and Fleming is in such a fuss that he is quite disagreeable – and as soon as I have finished this sheet and sealed it for
the post I shall set out for Wallace's lodgings in Clarges St. which is
our place of rendez-vous, where I hope to find F. North and Barker
and him ready. Adieu till Saturday at dinner.

*[The Journal resumes on 10 November]*

I left Ashborne, as you may remember, on the morning of Sunday,
Novr. 9th, and got that night to Stratford.

*10. [November]* Monday. At about 4 o'clock I arrived in Oxford.
My intention was to stay there a day or two – and my business there
was to call on the Dean – and other Christ Church people – and
particularly to see poor Dawkins, who has been most dreadfully ill,
and is now but just recovering. I found letters here, amongst them
one from Mr. Pitt, stating the importance of the business to come on
at the opening of Parliament, which induced me to alter my plan of
staying here, and to determine on setting-off the next morning, but

[302] He was re-elected for Norwich 1236 v. 700 following his appt. to office as sec. at
war. His main opponents were the Norwich radicals, see *Thorne*, v, 615

as I had promised to stop at night at Bulstrode[303] in my way with C. Greville and Lady Charlotte, and as I found here a letter from Ly. Charlotte, claiming my promise – I resolved to get to Bulstrode by dinner next day; and on Wednesday morning to proceed to London. This evening I called upon the Dean; and had a long conversation with him upon many subjects. I called also upon a variety of persons, young and old, and supped in the Common Room – where was Barker – and all the Masters of Arts, of whose number I now am one.

*11 [November]* Tuesday. Having obtained permission last night from Dawkins's physician to be admitted to see him, in consequence of his earnest entreaty, and of my promise not to stay long enough to flurry him – I was conducted by the physician this morning to his bedside and found him emaciated indeed most cruelly, and so weak as not to be able to lift his hand – but out of danger, as they tell me, and wanting nothing but strength for his recovery. Having paid this visit I had no longer anything to detain me in Oxford except to see the Barnards, to whom I went, and found them very well – and regretting that my business in London would not allow me to stay to dine with them. I walked back to my inn, William Barnard attending me, and set off for Bulstrode. There I arrived by dinner time. I found C. Greville and Ly. Charlotte alone – and passed a very comfortable evening.

*12. [November]* Wednesday morning. I got my breakfast early – and pursued my route to London – where as soon as I arrived I sent Fleming on in the chaise to Paper Buildings – and went myself to leave my name in Downing Street, where I heard that Mr. Pitt was in the country – and to call at Jenkinson's where, hearing that he was to dine at home and alone I left word that I would come and dine with him. I then called on Bobus Smith – from whom I learned that Frere is not in town – which is a great disappointment to me – and at 6 o'clock returned to Jenkinson's – dined and sat the whole evening, and supped tête-à-tête – which brought us to about 2 in the morning.

*13 [November]* Thursday morning I called in Downing Street – Mr. Pitt was not returned. I met Rose (the Secretary of the Treasury) at the door – and learned from him the sad news of the surrender of Maestricht and Nimeguen.[304] I had heard last night that Lady Malmesbury was in town at Mrs. Robinson's – so I called there – but she had set out into the country about an hour before. I called too on fifty other people, just to shew my arrival in town – and at Wood-

---

cock's – to enquire after his father – where I was informed that after
his dreadful illness of six months he had at last been released from all
his sufferings and died on Tuesday night. He is a cruel loss to his
family. He was a very good and a very able man – and so eminent in
his profession (as a solicitor) that he enjoyed from it a splendid income,
which must now of course cease in great part – and it is not known what
provision he may have left for his wife and children. The Chancellor,
however, who had some obligations to old Mr. W. in the earlier part
of his life, is behaving nobly to his family. He continues this second
son (a boy of about 19) in a place of considerable emolument under
the Great Seal[305] – and has provided for him a partner in the business
of his father – and is helping them in every way to carry it on. My
friend the eldest son was designed by his father, and his own choice,
for Orders – and the Chancellor has promised him every assistance
that he may have it in his power to afford him. So I hope they may
yet do well.

I went into Lincoln's Inn Hall to keep Term. Boringdon is come
to town – and has set up his establishment very splendidly – with a
good house in Hill Street, Berkeley Square – and a good cook to make
his house pleasant to his friends. There I dined to-day with a small
party consisting of Jenkinson, Morpeth and Edwd. Legge. We found
everything worthy of our approbation – and had a very pleasant
dinner. From thence I went in the evening – and supped no less
pleasantly with the Markhams. Alicia Markham is to be married
soon.[306]

*14.* [*November*] Friday morning I had a visit from Bootle – who is
just returned from two years and a half's tour on the Continent –
having travelled in that time all over the more usual northern route
of Sweden, Denmark, Norway, Russia – and besides into Siberia, over
Mount Caucasus, through Crim Tartary and God knows where. We
had much to talk of, after so long an absence – and so I agreed to
dine with him at the Piazza Coffee House – which I accordingly
did – and his fellow-traveller, a Mr. Parkinson of Magdalen College,
Oxford, an elderly tutor-like stupidish sort of man,[307] and a Mr.
Edmonstone,[308] who married one of Bootle's sisters (and a young
barrister by profession) – were of our party. In the evening I went
with Bootle to Newbolt's – where we met Sturges and staid to supper.
Newbolt, you remember from a letter of his which I shewed you, has
got a place under the Chancellor, which makes his circumstances very

[305] Elborough Woodcock, s. of Elborough Woodcock q.v., and sec. of Bankrupts and
register of Affadavits in 1795
[306] To the Rev. Henry Forster Mills
[307] The Rev. John Parkinson (1754–1840). Fellow of Magdalen Coll. Oxf. 1775–98
[308] Sir Charles Edmonstone 2nd Bt. (1764–1821)

comfortable – and his Julia is in high beauty, and seems to promise to add another comfort to his family.

*15 [November]* Saturday morning. I received a note from Woodcock desiring to see me. I went to him. It was rather a painful visit. I called at Mr. Pitt's. He was at home – but the Cabinet was with him – and as I had nothing to lay immediately before them, I would not interrupt their deliberations. I resolved, however, since he seemed so constantly out or engaged, not to call again till I heard from him – and accordingly wrote him a note to say that when he could appoint an hour at which he should be at leisure I should be happy in the honour of seeing him. I dined at the Chief Baron's – where was a very *young* and *gay* party – consisting of the Archbishop of Canterbury and Mrs. Moore, the Archbishop of York and Mrs. Markham, Mr. Justice Rooke,[309] and Mr. Cracherode,[310] an old lettered Christ Church man of about 70. There was Eliz. Markham to be sure – and we two seemed like the father and mother of the whole company – with very fine children about us. In the evg. I went to the Play – and from the Play to sup tête-à-tête with Jenkinson.

*16 [November]* Sunday I was at home almost the whole morning. I could not go to Wanstead being engaged from the moment of my arrival in town, to dinner. Sundry people called on me – among others Borrowes who looks very well, and I believe is thriving very well, as he appears one of the least desponding politicians that I have encountered – and Granville Leveson, who is just come to town from his Militia. I dined at the Master of Rolls's – with Bootle (Lady Arden, the M. of the R.'s wife, was a Miss Bootle, his sister), Mr. Parkinson, Mr. Abbot (a counsel[311]), Mr. Leicester[312] d°. – and H. Hinchcliffe.[313] In the evg. I went to the Archb. of York's – and supped there. Walking home after supper with O. Markham and another young Templar, we had nearly got ourselves committed to the Covent Garden Watch-house for the night by taking the part of a drunken blackguard whom the watchman was lugging before the constable of the night, and as we thought, very unjustly. We insisted upon accompanying the watchman and his prisoner, to the place where the complaint was to be made, and seeing justice done him. The inside of one of these

---

[309] Sir Giles Rooke (1743–1808). Judge in the Court of Common Pleas

[310] Clayton Cracherode (matric. Christ Church, 6 June 1746, aged 16)

[311] Probably Charles Abbot, 1st Baron Colchester, who had just been apptd. clerk of the Rules in the King's Bench

[312] Probably Hugh Leycester (1748–1836), counsel to Camb. Univ. until 1814; king's attorney, Chester circuit 1785–1801

[313] Henry Hinchcliffe (c. 1768–1848), e.s. of John Hinchcliffe, bishop of Peterborough and Master of Trinity Coll. Camb. by Elizabeth, da. of John Crewe of Crewe Hall. Fellow, Trinity Coll. Camb. 1789

nightly tribunals is truely curious. It is exactly such as you see it described in Fielding's *Amelia* – and I believe, had we not been by, the worthy magistrate who filled the chair this night would have made our drunken protegé (who by the bye was a red-hot Irishman) pay most handsomely for his release. We saved him however by our interference – but triumphing a little too loudly over the gentlemen in office, we had nearly drawn down the vengeance of their authority upon ourselves – and though we certainly might have punished them by due course of law, had they chosen to detain us in custody all night as they threatened – yet as it would have been rather an uncomfortable thing to have passed a November night in the black hole, and rather a ridiculous thing to avow it afterwards, as we must have done if we meant to pursue and obtain a reparation for the injury, I am rather glad upon the whole that we made a timely retreat from the watch house before we had irritated our judges quite so far as to make them lay their hands upon us.

*17 [November]* Monday morning – I called upon O. Markham to consult with him whether or no we had better go and lay a complaint against the watch before Mr. Addington,[314] the Justice – but upon examining all the grounds whereon we could build and sustain it, we found so many little flaws in our own conduct, and saw so clearly that if *they* had been *wrong we* had not been altogether quite *right* – that we thought it better to drop the business than to resume it.

Not having been able to go to Wanstead yesterday, and having heard that they expected me; and foreseeing that I might not have another vacant day before the meeting of Parliament, I thought I could not do better than set out at once this morning. I accordingly did so – calling upon Harry in my way – got there by two o'clock – dined there – and returned to town in the evening. I could not well stay there all night – and indeed if I had gone with that intention I should not have felt much inclined to adhere to it, seeing that it was unluckily the night of a great assembly at Wansted – where Hetty had assembled the neighbourhood to the amount of two dozen men and women to cards and tea and refreshments. I had almost forgot to say that in my way down I met Willy Canning trudging it away from home, where he had been yesterday, to his school at Hackney, with a pound of tea under his arm. I made him return with me to dinner at Wanstead – and brought him back to Hackney at night. Willy is really a very fine boy. They are going to act Cymbeline at Mr. Newcome's – and Willy is to be the Posthumus – which is very grand.

*18 [November]* – Tuesday I was at home all the morning busied

---

[314] William Addington, JP in Bow St. Office

about many and various things. Amongst other things I had promised when I left Trentham that I would write to Lady Sutherland – and tell her all the news of the town. Now this I had never yet done – and as she was to leave Trentham about the 20th, unless I did it to-day I should be too late – and at the same time I was not much in a humour to write as long a letter as I should have liked to have written – so I thought the best way was to write a little hurried note from myself saying that I had been so occupied, and was so still, that I could not perform my promise fully, but that I had ordered my servant (whom she had admired so much and taken such a fancy to him for being a Scotchman) – to put down for her information the most material articles of intelligence – which I now sent off to her, though without having time to read them over, and hoped they would prove satisfactory. Inclosed in this note of mine was Fleming's letter written in proper hand and spelling, and broken off abruptly at the end, without conclusion or signature as if I had just come in, and called for it in a hurry to seal and send it before I dressed. It informed her that 'his master was so *bizzy* that he had desired him to *right* the nuse of the *meatrawpullies*, being her lps. countryman of which he was very proud, not *douting* her la<sup>p.</sup> to be the same'. It stated 'that things on the *contanent* were in a bad situation – that Masturcht had *surreverenced* to the *anymy*, that Nimagain had *evacuated* also – and all *owing* to the *Asturians* not being able to keep their *ordures*'. 'that Horn Tucks'[315] trial was going on but slowly – because he every moment *embraced* (i.e. embarrassed) the Juges and Councillas with fulsome questions and made free with every *parson* that came in his way – that there were great fears of riots if he should be *acquainted* – for that when the *Jewry renounced* Hardy *non compass* they had filled the Court with the lewdest hussies (i.e. Loud huzzas) and *proclamations* – that he hoped the yeomanry went on well – but that his master's *unkal* Mr. Leigh had not yet been able to get a *prostitute* – and would be glad to know if Ld. G. had more than he wanted for his own *personal* service (wch. her La[*dyshi*]*p could probably tell*) – or where Mrs. L. could get for LOVE or *munny* to serve during the war'.

I dined at Boringdon's – with a larger party than before – Morpeth, Leveson, Edwd. Legge, Bootle, Wallace (who came to town yesterday) and Bartlam – whose name you may remember to have heard in my accounts of Oxford – a pupil of Dr. Parr's.

In the evg. I went to the Play – and from the Play came home.

*19.* [*November*] Wednesday[316] morning I went to the Old Bailey,

---

[315] John Horne Tooke (1736–1812), the radical politician who was tried for high treason but acquitted on 22 November 1794

[316] 'Wednesday morning ... own hearing' (p. 148), printed in *NER*, 531

and was there till past 9 o'clock at night. The evidence against the prisoner closed to-day, and Erskine opened his defence. I was very curious to see Horne Tooke – and it is not easy to see him to more advantage than he appears, in point of talents, on his trial. His mode of examining witnesses, his objections in law, and his whole manner of conducting the part in his cause, which he takes upon himself, is the most masterly, that I can conceive – infinitely beyond any professional counsel, that I remember to have seen. But then he is so insolent, and does and says things so unlike the usual conduct allowed in a Court of Justice, that it is evident Eyre[317] must be afraid of him, or he would feel himself called upon a thousand times a day to interfere. Erskine, whom I heard for about 4 hours, was *bad* beyond all belief – trash, nonsense, impudence and mischief – were what principally char-acterized his speech, and were relieved very little by any display of eloquence or ability. I should not have trusted to any other person's account that he had been *so* bad as I thought him myself from my own hearing. I was obliged to leave the Court before he had finished, that I might come home to receive the Irish Club – who were to sup with me tonight – and for whom Fleming had prepared a very splendid set-out. They came to the number of 7 – and talked Jacobin politics here till past 12. While I was at the Old Bailey to-day came the news of Parliament's being prorogued to the 30th December. It occasions of course many deep speculations. In peace *I* do not believe.

*20. [November]* I[318] did not intend to have gone to the Old Bailey again to-day, but Wallace came and persuaded me to go with him, by telling me that Pitt and Fox and Sheridan were to be examined. I went accordingly and staid till 1/2 past 4, during all which time I was entertained as much as before with Horne Tooke's able and acute remarks and examinations, but disgusted no less with the conduct of the Chief Justice – which can arise from nothing but absolute folly, or a silly courting of popularity, which is unworthy of his situation.

With such a judge to sum up, and with a jury, of which three members have been challenged by the Attorney General, there can be little doubt of his acquittal. Indeed I have not heard enough of the case on the part of the prosecution to judge how far the facts charged have been brought home to him – though I have heard enough of his defence to see that great part of it is very little to the purpose, and some of it such evidence, as an unbiassed Judge would not admit into a Court of Justice at all. He is accused of *deeds* in 92–3–4, and he brings evidence of his *professions* ten years *before* to rebut the accusation.

[317] Sir James Eyre, chief-justice of Common Pleas; counsel for John Wilkes in Wilkes v. Wood in 1763
[318] 'I did not ... worth attending' (p. 149), printed in *NER*, 531–2

And the Chief Justice does nothing but smirk and say 'how clever you are'. I heard the examinations of the Duke of Richmond, Mr. Pitt, Mr. Fox, and Sheridan, and then came away, to go and dine with Garthshore (whom I have before mentioned to you), a Ch. Ch. man, a great friend of the Dean's – formerly a tutor there to Boringdon and others – aftds. travelling with Lord Dalkeith – and now private secretary to Mr. Dundas, and married to a great fortune, daughter of Chalier, the wine merchant. He has a house in Manchester Square, and gave a very good dinner to-day to me and Harry Legge (the lawyer) and Robt. Markham.

In the evg. I went to Sir Ralph Payne's – and from thence with Wallace to White's – where we met Leveson and Morpeth – and would have supped, had there been anything for supper in the house. But there was not. White's is very ill attended – and unless *our* generation do something to support it, will soon not be worth attending.

*21. [November]* Friday morning – I went into the City and called on Borrowes – Maxwell and P. Patrick. I dined at Lambeth – there were the family, Sir Moreton Eden[319] (Mrs. M.'s brother), our Minister at Vienna – and his wife Ly. Eliz<sup>th.</sup> (neither of whom I ever saw before indeed they have been living abroad these many years at one Court or other, and I am not likely soon to see them again, as they set out in a day or two for Vienna) – Ly. Bridget Tollemache – Lady Errol – a very pretty brisk Irish girl though just married to a Scotch Lord, and some other people.

In the evg. I went to the Play – and from the Play to sup at the Law Club in Carey Street, which is better off in point of supper than I found White's last night – and from Carey Street home.

I found a note on my table from Mr. Pitt – informing me that he should be at home and at leisure the next morning – and hoping to see me. The prorogation of Parliament has explained to me the business and frequency of cabinets, which prevented my seeing him hitherto.

*22 [November]* Saturday morning – According to my appointment I went to call on Mr. Pitt and had a long conversation upon things in general that have happened, may happen, and ought to happen. The result is, to my mind, a vigorous prosecution of the War, *with* or *without* Allies. All the vulgar notion of a Treaty with France having been opened, or even thought to be opened, is nonsense. Mr. Jay,[320]

---

[319] Sir Morton Eden, 1st Baron Henley; envoy extraordinary to Vienna 1794–9. His sister, Catherine, had m. the archbishop of Canterbury in 1770

[320] John Jay (1745–1829). Chief Justice, U.S.A. 1787–95 and responsible for negotiating the commercial treaty with Britain, 1794, to which his name is attached

the American Ambassador, is no more gone, or going, to Paris than I am. Pitt is just as I would have him – open, free, ready to answer questions without reserve, or to say without reserve that they are such questions as he cannot at present answer.

I called at Lansdown House. Did I say in my last letter that I had received an invitation from Lord L.[ansdowne] to dine with him yesterday to celebrate Holland's birthday? – and how sorry I was that I could not go – because I knew that he had felt last year somewhat affronted at my not accepting one or two invitations that he sent me, and had, as I feared, attributed my declining them (which in fact was purely owing to my being engaged) to politicks? I called to-day to do away this impression – but did not find him at home. I dined with Borrowes – to the great anger of Leveson, Morpeth and Boringdon, who had made a party to dine at White's, of which I was to be the fourth – but I was engaged to Borrowes – and I never *cut* an engagement. At Borrowes's I met Paul Patrick and Mr. Jamieson[321] – and they talked politicks. Coming back in a hackney coach I was stopped at the end of the Old Bailey by the mob, who were waiting there for Horne Tooke's acquittal, and we (that is the coachmen, P. Patrick who was in the coach with me, and I) were made to huzza loudly. Paul was mightily delighted with my unwilling exultation.

I called on Jenkinson – of whom I had heard last night by accident that he was in town (I thought he was at Addiscombe) laid up with a broken shin, which he had got by riding against a buggy (as I say) a waggon (as he will have it) in the dark, – a pretty exploit for a Colonel of Cavalry. To punish him for not having let me know of his misfortune and consequent confinement I would not stay with him to supper, as he wd. have me, and as I should have liked to do, but left him in five minutes – and went to the Archbishop of York's. There I found the Greffier Fagel[322], whom, I knew a little at The Hague. He is come over to try to persuade us to join with Holland in negotiating a peace with France, in which I apprehend he will not succeed, or, failing that, to obtain our permission for Holland to negotiate a peace for herself, which she may do, and be d____d! I supped with the Markhams and came home.

*23 [November]* Sunday morning – I received a *nice* letter from Ly. S[utherlan]d, informing me that they were just arrived at Wimbledon – that she should be in town Monday morning at the *Chef Barren's*[323] – where she wished I would call on her – that they were

---

[321] Possibly Robert or Thomas Jameson (sic), merchants and Irish factors of 22 Ironmongers Lane, London

[322] Baron Henry Fagel (1765–1838), Dutch Minister in Britain

[323] Chief Baron of the Exchequer, Archibald MacDonald q.v., Lady Stafford's son in law

going to look out for a small house for themselves in London (hitherto they have been at Whitehall, Ld. Staff[or]d's, when in town) – and above all that she, and all Trentham, had been laughing to 'an unspeakable degree' at her countryman and correspondent's letter. You will easily guess my answer was that I could not possibly call at the *Chef Barren's* to meet her next morning. Poor little Charles Reddish called on me – I had heard from Paul, who you know got him placed with Mr. Popplewell for me, that he had been attacked with *fits* of a very unpleasant nature – and I wanted to see him that I might have advice for him. I wish this was all the mischief about him – but I hear also that he is much addicted to *lying* – and if so, I am afraid no advice that I can give or get for him, will save him from very sad scrapes – but I must try.

I went to Wanstead – and stayed there all night. I had taken leave of them when last I was there, as for some time – but the deferring of the meet[in]g of Parl[iament]t since then gave me an opportunity of seeing them again, and I was thought a very good boy for seizing it.

*24. [November]* Monday morning I breakfasted at Wanstead – and then returned to town by 12 o'clock – and as 12 was the hour appointed for Ly. S[utherlan]d's being at the Ch. Baron's, perhaps you will not be at a loss to guess where I went as soon as I came to town. I found her and Lord G. there – and settled with them to go to Wimbledon some day this week – and Granville Leveson and Morpeth with me. Ld. G. and Ly. S. went back to Wimbledon. Having no engagement to dinner and fancying I had much to do, I resolved to dine at home alone – I had no sooner made this resolution than I called on Bobus, and asked him to dine with me tête-à-tête. No sooner was this determined than Frere called on me, that moment come to town – and I kept him to make a trio – and scarce was the trio adjusted, when I saw a note on my table from Smith (the other Microcosm Smith) telling me that he was just arrived in London to stay a week or ten days – and so I sent to him to make up our quartetto – and so – as if *providentially* – here were the four Micro-cosmopolitans of a sudden brought together. We passed an evening such as rarely occurs, in talking over old times – and when they left me I walked to the other end of the town – and being there could not avoid calling on Jenkinson and supping tête-à-tête with him, before I came home.

*25 [November]* Frere breakfasted with me. Are you not glad to hear this? You will be still gladder to hear that I made him stay with me the whole day, talk, talk, talk – and dine with me tête-à-tête. – After dinner Sturges came in to us, and we all three went to the Play – and from the Play Sturges and I went to Carey Street, where we supped together – and then to the Temple – home.

Charles Reddish called on me in the course of the morning – and I sent him to Norris to be cured of his fits – and scolded him for lying – and had him measured by Cowley (my taylor) for a new coat and a pair of corderoy breeches.

This morning I had a letter from Charles Ellis – reminding me of my promise to come to him at Wootton – and from Ly. Malmesbury enforcing his suggestion and adding her commands that I should meet her there. I mean to do so. This morning too I went, making Frere go with me, to Messrs. Chipps and Long to see about your phaeton.

*26. [November]* Frere breakfasted with me. Norris called and told me what he had advised about C. Reddish – and how he hopes to cure him of his fits. I hope he will succeed – or Mr. Popplewell will hardly keep the boy.

I dined tête-à-tête with Jenkinson. In the evening I called at the Abp. of York's – and neglecting to ask whether anybody was at home I was ushered upstairs into a room where the old couple were sitting quite alone – and laying their heads together about the wedding, which (though I like a fool had forgot it) was to take place next morning. Not a soul besides in the house. I soon found that *I* ought not to be there to interrupt their arrangements – and so, as soon as I could decently find opportunity, I slunk away and returned homewards, supping at Carey Street in my way.

*27 [November]* Thursday morning. Having received from my poor mother a dreadful account of the illness of her son,[324] who is with Mr. Milner at Scorton in Yorkshire, I poked out a little bit of *paper* to send to him (the schoolmaster) in hopes that it might make him more attentive to the poor boy's cure. I went to see my aunt (my mother's sister) and grandmother,[325] at their lodgings at Somers Town. They have changed their situation since I saw them last – but are now very snug and comfortable. My poor grandmother indeed is dying very perceptibly, though slowly, and from mere decay, without any pain, or effort, and wishing most devoutly herself for her dissolution. Poor old soul she reads the psalms all day long – and they seem to afford her infinite consolation. My aunt in the meantime is mending Charles's stockings – which she complains he wears out very fast – and therefore asked my advice about *double-heeling* them – an expedient that in a great measure counteracts the rubbing of the shoe. I highly approved of it.

As soon as I returned from this visit, which however I did not do till I had furnished my aunt with the means of providing, and insisted

[324] William Hunn who d. Dec. 1794 see n. 239 and p. 000
[325] In a letter to his mother, 28 Oct. 1795, C. said they were normally to be found at 8 Ossulston St., Canning MSS (2)

upon my grandmother's taking, the only medicines that her decrepi-
tude and decay require, cordials and good fires – and as soon as I had
written to Charles Ellis and Lady Malmesbury (who were both to
come to town to-day – Charles from Wootton to meet Ly. M., and
Ly. M. to meet Mrs. Robinson and him – and to return with them in
a day or two to Wooton) – to give them my promise that I would
soon join them at Wootton – and that I would see them if possible
before they left town – I set off for Wimbledon – and arrived there
time enough to dress before dinner. To dinner came Leveson and
Morpeth – and Mr. Campbell[326] and Ly. Caroline Campbell (Morpeth's sister) and Mr. C. Greville[327] (not the D. of Portland's C.
Greville, Ly. Charlotte's husband, but a brother of Ld. Warwick's,
the same that I met at Castle Howard – the friend and constant
companion of Mr. Campbell and Ly. Caroline and Ld. Carlisle) –
and beside them from his house on the other side of the Common
came Mr. Dundas – with his wife Ly. Jane – and a daughter. The
dinner was very pleasant. I do not remember ever to have seen
Dundas in so easy and communicative a humour. He is always good-
humoured – to be sure – and chearful – but apt not to contribute
much to the conversation. To-day he was absolutely talkative – and
seemed to like to be brought out – which I accordingly set about –
and the more earnestly as Greville, who is an eternal talker, and
though a sensible, by no means an entertaining one, seemed very
much disposed to have more than this share of the conversation. Lord
Gower, you know, in a mixt company says little or nothing. But he
*understands* what is going on and feels it with a taste and *tact* which
makes it delightful to have him to refer to *silently* and take his sense of
things and persons, and compare it with one's own. He is very often
very right.

The evening was just what it ought to be. I had some private
conversation with Dundas, which I liked the better as it ended with
his asking me to dinner to meet Ld. Gower and Ly. Sutherland next
day. After supper, having something to say to Granville Leveson, I
went with him for a few minutes into his room in my way to my own –
and being there the *something* and the few minutes extended themselves
into a long talk till three o'clock in the morning.

*28 [November]* Friday morning. Morpeth, Leveson, Mr. Campbell,
Lady Caroline C. and Mr. Greville left Wimbledon immediately after
breakfast – and left Ly. Suth[erlan]d, Ld. G[owe]r and myself to pass
a long rainy morning, in which there was no possibility of stirring

---

[326] John Campbell, subsequently 1st Baron Cawdor, who had m. 1789 Lady Isabella
Caroline Howard, da. of 5th Earl of Carlisle. M.P. Cardigan Borough 1780–96
[327] Charles Francis Greville (1749–1809), 2nd s. of 1st Earl of Warwick

from the fireside. So much the better– for so comfortably did we pass it together that when the time came for dressing to go and dine at Mr. Dundas's we agreed that we had much rather have to stay quietly where we were. When we came to Dundas's however we found no want of agreeableness. The company consisted only of Dundas and Ly. Jane, Lady Erne (Ly. Bristol's daughter, as you know) who is living here on the Common with her mother and Ly. Louisa, and Fred. Hervey) – Mr. Pitt – Genl. Grant[328] (great fat laughing old man – a Scotchman and member for the County of Sutherland, and a great friend of Ly. S[utherlan]d's family for many generations) – and ourselves. This dinner was not less pleasant than yesterday's. Dundas was again open and talkative. Pitt in very good spirits – for even in these desperate times one is allowed to be very merry if one likes it. Genl. Grant is a sort of Falstaff, in one part of the character at least – for if not 'witty himself' he is the cause of wit in others – and affords infinite room for all sorts of bad jokes, which are lavished on him unsparingly. I do not think I ever had so much talk with Pitt as to-day, with Dundas certainly never – and between us we went on so well that we did not rise from our *bottles* till it was about time for Lady S. and Ld. Gower and me to set out across the Common home. We had pre-determined not to stay out to supper but to return to a snug little repast at home – which we enjoyed in the library (a room sacred to very private meals) and cozed very comfortably till bed-time.

*27th, 28th [November]*

As a sort of supplement to the account of these two last days, perhaps you will be glad to have an account of some of the topicks of the conversations which I mention as having taken place with Mr. Dundas one day, and with him and Mr. Pitt the other. Mr. Dundas, you know, was summoned as a witness by Horne Tooke on his trial, and attended, but was never called. I asked him if he could guess to what points he was to have been examined. He said that he could think of none (having never personally known Horne Tooke, nor ever having been, as Mr. Pitt and the D. of Richmond and others had, member of any Reform Society or other political Club) except that he might have been questioned as to the truth of what had been so often asserted in the course of the trials, the circumstance of *his* having had *spies* in pay in all the seditious Clubs, to watch over their motions, and give him information respecting them – and secondly, that Horne Tooke being his neighbour at Wimbledon (he lives next door to him, you may have heard me say, so near that their grounds and gardens join) – he might perhaps have been called to bear testimony to his

[328]James Grant (1720–1806). M.P. Sutherland 1787–1802

(H.T.'s) peaceable and quiet demeanour in the country. 'To the first of these questions (that respecting spies) I should have answered that I must certainly had thought it my duty as Secretary of State, and entrusted by my office with the preservation of [the] internal quiet of the country, to have a constant look-out after the proceedings of the Societies, which I believed to be meditating mischief and sedition, and that I therefore always had, and always would take care to have persons amongst them to watch their plans and to give me immediate information of every design that they had in hand. I should have said for instance that one day, one of these spies of mine, who was a member of the Constitutional Society, came to me with a copy of some Resolutions, which he said Mr. Tooke had composed, and he was now carrying them to him to look over. They were those violent Resolutions, read at Chalk farm,[329] I think. I desired him to carry them to Mr. Tooke – and then to come and report to me the conversation that passed between them. He did so. He returned and told me that he had found Mr. Tooke and Mr. Hardy[330] together – that Tooke had read the Resolutions over – and approved them, and said to Hardy, 'Now, Mr. Hardy, you had better sign them'. Hardy answered, 'Yes, Mr. T., and will not you sign them too?' Tooke replied, 'Why no, Mr. Hardy. *I* am, you know, a *marked man*, and must take care therefore to do nothing without a *Statute Book in my hand* (or some such expression). I must keep within the letter of the law – to be safe.' This wd. have been Dundas's evidence to the first point – and it would have gone farther to open the eyes of the public to Horne Tooke's real character, than anything that came out against him. It would have shewed the cool, deliberate and artful manner in which he went about all the mischievous designs that he formed himself, and got others to execute, and how, whenever there was anything to be done, which was likely to involve the doer of it in the smallest degree of personal danger, he took care to push other weak and uneducated people forward, and to keep himself snug and out of sight and out of risque. 'As to the second point', said Dundas, 'that of his character as a neighbour in the country, I must have owned that I never knew any harm of him here – for indeed I do not recollect even to have had any manner of intercourse with him but once – which was when his gardener came to mine one day to complain of a large tree of mine which hung over his wall, and dripped upon his vegetables, and spoiled them. And to this complaint I remember having answered in these words, 'Damn the rogue, though he *is* a traitor, I don't wish to spoil his green peas, so cut the tree immediately'.

[329] The Chalk Farm meeting took place on 14 Apr. 1794
[330] Thomas Hardy (1752–1832). Founder of the London Corresponding Society

The second day (Friday) after dinner at Dundas's, the conversation turned upon our conquests in the West Indies – and I asked their (Dundas's and Mr. Pitt's) opinions as to the *exactions*[331] of Sir C. Grey and Sir J. Jervis, on the estates in the conquered islands. It was a great satisfaction to me to find Pitt and Dundas thinking at least as ill of them as I did myself, and it was a still greater to hear that all that Sir C. Grey and Sir J. J[ervis] had done of that sort had been not only without the consent of Ministers at home – but directly against the positive orders and instructions that they carried with them – and the purport of which was that they should receive all the inhabitants who were willing to submit themselves, under the immediate protection of England, without touching one farthing of their property, or offering them the smallest violence or molestation – instead of which, not an estate in any of the islands, conquered or surrendered, but they have taxed shamefully and to an enormous amount to furnish prize-money for themselves and their troops. In their defence they plead – that having taken the islands by force, they had a right to plunder them, altogether, and that it was therefore a *lenity* and *mildness* in them to accept a *compensation* in lieu of the *whole*, which, by a conqueror's right, they might have taken. But this is utterly false in fact, and false in law – as the law of nations has been always understood – and as it certainly ought to be construed at this time particularly, when we are blaming the French so much for their extortions in Flanders and in Germany, and when it would highly become us therefore to hold ourselves out as an example of justice and moderation. The conduct pursued in this instance by Sir C. Grey and Sir J. J[ervis] forms a striking and most disgraceful contrast to the glory of their military achievements. The reduction of the West Indies, as far as our *arms* were concerned, is perhaps one of the most brilliant successes in our naval and military history, and does immortal credit to the troops and to the commanders who conducted them. But their subsequent oppression and rapacity, exercised as they were upon thousands, who, so far from resisting, did all in their power to further and promote our success, and gave themselves up voluntarily and eagerly to the protection of Great Britain – this throws as foul a disgrace upon our name and conduct, as not even the glory of the conquest can efface or compensate. It is to be hoped indeed that the exactions may not have been *levied* – since Pitt told us that immediate orders had been sent from Government here to forbid them from proceeding to levy them, and to express in very strong terms their disapprobation of the measures taken in the imposition. But even if

[331] In April 1794 Sir Charles Grey and Sir John Jervis had captured Martinique, St Lucia, Guadaloupe, and other enemy islands in the West Indies

this prohibition should fortunately arrive in time to prevent the actual payment of the money – it cannot be soon enough to prevent, what must already in great part have taken place, the alienation of the minds of the inhabitants from the English nation and Government – which may probably lead them to be as active in endeavouring to get rid of us, as they were, for the most part, willing and eager to receive us. And if that disposition should get head amongst them, farewell our acquisitions in the West Indies! Nothing will then remain of the event in which we so much and so justly gloried, and from which we fondly promised ourselves so large and permanent advantages – except enormous ill-gotten fortunes to the Commanders of the expedition – whom it would be but a poor satisfaction to impeach some day or other for their misconduct.

You will of course never mention the subject of this conversation – nor these my reflections upon it, to anyone.

Since the time of its happening *Guadaloupe is lost* – and without any fresh reinforcements having come from France to retake it. If so – see there a *change in the minds of the inhabitants towards us* wth. a vengeance.

*29 [November]* Saturday morning. I intended to have returned to town, and had engaged myself to dine with Mr. Campbell and Ly. Caroline – but being much pressed to stay I could not very long resist, and so sent Fleming to town with an excuse to Mr. Campbell – and to bring any letters that he might find at my chambers; and to put one for Ashborne into the post. He brought me back among others two or three from Charles Ellis and Ly. Malmesbury, informing me that they were to leave town for Wootton on Sunday, and denouncing eternal wrath against me if I failed to come there early in the week. Lord Gower and Ly. S[utherlan]d went to town to look at a house – but returned, as you may suppose, to dinner. In the meantime I paid a visit to Ly. Bristol, and passed great part of the morning with her and Ly. Louisa. What remained I dedicated to a visit to Putney,[332] where I had not been for God knows how long. I looked over the fields and peeped into the house – and was surprized to see how small everything was grown. I went also to the church yard where I followed poor Stratty[333] to his grave, now seven years ago. I found his tomb – with a simple inscription on it; and a tablet on the other side, which *was* to have been filled with one more splendid and more worthy of him in verse. So Sheridan promised repeatedly – but the promise has never been fulfilled.

I got back again time enough to dress before Ld. G[owe]r and Ly. S[utherlan]d came. There came nobody else to dinner but that old

[332] Where his uncle, Stratford Canning, had lived
[333] Stratford Canning had d. May 1787

Genl. Grant whom I had met yesterday at Dundas's – and he is so much one of the family that he is no interruption to a comfortable talk – and does not prevent our dining in the little library, with dumb waiters. In the evening indeed he plays picquet – but that is only so much the worse for Lord G. – who plays with him – and so much the better for Ly. S. and me, whom it leaves quite to ourselves.

*30 [November]* Sunday, however, even this interruption to a tête-à-tête was removed. Genl. Grant went away after breakfast – and the morning proving delightfully wet, so that there was neither stirring out nor receiving visitors (except Mr. Huskisson, formerly Ld. G.'s Secretary at Paris, now in Dundas's Office, who came for a quarter of an hour, and brought us all the news) – we were alone the whole day, with our books and our talk, without once separating, but for about twenty minutes before dinner to dress; and without moving except from the large library in which we sit, to the little one which adjoins to it, and where we dine so snugly without attendants – and then back again to the library, where the evening passed exactly as the morning had done. This was a day.

I had almost forgotten to tell you how much Ly. S. excels in that art, which I have more than once practised upon her with success – of writing sham letters. I wish you could have seen one which was delivered to Genl. Grant yesterday after dinner, as from Mr. Dundas, offering him the Govt. of Corsica[334] and a red ribband, and desiring him to prepare to set out immediately – the hand and style precisely like Dundas's – and the poor old Genl. for a time in a great quandary what to think of the offer, and what answer to return to it.

*1 Decr.* All days cannot be like yesterday, and so this morning I set out on my return to town. I called on Woodcock by appointment, to talk over his affairs with him. O! What a dreadful thing is the breaking up of a family by the death of its chief supporter, and what a painful thing it is to have nothing better to offer to a friend in distress than one's advice!

I dined with the Master of the Rolls – where were Bootle – C. Moore – O. Markham – Newbolt and Mrs. N. and Wallace. In the evening I went with Wallace first to Ly. Payne's – and aftwds. to Jenkinson's where we supped.

*2. [December]* Tuesday. Frere breakfasted with me. I called in the morning at Lord Abercorn's, to enquire whether he is at his house near London – meaning, if he were there, to pay him a visit of a day, before I leave London. I ought to have gone before. To-day he was in town it seems – so I can get no answer till to-morrow – on which

---

[334] He was already gov. of Stirling Castle, a less demanding one than the joke appointment suggested here

day I must go there if at all – for I have written to C. Ellis, promising
to be at Wootton on Friday.

I dined with Jenkinson – where were Mr. Lewis (of the War Office)
and his son[335] – who was at Ch. Ch. in our time – and Wallace.
Wallace and I stayed all the evening and supped with him. There is
news to-day of Guadaloupe's having been retaken by the French. The
Duke of York is expected home daily from the army: it is to be hoped,
not to return, for his unpopularity is terrible.

*3. [December]* Wednesday morning I called on Lord Abercorn –
and found him at home. He is not going to the Priory (that is the
name of his house near Harrow) to-day – so I have settled to go there
some day after my return to town. We are very good friends indeed –
though I am afraid his politicks are not at present strictly ministerial.

I dined at a Coffee house with Frere and Bobus and Easley Smith –
and afterwards went to the Play with Frere and supped at Carey
Street in my way home.

*4. [December]* Thursday – Frere breakfasted with me. I dined at
Mr. Pitt's with the Duke of Montrose[336] – Steele – Long[337] (sec. of the
Treasury), Mr. Hopkins[338] (an old Ld. of the Treasury), Mr. W.
Grant[339] (a lawyer and very good speaker in Parlt.) Mr. Smyth (Ld.
of the Treasury), Mr. Moreton Pitt[340] (a country gentleman) – and
Wallace. The dinner was pleasant enough – and a considerable quantity of wine was discussed – so much port by Pitt himself particularly,
that I think we left him a little unfit for business. I returned home to
do a good many little jobs before my journey – among other things
to send a set of the Microcosm to Ly. Sutherland – and 5th Friday
morng. I set out for Wootton.

*5. [December]* On Friday evening, Decr. 5th – after a cold and
tedious journey of about 60 miles, I arrived at 7 o'clock at Wootton –
and found Lady Malmesbury, Mrs. Robinson, Charles and Geo. Ellis
at dinner. It was pleasant to find such a party so occupied – and as
soon as I had thawed myself sufficiently I joined them with great
satisfaction – and took share first most ravenously of their dinner, and
afterwds. with more calmness, in their conversation. The time that

[335] Possibly David Lewis who matric. Christ Church, 23 Oct. 1788, aged 19. He was
subsequently rector of Mannington, Hereford
[336] Master of the Horse Dec. 1790–Mar. 1795; commr. Board of Control May 1791–
Oct. 1803
[337] Charles Long, 1st Baron Farnborough. M.P. Rye 1789–96; sec. to Treasury 1791–
1801
[338] Richard Hopkins (c. 1728–99). M.P. Queenborough 1790–6; lord of the Treasury
1791–7
[339] William Grant (1752–1832). M.P. New Windsor 1794–6; solicitor-general to the
Queen 1794–8
[340] William Morton Pitt (1754–1836). M.P. Dorset 1790–1826

passed at Wootton, passed so uniformly, as well as pleasantly, that
the description of one day will answer pretty nearly for the whole. I
need only say that on

6. *[December]* Saturday morning Mrs. Robinson went away, and
Sir Ralph and Lady Payne arrived – and then proceed to tell you
that this day and the whole of the following week down to Sunday
the 14th was spent in a manner which was more pleasant to experience
than it is lively to describe. The house is very sufficiently good – that
is – it has one large room, which next to the Gallery at Crewe is the
most *universal* sort of room that I know – but being only about a third
of the length, and better proportioned in breadth, is much warmer,
and better calculated for this season of the year than that at Crewe.
Adjoining to this large room, in which, as you may suppose, greatest
part of the day is passed – in which we breakfast, read, write, play
battledoor and shuttlecock in the morning, and cassino in the
evening – and sup at night – in short do everything but dine – and
play billiards – adjoining to this is the billiard room, which at night
is lit up with patent lamps – and on the other side of the billiard room
is the dining room – in which every day at about 1/2 pt. six is a table
covered with the best dinner and the best wines that one can find at
almost any table in England – and this I speak not on my own
authority but on that of Sir Ralph Payne, who being himself a very
exquisite giver of dinners, and a still more exquisite judge, pronounced
this to be his opinion – and to do him justice, proved his sincerity by
his performance every day. We rose at what hour we each liked best –
and came to our breakfast one after another, or all together, as it
happened. And here let me remark that this is the only house where
I have seen breakfast quite to my liking. At Trentham it is shocking –
at Crewe not quite so bad – but there is a helping, and slopping
*there*. Here – you find a large table with as many little separate
establishments of little teapot, cream-jug, sugar, tea &c. &c. – at
different parts of the table, as there are persons to breakfast, and in
the middle an urn with spouts looking E., W., N. and south – out of
which everybody helps themselves – makes their own arrangements,
and dispatch as silently and shortly and sulkily as you please, without
interfering one with another. After breakfast – letters received – and
written – newspapers – then billiards – battledoor – books – then a
walk if the weather permits – which however it seldom did permit in
that most execrable muddy county, to be extended beyond the gravel
walk – up and down which we used to trudge for two or three hours,
Sir Ralph assuring us that it was the only way to secure an appetite
for dinner. At 6 or 7 – dinner – and then billiards – cassino – and talk
and supper till bedtime. There was hunting two days – for the two

Ellises – but Sir Ralph's black sattins and star[341] were not calculated
for the field – and though I find it is reported in London that I was
seduced to the chace, and got a tumble, I have the best reason in the
world to know that it is a calumny.

This mode of life lasted till Sunday the 14th when Sir Ralph and
Lady Payne set off for London – meaning to make two days of the
journey. I thought their determination so wise that I was bent upon
accompanying them – but I was over-persuaded to stay on till Monday
morning – when it was suggested it would be very delightful to be up
at 6 – men and women (for Mrs. Robinson returned on Sunday to
accompany Lady M[almesbur]y to town) – and to set off pell-mell –
all at once – Charles, for Leicestershire, where he goes for more
hunting; and Ly. M., Mrs. R., George and I for town. I yielded to
persuasion – and accordingly Sir Ralph and Ly. Payne set off by
themselves – and left us there to talk them over when they were gone,
which we did very much to their praise. And if I have never spoken
fully of them till now it is fit you should know that our joint opinion
was that they are two of the best and worthiest people in the world.
Ly. Payne is a woman of fashion, more completely answering in every
point (except folly and vice) to that description than almost any
woman I know. She is a foreigner by birth (a Pole)[342] but married
very young, and has ever since (perhaps these 25 or 30 yrs.) lived in
England, in the very best company, knowing everybody and universally liked. Sir Ralph has his ridicules, particularly that of his
fondness for this *star* – but except in that point – unless the love of
good eating himself, and of giving it to others be a fault – I know
none that he has. He has lived long in the world – was many years in
Parliament, and in his younger days during Lord North's Administration, was Governor of the Leeward Islands, in which station he
acquitted himself very creditably. He knows everything, therefore,
and everybody, that has had anything to do in public or in fashionable
life for these many years – and is one of the most friendly and useful
persons in the world. It was at his table that Dundas and Lord
Loughborough met to concert the junction which has since taken
place between the D. of P.[ortland] and Pitt. If there was any one
question in the world that I wanted to have asked of anybody – I
should go to Sir Ralph – and he would get the answer for me. If there
was any man great or small, public or private, with whom I wanted
half an hour's conversation, but did not like to seek it – whom I
wanted to see, or hear talk, but did not wish to him to know that I

[341] He was cr. KB 18 Feb. 1771
[342] Lady Frances Lambertina Christiana Charlotte Harriet Theresa Payne was the
da. of Baron Heinrich Kolbel of Saxony

wanted it – I should go to Sir Ralph – and in a week's time I should be asked to dinner as if by accident, and the man whom I wished to meet would be asked *by accident* too.[343]

I hear Sir Ralph is going to be made an Irish peer[344] – and I wish he may with all my heart – not so much for the worth of the thing itself, as because it is probably that such an accession of title might decide an old relation of his,[345] who is immensely rich, and just dying, to leave Sir Ralph his fortune – and there are few men who would know better how to make use of a fortune, always excepting Charles Ellis.

Oh! I must not forget to tell you of C. Ellis – that I was a little solicitous to know whether or no *one* use that ought always to be made of riches had *occurred* to him – for if it had occurred I had no doubt of its being put in execution – but it is the sort of thing that generally suggests itself to a woman – but not so much to a young, unmarried man, with a French Maitre d'Hotel at the head of his establishment. I mean the *taking care of the poor* in the village near his house. I would not ask *him*, lest, if it should have escaped him hitherto he should think it a reproach, but I took an opportunity to enquire of Lady Malmesbury. 'Oh yes', said she – 'Charles has set about that in a *clumsy* way. He heard it talked of at Brookwood[346] – where it is done – as of course it is at all large and regular houses – but regularly and under the inspection of proper people, who select such objects as deserve relief and encouragement. But Charles was too proud to enquire particulars. I saw him catch at the idea – and was determined to let him go his own way – and so he has – for I find the first thing he did on coming down here was to throw the house open by general invitation on certain days to the whole neighbourhood without choice or exception – and if you will go to the back-door on such a day you may see all the poor of the country flocking round with their pitchers and pipkins. It was quite right and quite *like him* to set out in this way – but now that he has had his swing for a time, it will be right to teach him how to do it with more effect as well as economy – and so we are to have a consultation about it – and settle a regular plan for the distribution during his absence'. This satisfied me, as you may suppose.

I must not omit the substance of a conversation which passed between Charles and me – and aftwds. between him and Lady

[343] Payne had also invited William Windham, one of the leaders of the pro-war whigs, to dinner on 15 Aug. 1793 without telling him that Pitt was to be there, his object being to hasten the junction that eventually took place in July 1794, see *Thorne*, iv, 737
[344] He was cr. Baron Lavington 1 Oct. 1795
[345] Ralph Willett who left him only £1,500, see *Thorne*, iv, 738
[346] The Hampshire seat of the 1st Earl of Malmesbury

M[almesbury] upon another subject. I had heard so much in the course of the summer from different persons, from young as well as old, of the changes that were working in people's opinions about the War, that I scarcely knew whom to consider as stout and safe – especially as, to say the truth, the unexampled ill success of the campaign furnished to those who did not think very deeply upon the subject, a plausible and natural ground for calling out for peace. Under the impression of these sentiments I had, in writing to Charles Ellis, requested of him that he would give me an opportunity of seeing him, and having some conversation with him before the opening of Parliament (this was when Parlt. was expected to meet earlier) – upon this state of affairs – upon which subject I should be very sorry if our opinions should not agree. In answer to this I had received from him a warm and general assurance that he could not foresee any probability of our opinions ever materially differing. When we met at Wootton the subject of these letters was renewed. And one fine morning, as we were walking up and down the gravel walk of which I have made mention, and which runs before the windows of the great room – our conversation ran upon the War and publick affairs in general, into such length as to set Lady Malmesbury and Lady Payne (who were sitting in the great room, and before whose eyes therefore we were passing and repassing for the space, as they averred, of four hours) quite wild with curiosity – and I found afterwards that Lady M. had not let him rest till she had got every word of it from him. The result was the most perfect coincidence of sentiment upon every point in question – and the conclusion of the conversation on his part was that, after what had passed between us last year (which you may remember my stating to you at length) I need not have entertained any apprehensions of his dereliction of Ministry – for that, '*if* upon *public* grounds he did *not* fully agree with them (as in the present instance he *did*) *I knew* that there were *private* ties of a much stronger nature, which would keep him steady to the party to which *I* belonged'. You may imagine that I was pretty well contented with this declaration for himself – and you will understand too, how much more contented I must have felt when it was repeated to me a few days afterwards by Lady Malmesbury – who, in informing me that she had worked out of him all the particulars of our long conversation, repeated what he had declared to her as his determination – which was – 'that *I* need not have given myself so much trouble in talking over the propriety of the measures of Ad[inistratio]n, for that he was already of opinion that they were right – but that *if he had* ever entertained doubts upon the subject – I might have rested assured that *his* vote would never be given *against* the Party with which *my* interest and attachment went'.

But to quit Ch. Ellis and his house at last. On Monday morning we all rose and breakfasted by candle-light, and a dreary ridiculous business it was. We then set off – Charles Ellis towards Leicestershire – George Ellis and I in a curricle for the first two stages – (having sent on Fleming two hours earlier in the morning for the greater expedition) – and Lady M. and Mrs. R. following us in their chaise – towards town. We had no adventures by the way – but when we came within four miles of town – we found ourselves immersed in so thick a fog that literally speaking we could not see our hand when stretched out before us. I had heard of such a thing before, but had so little idea of it that I had considered the accounts of it as much exaggerated. But the reality went infinitely beyond them. The situation of us and our chaise (for we were now in a chaise, not a curricle) was very disagreeable and somewhat perilous. And soon after we got upon the stones we dismounted to grope our way – and after many turnings and windings and jostlings I made shift to guide the post boy to the Temple – where to my great comfort the first voice that saluted my ears was that of Fleming – who had come in Geo. Ellis's chaise with his man – and had got out earlier than we did, and found his way providentially to Paper Buildings about five minutes before my arrival. I dressed and then went, as I had engaged to do, to dine at Mrs. Robinson's in Privy Garden – though scarcely expecting to find them safely arrived. Beyond my hopes, however, I did find them – and so after all our perils and fatigue Ly. M. and Mrs. R. and George and I sat ourselves down to a comfortable dinner – and chatted after it till we agreed it was time to find our way through the fog to our respective beds.

*16. [December]* Tuesday morning my first business was to call on Jenkinson, to enquire into the state of an affair which I have never yet mentioned to you, though it has been going on this long time – but which, as it has got abroad into the world, and is now in some degree of maturity, I may mention without any breach of confidence or of propriety. You must know then that Jenkinson is, and has been since last winter, most devoutely in love with Lady Louisa Hervey. His passion grew, as most passions do, so imperceptibly that it had gotten entire possession of him almost before he was aware of it himself, much more before he had thought of making anybody acquainted with it. As soon as he did feel himself convinced how much in love he was – he made me his confidant. This was I should think about April – and from that time forward I used to receive from him regular intelligence of his progress with Lady Louisa (and she knew that I and nobody else, did so) – which was such – that when I left town for the summer – though she had not yet absolutely said *yes*, I felt pretty much assured that she would [not] very long defer saying so. During the summer I heard nothing from him – for Jenkinson never writes when he can possibly help it. At my return to town in November I found that all had been going on very prosperously – that the thing was settled as far as Ly. Louisa's assent was concerned – and that nothing was wanting to complete their union and happiness but the approbation of their respective fathers. It had been thought more prudent, and more delicate to Lord Hawkesbury that nothing should be said to him upon the subject until Lord Bristol's inclination had been sounded – Ld. B. being a man for whose possible whims and caprices there was no answering; and being at this time so far off and so uncertain in his motions, that had Ld. H. been previously spoken to, there might have ensured a painful and perplexing interval after *his* consent should be obtained, before anything could be known of Ld. B.'s opinion – and perhaps when his opinion did come it might be such a one as to throw everything into confusion – whereas, if he was first won over, and all his doubts and prejudices, if he should chance to entertain any, done away – Jenkinson might then go to Ld. H. with Ld. B.'s consent in his hand; and so having saved his father the uneasiness and perplexity of waiting after *his* consent was given, for that of Ld. B. – would no doubt receive his thanks for this delicate attention to his dignity and peace of mind – would obtain his full approbation without difficulty – and there would be at once a happy consummation. This plan was no doubt very nicely contrived and very finely reasoned – in pursuance of it Lady Louisa had written to her father – and they were then (in Novr.) impatiently expecting his answer. It had not yet arrived when I went out of town to Charles Ellis's. This morning I went to Jenkinson – he told me that Lord Bristol's letter was come – that it was favourable beyond their warmest expectations – that in consequence of it, he had written to his father – an interview had taken place on Saturday in which Lord H. urged indeed many very loud objections to the match – which he seemed to consider as imprudent and ineligible in many respects – but concluded the conversation with desiring that Jenkinson would turn these considerations in his mind – and give them what weight he thought they merited – that if after due reflection he should not think them of sufficient weight to alter his intentions, and that his happiness was unalterably fixed upon the marriage – why then he (Ld. H.) must give away. He seemed a little offended at having been kept so long out of the secret – and did not give much attention to the reasons of delicacy on which that part of Jenkinson's conduct towards him was founded. He said that it had indeed come to his ears in the course of last year – but that he had not believed it. His wish, he confessed, had always been that J. should not marry before he was 30 – *unless he married a fortune* indeed (for that would alter the case). He did not much like the *connection* – but of Lady Louisa herself he had heard the highest character. He hoped upon the whole that J. would be able to get the better of his inclinations – but concluded as I have before said. This conversation upon the whole struck me as being pretty much such as one might have expected from a man of Ld. H.'s character, hearing for the first time a piece of intelligence, which, though he had no right to be displeased with it, yet it certainly appeared, was not delightful to his feelings – as not very favourable indeed, nor indicative of a very speedy and sanguine acquiescence in his son's wishes – but certainly as not giving room, on the other hand, to look for a positive and final opposition to them.

I dined with Lady Malmesbury tête-à-tête. It was in the long conversation which this tête-à-tête afforded that we talked over C. Ellis, and I learnt from her particulars which I have already mentioned. In the evening I returned to Jenkinson and resumed with him the discussion of his affairs.

*17. [December]* Wednesday morning I called on Mr. Pitt to let him know that I was in town, but having nothing particular to say to him I did not call at such an hour as to be admitted. I dined at Sir R. Payne's – with Lady Malmesbury, Mrs. Robinson and Geo. Ellis – and Captn. Payne[347] – who is just setting out to bring over the Princess of Wales. In the evening I went to Jenkinson's to sup and to discuss, as before. He is to see his father to-morrow.

*18. [December]* Thursday. Frere breakfasted with me. Before he was gone Jenkinson came in – so miserable and woe-begone in his appearance, that it was evident his late conversation with his father had not confirmed the hopes which we had thought ourselves warranted to entertain from his first reception of the matter. Having got Frere to go away I proceeded to enquire into particulars. The result appeared to be that Lord H. was furiously and obstinately determined against giving his consent; and positively commands J. to think of the matter no more. His manner is quite changed since the first conversation – nothing mild – nothing indulgent – nothing reasonable – but all authoritative and inflexible. His old objections – of the connexion – of the prudential reasons (and yet Lord B. will give her £10,000) and of his wish that J. should not marry so young, are much fortified – and he is fifty times more violent than before upon the subject of his having been so long kept out of the secret. This comes of their *delicacy* towards him, from which we all promised ourselves

[347]John Willett Payne (1752–1803), half-bro. of Sir Ralph Payne and M.P. Huntingdon 1787–96. Apptd. Cpt. 1780, he became the private secretary of the Prince of Wales in 1785 and in Dec. 1794 was put in command of the squadron escorting the future Pcss. of Wales to England, see *Thorne*, iv, 736

such fine effects. What to do? I, who am rather a rebel in my opinions upon matters of this kind, am for J.'s speaking out – and saying at once *I will*. But perhaps it might be more adviseable to *manage* a little first. Our first motion was to send an express to Fred. Hervey at Wimbledon desiring him to come up to town immediately, and meet in consultation at Jenkinson's house. Next I set off to see Lady Jane Dundas (Dundas's wife, who is Lady Louisa's dearest friend, and as well as D. himself takes infinitely great interest in the success of the match with J.) to report to her the result of the interview of this morning; and with her I found Lady Erne. They were both astonished at the sudden alteration of Lord H.'s tone. And after much condolence and deliberation I left them, to return to J. – whom I then sent to tell his own story to them and express his own feelings – promising to join him and Fred. Hervey at 5 o'clock in Conduit Street. I did so – we dined together in rather a melancholy way – though I could at times hardly help laughing a little inwardly at the *lover*-like sighs and groanings of poor J. F. H[ervey] returned to Wimbledon to convey the sad tidings to his sister. I sat with J. till night and we then parted without having settled the line of conduct which he ought to adopt, I being for *vigorous* measures – and he relying rather more on the affection of his father and his hopes that he would at length be brought round by persuasion.

*19. [December]* Friday morning Sir Ralph Payne called on me – while Jenkinson was here talking over his grievances. It occurred to J. and me that Sir R. P. being, as I have before described him to be, one of the very best-natured men in the world, and ready to undertake anything for the service of a friend – would be the man of all others to talk Ld. H[awkesbury] over and bring him to reason. So Jenk. went away and left me to open the case to Sir R. which I had no sooner done than he entered most warmly into all our feelings and interest about it – and offered his services in any way that they might be useful. There is at least this advantage in employing him – that if he should not be able to bend Lord H., he and Ly. P. see all the world – and will get all the world on Jenkinson's side in the dispute.

I dined at Ld. Stafford's – none but the family. Afterwards I went to sup with Jenkinson.

*20. [December]* Jenkinson, you see has occupied almost all my time and attention since my return to town – and indeed his situation is so very perplexing, and the agitation which he suffers, so great, that I do give myself up as much as I can to the consideration of his concerns, and to soothing and comforting his affliction. To-day however I was obliged to set apart for the execution of a promise made long ago to Lord Abercorn, that I would visit him at the Priory (a place of his about 10 miles from town where he lives in great state and receives all comers) and which I was the more anxious to do, as I had heard that he was *wavering* in politicks, and thought he might very probably attribute any accidental omission of civility on my part to design. I called on Jenkinson in my way out of town – and got to the Priory by dinner-time. I found a multitude of people, but none, I think, whom it would much interest you to hear described – nor any, whom you have heard me mention before, except Steele (the Paymaster). I stayed at the Priory all

21 *[December]* Sunday, and on

22 *[December]* Monday morning I returned to town. I found a note on my table from Boringdon saying that he was coming to town that day, and wanted me to dine with him. I found also one from Ly. Sutherland – informing me of their having taken a house in Albemarle Street, to which they were to come up by Monday – the day before the meeting of Parliament.

I dined with Boringdon tête-à-tête and talked over with him at great length the whole of present politics. He is, I am sorry to say, one of those who have got their heads puzzled about peace – and though wishing well to Pitt, and detesting Opposition, he is yet disposed to vote against the continuance of the war, on which Pitt's judgement is fixed, and his character and situation staked – and this he thinks he may do, consistently with his desire to keep Pitt in and the Opposition out. I have been trying to shew him the impracticability of this conduct – as well as to convince him of the necessity of going on with the war till we can have something like security for peace, if we should make it – but hitherto without effect. It gives me great concern to find him in this temper – more especially as I am afraid that Morpeth and Leveson may be a little infected by it (for they live constantly together) and it would be a heartbreaking thing to have our young set split, the very first parliamentary campaign that we meet. My comfort is that Charles Ellis is *firm*; Jenkinson and Wallace of course are so.

Did I ever tell you a matter of accusation against me, that I first heard from the Dean of Christ Church, as having been related to him by good authority – but which authority he would not give up? I heard it again to-night from Boringdon – he too had it from authority. I cannot think how – or what it means – but the world is very ill-natured. The accusation is this – that[348] my manner with Pitt in the House of Commons is too familiar – that whereas other persons, country gentlemen and others, some of great consequence, and who have known and supported Mr. Pitt for years – treat him with the utmost respect and distance; and if they venture to address him at all,

---

[348] 'that my ... be altered' (p. 169), printed in *Marshall*, 90–1

do it in a manner the most humble and deferent, I, it seems, stand in no awe whatever – but talk to him without reserve or hesitation at all times, and laugh and make jokes – and *once* was seen, when I wanted to speak to him, and he was looking another way, to put my hand upon his shoulder. How can you conceive a more silly thing to trouble people's heads than this? I really scarcely know what part of my conduct it may be that gives so much offence – and as for the one flagrant fact of putting my hand upon the shoulder, it may have happened, for ought I know, not once but twenty times, as it is the most natural way of calling anybody's attention, who is sitting near you, and to whom you must not cry out by name – as that would interrupt the debate. I know indeed that I have, with people whom I like, old or young, great or small, something of a *caressing* manner (I think I must call it so, for I do not recollect any other word to express it) and so have a great many other people – a great many have it *not* – and with *that* class it is not right to make use of it. Recollect among your acquaintance any ten or twelve persons – and you will find that there are some whom you never meet without shaking hands, perhaps, or some other trifling salutation, if you meet them even ten times a day. You will find others whom you like perhaps in all respects equally well – but with whom you never think of exchanging any sort of *corporal* civility – even if you have not seen them for a week. Do you understand me? If you do, you will comprehend that one mistake of these good folks who are out of humour with me, is that they consider Mr. Pitt, naturally enough, as one of the latter class, the *non-shakers* – whereas he is in fact a very hearty, *salutation-giving, shake-handy* sort of person – and one therefore whom I feel it as natural to take by the arm or to *touch upon the shoulder even* (which is the great offence) as I do with Leveson or Frere or anybody that I most like, and towards whom I act most familiarly. But if it be wrong, it must be altered.

From Boringdon's I went to sup with Jenkinson. I found that nothing material had passed within these three days.

*23. [December]* Tuesday. Frere breakfasted with me. I received a note from Mr. Dundas, saying that he wished very particularly for some conversation with me, and desiring that I would, if possible, come and take my dinner and my bed to-night at Wimbledon. I had engaged with Boringdon to dine at Whitehall, but, guessing that what Dundas had to say, respected Jenkinson and Lady Louisa, I sent to put off my engagement – and set out for Wimbledon, where I arrived by dinner-time. There was nobody there but Dun[das], Lady Jane and some Dundasses and other Scotch relations, who live in the house with them. In the evening I had a very long conversation with Dundas, from which I learnt that he felt himself extremely interested in all that concerned Lady Louisa, and little less so for Jenkinson – and that it was his decided opinion, as well as Mr. Pitt's with whom he had talked much upon the subject, and who is himself a very warm favourer of the match, that there was little hope of Ld. H. being softened by entreaty and submission, but that if Jenkinson hoped to gain the point, it must be by vigour and determination. This coincided perfectly with my own opinion.

*24. [December]* Wednesday morning, I called at Lady Bristol's and had a conversation with Lady Louisa. She is disposed to act in every way as may best conduce to Jenkinson's happiness – with Lord H.'s consent, if any means can be found to obtain it – and I am not without hopes that she might be persuaded to *wave that* condition if his obdurate inflexibility should make it necessary.

I returned to town and related to Jenkinson the result of both my visits. There was another visit at Wimbledon which I should probably have made, not for his sake, but my own, and which you might well be surprized at my omitting – but Ld. G[ower] and Ly. Suth[erland] were absent upon a visit elsewhere.

I called this morning on Mr. Pitt – but without finding him at home. I dined at Lord Stafford's with only the family and Lord Garlies (son of Lord Galloway, Ly. Stafford's brother) – a sailor – and who has behaved very gallantly in his profession – particularly during the late expedition in the West Indies – rattling but sensible and good-humoured. In the evening I went to Jenkinson and supped with him. On my return home at night I found a note from Mr. Pitt, saying he should be at home at one to-morrow.

*25. [December]* Thursday morning little Charles Reddish called on me, that I might send him to Cowley to be measured for mourning on the death of his brother. Did I tell you that his brother – a boy about a year younger than himself, and who was at school in Yorkshire, had been very ill some time – and that about ten days ago I received the account of his death? This is another dreadful stroke to my poor mother in a very short space of time. I went at one o'clock according to my appointment to Downing Street. I had a long conversation with Mr. Pitt, and he shewed me the rough draft of the King's Speech, which he was preparing for Tuesday. It is spirited and resolute. Holland is gone, but war we must have, unless we are contented with such a peace as Holland is likely to make for itself. Pitt is stout and undismayed. As soon as I had left him, having previously settled to call on him again on Saturday or Sunday, I set out for Wanstead to spend my Christmas, according to a promise made when last I was there. I got there to dinner. There was Harry and T. Sheridan. I made my arrangements on leaving town for staying over to-morrow, though I will confess I almost wished I had not done so, when I found that instead of a quiet snug family party, which I had anticipated with great satisfaction – we were to have about *forty* strangers to-morrow evening – every one of whom they assured me were very pleasant – but *being strangers* was enough to make me disrelish their company.

*26. [December]* All Friday I stayed at Wanstead – and passed the morning, and dined comfortably with *ourselves*. But in the evening came the company, not quite 40 indeed, but literally *nine* persons, eight of whom I had never seen before – and poor Hetty was surprized – and I believe rather mortified, that I could not find it all very agreeable. But for my life I could not. I did my best however by playing for four hours at Cassino – with an old lady of ninety – and then came supper – and then most happily came the time for going to bed.

*27. [December]* Saturday morning I left Wanstead – and left poor Hetty, I am afraid, not so satisfied with my visit as I could have wished her to be – because I could not take share in the jumping and skipping and other animal exertions of Tom Sheridan and Harry and the seven Miss Bs.[349] She quoted against me the romps which she had heard of at Ashborne – and it was in vain to urge the difference of a society in which one knows and likes everybody – and one, where for three that one loves, there are nine that never come in one's way before. It seems it had been all planned as a fête; and I came down looking for quiet, placid conversation, for a talking over of all our old stories and family matters – for which Hetty always complains she never can find opportunity with me – and sure enough she never will if there is such a festivity whenever I go to her. I had scarce time to inform her of Sheridan's approaching marriage with Miss Ogle, daughter of the Dean of Winchester – which is in contemplation, as I am informed from very good authority, and wants nothing but the old man's consent to confirm it.[350] It is a subject to Hetty, as you may suppose, of great surprize and concern.

On my arrival at my chambers I was delighted to find Frere sitting by my fire. I kept him all day – and we dined comfortably tête-à-tête. At night I went for five minutes to the Opera – and from thence with Wallace to sup at Jenkinson's. Wallace, is *now* in the secret of J.'s situation.

*28. [December]* Sunday morning I called on Mr. Pitt and found a message left for me – that he was just then very busy – but that if I could call at about 4 o'clock he should be happy to see me. At a little

[349] If all the Patricks were present there would have been 4 Miss Bs or Elizabeths, namely, Hetty's sister and her own, Robert's and Paul's daughters. The identity of the other 3 has not been established

[350] R.B. Sheridan m. Hester Jane Ogle, a da. of the Dean of Winchester on 27 April 1795

after 4 therefore in my way out to dinner, I called again – and [351] talked over with him all the material points of the debate for Tuesday[352] which occurred to me – saw the Speech, which was now finished – and happening to ask him who was to move, and who to second the Address, he informed me that Sir Ed. Knatchbull, member for Kent, was to move – but that a seconder was not yet fixed. 'He will have but short notice', said I. 'Very short indeed' replied he, 'for whoever he is, he must be dining in this house by about this time to-morrow'. From this conference I went to dine at Lord Stafford's – where were Boringdon, Morpeth and Granville Leveson, who came to town a day or two ago. After dinner the conversation turning upon the debate of Tuesday, everybody was guessing at the mover and seconder of the Address in the House of Commons. In the House of Lords they were known to be Ld. Camden and Ld. Bessborough – and as I had just been with Mr. Pitt, it was supposed I could let them into the secret of the H. of C. I repeated what had passed between us on the subject, and certainly at that time had as little notion as anybody with whom I was talking, how nearly I was interested in it. In the evening I went to the Abp. of York's, where I found many persons, and among them the Abp. himself, upon the same topic – I was applied to for information – and I could tell them no more than I knew, that Sir E. Knatchbull was to move, but who to second, was undetermind. Little did I think that the first thing I should find on my return home would be a note from Pitt in nearly these terms. 'In the uncertainty of finding a good seconder, I should be very much obliged to you if you would undertake it. I think indeed that I should have rather wished you to take your part in the course of the debate, but I see so much use in having the matter well stated at the beginning, that &c. &c.' The first thing that struck me upon reading this – was how foolishly mysterious I should appear to all the people with whom I had conversed this night upon the subject of the Address, and how difficult I should find it to persuade them that I was in fact as ignorant as I pretended to be. The next thing was the difficulty of the undertaking itself; and the awkardness of performing it in *a dress coat*. These and other reflections contributed to make my repose of Sunday night less refreshing than it ought to have been preparatory to making a speech of such importance.

29. *[December]* Monday morning Frere came to breakfast with me; and received with surprize the account of the task which was imposed on me. I could not stay long with him to discuss the nature of it at that time, as I had to call on Mr. Pitt – and talk over with him the

---

[351] 'and talked ... importance', printed in *Marshall*, 76–7
[352] On the Address of Thanks for the King's Speech

line to be taken in explaining the Address; and also to assist in
preparing it. I[353] called therefore accordingly, and the Address was
prepared – a process not very difficult as it consists only in turning
the King's Speech into the second person instead of the first, and re-
echoing the sentiments, and, as nearly as can be done consistently
with grammar, the words, which he has delivered. I lamented most
feelingly the necessity which I had heard there was, for being full-
dressed the next day in the House of Coms. Pitt was of opinion that
it might be dispensed with – but Long (the Secretary of the Treasury)
averring that to come in a frock to second an Address would be such
a departure from the established usage of Parlt. as in these times to
threaten the downfall of the Constitution, I submitted – stipulating
only that I would put off the evil as long as possible, and would not
therefore come full-dressed to the dinner at Pitt's to-day (where my
attendance as he had said yesterday was necessary, to proceed from
thence to the Cockpit.[354]

I returned home calling on Frere in my way, and bringing him
with me – and there, going over, once for all, the sort of train of
argument that I intended to pursue, and appealing to his judgement
(than whom nobody has better) for the force of such and such a way
of stating, or such and such a way of illustrating my subject. Having
done this, I determined to dismiss all thoughts of the matter from my
mind, and not to recur to it again, till I entered the doors of the House
of Commons.

At 5 I went to Pitt's dinner – which was attended by all the Privy
Councillors and official people in the House of Commons – amounting
to about thirty – and getting into a knot at the top of the table –
consisting of Pitt – Windham – Ryder – the Speaker (who is a very
pleasant man and good Classic) and Ld. Gower. I do not remember
to have had a pleasanter dinner for a long time. After dinner – about
nine o'clock, comes the news that the Cockpit (which is a room in the
Treasury, adjoining to Mr. Pitt's house) was filling with members.
We all get up – and drink our coffee and set forward – to hear Pitt
read the Speech and the Address. In the middle of the room is a long
table, round which are crowded all the members, who are friends of
Govt. At the upper end – Pitt and the Speaker take their stand – the
mover at their right hand – the seconder at their left. Mr. Pitt reads
the Speech over twice – then the Address once and concludes with
saying 'This Address, gentlemen, Sr. E. K. has kindly undertaken to
move and Mr. C. to second'. And so the ceremony ends.

[353] 'I called ... innocence' (p. 174), printed in *Marshall*, 77–8
[354] The Cockpit was a room in the Treasury where supporters of the administration
heard the King's Speech and the Address

From the Cockpit I went with Lord Gower to Whitehall – and there finding Lady Sutherland I went with them to see their new house in Albemarle Street – which is small but very pretty – and I trust they will live at home a great deal, and be very comfortable people to go to. Their supper was coming up, and looking so nice, in her little dressing-room, which is the only room yet quite finished – that I could hardly resist staying, though I was under a promise to sup with Jenkinson. I went away however to keep my engagement. From Jenkinson and Wallace, whom I found with him, I had many reproaches to undergo for having kept my undertaking of to-morrow so profound a secret. I had been overwhelmed before to-night, at Whitehall, with reflections upon my hypocrisy at dinner yesterday in pretending to know so little about the seconder of the Address, and had great difficulty there, and almost as much with Jenk. and Wallace, to clear my innocence.

Jenkinson's affairs stand still. He has written to his father again – without any good effect. It has been settled now, as the most likely method to rouse Ld. H.[awkesbury] – that he should stay away from Parliament under the plea 'that the state of his spirits is such as to render him unequal to any parliamentary exertion, and that the only hopes which he can have of being again able to exert himself, rested on the chance of his father's being brought to consent to his happiness'.

This plan I mentioned to Mr. Pitt and to Mr. Dundas – and they both agreed in thinking that it was more likely to work upon Lord H. than almost any other – as in his mind the pride which he feels in his son's consequence, is a passion much more powerful, and to which it is much more prudent to appeal, than his affection. In pursuance of this plan Jenkinson declared to his father that his health and spirits making it absolutely necessary for him to absent him from Parlt., he is going to-morrow morning into the country – and this declaration is to be conveyed to Ld. H. in a note to-morrow – which he will receive just about the time that he fancies Jenkinson going down to the House, and preparing to drown the thoughts of his love in politicks. For on that remedy Ld. H. relies – and we think that the absolute failure of it will be a thunderstroke to him.

*30. [December]* Tuesday[355] morning I got up rather late after a night of less rest than reflection – and sent Fleming with my dress black clothes to Wallace's house in Clarges Street – where about two o'clock I followed him – dressed myself – and about half-past three went down with Wallace to the House of Commons. The apprehensions which I felt on this day, though by no means equal to those of my first appearance, yet were not small. To open the Session – as it were –

[355] 'Tuesday morning. ... Lords and Commons', (p. 176) printed in *Marshall*, 78–80

to get up in cold blood, with everybody expecting one with nothing preceding in the debate to answer, no warmth excited in the audience to animate one's feelings, is a situation very embarrassing. And the task which I had undertaken, in a time so difficult and disastrous, of stating the grounds of the continuance of the War, and laying the foundation as it were, of the debate – and upon which the whole question of such magnitude would rest – appeared to me a task of considerable moment, and the rather, as I found that everybody about me looked upon it in that view. There was a little skirmishing conversation before the business of the Address began[356] – which though it was in some degree distressing, as it kept me in hot water much longer than I had expected – yet perhaps was upon the whole not amiss, as it in the same degree warmed the House and broke the silence. Sir Edward, my worthy mover, rose, and talked of 'old England' and sundry other topics – with great fluency. Then he read the Address[357] – and then upon the Speaker's queston of 'Who seconds this Address?', up rose I. The faults which had been most frequently attributed to me in the course of last Session were too rapid a pronunciation and too violent action – so I set out determined if possible to avoid these extravagancies and accordingly proceeded with caution and good head through half a dozen long rounded sentences till I got towards the marrow of the subject. I believe my caution may have forsaken me a little in the subsequent course of my speech – but I fancy never to any very violent degree – as I certainly never lost the complete possession of myself – and I have indeed since had the satisfaction to hear from many quarters that if not completely reformed in those particulars, it was at least plain that I had attended to the advice which had been given me, and had gone a good way towards a reformation. I spoke for about three quarters of an hour – and I have every reason to believe with success proportionate to my greater self-possession, and to the desire which I felt to be successful.[358]

[356] Sheridan objected to the first reading of the Clandestine Outlawries Bill which customarily preceded the debate on the King's Speech and he, and subsequently Fox, introduced the topics of the suspension of Habeas Corpus, the treason trials and the junction between ministers and the Portland whigs, see *Parl. Hist.*, xxxi, cols. 994–1005

[357] The Address was devoid of any stirring reflections or prognostications and, against the background of the reverses in Flanders and the expected capitulation of the United Provinces, exhorted the country to continue the war and, by implication, not to consider a peace settlement, see *Parl. Hist.*, xxxi, cols. 1006–8

[358] C.'s speech was directed against those who felt that the downfall of the Jacobins in France (the Jacobin Club closed on 12 Nov. 1794), opened the way for peace negotiations. His main points were: (a) there was no guaranty that the Jacobins's successors could provide a more stable form of government; (b) there could therefore be no secure peace; and (c) that the French deserved a more stable form of government than either the Jacobins or their supposedly more moderate successors could provide, see *Parl. Hist.*, xxxi, cols. 1009–16

Wilberforce, who answered me, did it with the handsomest acknowledgements &c &c. Pitt – who spoke soon after him, went over almost the same grounds that I had taken, adopting confessedly the topics of my speech, and nearly the method of my arrangement – and Fox, by the angriness of some of his allusions to what I had said, showed me that in one or two material points, I had anticipated exactly (as I meant to do) what he would have said – and taken out of his mouth some topics of abuse (particularly respecting predictions &c.)[359] which he would have been glad to have had left untouched for himself. Windham and Pitt and Dundas sat below me – and turning round to me when I sat down, 'This was exactly the right *tone* to take – it could not have been stated better' – and so, as I have before told you, I feel myself most completely satisfied, and as the event has turned out, would not for the world but have had the opportunity which seconding the Address gave me, though I had looked forward to it as a thing nowise desireable. The only thing that I had to regret on that night was a most violent cold, which I caught in passing to and fro between the Houses of Lords and Commons. In the House of Lords Ld. Abercorn spoke – in a manner rather unfriendly to Ministry – but did not vote against us. Boringdon spoke too – but not so decidedly as to pledge himself either way. I hope with care we may yet save him. Our division, 246 to 73. They gain abt. a dozen – but still we are 3 and 1/2 to 1. After the debate I supped with Dundas at his house in Somerset Place in may way home.

*31. [December]* Wednesday morning I lay in bed some time to recover myself from the fatigue of yesterday, and to indemnify myself in some degree for the want of rest which I had unavoidably experienced on the two preceding nights. Frere came to breakfast with me, and to tell me how well he thought I had spoken – for he was in the Gallery to hear me. Bobus Smith would have been there had he been in town. But he was obliged to go out of town a day or two ago to see his father at Bath. Mr. Debrett called on me to request that I would correct a copy of my speech for his Parliamentary Register.[360]

At the House of Commons there was nothing but the Report of the Address, which was ordered to be presented to the King to-morrow.

[359] C. had criticised Fox and the Opposition for predicting the defection of Britain's allies, Prussia and the United Provinces, see *Parl. Hist.*, xxxi, col. 1010 and for Fox's response, col. 1055

[360] The version of C. 'speech in Debrett's *Parl. Reg.*, 2nd series, vol. 40, pp. 20–7 differs from that in *Parl. Hist.*, above, in the opening statements. In the former, while the underlying argument is the same, he is harder on the failures of the allies and the extremism of the Jacobins. It therefore seems likely that he did 'doctor' the opening passages for Debrett but left the rest substantially the same either because he found it satisfactory or because he ran out of time. The versions in *Woodfall*, vol. 5, 78–82 and *The Senator*, vol. 11, 61–5 are digests of the longer versions in the above two sources

I dined at Boringdon's – where were Morpeth, Granville Leveson, C. Ellis, Fred. North, and Sir C. Hamilton[361] and Captn. Pole,[362] two Navy officers. From Boringdon's I went with C. Ellis to call on Jenkinson – who is not yet gone out of town, tho' he proposes going almost immediately, having written to his father to that effect. There we found Wallace, and I should have liked to stay and sup but that my cold was so bad that I felt it much more prudent to go home to bed.

*1st January* Thursday morning[363] I felt a very strong disposition to stay at home and nurse my cold, instead of encreasing it by going full dressed to the House of Commons, and from thence with the Address to St. James's. But on these occasions the attending of the Seconder, it seems, is indispensably necessary. And so, much against my will, I got up and dressed myself – and went down to the House. From the House we set out in procession at about 1/2 past three for St. James's, the Speaker in his gingerbread coach leading the way, Sir E. Knatchbull and I following next in his chariot, and then as many other members as thought it worth while to join in the procession. This being New Year's Day, and the Court in consequence much crowded, we waited hours in a cold anti-chamber before we were admitted with our Address – not much to the emolument of my cold, which was every moment perceptibly encreasing. At length our gracious Sovereign was ready to receive us. We marched up through the apartments – the Speaker in the front was supported by the Mover on his right hand and the Seconder on his left – next to us the Ministers, and then the crowd of the House of Commons – bowing – bowing – bowing – till we approach the footstool of the great chair in which the King is seated, surrounded by his courtiers, and sticks white and gold.[364] The Speaker with an audible voice reads the Address – which by the bye the lateness of the hour and the darkness of the day obliged him to do by a candle (the first instance, old courtiers say, in which a candle has ever been known to be admitted into the Levée Room) and the K. returns his answer. Then bowing – bowing – bowing – as before, we retire backwards out of the apartment. Amongst the crowd which surrounded us I had just time to get

---

[361] Sir Charles Hamilton 2nd Bt. In 1794 he was a Cpt.

[362] Probably Sir Charles Morice Pole 1st Bt. In 1794 he was a Cpt., and groom of Bedchamber to the Duke of Clarence.

[363] 'I felt ... had done (p. 178)', printed in *Marshall*, 80–1

[364] The White Rod was carried on ceremonial occasions by certain officials such as the Lord Steward of the Household and the Lord Chamberlain. The Gold Stick was reserved for the office of Captain of the Yeoman of the Guard which was occupied in 1795 by the Earl of Aylesford

a glimpse of Ly. Suth[erlan]d – and to receive her congratulations on having spoken so *slow* and so well as she heard I had done. From St James's, seduced rather by the offer of being carried, than from being in a humour to enjoy either dinner or company, I went home to dine with Sr. W.W. Wynne.[365] You of course know who he is – but as you perhaps have never heard me mention him, you may not know that he was contemporary with us at Christ Church, and acquainted, though not very intimately, nor at all as one of our set, with C. Ellis, Leveson, Boringdon, &c.

Morpeth, Leveson, Boringdon and Newbolt dined here – and it would have been very pleasant had I not been so unwell as to think nothing pleasant but going home and to bed, which I did as soon as possible.

$2^{d.}$ [*January*] Friday morning I woke with a determination to stay at home all day; which was not a little strengthened by Frere's coming to breakfast and promising to stay all day with me. I sent for Norris to consult – and got from him the usual prescriptions of temperance and tranquillity which I promised strictly to observe and did so. And so Frere and I sat and read and talked till it was my bed-time.

$3^{d.}$ [*January*] Saturday morning – I should have kept as closely at home as I had done yesterday – but that I received a message from Mr. Dundas, desiring to speak with me – and as Somerset House is not two hundred yards off, and I knew that he wanted to talk about Jenkinson's affairs, I wrapped myself up in my great coat and went to him. Jenkinson is intending every day to set out for Croydon, where his regiment of Fencibles is quartered, but wishes to hear something more from his father before he goes. This resolution not to attend the House of Commons certainly struck Ld. H[awkesbury] exceedingly, but he seems stubborn and self-willed in the business – and I am afraid is not to be conquered but by *vigour* and perseverance. If he will not consent handsomely in good time, the step must be taken *without him*. This is my opinion; it is Mr. Dundas's; it is Ly. Jane Dundas's, with whom also I had some talk about it this morning; it is Mr. Pitt's, with whom I have conversed about it two or three times; it is Wallace's – and though Jenkinson having, as is natural and laudable in him, a better opinion than we have of his father's tenderness and flexibility, is not yet quite prepared to think such a step necessary – it will come to be his opinion too when he sees how hopeless all other means turn out.

Except this visit to Dundas I did not stir out to-day, but sent an excuse to Sir R. Payne's where I was to have dined – and was at home

[365] Sir Watkin Williams Wynn 5th Bt. M.P. Beaumaris 20 Oct. 1794–96

alone from morning to night. This day came the confirmation of the news that the French had crossed the Waal.

*4th. [January]* Sunday morning came a message from Mr. Dundas, desiring me to dine with him to-day to meet the Speaker. I should have liked very well to do so – but I thought one more day's care might be decisive as to my cold, and so I excused myself – which I did indeed the more willingly as Frere and Easley Smith were come to breakfast with me – and I meant to persuade one or both of them to stay and dine also. Frere stayed with me the whole morning: in the course of which Ld. Gower called – and I was glad to have an opportunity of making him and Frere acquainted. They liked each other very much. Fred. Hervey called here – Lady Louisa, he tells me, is much agitated and perplexed by the awkwardness of her present situation: at which I cannot wonder – but I trust it will not be of very long continuance. Easley Smith returned to dinner – and he and Frere remained with me till they thought it time that I should be sent to bed.

*5th [January]* Monday morning my cold was not so much better but that I thought it prudent to lie in bed till it was time to set out on my road to the House of Coms. I called on Jenkinson in my way. He has seen his father again, who has again refused his consent. He has now resolved upon going to his Regiment to-morrow or next day, not to return to town or to attend Parliament till the matter shall have come finally to issue.

In the House of Coms. was a motion by Sheridan for the repeal of the Act passed last Session for the suspension of part of the Habeas Corpus. As it seemed to promise a long debate, and I had no thoughts of taking any part in it, nor much disposition to sit it all through – I willingly accepted Lord Gower's proposal to go home and dine quietly with him and Ly. Sutherland – and return to the House after dinner. We dined very comfortably – though their house is not quite got into order yet – but they understand the arrangement of a house thoroughly, and when settled, it will be a great gain and comfort to me. I found that Ld. Gower had been reporting very favourably of Frere – and had been particularly struck with the use and consolation of which he appeared to be to me during my indisposition, when he heard us talk of the books that we had been reading *such* a day, and the conversation that we had had on *such an* evening. 'What a delightful, comfortable friend he must be to you, to be with you this every day and all day long – and take such care of you, and amuse and entertain you so constantly'. And upon my saying in answer to this that there was no sort of day that I liked so much as one passed within doors, with one or two pleasant persons reading and communicating one's remarks to each other, and without interruption from the world or anything belonging to it – 'If that be the case, why should not we have a week of such days at Wimbledon? There is to be nothing of any consequence in the House till Grey's motion of which he has given notice for the 20th. Let us go out of town on Sunday next – and stay till the Sunday following – the day before the [Queen's] birthday'. You may suppose I was not slow to agree to this proposal. Sunday indeed I could not leave town, as I was engaged to dine with Dundas – but on Monday I promised to join them – and we would live so snugly, and not let a soul come near us. After making this agreement and finishing our dinner, Lord Gower and I returned to the House – and found that Sheridan had made a very brilliant speech, and Windham a very able answer to it. I was very sorry to have missed them and it is quite against my rule to absent myself from any part of a debate – but this one time I made my excuses to myself not only on the score of my cold but because the interval had been passed to so good a purpose. The debate continued till about 3 in the morning. In the course of it Serjt. Adair[366] made one of the very best speeches, whether as a parliamentary oration or as the argument of a lawyer, whether for eloquence or for effect, that I ever heard in my life. It far surpassed my opinion of the learned Serjt.'s oratorical powers – and the conviction which it carried to the House was perhaps the most strong and clear and conclusive that ever was produced by a speech in Parliament. The division was 185 to 41. Among all the foolish things that Sheridan has done, perhaps there never was anything more foolish and ill-judged than the bringing on this question. If there was one point upon which the minds of the House and of people in general out of doors, were more completely made up than another, it was upon the existence of dangerous designs in the country, and the effect of the late trials, though they had terminated in the acquittal of the individuals, had been to confirm more and more the belief of mischief having been planned, though providentially prevented from being carried into execution. To counteract an impression so general, is always an unpopular, and can never be a successful, undertaking – and as to the suspension of the Habeas Corpus Act, if Sheridan thought *that* an unpopular measure on the part of Govt., his best game, and that of his Party, would have been to wait the expiration of the Act of Suspension (which expires by the Bill of last year on the 1st of Febry.) and then to have made the attack when Govt. should move the renewal of it (which they certainly must do) – instead of which, by making the debate *now* upon the repeal, proposed by them, instead of upon a *renewal* to be proposed by Govt., they took upon themselves

[366]James Adair (?1743–98). M.P. Higham Ferrers 1793–8 and sejt.-at-law 28 Apr. 1774. He spoke in defence of the suspension of Habeas Corpus

all the *onus probandi* – irritated the House, who are tenacious of their own acts and opinions, and do not chuse to rescind them – and paved the way for the renewal, which is to come, making it an *expected* and *foreseen* matter,[367] instead of a sudden and unlooked-for one, as it might have been if they had kept themselves quiet. I believe that Fox and others of Opposition saw the subject exactly in this point of view, and were very earnest with Sheridan not to bring it forward. But he was determined to make a grand speech, and nothing could dissuade him.

After the debate I asked Dundas to carry me home. When we came to his door he would have had me come in to sup with him – but I was virtuous and abstained, and went home supperless to bed.

*6th [January]* Tuesday morning I found myself very ill rewarded for my virtue and abstinence of last night, by a return of my cold, accompanied with a headache.

I lay in bed till 3 o'clock, not sleeping indeed all the time but receiving visitors. Frere was among them – and so was Woodcock. I have not mentioned him and his family for some time. I do not see much of them, as you may suppose, for they do not yet admit visitors. I am happy to hear, however, from Woodcock that his father has left his affairs, though not in a splendid state, yet very comfortable. His mother will have income enough to live as well as she has always been used to do, and to keep her children about her. His second brother (about 19 or 20) goes on with the business in partnership with a very worthy and sensible man, a relation of the Chancellor's (Mr. Cotes),[368] and the Chancellor continues to him a place worth about £800 a year, which was held by his father. He himself (Woodcock) has taken Orders, and has received from the Chancellor renewed promises of preferment. So all is pretty well.

When I got up I felt very little disposed to dress and go out to dinner – and was just about to send an excuse to Lord Stafford's – when finding that Frere could not stay with me – and being very much urged by Fleming not to yield to my complaints but fight up against them, I dressed, and set out for Whitehall – going indeed for a quarter of an hour to the House of Coms. in my way. It was a quiet family dinner, such as exactly suited me to-day – Ld. and Ly. Stafford, Ly. Susan, Granville, Ld. G.[ower] and Ly. Suth[erland]. Poor Lady

---

[367] The second reading of the Bill to continue the suspension of Habeas Corpus was debated on 23 Jan. and passed by the substantial majority of 239 v. 53

[368] John Cotes (?1750–1821) of Woodcote, Salop, M.P. Wigan 1782–1802, was the Lord Chancellor's brother in law. As he had been adm. Middle Temple in 1770 it is possible that it was he who went into partnership with the Woodcocks' firm of solicitors. However, as he was a substantial country gentleman, C. may have been referring to a brother, Washington Cotes, recorded as a K.C. of 10 Lincoln's Inn, Old Sq., and who was the Lord Chancellor's principal sec. in 1795

Georgina is not yet recovered from the illness which confined her when we were at Trentham – but Sir Lucas Pepys[369] promises that she shall get better soon. Lady Susan is looking so remarkably well that people are all talking about her – and almost wonder that they should never have thought her handsome before. I stayed some part of the evening at Whitehall – and then came home directly to my bed.

Granville goes out of town to-morrow to Lichfield to be elected.[370]

*7th. [January]* Wednesday morning – I thought a walk would do me good, and so set out into the City and called on Borrowes to make my excuses for not dining with him to-day, as I had provisionally promised to do. There is business in the House. I fixed Saturday instead. The business in the House was to vote the Navy – 100,000 seamen voted – but we must have more before we have done. There was much discussion of course upon Lord Chatham's conduct at First Lord of the Admiralty – from which discussion his character and conduct appeared to come out more clear and even praiseworthy than I, though a friend of Govt., could have hoped or imagined. It is however a good thing after all that he is gone – for the voice of the publick was against him, and that is reason enough.[371]

I dined at Lord Digby's. I must have mentioned him to you before. He is a contemporary of our youngest set (Morpeth, Holland &c.) at Christ Church – now come to his seat in the House of Peers, and a plentiful fortune, and living in a manner that becomes his situation. He is a good, stout politician. There were Morpeth, Newbolt, Augustus Legge, and two or three other people. In the evg. I called at Lady Payne's – and then came home.

*8th. [January]* Thursday I was at home the whole morning – there being no House to call me out. I dined at Boringdon's – where were Morpeth, Ryder and Arbuthnot, and Mr. Greville (the C. Greville that I met at Castle Howard). In the evening I went to the Markhams, whom I have not seen this long time, never having been out of a night – and never going to them except when I felt stout enough to stay the whole evening and sup with them. They would think an evening *call* formal. To-night I felt stout enough, and therefore went and stayed and supped.

[369] Sir Lucas Pepys 1st Bt. Physician-in-ordinary to George III, 1792 and physician-general of the army, 1794

[370] Lord Granville Leveson Gower was returned for the family borough of Lichfield on 14 Jan. 1795

[371] Sir John Pitt, the 2nd Earl of Chatham, the prime minister's elder brother, was first Lord of the Admiralty 1788–94. The Opposition claimed in this debate that he had been ineffective in this role, particularly in respect of providing protection for merchant shipping, see *Annual Register*, 1795, 31–3

*9th [January]* Friday Frere breakfasted with me, and stayed the whole morning till it was time for him to go home to dress for dinner at Easley Smith's – where we had promised to dine to-day. Charles Ellis called on me – being just come up to town. Perhaps I have not mentioned that he had gone out of town. He did go within a day or two after the first debate, to his brother's in Hampshire – leaving, as usual, full powers with me to summon him to town for any question that I thought required his attendance. These powers I put in practice for last Monday, the day of the Habeas Corpus debate – and mark the good faith and stout zeal of his conduct. Tuesday was the anniversary of his brother's wedding day,[372] and it was to be kept with great festivity. Yet no sooner did he receive the call to his parliamentary duty, that he got into his post chaise on Monday morning came up to town time enough for the debate, stayed to give his vote till 3 o'clock in the morning, – and then, after a few hours' rest, set off back again into the country, 60 miles, to be present at his brother's wedding night celebrity. What brought him to town now so soon again was his brother's little boy being ill. John Ellis and Mrs. Ellis came to town for advice, and Charles of course accompanied them. I dined at Easley's – wth. Easley's mother and aunts, and Frere. In the evening I went to Whitehall – and afterwards to Charles Ellis's – to sup with him, his brother and Mrs. Ellis.

*10. [January]* Saturday morning I was a good deal taken up with Jenkinson's affairs, receiving a letter from Fred. Hervey to tell me that all circumstances considered they thought it best to wave the delicacy which they had felt at first about Jenkinson's coming in person to Wimbledon – and that they were now ready to see him, finding that it was difficult to understand each other so clearly as they ought to do, at a distance. In consequence of this letter I called on Lady Jane Dundas to consult with her upon the subject, and finding her of the same mind with F. H. I wrote to Jenkinson at his head-quarters at Croydon to desire that he would cross the country to Wimbledon with all the possible expedition – and to inform him that if after the conversation which he would have next day with Lady Louisa, there should arise anything in the course of the next week that he particularly wished to the communicated to her, I should be the whole of that week within a hundred yards of her, and could easily execute his commission.

I dined to-day at Borrowes's with a large City party – and went afterwards to the Opera, where I found it so cold that I determined not to go there again till spring.

*11. [January]* Sunday morning Frere breakfasted with me. After

[372] John Thomas Ellis q.v., for whose m. see p. 38, n. 61

breakfast I went to keep an appointment which I had made some
days ago with Boringdon to discuss the present state of politicks
internal and external, and to try if we could not bring our opinions a
little nearer to each other. I have already told you that he is one of
those who, in the course of the summer, have got a puzzle into their
heads about peace – the necessity of it soon – and the possibility of
obliging Pitt to set about making it against his own opinion, without
turning him out of office. For to Pitt he still looks as the only man fit
to conduct the affairs of the country – at the same time that upon the
one great measure of the war, he has persuaded himself to form an
opinion directly contrary to that which Pitt entertains, and upon
which he (Pitt) will act, at least for the present, and stake his situation
upon the consequences. Under these impressions Boringdon, while he
continues to *vote with* Government in Parlt., because he wishes not to
turn out Pitt, yet *talks* and *thinks against* them in private, because he
wishes peace to be made – an inconsistency, which not only makes
him appear in a very disrespectable light to others, but makes him
feel also, as he has often confessed, very uncomfortable to himself. In
my[373] conversation with him to-day I had in view – first to persuade
him of the utter impossibility of making peace at this time; and
secondly to shew him that the conduct and conversation which he
was now holding could not, in any case, or under any opinion that
he might entertain, be prudent or creditable. As to the first point I
made use of but few arguments, feeling much less interested about his
publick sentiments than about his individual character. That which
seemed to weigh with him most, and which I do think is the most
sober, rational and straightforward way of considering the subject is
simply this. 'I care not about the internal state or government of
France one farthing – whether republic – anarchy – monarchy or
what not – it does not signify for my argument. I only desire you to
look at the map of Europe – see what France has done – what she is
gaining – and of what she is already in possession – and then tell me
if there ever was a period of our history at which England could
reasonably consent to make a peace with France in such a state of
power and aggrandisement. Tell me if any statesman that ever lived,
on being shewn that France was mistress of the Netherlands and of
Holland – no matter whether with Louis the 14th – or with Tallien[374]
and the Committees at her [sic] head – would not exclaim at once,
'Then England *must be* at war with her'. As to the second point, I

[373]'In my ... and cordiality' (p. 188), printed in *Marshall*, 91–6
[374]Jean Lambert Tallien (1767–1820). A member of the Committee of General
Security, 1792, who subsequently figured prominently in the Thermidorian reaction
and became a leading critic of the Jacobins

pressed it, as I felt it, nearly upon these grounds. 'You wish for peace, and you think it may be had immediately and securely. At the same time you have the highest possible opinion of Pitt, and would not for the world that he should be removed from Administration. Be it so – with these, or any other opinions I have at present nothing to do, as to their propriety. I have only to shew how a man, having such opinions, ought to act in consequence of them. You must see, I think, that there are but *two* lines of conduct which a man can pursue in public life. The one is to dismiss from his mind all party and personal feeling – to look at *measures* only, and not to *men*, and to give his judgement and his vote upon every measure that comes before him, exactly according to his own view of the subject, and without reference to any man or set of men whom he may serve or injure by doing so. The other and the more general line – is to attach one's self (not slavishly and exclusively and eternally but with room left for the fair exercise of one's own reason, and with the power and determination to break off such attachment if any question should arise of *sufficient importance*, and any difference of sentiment *sufficiently wide* to make such a step necessary) to attach one's self generally to that Party whose principles and conduct appear *upon the whole* best calculated to promote the real welfare of the country, and in pursuance of such a connection it must no doubt happen sometimes that one's private feelings will be overborne by the consideration of the general utility, and one's individual opinions given up to the general opinion of one's Party. Now, if you are prepared to take the *first* of these two lines of conduct – a difficult and bold one, I confess, and one which requires great firmness, great circumspection and great judgement to make it respectable in itself or useful to the country – but one nevertheless which your situation as an independent and unconnected man, with a perpetual seat in Parliament, with an ample fortune, and with talents such as I think yours to be, will enable you to pursue, if you please. In that case, I say – you have nothing to do but to make up your mind upon the subject of the war, and act for yourself at once, by your own judgement and authority – and it is your business therefore, if you are really and thoroughly convinced that peace can be made with advantage immediately, to express that conviction in the very first *vote* that you give in the House of Lds. You *ought to have* voted against the Address on the first day of the Session. But if, as I rather believe, you are not prepared to take his high and self-dependent tone – but mean, like other public men, to mix a little of party and personal consideration with you own opinions – if, for instance, you have such respect for Mr. Pitt as induces you to think him generally right, and his Administration essentially useful to the country – then it will become you to put these questions to yourself.

'Am I *so* convinced of the justice of *my own* opinion about peace, that all the arguments against it, backed by the confidence which I have in Mr. Pitt's judgement and integrity, cannot shake that opinion? Or, ought I not rather to *distrust* a little my own judgement, when not only that of so many persons whom I respect, but that of Mr. Pitt, in whom I have so much confidence, is against me?' And your conduct in and out of Parliament should be the result of the answers which you find yourself able to give to these questions. But depend upon it – the conduct which you are now pursuing is exactly the *only one* which *can in no case* be right – which, whether you consider yourself as an independent individual or as a partizan of Govt. you will find it equally impossible to justify. To vote *one way* in Parliament and talk *the other* way in private company, is neither fair to your own character, if you look to yourself only, nor fair to Mr. Pitt, if you take him and his Government into your contemplation. It is not fair to *your own character*, for see what people must think of it.

They must think either that you *act* in public, in a manner which you are ashamed in private to defend – or that you hold *opinions* privately, which you are afraid publicly to carry into action. They will say, and I must say *with* them – not perhaps that YOU adopt this mode of proceeding with the view of keeping well with Mr. Pitt so long as he *continues* Minister – by your *vote* – and at the same time of laying the foundation of amity with Opposition – whenever they may *become* Ministers – by your *conversation* – because *I* know *you* too well to suspect *you* of being actuated by such motives – but that a man, who *was* actuated by *such motives*, could act *no otherwise than as you are doing*, is what the world will say, and what I should find it hard to deny. It is *unfair to Mr Pitt* in a *double* point of view – *first* as it affects his permanency as Minister – by giving him a false idea of his strength. For what does a Minister calculate? He reckons his *majorities*, and says, 'Thus supported I may safely persevere'. But if of those majorities part is composed of persons like you, *voting with* them, but *thinking* and *talking* against him, he builds upon a hollow foundation, which some fine day will deceive him when most relying on it, and you, as far as your own vote goes, are guilty of involving him in his error. *Secondly*, as it affects his reputation – for are you not aware that every word that is uttered *against* any man comes with double force if it proceeds from the mouth of a friend? When Sheridan or Grey accuse Mr. Pitt of mistake or misconduct in private company – the company look to their parliamentary enmity and give the accusation the less weight – but when *you* professing yourself a friend, and supporting his measures in Parliament, give an opinion against them, those who hear you naturally say, 'Aye, indeed, there must be something *very wrong* – for you see here is a *friend* of Mr. Pitt's, that condemns him!!

So that if I were arguing this point with you, not for your own sake but for Mr. Pitt's (and I confess I do feel a little for *his* interest involved, as it is, in the argument) – I should say, 'My dear B[oringdon], I would certainly rather have you with us, both in publick and in private, than against us – but if we cannot have you in both, for God's sake do not let us have you in either. If you cannot bring yourself to approve the measures of Govt. in private society, pray do not support them in Parlt. – if you must abuse us, I beg of you at least not to call yourself our friend'. If I were to add another consideration, of somewhat less importance indeed, though by no means unworthy of attention, it would be this – that a person in your state of mind, acting contrary to his opinions, and talking contrary to his actions, is of all others the most unpleasant in society. With decided political friends one is of course easy and unembarrassed – with *decided* enemies one always knows one's ground exactly, and can get on very well, joking and abusing each other in perfect good humour – but with an ambiguous friend and *half* enemy, there is no knowing what tone to take. Such a person is always *fidgetty* and irritable – always on the watch for opinions to confirm his own, or for instance to authorize his mode of acting – always having something to explain, something to distinguish, something to reconcile, always endeavouring to compensate for the indecision of his actions by the violence of his words, for nothing is so violent in *abuse* as a *candid friend* – in short, nothing but plain sailing gives a man comfort to himself or with others. And I protest, though I should be much grieved at a separation among us at so early a stage of our public lives, and tho' I had fixed much of my hopes on our all going on pleasantly and cordially together, I had rather see you (and Morpeth, if he thinks with you, as I am afraid he does – and Leveson, if you should corrupt him between you, which however I do not think you will) at once in bold, barefaced opposition, than in a state of puzzle and perplexity, in which one knows not where to have you or how to talk to you. The sum of my opinions upon this subject, then, is this. First, that you ought to revolve the matter over and over again in your mind, before you take up finally an opinion upon so vast and complicated a subject, in opposition to that of those with whom you have been in the habit of agreeing, and whom you generally respect and esteem. Think, whether it be not *possible* that *you* may be *mistaken*, and Mr. Pitt after all, in the *right*. I am sanguine enough to flatter myself still, that you may come to *this* conclusion. But if you should not – and yet should determine to vote with Mr. Pitt, tho' differing from him in opinion – it is absolutely *necessary* that you should have an explanation with him, that he may not be deceived in reckoning too far upon your subject. Lastly, for your own sake, for the sake of Mr. Pitt, and for that of society, I do most sincerely hope and recommend to you that you endeavour at least to reconcile your language and your conduct, so that whatever the one may be, the other shall not appear to be at variance with it'.

This was nearly the purport of my share in a conversation which lasted some hours – and which was borne on both sides with the most perfect good humour and cordiality. For of all the men, old, or young, whom I ever knew, B. is the one who takes in the best part, or rather, seeks and courts with the greatest eagerness any advice or comment on his conduct. And indeed, but for his seeking it, you may imagine I should hardly have spun out so unmerciful a dissertation on such a subject.

The answers on his side to the propositions with which I concluded – were, first, that he would most undoubtedly think over again with the utmost care and attention the whole of the subject of peace and war, giving to the arguments which he had heard, and giving to the high authority of Mr. Pitt's opinion all the weight that they naturally merited – and he would make me acquainted with the result of his reflections. Secondly, if he continued in the same mind as to Peace, and continued as even in that case he certainly should, to support Government with his vote, he would assuredly see Mr. Pitt, and explain to him the ground of his support, and the tenour of his opinions. Lastly, as to his private conversation, he saw the impropriety of *that* in the same light that I had represented it – he would talk that part of the subject over with Morpeth, who was in some measure implicated in the same fault, and whatever might be the event as to the other points upon which we had gone into discussion, upon this at least I should have no reason to differ with him henceforward.

From this long conversation I returned to dress, and then went to dine at Mr. Dundas's. There were Lady Jane, Lady Anne Barnard[375] (do you know her?), her sister Lady M. Fordyce,[376] Lady Catherine and Mr. Douglas (Silvester Douglas, that married Lord Guilford's daughter and was in Ireland Secretary last year, and is to have £2,000 a year pension and a seat in Parlt. here,[377] and I know not what else

---

[375] Lady Anne Lindsay, e. da. of the 5th Earl of Balcarres m. 31 Oct. 1793 Andrew Barnard. She was a close friend of Dundas who, in 1797, appointed her husband sec. to Lord Macartney, the first Governor of the Cape of Good Hope. The author of the ballad *Auld Robin Gray*', she and her sister [see n. 376] made their house in Berkeley Square one of the social centres for the foremost political and literary figures of the day, see W.H. Wilkins (ed.), *South Africa A Century Ago: Letters ... By The Lady Anne Barnard* (London, 1901), 3–36

[376] Lady Margaret Lindsay, 2nd da. of the 5th Earl of Balcarres m. 20 June 1770, Alexander Fordyce of Roehampton

[377] He was returned for Fowey on 14 Feb. 1795 on the recommendation of the Treasury and granted a pension of £600 for his life plus £600 in survivorship for himself and his son on 21 Mar., see *Thorne*, iii, 611

besides, as a reward for about six weeks' services, and was not worth half as much if his services had been for 16 years) Fred. North, and Wallace. In the evening Wallace and I, in our grand full dress, taking up Charles Ellis, as grand as ourselves, in the way, went to pay our respects to the Speaker and to the Chancellor.

From these visits I returned home with Charles Ellis – and talked over with him the conversation which I had held with Boringdon this morning – and agreed with him (for he is a great friend and well wisher of Boringdon this morning – and wishes as earnestly to see him in the right way as I do) that he should seek an opportunity of having some discussion upon the subject – and should send me an account to Wimbledon of the temper and turn of mind in which B. seemed to be. To settle this took almost as long as the original conversation had taken in the morning, and it was some hours after supper that I set out for home.

*12. [January]* Monday was the day that I had fixed for being at Wimbledon – and to which therefore I had looked forward with some degree of impatience. I ordered Fleming and my chaise to Charles Ellis's, and set out to walk there, meaning to arrange with him still more accurately the nature of the conversation which it would be adviseable for him to begin with Boringdon. In my way there I met Boringdon himself, and as honesty and openness always do their work better than anything else, I thought it best at once to tell him that I had been talking him over with Charles Ellis, and that I had made him (C. E.) promise and hoped he (B.) would accede to the engagement to give the subject a very full discussion, some fine morning in the course of this week – which I found, as I had expected, to be the very thing that B. himself had in his contemplation. For of C. Ellis he thinks almost as highly as I do, and is besides well assured of his kindness and sincere good disposition towards himself. Boringdon went with me to Ch. Ellis's – but he was, like a great child, gone out skaiting, so I had no opportunity of getting their joint promise face to face – but left town pretty well contented with the arrangement, as it was made – and not without sanguine hopes of the effect which might be produced on B.'s mind by his own reflections, and C. E.'s conversation.

I arrived at Wimbledon to dinner – and why is it that I shall be able to get this day and all that follow – Tuesday, Wednesday, Thursday, Friday and Saturday into this one side of a half sheet of paper? It is because the perfect, calm, tranquil enjoyment of that time leaves behind it a pleasing, quiet, unbroken recollection, which admits of no description, affording no variety – breakfast, books and conversation – dinner in the little library, conversation and books again – and supper with dumb-waiters – are the elements of the history of every day. The only diversity that I have to mention is that for one whole day and part of a second the *tête-à-tête* was interrupted by the presence of Mr. Huskisson (Ld. Gower's private secretary) but he went away again. You may be sure that one morning I spent with Lady Bristol and Lady Louisa, and another was sent for to their house to see Jenkinson, who came over to them from Croydon for an hour or two. The only event was the arrival towards the end of the week, of a letter from Charles Ellis containing a full and satisfactory narrative of a conversation which he had, according to their respective promises, held with Boringdon – the result of which appeared to be that B. had come *right* again, beyond my most sanguine expectations – that he thought of the War *rationally and firmly* – was prepeared to *support Government* on *Government's own grounds* – so much so that it became quite *unnecessary* for him to *speak to Mr. Pitt* – and as a *proof* of the tone which his general *conversation* had assumed in place of the *old* abuse of the measures of *Administration*, C. Ellis added that Wallace had said to him (C. E.) one day with such surprize and admiration '*What a* WARRIOR B. *is become all of a sudden!*'

This letter gave me so much satisfaction – and in addition to the agreeableness of its contents was so well written, and in a strain of proper feeling and sense so creditable to the writer – that I could not deny myself the pleasure of communicating it to Ld. G[ower] and Ly. S[utherland] – and with it such a character of the person from whom it came, that they exacted from me a repetition of the promise which I had before willingly made, to make them acquainted with C. Ellis.

When I said this letter was the only *event* of the week – I ought to have made an exception in favour of publick events, which indeed were many and most distastrous. The repeated attempts of the French to cross the Waal – their ultimate success – and their progress into Holland, were detailed to us from town day after day, and *ought* to have made us very melancholy.

*18th. [January]* Sunday I returned to town – and so did Ld. G. and Ly. S. I dined at Charles Ellis's with Boringdon, Morpeth and Leveson. The latter just returned from his election at Lichfield. Morpeth's election for Morpeth came on last week, and he took his seat on Friday. I promised to introduce Leveson to his seat with the help of Ld. Gower (for two introducers are required) on Tuesday. After dinner my first care was to seize an opportunity of having five minutes' conversation with Boringdon which confirmed all that C. Ellis had told me. In the evening I went to Whitehall – and from thence returned alone to sup and hear the particulars of all that had passed between B. and him, from C. Ellis.

*19. [January]* Monday Frere breakfasted with me. I was to have dined with Mr. Dundas, in celebration of the birthday[378] – but the

[378] Queen Charlotte's birthday was traditionally celebrated on 18 Jan.

death of a brother[379] of his obliged him to put off his party, and left me at liberty to dine with Charles Ellis, where I met Morpeth, Wallace, Mr. Mundy (of Shipley) and his namesake the young Mundy of Marston.[380] In the evening I went to the Markhams, whom I had not seen for 10 days, and supped there.

*20. [January]* Tuesday. I went early to the House of Commons to help Leveson to take his seat. Grey's motion, which stood for this day.[381] But the Call of the House, which had been appointed as preparatory to it, to procure a full attendance, took place. This Call, among many others whom I suppose it put to inconvenience, reduced Jenkinson to a dilemma. He had till now absented himself from Parliament under the pretext (to the world) of being unwell; in reality, and as he had said to his father, from not having spirits, under his present uncertainty, to exert himself, if he attended. Now the Call admitting no excuse but serious illness, authenticated by a physician, he could not continue to absent himself; and yet to come out and attend Parlt. was like giving up the point, and might be construed by his father into an acquiescence with his determination. To prevent this the only expedient was to write to his father, explaining the circumstances, that the Call making his appearance absolutely necessary, he was obliged to come out, but that lest *he* (Ld. H[awkesbury]) should construe his doing so as a giving up of his former wishes &c. he felt himself bound to inform him that he had *finally made up his resolution* – in short, that the thing *must be.*

I dined to-day at Boringdon's with Leveson, Ch. Ellis and Lord Garlies.[382] In the evening I called at Lady Payne's – and in my way home supped at Carey Street.

*21. [January]* Wednesday Frere breakfasted with me. In the House of Coms. the Army Estimates were to be voted. Not thinking it likely that there would be any very interesting debate upon that subject, I suffered myself to be seduced by Leveson and Morpeth to go and dine at Sir W. W. Wynne's – where C. Ellis also – and a large party of young Ch. Church M.Ps. came to dinner. I felt that I was doing wrong in going away during the debate myself, and much more so,

---

[379] As Dundas' only brother, Lord Arniston had d.1787, C. must have been referring to one of his numerous kinsmen. The only one who seems to qualify is Maj. Gen. Thomas Dundas, b.1750 and d. 3 June 1794 on active service in Guadaloupe. Dundas was possibly attending a memorial service

[380] Either Edward Miller Mundy (d.1834), e. s. of Edward Miller Mundy q.v. or possibly their kinsman, Francis Mundy (1771–1837) of Markheaton Hall, Derbyshire which was near Marston in that county

[381] The motion – that the politics of the existing govt. of France should not preclude a peace negociation – was held over to 26 Jan.

[382] He was to vacate his seat for Saltash in Feb. 1795 following a vote against gvt. on the Address, 30 Dec. 1794, see *Thorne,* v, 272

in countenancing such idlesness in Leveson and Morpeth, whom I
ought to have taught better behaviour – and wrong indeed I had
done – for on my return in about two hours I found that Pitt had
been speaking most brilliantly. The House was just then up – and so
as a punishment for my fault I went to Whitehall to get myself scolded
by Lady Stafford, whom, when I came in, I found in the very act of
scolding Granville, and saying I am sure Mr. C. never would do such
a thing'. 'Indeed, but he would, and did too, for he went with us',
was the reply – and I came just time enough to plead guilty to the
charge, and to submit myself to the indignation which it merited.
From Whitehall I went to sup with C. Ellis.

22 [*January*] Thursday morning, I went according to an appointment, which I had made yesterday, to call on Mr. Pitt – and talked
with him on the subject of Grey's motion, which now stands for
Monday. From Downing Street I sent to Ch. Ellis, having prepared
Lady Sutherland yesterday for his introduction to her. I took him
with me to Albemarle Street, where he was received as he deserves –
and I hope they will be well acquainted. She tells me that she likes
his first appearance of all things. Returning from this visit to Charles
Ellis's, we found dinner ready (for expecting the debate to last long,
we had agreed to dine before we went down, and to sup afterwards –
Morpeth, Leveson, Boringdon and I wth. C. Ellis) – and I found also
Willy Canning waiting to partake of it. I had promised him when I
was at Wansted, that he should come up to a debate before he went
back to school – and to-day having been fixed for his coming, I had
left word for him at my chambers to follow me to Park Place. We
went down to the House, but in our debate – which was to be on the
Atty. Genl.'s motion for the further suspension of the Habeas Corpus,
we were disappointed. There was so much previous business as to last
till 9 o'clock, and then it was thought too late to begin upon so
important a subject and the Habeas Corpus was put off to to-morrow.
Among the previous business of to-day was one thing, which I was
very sorry to have missed – a Petition from Carlisle,[383] or rather a
Protest against a Petition sent up from that place for Peace – which
(Protest) Morpeth introduced in a little short speech, so well delivered
and in such good taste altogether, that when I came down I found
everybody talking of it, and Pitt told me it was one of the *prettiest*
things to see and hear that could be imagined. Wallace who had
spoken (also before I came down) on the same business, had not
acquitted himself in quite so *pretty* a manner, for he had got into a sad
scrape by mistaking one business for another, and told a long story

[383] A petition from the freemen of Carlisle against the war, 22 Jan. 1795 see *The
Commons' Journal*, vol. 50, 87

about a James Smith, a barber of fifteen years old, whom he averred to have signed the Petition of the democrates [sic] – and when the list of signatures came to be examined, lo! there was no such name – so that I found everybody laughing at Wallace in the same proportion that they were praising Morpeth.

The House being up so early, I sent Willy off to the Play with injunctions to come to me again to-morrow. And I went, with Leveson, and made him bring C. Ellis to Whitehall to be introduced – for there also I have talked of him a great deal and made them desirous of being acquainted with him – and so has Leveson, who next to myself, has I think the justest notion of his value. We staid at Whitehall till joined by Morpeth and Boringdon – then proceeded to White's – and from White's to sup at Charles Ellis's – where I staid some hours longer than a prudent consideration of my cold, still bad, and the prospect of so late a night in the House of Coms. to-morrow, should have permitted.

*23. [January]* Friday. Willy came punctually to his appointment. I gave him some dinner here – and took him down to the House. The Attorney General's motion[384] occasioned a debate which lasted till 3 o'clock in the morning, but in which, as it was managed chiefly by lawyers on our part, the Atty. and Solr. Genl. and Serjt. Adair, I felt no inclination to take any part till towards the end – when upon Grey's getting up I proposed to Pitt to answer him, if there should appear occasion. Occasion there was none, however, as he spoke but for a few minutes, the House becoming very clamorous for the Question. The division was 239 to 53 – for on this question, and others of the same sort, the Opposition have no proselytes.

Charles Ellis had offered Willy a bed at his house, and ordered a supper to be ready for him when he should come home, so when the strangers were sent out of the House upon division, I bade Willy make the best of his way to Park Place, where, as he informed me the next morning, he supped and slept like a Lord. Charles Ellis and I, with Morpeth and Leveson and half-a-dozen more people supped at White's – another irregularity in addition to that of last night, which prudence and my cold ought to have prevented.

*24. [January]* Saturday Jenkinson was with me greatest part of the morning, talking over the *final* letter which he has written to his father, and to which he has received no answer, written or verbal, though they have met once or twice, and conversed upon indifferent subjects. My belief is that he will hear nothing more upon the subject till the *thing is done*; that Lord H[awkesbury] sees it *must be* – but that though he finds it useless to withhold his consent, he does not like positively

---

[384] For continuing the suspension of Habeas Corpus

to give it – and will rather pardon the crime after it has been committed than authorize it beforehand.

I dined at Lord Abercorn's – where were Lord Bathurst (he was Lord Apsley last year, and I have mentioned him under that title as a guest at Pitt's table) – Steele and Arbuthnot. I spent the evening and supped with the Markhams.

*25. [Janauary]* Sunday I was at home all the morning till it was time to dress for the Speaker's dinner. And then sending Fleming with my dress clothes to Charles Ellis's, I went to make my toilette there; and we went together to dinner. There were about 16 other members of the House of Commons, and it was altogether as pleasant as an entertainment necessarily somewhat formal can be.

In the evening I went with Ch. Ellis to Whitehall – his first visit since his introduction there – then to Lady Payne's – and then by myself to sup with Mrs. Crewe – who came to town a few days ago.

*26. [January]* Monday morning I received a note form Mr. Pitt desiring to see me in Downing Street at 2 o'clock. I went there at the time appointed – and found members of the House of Com<sup>s.</sup> – Attorney and Sol<sup>r.</sup> Gen<sup>l.</sup>, Serj<sup>t.</sup> Adair, Anstruther,[385] Steele, Master of the Rolls, Ryder, Jenkinson. And the purpose to treat Grey's motion in the House to-day, and to consider of the Amendment which was to be moved upon it. Grey's motion went to declare that 'the present form of govt. in France is not at this time an impediment to a negotiation for peace' – and the meaning of his moving it is to endeavour to persuade the House and the people that ministers *do* really insist upon the establishment of *monarchy* in France as an *indispensible* preliminary to peace, if they should reject his motion, as he expectd, by a *previous question*, or meet it with a *positive denial. One* of these modes most certainly would be adopted if these were common times, or this an ordinary occasion. But as it certainly has so happened, partly by misapprehension on the part of well-meaning persons, but principally from studied and diligent misrepresentation on the part of Opposition, that a notion has prevailed both in and out of the House, of Pitt's having determined not to treat with any other than a *monarchy* – and as nothing *is* more *false* or could be more *foolish* than his having made *anything like any such* determination – it appeared more adviseable to clear up these mistakes and confute these malicious perversions by a *plain declaration* once for all, of what always had been, still is and ever will be the sentiments of Pitt and of those who support him, with respect to a treaty with France – namely, that it is not the *form* of the Govt. there, but its *power* and *will* to afford and maintain *security* to

---

[385] Sir John Anstruther 4th Bt. M.P. Cockermouth 1790–6; solicitor-gen. to the Prince of Wales 1793–5; counsel to Board of Control 1794–7

other countries, that we consider as *indispensable* – that about monarchy, or republicanism, or Revolutionary Committees, or this or that set of men or set of principles, we have no care nor consideration – *further* than as they go to promise or to make improbable, the secure maintenance of peace, if on other grounds peace should be desirable. To declare, therefore, as Grey proposes, that *this form* of Govt. is not of itself an insurmountable objection – is to declare *too little*. We say at once that *not any* form of Govt. is an objection, merely as *such*. It is an objection *only*, if it be incapable of affording safety and reliance for other countries – and with *any form of Govt. whatever*, that can afford *that*, we are as *ready to treat* for peace (when peace is proper to be treated for) as with a *monarchy* – if Louis the 17th were on the throne. For this purpose Pitt had drawn up an Amendment – which he was to move himself. He read it to us. Some alterations were suggested by one or other person here and there in the wording of it – and then we separated to meet in a few hours on the Treasury Bench in the H. of Coms.

My separation from Pitt was not quite so long – for having heard him say that there would be dinner ready at his house for anybody that liked it at half past three – I thought I could not do better than return there at that time to fortify myself for the fatigues of the day – and so I dined hastily with him, and Eliot[386] and Ryder – and then we went down to the House. I never went down more fully determined to speak than on this occasion. And it was not my fault that I did not. Twice I rose – after Wilberforce the first time, whom of all persons I most wished to answer – and again after his seconder, Mr. Thornton[387] (for *he*[388] moved an amendment) but neither time was I lucky enough to catch the Speaker's eye. I should have risen a third time – but having seen Fox get up I would not contest the *parole* with him – because I think it an ungracious thing for a young man not to yield to one of his rank in the House – and because the House is never very favourably disposed to hear a person who interferes with Fox on the one side, or with a Minister on the other, well knowing that a speech from one of them leads to what beyond all things else the greater part of the House – anxiously wishes, a speedy conclusion of the debate. Pitt, by whom I was sitting, who had been solicitous for my speaking before, thought however that I was perfectly right in giving way in this instance. I was certainly very far from pleased at having missed

---

[386] Probably Hon. Edward James Eliot q.v.

[387] Henry Thornton (1760–1815). M.P. Southwark 1782–1815. Thornton was Wilberforce's cousin and acolyte.

[388] Wilberforce's amendment took a middle line between Grey's and Pitt's and supported a peace negociation consistent with 'the safety, honour, and interests of Great Britain', *Parl. Hist.*, xxxi, col. 1231

the opportunity. The debate lasted till past 5 o'clock. There were two divisions – the first on Pitt's amendmt. to Grey's motion 268 to 86[389] the second on Wilberforce's amend[ment] to Pitt's amendt., in which Opposition were reinforced by 4 or 5 seceders, 254 to 90.

Lady Sutherland had written to me yesterday to desire that I would come home with Lord Gower to supper after the debate – promising to sit up for us. It was now too late to expect that she should have kept her word. I went home however with Ld. Gower – as did Leveson and Ch. Ellis and Villiers – and we supped – ravenously – and for my part I was not fairly in bed till near 8 o'clock in the morning.

*27. [January]* Tuesday I found the consequences of my sitting up such as might fairly be expected – that I was very much *fagged* and worn indeed. Perhaps if Frere had not called on me I should not have thought so much of it – but having him to keep to dine and stay all day with me, I easily persuaded myself that I was too unwell to go out – and sent an excuse to Whitehall where I was to have dined – and spent a quiet day and sober tête-à-tête evening.

*28. [January]* Wednesday morning I found myself quite recruited. The Second Reading of the Habeas Corpus Bill was to come on – and they had threatened again to debate it. In the apprehension of a long night I eat a little something before I went down – but I found my precaution unnecessary. They did not make any debate. The House was up at 7 and then rather for want of something to do, and for the sake of society, than with any want or desire of more dinner, I went home with Rose (of the Treasury), as did Wallace, and Smyth (of the Treasury) and Mr. Orde[390] (the Irish Secy.) – and coming away from there early in the evening, I made the best of my way quietly home.

*29. [January]* Thursday there came on the Third Reading of the Habeas Corpus Bill. It met with no opposition but passed – and was sent up to the Lords.

I dined at Mrs. Crewe's with Miss Fox[391] – Pelham and Fred. North. In the evᵍ· I went with F. North for a little while to his mother's – and afterwards supped with Jenkinson – as did Wallace.

*30. [January]* February Frere breakfasted with me – and in the morning I took him, according to my promise made some time ago, to call on Lady Sutherland. We found her at home, and she received him very good-naturedly – and promises that she will like him very much.

I dined at Lord Abercorn's, with pretty much the same party as

---

[389] 269 to 86 according to *Parl. Hist.*, xxxi, col. 1246

[390] Thomas Orde, subsequently 1st Baron Bolton. M.P. Harwich 1784–96; chief sec. [I] 1784–7; member of the Board of Trade 1786–1807

[391] Probably Hon. Caroline Fox, e. surv. da. of the 2nd Baron Holland

last week. Lord A., I am sorry to say, is going terribly astray in his
politicks. On a motion which the Duke of Bedford brought on Tuesday
into the House of Lords, similar to that of Grey on Monday in the H.
of Coms. – Lord A. both spoke and voted in the minority.[392] It is very,
very bad, for there is no man in England for whom Pitt has done so
much, and in doing it incurred so much odium, as for Ld. Abercorn.
Boringdon, I am happy, has *voted quite right*, and *talks quite as he should
do*, and seems to *retain nothing* of the *perversity of his former opinions*.

In the evening I called at Whitehall and then came directly home.

*31. [January]* Saturday. I dined at Boringdon's – with his aunt Mrs.
Robinson – and another aunt of his – and his sister – and Mr. Lee[393]
(Clerk of the H. of Coms.) who was his guardian – and Ed. Legge.
In the evening I went to Markhams and supped there. Walking
home after supper I passed through Albemarle Street just as Ly.
Suth[erlan]d's carriage was stopping at her door – when to her utter
surprize she found me, as if waiting to hand her out. Lord Gower was
there too – and though *I had* supped I could not resist the temptation
of going in and staying to see them sup, till about 2 in the morning.

*1st Febr*[y] Sunday morning I found my cold so bad that I resolved
not to stir out all the morning; and should have extended my resolution
to the whole day had I not been engaged to dine with the Duke of
Portland, whom I had not seen before since he became a Minister.
Bobus Smith was with me the whole morning – and we talked over
times past, present and to come. You must have observed that his
name does not appear so often in my journal as from our intimacy
you might have expected. The sole reason of which is, that our
different ways of life throw us very wide from each other, without any
fault in either of us. He is special pleading, and I attending the House
of Commons – and either of these occupations accounts for by far the
greater part of every day. At dinner we do not happen to meet
very often, because we do not happen to have many dinner-giving
acquaintance in common, and besides, Parliament introduces such
an irregularity in hours, that, if we make an engagement, as we
sometimes do a week beforehand to dine together on some particular
day, it is ten to one but there comes on something, when the day
arrives, which detains me in the House of Commons beyond the time
to which any reasonable man, out of Parliament, will consent to wait
for his dinner. Our meetings therefore depend in a great measure
upon accident, and take place, usually, by his happening to call on
me or I on him in a morning – and as such do not make any figure

[392] Of 15 to 88
[393] John Ley (not Lee), (d.1811), e. s. of John Ley of Trehill, Devon. Clerk Assistant
of the Commons, c. 1764–1811

in the history of a day upon paper. It is in some degree the same with regard to Frere – that our hours and ways of life lead us very wide of each other except in the mornings. But then Frere being comparatively an idle man, can accommodate his times to mine more easily, and so of him, as you know, I see more than almost of any other human being. Bobus cannot afford his mornings, which are his working time – and so of him I see comparatively but little. The consequence of this, however, is not any diminution of our regard or confidence – but that when we do accidentally come together, we have abundance of matters to recapitulate, and a thousand questions to ask, and comments to make – that one conversation may last us for a considerable time, taking it up always, where the preceding one ended, and leaving it to be resumed again at some distant opportunity. Bobus is a man of the very first-rate talents – and of all others the one whom I most confidently expect to see at a very high eminence in this country.

I dined at the Duke of Portland's – with Mr. and Mrs. Crewe, T. Pelham and Mr. Hare[394] – a mixture of all parties, you see – Hare being a *Jacobin Oppositionist*, Crewe a *moderate* one, T. Pelham an *alarmist, out of place*, the D[uke] an *alarmist* in *place*, and your humble servant a ministerialist. The dinner was exceedingly pleasant, and I wished my cold had been kind enough to allow me to enjoy it to the full – but it had now got into my eyes and head and nose and every part, and so plagued me that as soon as dinner and coffee were ended, I got into a hackney coach and came straitway home to bed.

*2. [February]* Monday morning I found that a long night's rest and some hot stuff taken at going to bed, had been of much service to my cold – and thinking that a long walk might do me good – and feeling that I ought to go and make my personal enquiries after C. Moore, who has been laid up with a cold at Lambeth for this fortnight – I sallied out with Sturges for my companion – and found upon our arrival there, that C. Moore was well enough to have left Lambeth for Lincoln's Inn three or four days ago. Thus we had our walk for our pains – but I had done my duty in calling upon the Archbishop and Mrs. Moore, and besides had done myself as much good as a long walk in the fall of snow could afford me.

In the House of Coms. Pitt moved for leave to bring in his Bills for manning the Navy – 1st by men to be furnished by shipowners in proportion to the tonnage of their ships – and 2dl.ʸ· men to be raised in the counties, at the rate of one man for about every 68 rateable houses – in all about 10,000 men, there being 680,000 rateable houses

---

[394] James Hare (1747–1804). M.P. Knaresborough 1781–1804. A staunch Foxite whig and a firm opponent of the war

in England – the other to amount to about 18,000 men – perhaps not quite so much.

I had engaged to dine with Mr. Maxwell in Camomile Street to-day, if I could get away from the House time enough to be with him by 5 o'clock. And that being by no means likely, I had made another provisional engagement to dine at Lord Stafford's if the House was up soon enough for me to reach Whitehall by dinner-time. The House perversely sat an hour beyond this latter period – and so I had nothing left for it but to dine upstairs with Jenkinson. In the evening I went to Whitehall for a little time – and then home to hot stuff and bed.

*3. [February]* Tuesday Frere breakfasted with me. Charles Ellis came to me, on his arrival in town from Bath. Perhaps I may have omitted to mention that he had gone out of town again and to Bath. The truth is that he had done so the very day after Grey's motion – and is likely to do so again tomorrow – and to stay out of town, and at Bath, I am afraid the greater part of the winter. Lady M[almesbur]y is there, you must know, and very ill, and would be quite alone too – but that Geo. and Ch. Ellis go to take care of her. When first I heard from Charles that this was likely to be the case – and that there was no chance of his being settled in town the Lord knows when – I was a little vexed, I must confess – but I was not unjust enough to be vexed long – but wrote to Ly. M. to desire that she would keep him as long as he was of any comfort to her, on condition that she would let him come up for a day or two whenever I should send him a summons, intimating that his attendance in Parliament appeared necessary. To this condition she chearfully subscribed, and you see it has been always religiously fulfilled on his part. Today however he came up, not in consequence of any summons from me but for a Call of the House which had been fixed for to-day, and which, though he could not know it, nor could I write, time enough to prevent his journey – was yesterday discharged. Here therefore he had come with all diligence and propriety 120 miles for nothing, and he came to me to shew himself, and to boast, and to complain, and to put me in mind that I had promised long ago to dine with him to-day – as had Morpeth and Leveson and Boringdon. This promise I had totally forgotten – and had promised yesterday to dine with Jenkinson, to talk over all that has happened in his history of late. One part of this subject which I purposely mentioned to Ch. Ellis, that he might make exactly the answer that he did make upon it, was that Jenkinson was in great doubt where to go, immediately upon his marriage and London or Wimbledon or any place within reach of London would not do at all. 'But why not Wootton?', says C. E. 'It is only a short day's journey from here, or from any place where they will be married. The house is perfectly ready for them at a day's warning. There is the blue room (or red room or whatever it is) – and then I will send down my cook and two or three servants, and they may stay there as long as they like'. This was the very thing of which I had been thinking, and so I closed with him at once – and agreed that he should call on Jenkinson and make the offer in person – or if he did not find him at home I would do so in his name. When I came to dinner with Jenkinson I heard from him that Ch. Ellis had been there and had made his offer of Wootton, and that he had accepted it gladly and thankfully.

Fred. Hervey dined with us – and he also on his sister's part approved the arrangement entirely; which appeared to us all the more acceptable, from the circumstance of C. Ellis's *not being acquainted* wth. Ly. L[ouisa] or any part of her family – so that it could not appear to Ld. H[awkesbury] (who would be apt to seize on any little thing that might seem to favour the idea of *plot* and *cabal*) that there had been any contrivance of the Bristols to facilitate the accomplishment of the marriage.

In the evening Jenkinson and I went together to C. Ellis's – and supped there with Morpeth and Leveson – and then I took leave of C. Ellis, who returns to Bath to-morrow, and came home much later than I ought to have done, to bed.

*4th.* [*February*] Wednesday I was at home all the morning – walked down to the House of Coms. where there was nothing to do – and then went to dine at Ryder's. This ought to have been a very pleasant dinner – but a bad cold and a cold place at table in a cold room, in cold weather, make one but sorry company. Here were Jenkinson, Wallace, Boringdon, Leveson, Arbuthnot, Ld. Belgrave,[395] Ld. Worcester, Mr. Eliot (a son of Ld. E.'s, just returned from The Hague with the Stadtholder)[396] and Ld. Gower. After dinner I went with Lord Gower first for a little while to Whitehall – and then home to Albemarle Street – where we found Lady Sutherland, expecting us to supper.

*5th.* [*February*] Thursday[397] morning I went to Mr. Pitt's by appointment at 11 o'clock to talk over with him the subject of the Austrian

[395] Robert Grosvenor, styled Visct. Belgrave 1767–1802, and subsequently 2nd Earl Grosvenor and 1st Mq. of Westminster. M.P. Chester 1790–1802; commr. Board of Control 1793–1801

[396] Hon. William Eliot, 2nd Earl of St. Germans. M.P. St. Germans 1791–1802. Eliot had served as sec. of embassy at the Hague 1793–94 and was sent to Yarmouth on 20 Jan. to receive the Princess and Hereditary Princess of Orange following their flight from invading French forces. The Prince Stadtholder made his way to Harwich, see A. Aspinall (ed). *The Later Correspondence of George III*, (Cambridge, 5 vols. 1962–70), ii, 294–95, [1194]

[397] 'Thursday morning ... passed', printed in *NER*, 532–33

loan,[398] which comes on today, and again at 2 o'clock to a meeting at
his house upon the same subject. At the meeting were, as before, the
Atty. and Solr. Genl., Serjt. Adair, the Master of the Rolls, Anstruther,
Ryder, Jenkinson, and T. Grenville[399] – in short most of the friends
of Govt. in the House of Coms. who are in office, or in the immediate
confidence of Ministers without being Ministers. From the meeting I
went to dine with Ld. Gower, Ly. Suth[d.] having promised last night
to have a little dinner for us at 4, before going down to the House,
preparatory, as we thought to a long night – and, as I hoped, to
my speaking. The debate, however, disappointed these hopes and
expectations. The Austrian loan – of 4 or 6 millions (for it is not yet
determined which it is to be – the Emperor's demand of 4 – and *our*
offer of 6 – having crossed each other upon the road) passed as easily
as you would borrow half-a-crown to pay a hackney coachman.
Sheridan, I suppose because he is a friend to loans, went away before
the debate began. Fox was the only speaker on their part – and
Pitt, who brought the business forward, on ours, except one or two
straggling country gent[leme]n. And the whole was over a little after
9 with a division of 173 to 58.

I called at Whitehall – and then went to the Play in hopes of finding
Ly. Suth[erlan]d who, I knew, was to go there to-night. But when I
arrived the Play was over, and so I came home.

*6th [February]* Friday morning Frere breakfasted with me and Bobus
came in to read the newspapers, in one of which he made the discovery
of that curious epistle to me which I sent you some days ago.[400] At
two o'clock I went to a meeting in Downing Street on the subject of
Grey's motion,[401] which comes on to-day, and of which, being only a
repetition of his old one, whereon the House has so lately decided, it
is resolved to get rid by the *previous question.* I was very anxious indeed
to speak to-day, and in talking with Pitt yesterday upon the subject,

[398] The government proposed to guaranty a loan to the Habsburg Emperor raised on
the London money market. A treaty was signed on 4 May by which Britain guaranteed
an Austrian loan of £4,600,000 on condition that the Emperor maintained 170,000
troops in Germany

[399] Thomas Grenville (1755–1846). M.P. Aldeburgh 1790–96. A brother of Lord
Grenville, the Foreign Secretary, Grenville accompanied the Portland whigs in supporting ministers in 1794 and from July to October had been minister extraordinary
to Vienna to assist in negociating a treaty with the Emperor. Although not mentioned
by C. as having been at the previous meeting on 26 Jan. (p. 194), his presence was
obviously required in view of his mission to Vienna

[400] C. was referring to a letter from a Mr. Harrington published in *The Telegraph*, on
5/6 Feb., see Canning MSS, (13) Canning to Rev. William Leigh, 7 Feb. 1795.
Unfortunately no copy for those dates has been found

[401] '... that the government now existing in France is competent to entertain and
conclude a negotiation for peace with Great Britain.'

I had expressed my wish to have the moving of the previous question. He was very ready and desirous that I should have it, but told me at the same time that Mr Dundas[402] had expressed the same wish with myself; and that it must therefore depend on him. Dundas, I found to-day, had by no means given up his intention and with a Minister there is no contending – so I was obliged to give up mine. I still trusted, however, that the debate would be long enough to afford many opportunities of speaking – and as I was dining with Jenkinson, previous to our going down to the House, we settled that – as some Opposition man would probably follow Dundas – he (Jenkinson) not having yet spoken this Session, and wishing to do so – I would willingly yield to him the opportunity which would arise of answering that Opposition man, whoever he might be, and would wait myself for the next – or would follow *him*, as I should see occasion. With this determination we went down – Grey spoke shortly – Dundas shortly – and then Whitbread at some length. While Whitbread was speaking – Jenkinson consulted with Pitt upon the propriety of answering him – and Pitt gave it as his opinion – that as the debate seemed to be so languid, and the House so little disposed to attend, as to make it more prudent to let the division come on as soon as it could, without attempting to revive the discussion on our part. After this opinion, Jenkinson was not disposed to risque the revival upon his own responsibility – nor is it pleasant at any time to interpose ones-self between the desire of the House and the putting of the question – and so our plans fell to the ground – I do not know when I have been more angry. There came then a few skirmishing little speeches of five or six minutes each – and then the division which was 190 to 60 – and all was over by 10 o'clock. So angry was I – that I felt very little disposition to go home with Pitt to supper – when he asked me. I did go, however, as did Jenkinson – and we supped and sat till it was full time to betake ourselves to our night's rest. When there will be anything like another debate – the Lord knows – I see no prospect nor hear no threat of it. There is Wilberforce's motion about the Slave Trade indeed – but upon *that* subject I do not intend ever to *speak*. It has been already and so often discussed and decided in the House of Coms. that there is nothing to be added upon it. And I shall content myself, therefore, as often as it comes on, with giving my vote, without my arguments, for the immediate and unqualified abolition.

7. [*February*] Saturday I was at home all the morning. I dined at Lord Gower's – where were a Mr. and Mrs. Craufurd of Rotterdam, of whom you must probably have heard, as he was a correspondent of my uncle's – and Geo. Craufurd, the brother (who is still at

---

[402] 'Dundas had ... of it', printed in *Marshall*, 82–83

Rotterdam, taking what care he can of the house and property left behind) was a frequent visitor in Clement's Lane.[403] Mrs. C. was with Lady Suth[erlan]d at Paris, where Mr. C. saw and afterwards married her. There was also old Mr. Gilbert[404] – and older Ly. Alva, Ly. Suth[erlan]d's *grandmother*,[405] who bred her up from a child – and instructed her in everything, I suppose, except her own broad Scotch, which she seems to have kept pretty much to herself.

In the ev^g. I went to the Opera, and then home.

*8th. [February]* Sunday morning Mr Borrowes called on me about a letter which he has received from Mr. Bradish, offering to take my lands[406] when the leases are to be renewed in a year or two, paying I know not what fine – and lowering the rent proportionally. This offer was tempting enough, but there was one obstacle to it that did not occur immediately indeed, but is no less conclusive – that by my grandfather's[407] will I am not empowered to let leases for more than one life, or 21 years – and such a lease is not the sort of thing which Mr. Bradish would want, as he could not turn it to any great advantage. Besides, upon reflection, it may perhaps be as well for my interest, as it most certainly is rather more fair, to give the old tenant, or tenants, the option of renewing upon terms of reasonable advantage to me and to themselves – and as the leases not expiring are leases of 31 years, and during that space of time the value of Irish property has encreased so considerably, I flatter myself that the rise in my new rents may be something.

I dined at Mr. Dundas's – where were Leveson, Arbuthnot, Mr. Campbell[408] and the Duke of Buccleugh. In the evening I went with Leveson to Whitehall – and from Whitehall came early home.

*9. [February]* Monday I was at home all the morning except taking a walk to Newbolt's in Bedford Street to enquire after Mrs. N., who lay in yesterday – according to his prophecy communicated to me in

[403] Mr Crauford and his brother, Lt. Col. George Crauford, were probably descendants of James Crauford, 4th s. of Patrick Crauford of Auchenames, Ayrshire who m. Elizabeth Andrews of Rotterdam. They were kinsmen of John Crauford,, q.v.

[404] Thomas Gilbert (?1720–98). Gilbert had sat as M.P. for Lichfield 1768-Dec. 1794 on the interest of the 1st Mq. of Stafford, Lord Gower's father. Gilbert had m. Mary, a da. of Lt. Col. George Crauford who was a brother of James Crauford see n. 403

[405] Elizabeth Maxwell of Preston, Kirkcudbright who must have m. (2) James Erskine (1722–96), a Lord of Session [S] which brought with it the title Lord Alva. Her da., Lady Sutherland's mother, d.13 months after Lady Sutherland's birth

[406] C.'s estate consisted of approximately 250 acres at Kilbraghan in the barony of Cranagh, co. Kilkenny, see Canning MSS (141) where two maps of it, one of 1785 and another of 1796, can be found. Mr. Bradish has not been identified

[407] C.'s grandfather, Stratford Canning. (d.1775)

[408] John Campbell, 1st Baron Cawdor. M.P. Cardigan Boroughs 1780–1796

a letter last autumn – but not in completion of every part of that prophecy – of a boy – but a very fine girl.

I dined by very old engagement with P. Patrick – where I met Robt. Patrick[409] and Mr Higginson and one or two others – but not Harry, who is destined this day at Wanstead to be nursed for a cold. I took advantage of the earliness of the evening to go to the Play, where I have not been a long time, and saw the new Pantomime much to my satisfaction – and from the Play I came home.

*10 [February]* Tuesday. In my way down to the House I called on Wallace, having heard that he was not well, and found that he had been for some days very seriously ill indeed, and was still confined to his bed, and could not see anybody. One loses sight of people so completely in this great town sometimes, that one hardly knows what becomes of one's most intimate acquaintances for days together. I had not seen Wallace since we dined together at Ryder's last Wednesday – but I had attributed it merely to accident – and not thought much about it.

In the House there was nothing. A ballot for an Election Committee stood for the day – which, as it requires 100 members to make a House (instead of 40, the ordinary number) and as people hate of all things to be on an Election Committee, naturally produced this consequence, that a House was not made. I did my duty, however, in going to help to make one.

I dined at Sir Ralph Payne's – with Mr. and Mrs. Crewe, Morpeth, Lord Palmerston,[410] J. Payne, and Mr. Craufurd (not the Rotterdam one – but the old gent., whom I have often had occasion to mention before). In the evening I went to the Markhams and stayed there to supper.

*11. [February]* Wednesday morning I went with Sturges to Lackington's,[411] a new bookseller who has lately made himself famous by an immense establishment near Moor Fields – where he sells books cheaper, as he contends, by I know not how much per cent than any other of the trade. His shop is really a curious sight, from its size and uncommon arrangement. I was tempted to buy more largely, but I believe upon review of my purchase, less cheaply than I intended.

I called on Wallace in my way to the House – and found him up – and much recovered. The House was like yesterday's – that is – none – and for the same reason.

---

[409] Probably Paul Patrick's nephew, s. of Robert who d. 1797. He was a Lt. in the Army

[410] The 2nd Vsct.

[411] James Lackington (1746–1815) established a bookshop in Finsbury Square known as the 'Temple of the Muses', and as one of the sights of London. His cousin, George Lackington (1768–1844), entered the business in 1779 and became its head in 1798

I dined at Lord Carlisle's – a large and pleasant party – Leveson, Morpeth, Boringdon, Edwd. Legge, Ld. and Lady Worcester, Ld. Gower and Ly. Sutherland. In the ev^g· I went to Whitehall – and afterwards went and supped with Mrs. Crewe. Mrs. Crewe is going down to-morrow to see Mr. Burke at Beaconsfield – and I promised to dine with her on Saturday and hear all about him.

*12. [February]* Thursday morning Robt. Patrick called upon me to desire that I would present a memorial from him to Mr. Windham, complaining of a circumstance which does in truth seem rather hard. His Regiment was sent last year to the West Indies. He was embarked with it but received orders, when they were just upon the point of sailing, to stay behind on the recruiting service. He did so. In the course of the service of his Reg. in the Wt. Indies, a vacancy happened by the death of a captain, which Sir C. Grey, as Commander-in-Chief, empowered to fill vacancies, filled up by giving the captaincy to the next Lieutenant (junior to Robt. Patrick) without purchase. Had Rt. P. been there, no doubt it would have been given to him, but it is hard that the accident of his being *ordered* to stay at home on an unpleasant service should put him out of the way of the promotion to which he was entitled, and wch. he wd. otherwise most certainly have had. I do not know what remedy there is to be obtained for him, but I promised to present his memorial though warning him at the same time that I could not presume to do more than barely present it. To-day as yesterday and the day before, the dread of the Seaford Committee[412] prevented the making of a House. I was kept away, though not by the same dread, but by the necessity of going to do certain formal exercises in Lincoln's Inn Hall, which are necessary to be performed before one can be called to the Bar. I dined at Lord Stafford's with Leveson, Morpeth and Ed. Legge. There was a debate in the House of Lords to-day upon the Duke of Bedford's second motion (similar to Grey's) in which we had reason to expect that Boringdon would speak. After dinner therefore we all went down there and arrived just time enough to hear that Boringdon *had* spoken. He had spoken pretty well as I could gather from all reports of him, but what was better than well – he had declared sentiments perfectly correct and unequivocally in favour of Administration. I went with Morpeth and Leveson to White's for a short time – and then proceeded to Albemarle Street and supped with Ld. Gower and Ly. Sutherland.

*13. [February]* Friday morning Frere breakfasted with me. I called on Wallace in my [way] down to the House – and found him getting much better – so much so that he will be stout and well again in a

---

[412] C. feared being balloted on to the Commons' committee established to investigate irregularities in elections for Seaford, one of the Cinque Ports

short time. At[413] the House we were at length fortunate enough to have a sufficient number of members to ballot for the Seaford Election Committee. The ballot is conducted in this way. The names of all the members of the House of Cms. are written on little bits of paper – and put into separate jars. The Clerk draws them out one by one, and reads them aloud till out of those present in the House, 49 have answered to his calling. The list of 49 is then given to the parties (of petitioners and petitioned against) or their counsel – and they strike out names alternately till the number of the list is reduced to 13. To these 13 each party adds one person of its own choice, called their nominee – and these 15 constitute the Committee – who try the merits of the election. I was lucky enough not to have my name drawn from the jar.

In the House I took an opportunity of speaking to Windham upon the subject of Robt. Patrick's memorial. He tells me that it is not in his province but that of the D. of York, the Commander-in-Chief, to redress grievances of this kind. I shall send the memorial nevertheless, that I may satisfy Robt. Patrick by a written answer.

I dined at White's with Leveson and Morpeth – and sat there till it was time to go and sup with Jenkinson tête-à-tête.

*14. [February]* Saturday I was at home the whole morning till I set out to dine at Mr. Crewe's. Mrs. Crewe was not returned from Beaconsfield, being kept a prisoner there by the floods. In the evening I called on Wallace, who gets strength daily and will be about again very soon. I then went to The Opera, but finding it very cold, stayed only a short time and came directly home. To-day I sent Robt. Patrick's memorial wth. a letter, to Windham.

*15. [February]* Sunday morning Harry Canning called upon me to consult with me for his mother upon the propriety and prudence of sending little Stratty[414] to Eton, and putting him upon the foundation – and to desire me, if I thought the plan a good one, to apply to the Provost of Eton (Dr. Davies who was Master in my time, is now Provost) for his *nomination* for Stratty at the next election of Collegers. I do think the plan a very good one, for if he turns out a clever boy, as he promises to do, it opens to him a field for a very distinguished exercise of his talents, in the course of his education there; and if he should be fortunate enough to go to King's Coll., Cambridge (as from his age he has a fair chance of doing) there is the further prospect of an establishment for life, sufficient if not for his

---

[413] 'At the House ... the jar', printed in *NER*, 533
[414] Stratford Canning, 1st Vsct. Stratford de Redcliffe, 3rd s. of Stratford Canning, C.'s uncle

whole support – at least whereon to build his fortune. I called on the
Provost (who is in town) but did not find him at home.

I dined at Mr. Bootle's in Bloomsbury Square – with a large party
of all sorts and sizes – Bishops and barristers and members of Parlt.,
a jumble altogether, which now and then I think very amusing, but
it makes one drink too much wine. In the evening I went first to
Whitehall – and then to the Markhams where, as usual, I stayed
supper.

*16th. [February]* Monday morning Frere breakfasted with me. And
we amused ourselves with reading Mr. Halhed's[415] strange book in
defence of Brothers's[416] *Prophecies*. This rascally Brothers has been
prophesying in print, and by word of mouth for these last three months
or more; and has, I am afraid, done a great deal of mischief among
the lower sort of people – though I never heard much of him till this
publication of Mr. Halhed. The point to which all his forebodings go,
is the certain *demolition* of this country and its present establishments,
*by the French*, under the immediate guidance, and in fulfilment of the
declared Word of God – and the lesson which he inculcates in pursuance of this creed, and which if it were to gain ground, might be
productive of serious evil, is the necessity of *submitting without a struggle*
to misfortunes against which all resistance must be vain. It is always
a considerable doubt whether the taking any notice of these sort of
things may not do more harm than good. Indeed, if one were sure
that Brothers is only a madman I should be clearly for letting him
alone – but I hear in many places that he is an instrument in the
hands of the English Jacobin Societies. It is clear that somebody must
support him or he could not give away his books for nothing: and
yesterday a person in company at dinner informed us that he happened to lodge in the same house with Major Cartwright (the notor-
ious Reformer) and that his servant the other day came upstairs to
him in a great hurry to say, 'Sir, if you wish to see the Prophet that
they talk of so much, he is now in this house on a visit to Major
Cartwright,[417] and is so, very often' – a circumstance which makes it

[415] Nathaniel Brassey Halhed (1751–1830). M.P. Lymington 1791–96. Orientalist and
a friend of R.B. Sheridan since their days at Harrow. In Jan. 1795 he read and was
smitten by Richard Brothers's *A Revealed Knowledge of the Prophecies and Times, wrote under
the direction of the Lord God*, (1794) in which the latter prophesied, *inter alia*, that the
seventh chapter of the Book of Daniel was about to be fulfilled. In March 1795, Halhad
moved in the Commons that his pamphlet on Brothers's prophecies together with the
latters's own work be laid on the table. The motion was not seconded, see *Thorne*, iv,
122
[416] Richard Brothers (1757–1824), see n. 415. In 1795 he was arrested on charge of
treasonable practices and confined as a criminal lunatic
[417] John Cartwright (1740–1824). Major of milita 1775–90 and a leading radical
politician

very suspicious that Brothers is not merely an enthusiast, or that if he is, there are those who mean to turn his enthusiasm to their own account, and to the mischief of the country.

In the House of Commons – nothing. I dined with Lord Digby – so did Leveson, Boringdon, Beauclerk[418] and Cartwright[419] (not Major C. of whom mention is made above, but a Christ Church contemporary and acquaintance of ours). In the evening I called on Morpeth, who is not well – then went for an hour to Whitehall – then for half an hour to White's – and finally from White's to sup with Lord Gower and Ly. Sutherland.

*17th. [February]* Tuesday morning Bootle breakfasted with me and talked over his Russian and Siberian travels. By the bye I forgot to mention to you a bright remark of a Bishop, which was made upon this same subject at Bootle's house on Sunday. We were discoursing of Russian manners and politicks, and making enquiries after the principal persons of the Court of Petersburg, of whom we had heard, either as favourites or politicians, among the rest, of the Princess Dascow,[420] who was one of the chief promoters of the Revolution by which the present Empress ascended the throne, and has figured more or less in that country ever since – and Bootle, who knew her personally, was describing to us the life which she leads, and the degree of credit in which she stands with the Court at present. 'Is it the Princess Dascow you are mentioning?' said a mitred head at the upper end of the table. 'Yes, my Lord'. 'She was in England once, I think, was not she?' 'Oh yes, my Lord, some time'. 'Aye, I thought so – a friend of mine at York sent me the other day a receipt of hers for a sauce for cold meat, which she used to like – you take horse-radish and scrape it, and put a little vinegar (&c. – going through all the ingredients) and it is called the Princess Dascow's sauce. I have used it often myself and found it very relishing'. A company of about 16 people listened to the Revd. Prelate's illustration of Russian history with the admiration which it deserved. I longed for some people to be present whom it would have delighted beyond measure – among the rest for Lady Suth[erlan]d, to whom I resolved to convey it the very first opportunity, as a companion for that famous trait of epis-copal brilliancy which we heard together last year (about asparagus). The present Bishop was Madan, Bp. of Peterborough.[421]

[418] Probably Charles George Beauclerk (1774–1845), later M.P. Richmond 1796–98. C.'s contemporary at Christ Church
[419] William Ralph Cartwright (1771–1847), later M.P. Northamptonshire 1797–1831. C.'s contemporary at Christ Church
[420] Princess Catherine Dashkova, a sister of a mistress of Tsar Peter III whom she helped to overthrow in favour of Catherine II in 1762
[421] Spencer Madan (1729–1813). Bishop of Peterborough 1794–d.

This morning I wrote to the Provost of Eton to ask his nomination at the next summer's election of Collegers for Stratty – and received an answer from him, promising that, and his protection into the bargain. I forwarded his letter to Hetty – and trust that it will go some way towards determining her.

At the House of Commons there was nothing to do. I met Lord Gower there, and went home with him to dinner – and having dined comfortably after a Wimbledon manner, he and I and Lady Suth[erlan]d only – I felt much more disposed to spend the whole evening after the manner of Wimbledon also – than to go gadding about the town. I stayed therefore till it was time to come home for the night. Lady Suth[erlan]d leaving us for a few hours to go [to] the Opera, but returning properly and dutifully to supper.

*18. [February]* Wednesday morning the Provost of Eton called to confirm his written promise of yesterday. At home all the morning. Nothing particular in the House. I dined at Lord Carnarvon's – at the invitation of his son Lord Porchester – the history of which is this. I remember the son, a little boy, at Eton – but knew scarce anything of him there, and have seen nothing of him since. However he came up to me in the House of Coms. some time ago, and desired of me to fix a day for dining with his father and him, and he would ask Bobus Smith and an Eton party to meet me – and after fixing and unfixing one or two other days, at length the fated day came, and there was a great dinner, and Bobus Smith and Beauclerk and half a dozen other quondam Eton boys – and it all went off as well as a dinner can do, where one goes *to be shewn.* Lord Carnarvon seems a very sensible man. In the evening I went to Whitehall and at night supped with Mrs. Crewe.

*19. [February]* Thursday Frere breakfasted with me – and I was at home all the morning till it was time to go down to the House of Commons. Morpeth and Wallace had a petition to present to-day from some persons at Carlisle, complaining that their names had been affixed without their knowledge, and against their inclination, to a petition for peace from that place, and begging that they might be erased. A Committee is appointed to examine into this fact and to bring the *forgers,* whoever they may be, to punishment. I wish with all my heart they may *not* turn out to be *friends* who signed the names of absentees, *on purpose* that the false signatures might be discovered, and so discredit the whole of the petition.

The Bill for raising men in the counties for the service of the Navy, came on. I found the whole discussion of the day likely to consist in county members objecting to the several proportions of their respective counties, one after another – and as this did not promise any very interesting debate, nor threaten any division, I thought I might spare myself the trouble of attending it. It was now about the Whitehall dinner-time, and having no engagement, I did not see why I might not take my chance of a dinner there. I did so, and found Lord and Lady Stafford and Lady Georgina just sat down. Granville and Lady Susan dined out. Ly. S. and Ly Georg[in]a went out after dinner – and I sat tête-à-tête with Lord S. discussing many topics and much claret till a late hour – and then came quietly home.

   *20. [February]* Friday I was at home all the morning. In the House the Army Extraordinaries were to be voted – and in the course of the voting of them – there were two little divisions. I was engaged to dine at Boringdon's but the disposition to divide, which manifested itself in Opposition, and the thinness of the House, which made every individual's absence hazardous – kept me and Jenkinson, who was engaged to the same place, at our posts – till it was too late to hope for more than half a dinner – and then Dundas asking us to come home with him after the House was up, we thought it worth while to wait another hour for a whole dinner – and got to Somerset House about 9 – with Dundas and Mr. Pitt, and Wm. Dundas,[422] the nephew – and dined very pleasantly – and after dinner I came immediately home.

   *21st. [February]* Saturday morning Jenkinson called on me – and we had some conversation upon the present state of his affairs. Ld. H.[awkesbury] seems to be coming round. A very great advocate, it seems, has taken up the cause – and which gives his interference the more effect – without being solicited to do so. This advocate is no other than the King. The symptoms that appear of Ld. H.[awkesbury]'s softening, are his having complained to a third person that Jenkinson does not deal openly enough with him, that he does not come to him and state his wishes and intentions clearly. To remedy this defect I wrote this morning a letter recapitulating his former arguments, and re-stating his wishes and the resolution which he has taken in consequence of them – leaving it open to his father to consent still, if he shall be inclined to consent – but intimating the continuance of his own determination to marry, whatever may happen. I have little doubt but, now the thaw is begun, it will proceed very rapidly. And it will certainly be infinitely better for all parties that the marriage should be an amicable and approved transaction, than otherwise – but it must *be*.

   I dined with Mr. Campbell and Lady Caroline,[423], Morpeth,

---

[422] William Dundas (1762–1845). M.P. Anstruther Easter Burghs 1794–96
[423] John Campbell q.v. (p. 204, n. 408) had m. 28 July 1789, Lady Isabella Caroline Howard, da. of Frederick, 5th Earl of Carlisle

Leveson, Boringdon and Mr. Greville. The Opera – and after the
Opera I supped with Ld. Gower and Lady Suth[erlan]d.

*22. [February]* Sunday Frere breakfasted with me and stayed all the
morning. I dined with Mr. Edmonstone[424] – who married one of the
Bootles. There were Sturges and H. Legge. In the evening I went
with Sturges – first to the Bootles (who besides their Sunday's dinner
have, like half the world, a Sunday evening to which they wish people
to come – and it is necessary to pay one's respects there *once* in the
course of the winter) and then to the Abp. of York's – where we stayed
supper.

*23. [February]* Monday Frere breakfasted with me, and I was at
home all the morning till it was time to go down to the House of
Commons. This day Mr. Pitt brought forward the Budget. The
expences to be provided for were indeed tremendous, and the provision has been made in a way manly and full and satisfactory, and
against which either in the whole or in detail little if any exception
can be taken. You know that by an Act of Parliament of Pitt's own
framing,[425] it is enacted that for every fresh loan, such a quantity of
taxes shall be laid as to answer not only, as was formerly thought
sufficient for the *annual payment* of the *interest* of the sum borrowed, but
for the *gradual* liquidation of the *principal* also – at the rate of *1 pr. cent
pr. an.* Thus *1 per cent* on the loan of 18,000,000 was to be added to
the *5 per cent* or thereabouts to be raised for paying the *interest* of it –
encreasing of course, by one sixth part, the difficulty of the business
of the Budget. And thus, in this instance, and in every other that shall
follow, is it contrived that the expences, whatever they may be, that
are incurred by a war, shall in due time be discharged *altogether*, and
not remain, as hitherto they have been suffered to do, a *permanent*
burthen upon the country. Indeed the best part of Pitt's character as
a Minister, is the fair, bold way in which he meets, without shrinking,
the necessities of the times – not under-rating expenditure, that he
may have the less income to find – not over-rating income, that he
may seem the more easily to find it – but calculating every call at its
full extent, and providing even beyond that extent for answering it.
The taxes of this year about which one hears any complaint are the
tea tax, which it cannot be denied, will be felt in some degree by the
lower orders of society – but, if of all the taxes contained in a Budget
of a million and a half, *one* only appears likely to press upon the poor
at all, it may be lamented that any one should do so – but it cannot
be denied to be in a very small porportion, small beyond all precedent,
to former plans of taxation. The powder tax is perhaps an *experiment*,

---

[424] Sir Charles Edmonstone 2nd Bt. q.v.
[425] 32 Geo. III, c. 55

of which the success may not be quite certain. It may be evaded perhaps or imperfectly collected – but if it be collected at all regularly, it cannot fail, one should imagine, to exceed the amount at which it is calculated. There is much grumbling and much discussion about it, at present, in every company. What to do about servants is the universal doubt. One thing is clear, that for whatever servants you do pay you must do it by adding *a guinea* to their *wages* – *not* by directly *paying for their licence* – for in the latter case you would have a *fresh licence* to take out for every *new head* if they were to be changed once a week throughout the year.

After the Budget I went home with Jenkinson to dinner. Wallace came in some hours after, and we sat till we separated to go to our respective homes.

*24. [February]* Tuesday morning I walked into the City and carried with me to Robt. Patrick a letter which I received yesterday from the War Office in answer to his memorial, and to my letter that accompanied it. It is unluckily no very favourable answer. His case, Windham says, admits of no remedy, Sir C. Grey having done no more than he was empowered to do in filling up the vacant commission as he thought fit – and he adds too (what I am persuaded cannot be fact, but must be error or misrepresentation in the Returns) that from the Returns in the Office he finds Robt. Patrick to have been for near two years absent from his Regiment *without leave*. I did not find Robt. P. at home but left the letter for him, though I had a great mind to have withheld it from his sight, in apprehension of the indignation which he would feel from the persual of it. I thought however, that upon the whole it would be better he should see it, that he might be prepared to meet and refute the charge conveyed in it, if that charge should get before him in his application to the Duke of York.

In[426] the House was the Report of the Budget, and some little discussion upon the several articles of it, particularly that of franking. The restrictions in this article will indeed fall somewhat heavy upon County members perhaps, and members for large commercial towns. We are to be allowed no more than 10 letters a day (either to send or to receive) and each letter of no more than 3 qrs. of an ounce weight. All above that number or above that weight – whether addressed to us, or franked by us, to be charged. So you must keep a wary hand upon your packets and papers for the future. No more pounds of journal to be sent at a time. No more such *voluminous* epistles as have lately gone between Ashborne and Ashburton can pass free after the time of this Act being passed. You had better make haste, therefore, and *clear* away while you have yet the opportunity. To us private

---

[426] 'In the House ... popular' (p. 213), printed in *NER*, 533

gentlemen, indeed, with no very numerous constituents, ten letters pr.
day may be upon an average a sufficient allowance. But to members
for Bristol, and members for Lancashire, I apprehend it may be a
serious charge and inconvenience. It does no small good however in
putting an end to the fraudulent use made of the Privilege by bankers
etc. – and besides it looks like something of a sacrifice on our part,
and is therefore popular. These and similar arguments, I suppose,
were employed pro. and con. in the House to-day, but I did not stay
to hear them, not caring two-pence which way the matter ended, and
being better engaged to dine at Whitehall – where besides the family
were Boringdon and Morpeth and Mrs. Lloyd. Leveson and Boringdon had been to-day to see the Prophet Mr. Brothers – which,
while I condemned, and in very strong terms, as tending to give the
imposture a degree of éclat and thereby contribute to its success with
the common people, this description of their visit, and particularly of
a dispute into which Boringdon had fallen with the Prophet and his
converts excited my curiosity so strongly, that I made a private
agreement with Morpeth, who had not been any more than myself,
and thought it equally wrong, to go and see him together to-morrow.
In the evening I went for half an hour to Lady Payne's – for about
the same time to White's, and then came home.

25. *[February]* Wednesday morning. I called on Morpeth, in pursuance of our agreement, and we went together to see Mr. Brothers.
Being the day of the fast,[427] and consequently an idle day to all
shopkeepers and handicraftsmen, the Prophet's house was crowded
with a multitude of all sorts of people – gaping and staring, and
putting questions of various kinds, some with a view of making sport
for the audience, others more gravely as if detecting the imposture,
and not a few in sober earnest looking for something of inspiration
in his answers. Brothers is a quiet, decent, unaffected, man in his
appearance, with an air of simplicity and humility – which would
incline one to have compassion on him, if one were not persuaded of
the mischief which he is endeavouring to do, and in some degree
apprehensive of his success. But with those impressions one feels more
disposed to wish him, with all his simplicity, tied to a good cart's tail.
He does not seem of any very lively parts. The only answers that I
could get from him to any questions that I put, were – by referring
me to his book or to the Bible. All that he ventures to assert positively
is that 'all will be made manifest before June' – and that 'soon after
the manifestation he shall be constrained to set out for Constantinople'.
I could not prevail upon him to let me know if his convert Mr. Halhed
meant to favour the House of Commons with a vivâ voce warning –

---

[427] The first Ember-day

which I should really have been very glad to learn: as I had remarked Mr. H[alhed] two or three days since in the House, watching the Speaker's eye with great earnestness and anxiety, as if *he* was bent upon seizing the first opportunity of indemnifying himself for the long silence which he has so unwillingly preserved for these three years. I was not so wholly occupied with Mr. Brothers himself – but that my attention was diverted by a dispute which arose in a corner of the room between an enthusiast who professed himself a strenuous believer in Brothers's divine mission – and an honest coachman, who with all the firmness of incredulity was opposing to the ravings of the convert some of the soundest logick that I ever heard in a publick assembly. It was impossible to help taking part with the coachman when I saw him nearly overpowered by the numbers of proselytes who flocked to the assistance of his antagonist – and in taking his part I found myself, before I was aware of it, entangled in an argument from which, as well as from the crowd which gathered round us, it was not without some difficulty that I could extricate myself. I now understood how it was that Boringdon had got into the argument yesterday, for which I had blamed him so much. It really is impossible to resist the temptation that one feels, to check the nonsense and blasphemy which is poured out around one – especially when one sees all the effect that it unquestionably produces upon the poor ignorant folks who come there, the first time perhaps merely out of curiosity – but again and again, from a growing conviction of the truth of the doctrines delivered to them. I came away almost decided in opinion that some steps ought to be taken for promoting the prophet from his present lowly situation to the pillory – and still more decided that it was very wrong to visit him.

Being Fast day I had no engagement to dinner, and hearing that there was to be a dinner at White's for those who were not engaged elsewhere, I called to look at the list of people who meant to attend it. I found that Boringdon had been there on the same errand before me, and that not liking the list of the company very much, he had left a note for me in case I should call, to desire that I would dine with him instead of joining the White's party – and Leveson should do the same. I did so – and we sat longer, and drank more wine than became the avowed purpose of the day.

In the evening we went to White's, which was more brilliant to-night than I have ever yet seen it. The faro table was open for the first time that I remember since I have been in the habit of going there. But I feel no manner of temptation to assist at it. From White's I went with Wallace to sup with Mrs. Crewe.

*26. [February]* Thursday Frere breakfasted with me. At home all the morning. In the House of Commons Wilberforce made his motion for the abolition of the slave trade – which, to the disgrace of the House, was negatived by a majority of 78 to 61, in defiance of plain justice and humanity, and in direct contradiction to their Resolutions of former years. For[428] my own part the Slave Trade is a question upon which I find it so difficult to conceive how there can exist but *one* feeling – and that so plain, so obvious, and so little capable of being *enforced* by argument – that, determined as I always am as to my vote upon it, I never have the least inclination to accompany my vote with a speech. The *policy*, *prudence* &c. may be viewed in this or that light, as people's fancies or prejudices or supposed interest may incline them – and upon that part of the subject, if one were inclined to enter upon it, and had made one's self perfectly acquainted with the nature and circumstances of colonial possessions and politics – one might, I suppose, find materials for speeches enough, much to advance and much to answer. But to that part of the subject I do not look – first because it has been already so often treated and so completely exhausted for years before I came into Parliament that all I could hope to do upon it would be to repeat arguments that have been used a hundred times myself perhaps fancying them new – but principally because those secondary considerations make but little part of the reasons which influence my decision. That rests simply and almost singly on this ground – that when the question is put to me 'Shall such enormities go on – for *any* purpose, under *any* circumstances, to *any* degree?', I feel myself compelled at once, without looking to the right or to the left, or taking any other than a straightforward view of the matter, to answer with an unequivocal and unqualified 'No', and that 'No' dictated by such feelings, and no other, could receive no illustration and gain no support from any speech that might accompany it. With this impression on my mind I did not scruple, upon this debate, to do what it is quite against my rule to do upon any question of importance – I mean to attend less to the discussion than to the division – and so, after hearing Wilberforce's speech I went away without much remorse or compunction of conscience to dine at Sir Ralph Payne's – and came away after dinner with still less compunction to be in time to vote for the abolition.

It is curious, on a question of this sort, where there are no party feelings or interests that keep men together, to see how individuals split and run different ways, who never on any other night of the Session are seen to go but with one another. Of leaders, you know, Pitt is one way and Dundas the other. Fox is violently for the abolition, I rather suspect that Sheridan has some little doubts upon the subject. But he was not present – indeed I do not think he would *divide* against

---

[428] 'For my ... the division', printed in *Marshall*, 86–87

the measure even if he *thought* against much *more* decidedly than I
suspect him to do. Of us younger ones – Jenkinson is a slave trader –
so is Ch. Ellis (being a West Indian – but he was not in town – though
I had very fairly given him notice of the question having to come on,
that he might come up in time to vote, if he thought it put his property
in danger) and so is Gr. Leveson – for such is his father's, mother's
opinion, and that of all his kindred (except Lord Gower – who does
not speak out upon the subject, sufficiently to authorize me to say
that in his heart he is *determined for* the abolition. But I have great
reason to *think* he is at least *not determined agt.* it. He has never voted
one way or other, but always absented himself from the discussion –
and this is a conduct *natural* enough, if he *differs* from Ld. Stafford in
opinion – but for which it would be hard to account, if he *agreed* with
him. Lady Suth[erlan]d too, I am almost sure, is *right*. Wallace and
Morpeth and myself voted as we ought to do. I was rather doubtful,
at first, how Morpeth would go and went across the House to him –
just as the division was beginning – to be satisfied. Seeing *Leveson* near
him I began to remonstrate with *him* jokingly upon his savageness in
dividing so improperly, and was making as if I would persuade him
to *stay in* with us instead of *going out* (which is the form of the division) –
when a man whom neither of us knew, happening to pass by, took
him by one arm, as I had hold of the other, and calling out, 'Don't
mind him, Ld. G. L. Come along and vote as you like, *don't be fettered*',
and carried him out in triumph, really thinking, I believe, that he
had but just saved him from being perverted. There was a comical
impudence in the man's manner, which makes us both anxious to find
out who he was – but we have lost sight of him. After the debate I
went home with Leveson to Whitehall – and finding nobody at home
but Lord and Lady S. I stayed and played cassino with them till it
was the old man's supper time – then went for half an hour to White's,
and then came home. I ought to have mentioned that the company at
Sir R. Payne's to-day were Ld. and Ly. Hawkesbury, Mr. Fawkener,
Wallace, Lord Clive and Lord Macartney (and two or three more).
Ld. M. I have not seen before since his return from China. He has a
history of his Embassy ready for the press, but he waits for engravings –
and what may be more tedious, for the revision of Government before
he can publish it.[429] Ld. Hawkesbury I have not met since Jenkinson's

---

[429]The 1st Earl Macartney was the first diplomatic representative sent to China,
being ambassador extraordinary 1793–94. In 1795 he published under cover of the
name A. Anderson *A Narrative of the British Embassy to China in 1792 ... 1794* and in 1797
Sir G.L. Staunton published in two volumes *An Authentic Account of an embassy from the
King of Great Britain to the Emperor of China.* Macartney was an old student friend of C.'s
father (they had been at Trinity College, Dublin and at Middle Temple at the same
time) and in 1787 he had tried unsuccessfully to persuade C. to become a Gentleman

affair has been in agitation and I thought, that from his behaviour to *me* I might judge in some degree how he stood inclined to it. By that test I should imagine that he was very nearly reconciled to the business – for his manner was all civility. And Mr. Fawkener[430] (who is the person most in his confidence, being Secretary to the Board of Trade at which Ld. H. presides, and otherwise much connected with him) took me aside before dinner to enquire how the affair was going on, professing himself to be quite ignorant of all the circumstances, but expressing very warmly his hope and expectation that it would all come right at last, and be concluded with consent and approbation, as it was best for all parties that it should be. And from this I augur well.

*27. [February]* Friday I was at home all the morning. I dined at Whitehall with only Ld. and Ly. Stafford. Ly. Susan (Granville Leveson was obliged to dine out, and Ly. Georg[ian]a is again ill). In the evening I went to the Markhams and stayed supper.

*28th [February]* Saturday at home all the morning. I dined at Lord Gower's where I met the D. of Bridgewater[431] (who is Ld. G.'s uncle, you know – and likely I suppose to make him his heir) – a plain, sensible man, and upon all that concerns his own pursuits – canals – and the subjects connected with them, the internal commerce and state of the country, peculiarly well-informed and communicative. There was the fat General Grant also (and one or two others). We sat after dinner till we were surprised to hear it strike twelve. And then everybody else going – I stayed for Lady Suth[erlan]d's coming in from the Opera or wherever she had been – and then Ld. Gower and I went upstairs to her, feigning ourselves (as we had a *right* to be, but were not) exceedingly drunk – till, having annoyed her sufficiently, we laid aside our disguise, and supped and conversed very soberly for an hour or two longer.

*1st March.* Sunday I spent in a quiet tranquil manner, just as Sunday ought to be spent – except indeed that I did not go to church but I read and meditated and conversed soberly all day at home. Frere came to me in the morning – and stayed with me the whole day – and we did not stir from the fireside but for about an hour before dinner, in which we walked to Albemarle Street and called on Lady Sutherland. We then returned to dinner, and after dinner resumed

---

Commoner at Christ Church. William Leigh had also suggested Macartney would be a suitable guardian for C. See Canning MSS (12), C. to William Leigh, 5 Nov. 1787 and *Marshall*, 14

[430] William Augustus Fawkener (d.1811) clerk of the Privy Council and one of the secs. of the Board of Trade. A s. of Sir Everard Fawkener

[431] The 3rd and last Duke, famous for his canals from Worsley to Manchester and from Manchester to Liverpool

our book and read till it was time for him to go home and me to go to bed.

*2nd.* [*March*] Monday I was at home and alone all the morning till I went down to the House of Commons. At the House there was nothing to keep me – and so I went to dinner at Mrs. Crewe's – where dined Lord Palmerston, Sir Ralph Payne, T. Pelham and T. Grenville. My cold is not yet so well, but that it sometimes comes heavily upon me in an evening – and when I find it approaching I make a virtue of necessity and come home immediately after dinner. I did so this evening and read quietly till bed time.

*3rd.* [*Tuesday*] Frere breakfasted with me. I was at home all the morning, and did not go down to the House at all (where nothing but Tax Bills were to come on) being engaged to dine at Borrowes's. There was a large City party, and among them some Dutch and Portuguese merchants, with whom I talked a good deal, and collected several little bits and scraps of information. From Borrowes's I went to the Play – and from the Play to sup with Mrs. Crewe.

The whole talk of London now is a rumour, long[432] floating, but lately confirmed, of a disagreement between Lord Fitzwilliam and the Cabinet here.[433] It is said to arise from Ld. F.'s having either completely misconceived or wilfully exceeded the powers given to him on going to Ireland – and having hurried forward the Catholic business, which it was intended he should keep back – and turned out at once all the old supporters of Mr. Pitt's Administration, whom, though it was understood he was to fill up their places with his own friends by degrees as they retired – yet he was by no means authorized to drive out, bag and baggage, immediately upon his arrival. Lord

---

[432] 'long floating ... clearly explained' (p. 219), printed in *Marshall*, 97–98

[433] The dispute had its origins in the junction between Pitt and the Portland whigs in July 1794. One of the results of the junction was that Earl Fitzwilliam, one of the Portland whigs, was appointed Lord Lieutenant of Ireland. In November 1794 he had discussions in London with Pitt and other senior members of the administration on his future policy but each party to them came away with different impressions of what had been decided. On reaching Dublin in December, Fitzwilliam proceeded to dismiss senior members of the Irish administration who were identified with Pitt and to replace them with those identified with the English whigs. In addition, he did not stand in the way of the decision of Henry Grattan, the chief Irish author of the constitutional adjustment which had taken place in 1782, to introduce a bill in the Irish Parliament enabling Catholics to take seats there. Pitt, believing that Fitzwilliam had exceeded the terms of the agreement reached in November and that the Catholic Relief Bill would alienate both a powerful section of the Irish Aristocracy and the King in almost equal measure, issued notice of his recall in a despatch of 23 February 1795. An excellent account of the 'Fitzwilliam episode' is to be found in E.A. Smith, *Whig principles and party politics. Earl Fitzwilliam and the Whig party 1748–1833*, (Manchester, 1975), 175–218

Fitzwm., it is now certain, is to come back, whether in consequence
of recall or resignation is not clearly explained.

*4. [March]* Wednesday morning I devoted to a visit to Lambeth –
where Charles Moore is confined by an illness though not very severe,
yet very alarming, as it has hung upon him for these two or three
months past – and neither its nature nor origin appear to be known
to his physicians. *Confined* indeed I ought not to have said – for he is
allowed and even enjoined to go out whenever the weather is
sufficiently mild to allow of it – and accordingly this morning, as well
as several other days that I have been to see him, I have taken the
journey in vain. Part indeed and one most unpleasant part of his
complaint is an invincible aversion to society of any kind except that
of his nearest relations – among whom he sits all day coddled up, and
apprehensive to a degree of nervousness of the approach of any other
human being. Poor fellow! I trust his *corporeal* ailments are not very
serious – but this disease of his spirits really alarms me, and may have
consequences no less fatal than more substantial and describable
malady.

I dined at Lord Gower's with all the officers of his yeomanry –
whom he had been conducting to Court this morning – and Granville
Leveson – and Sir Edward Littleton[434] (Ld. G.'s colleague for the
County of Stafford) who, in a fit of sudden generosity asked the whole
company to dine with him next Sunday – which I had as lief not do –
one yeomanry dinner being quite enough for the winter. There was
also little Mr. Monckton[435] the member for Stafford – who seems a
very good sort of little man. In the evening I went to White's for a
few minutes – and from White's came soberly home.

*5th. [March]* Thursday – at home all the morning. In the House
there was nothing but some Tax Bills, but one of them (the Wine
Tax) was so tediously discussed and a division upon it expected (which
indeed took place and was 70 to 30 or thereabouts) that in waiting to
divide (like a good ministerial member) upon a clause of which I did
not understand the first letter, I very near lost my dinner at White's,
where I had engaged to dine with Digby and Gr. Leveson. Gr. Leveson
was in the same scrape however – and so Digby alone was the sufferer –
for having waited an hour to two, his patience was exhausted and he
had sat down by himself, and was just finishing his cheese when we
came to join him. Boringdon and Morpeth joined us soon after we
had got to our wine – and after that, though not very soon, I left them
to go and sup with Jenkinson. His affairs wear a favourable aspect.

[434] Sir Edward Littleton 4th Bt. M.P. Staffordshire 1784–1812
[435] Hon. Edward Monckton (1744–1832). M.P. Stafford 1780–1812. He was known
by R.B. Sheridan, his colleague for Stafford, as 'Little Monckton', see *Thorne*, iv, 612

*6th [March]* Friday. At home all the morning. At the House nothing but common business. The news of the day is that Lushington[436] (the ministerial candidate) has carried his election for the City of London, against Ald. Combe[437] by a great majority. This is of some consequence to Govt. and to the War, as the opinion of the City goes a good way throughout England.

I dined at Whitehall – nobody but the family. In the evening went for a little time to White's – and afterwards supped with Ld. Gower and Ly. Sutherland.

*7. [March]* Friday. At home all the morning. Dined at Mr. Smyth's (of the Treasury) a mixed company – men and women – his wife Ly. Georgina is a daughter of the D. of Grafton. There were Mr. and Mrs. Rose and their son young Rose[438] – with whom I was at school long ago, at Winchester – lately come into Parlt. for Southampton – Lady Arden (the Master of the Rolls's wife) – Mr. Banks[439] – Ryder – and Pybus[440] (a Lord of the Admiralty). A pleasant dinner enough. In the evening I went to White's – and afterwards supped with Mrs. Crewe. People would have it for this month past that I was to be a Lord of the Admiralty. I am not sorry for the universal prevalence of the opinion – as it shews that they think I ought to be something soon, and have a claim to the first – or one of the first, vacant offices. But then it must be an office in Pitt's disposal – and these Admiralty changes are solely and exclusively the province and choice of Lord Spencer[441] – with whom I have nothing to do. All in good time. An office to be sure is a good thing in many respects, but I am in no such violent hurry – and I have no doubt as to its being done as soon as circumstances put it in Pitt's power to do it. In the meantime to have *earned* it well, not only in his opinion but in that of the world, is a more solid satisfaction to me than it would have been to have come into it earlier without being thought to have deserved it.

*8th. [March]* Sunday morning Borrowes called upon me, and so did Mr. Higginson – and they both brought me alarming accounts of the ferment raised in Ireland by Lord Fitzwilliam's recall, and the

[436] William Lushington (1747–1823). M.P. London 12 Mar. 1795–1802. His majority was 2334 to 1560. He was associated with the banking house of Boldero, Adey, Lushington and Boldero of Cornhill and was a recent convert to the virtues of the war against France, see *Thorne*, iv, 475

[437] Alderman Harvey Christian Combe (1752–1818), who was returned for London at the general election of 1796

[438] George Henry Rose (1770–1855). M.P. Southampton 1794–1818

[439] Unidentified

[440] Charles Small Pybus (1766–1810). M.P. Dover 1790–1802; ld. of Admiralty 1791–97

[441] Spencer was appointed 1st Ld. of the Admiralty in 1794 as part of the junction between Pitt and the Portland whigs

consequent apprehensions entertained that the measures brought forward, under his auspices, are to be abandoned. Meetings[442] in all parts of the country – Addresses – delegates coming over here – in short all confusion, and upon my word it is difficult to form a conjuncture at this distance, and in this uncertainty, how it will end. It must have been a grave and weighty consideration that induced Pitt to risque so much – and I have no doubt but that the firm persuasion entertained by Lord F. and his friends on the other side of the water, that he (Pitt) would not dare to encounter such a risque, is the very thing that has emboldened them to act as they have done, and set him at defiance. In this case he has acted wisely and spiritedly, and it is to Ld. F. and his advisers that the responsibility for what may happen, must attach.

The rest of the morning being fine and sunshiny, and a Sunday withal, which is a very lawyer-like day for paying visits, I went up and down the town discharging all my arrears in that business. I dined according to the engagement contracted last Wednesday at Sir Ed. Littleton's – with the same party whom I had met at Lord Gower's – excepting Gr. Leveson, who had been wise enough, though taken on the sudden on Wedy., to say that he was engaged. Poor Sir Ed., who is a quiz of the first magnitude, and who I believe had not given a dinner for twenty years before, was all bustle and anxiety during the whole of the entertainment. He informed us at the outset that he had been able to get but two bottles of champagne, and he seemed to take it much to heart when anybody shewed a disposition to drink other wine in a much larger proportion.

I went away as soon as I could after dinner, and called at Lady Payne's. From Lady Payne's I proceeded to White's – and after lounging there half an hour, went to the Archbishop of York's, where I found a multitude of people assembled, but a few of whom staid, like me, to supper.

*9th. [March]* Monday morning Frere came to breakfast with me – and I found no difficulty in persuading him that the day was too wet and dreary for him to think of going away again without his dinner – nor indeed after dinner – till he should feel inclined to go home to bed. We therefore arranged ourselves with our books for the whole day – and except that about 4 o'clock I walked under my umbrella down to the House of Coms, and back again (finding nothing there for which I need stay) we did not feel any inclination to leave the armchairs in which we had planted ourselves about eleven in the morning, till considerably past the same hour at night.

*10. [March]* At home all the morning – with no particular event

---

[442] 'Meetings in ... must attach', printed in *Marshall*, 98

but a letter from Fanny announcing your arrival at Bath. At the House there was nothing but common business. I dined with Mr. Abbot (whom I have often mentioned my meeting at dinner, though I believe not my dining with him before – for till lately he was not much in the habit of keeping house. He was at the Bar – but has lately quitted it for a place in the Court of King's Bench – which is worth to him, as I hear, about £2,000 a year for life – a sufficient reason for pleading no more). The company were Bootle, Garthshore, O. Markham and a Colonel Bentham[443] – a very sensible well-informed man, half-brother I believe of Abbot, a Col. in the Russian service – of two Regts., one of which is at present quartered on the frontiers of China. It strikes me that I have met him somewhere before and given you the same account of him.

In the evening I went to White's for a little time – and then to supper with Mrs. Crewe.

*11.* [*March*] Wednesday morning I again called at Lambeth, but again without seeing C. Moore. I dined at Mr. Villiers. There were Ld. and Ly. Bathurst, Capt. Berkeley, Adml. Sir Geo. Keith Elphinstone[444] (who pleased me very much as a well-informed talking man – only he would insist upon calling me My Lord all dinner time – and I could not make out for whom he was mistaking me), Gr. Leveson (who was enjoying my impatience under my new title exceedingly, and would not help me out of the scrape), Ld. Gower and Lady Sutherland.

In the evening I went to White's – where all the talk was of Lord Fitzwilliam's coming over from Ireland – and Lord Camden succeeding him with T. Pelham, as his Secretary. Among other people I had a long conversation with my friend Lord Abercorn upon the subject – whom I find to be most violently Fitzwilliam*ish* – and anti-Pitt, upon this as indeed he is the latter upon most other occasions. I am sorry he has taken such a turn. From White's I went to sup with Mrs. Crewe. She too has got a Fitzwilliam tinge – which she derives from Mr. Burke, who cannot hear of an Old Whig being in the wrong. But her friend the Duke of Portland is so plain and decisive in his opinion agt. Ld. F. that upon the whole, I expect, she will be kept pretty right in her politicks.

*12.* [*March*] Thursday Frere breakfasted with me. Letters from Bath: one from Leigh, apprizing me of his intention to be in town

[443] Sir Samuel Bentham (1757–1831). Sir Samuel was a distinguished naval architect and engineer and had studied and served in Russia 1780–91, receiving from Prince Potemkin the rank of Lt. Col. and the post of superintendant of the shipbuilding yard at Kritchev. In Nov. 1795 he was apptd. inspector-general of navy works, a position which he held with distinction until 1807. Abbot was his half-brother
[444] Subsequently 1st Vsct. Keith

some day or other; one from C. Ellis, in answer to a summons that I had sent him for Fox's motion upon the State of the Nation, which is to come on next Monday, informing me that he is so unwell, and Ly. M[almesbur]y so very ill, that he cannot possibly, 'indeed he cannot in justice to himself, or in good nature to her', obey my summons this time. If I hear from Leigh that he is seen prancing about the rooms or about the streets at Bath, I shall give him a fine lecture in reply to his excuses.

At the House of Commons there was or rather there ought to have been a ballot for a Committee to try the Westmr. Right of Election – but 100 members not being present at 4 o'clock the House of course adjourned.

I dined with Woodcock tête-à-tête. He is recovered in some measure from the state of misery into which the death of his father had thrown him. He has taken Orders – and the Chancellor, I hope, remembers his promise to provide for him.

In the evening I went to Whitehall – and from thence came early home.

*13.* [*March*] Friday I was at home all the morning till I went down to the House of Commons – where there were not 100 members – and again an adjournment took place. I dined at Mr. Crewe's – nobody but themselves. In the evg. I went for half an hour to Lady Payne's and then to supper with the Markhams.

*14.* [*March*] Saturday Frere breakfasted with me. I was at home all the morning – dined at Whitehall – nobody but the family – and supped with Jenkinson tête-à-tête.

*15.* [*March*] Sunday morning Borrowes called on me – as did Mr. Higginson – and each of them brought with him packets of news from Ireland. Some of the delegates who are coming over with petitions to the King against the removal of Lord Fitzwilliam, are friends of Borrowes's – and he wants me to dine with him some day next week to meet them. I[445] am not sure that I shall much like going through that ceremony. A delegate, hot from our dear country, with all his passions and prejudices in a state of inflammation and irritability must be rather a formidable person to meet at dinner. Petition as they may, Ld. F. is as good as come back already – and Ld. Camden is to set out in a day or two. It is to be wished that the first brush on his arrival were well over. I wonder whether they will tar and feather him. He would look well so.

I went to Wanstead – dined – and stayed the evening there. All well – and returned to town at night – bringing Robt. Patrick with me.

[445] 'I am ... well so' (p. 224), printed in *Marshall*, 98–99

*16. [March]* Monday Frere breakfasted with me. I was at home all the morning and went down to the House of Commons – where a 100 members were at last assembled – and the ballot for the Westmr. Election Committee came on. Fox's motion, which stood for to-day, was deferred on account of the Ballot – and with a view I suppose of giving Ld. Fitzwm. time to arrive in London before it comes on, Fox named some day next week, I believe Tuesday, for making it. I went home from the house with Jenkinson to dinner. All is nearly settled in his business, except the exact day on which the nuptials are to be celebrated. His father is atoning by his present behaviour for his past harshness, and the settlement which he agrees to make, though not *magnificent*, is yet very sufficient.

In the evening I went to the Play by appointment to meet there Ly. Charlotte Greville and Leveson – and from the Play to White's – and from White's home.

*17. [March]* Tuesday. At home all the morning. In the House nothing particular. I dined at Digby's – a large young Christ Church party – Boringdon, Leveson, Morpeth, Beauclerk, Dawkins and the Duke of Somerset, who has just left Christ Church, and intending to go abroad, has provided himself with a tutor for that purpose – but, travelling on the continent being now a matter of no small difficulty, his journey is deferred, and he has the tutor upon his hands in London; and whether it be that he does not know what else to do with him, or that the tutor himself chooses it, or that the old Duchess insists upon it for some wise reasons of her own, wherever the D. goes, there the tutor must go also. From this circumstance the poor little parson gets into many companies and hears many conversations which can set him very little at his ease. To-day for instance it must have been evident to him that accompanying his pupil to dinner, as he did, without invitation, he was not very welcome – as there soon discovered itself among the young ones a very determined plan of quizzing him. I, who was not in the secret either of the plan or the motive of it (for this history of Mr. Mitchell[446] I did not hear till after dinner) was for some time amused by the spirit with which the quizzing was carried on – but soon began to take compassion on the little priest – and finding him to have been educated at Eton – and that we had therefore some common topics of conversation, I relieved him from his embarrassment by giving him an opportunity of talking for himself – for which service he expressed his gratitude by falling upon me with such a strain of barefaced flattery – loud and long – as completely put me out of countenance, turned the laugh against me, and occasioned them all to swear afterwards that I had bargained to defend him on

[446] Unidentified

condition of being thus *toaded* in return. After dinner I went to the Opera – and from the Opera to supper with Mrs. Crewe.

*18. [March]* Wednesday Frere breakfasted with me and stayed the whole morning – walked down with me to the House where I found nothing to do, returned with me to a quiet dinner and to our book, which lasted us till 12 o'clock at night.

*19. [March]* Thursday I was at home the whole morning and alone too, for a very good reason – that having thought it expedient to take a dose of salts I should have been little sensible to the charm of 'sweet society'. My only visitor was a letter from W.[illiam] L.[eigh] informing me of his intention to be in town on Monday.

I went down to the House, where was nothing but common business, dined at Whitehall, where was only the family, and in the evening went for a little while to White's, and then came home. Fox's motion on the State of the Nation is fixed for Tuesday. Lord Fitzwilliam certainly will not be over here by that time, so that Fox must make out about Ireland as well as he can without him. I made an appointment to-day at the House to call on Mr. Pitt on Saturday morning to talk it over.

*20. [March]* Friday. Frere breakfasted with me. At home all the morning. In the House nothing but common business. I dined at Boringdon's – the same party as that at Digby's on Tuesday – Leveson, Morpeth, Dawkins, D. of Somerset and his little tutor, who seemed to want my protection less to-day than he had the last time we met – and indeed I should have been afraid to lend it to him again, lest it should be repaid in the same manner to my utter confusion. Not but I like being flattered very well, but ridiculous, downright daubing is the devil. There were besides Bootle, the great traveller, and a greater traveller still, Berners,[447] who was at Christ Church in my time – and since his leaving the university has been sojourning in Egypt – at Jerusalem and the Lord knows where. From dinner at Boringdon's I got just in time, the length of half a street, to supper at the Abp. of York's.

*21. [March]* Saturday morning I called on Mr. Pitt and had a long conversation with him upon all the topicks likely to be comprehended in Fox's speech upon the State of the Nation on Tuesday – the War – Ireland. Upon this subject of Ireland Pitt seems stout and in heart even beyond what I should have expected from his firmness. He appears convinced that the apprehension of any serious disturbance is very ill-founded, and that the struggle is whether the *English Govt.* or *Ld. Fm. and Grattan* shall be uppermost in Ireland – in short, that

[447] Probably Charles Berners (c. 1768–1831) of Woolverstone Park, Suffolk. Matric. Christ Church 2 June 1785, aged 17

Lord F. had staked his personal interest against the general interest of England in that kingdom. He has no fear about the event.

There was another subject upon which I had to speak to him of a more private nature. Arbuthnot, whom I have often mentioned, has a place in Lord Grenville's Office,[448] answering in some degree to that which Frere has in the Home Office, but in many respects infinitely more desirable, from the nature of the business done in the Foreign Office [being] so much more interesting, than that in the Home – and a variety of other reasons, among the rest, the salary being somewhat larger – Arbuthnot is coming into Parliament and cannot keep his place any longer – and I thought it would be a pleasant thing for Frere to be appointed to it, instead of the one which he now holds. I accordingly asked Pitt if it could be done – and he answered that it was not in *his* power but wholly in Lord Grenville's to do it – but that he would speak to Ld. Grenville the very first time that he saw him – and if no arrangement had been already made by Ld. G. for a successor to Arbuthnot, he had no doubt but that his recommendation would procure the succession for Frere.[449] It is no mighty matter in itself whether it be done or no, nor is Frere so bent upon it that he would feel the failure as any great disappointment. But I was much pleased with Pitt's manner of receiving the application from me, which was such as to persuade me that if it depended upon *him*, it would be done as I desired – and such as to soften and make easy what is in itself by no means a pleasant task, though in this case it was one that I gladly imposed on myself, the asking a favour.

I dined with C. Greville and Lady Charlotte – there were only Granville Leveson and Arbuthnot, and a pretty French woman, an emigré friend of Ly. Charlotte's. In the evening I went to the Opera, and from thence came home.

22. *[March]* Sunday morning I spent wholly at home and alone, my outer door being shut to exclude visitors from the same cause that operated to that effect on Thursday last.

I dined at the Master of the Rolls's. There were people that I did not know – Ld. Curzon (a new-made peer and who seemed to recollect his peerage), Ld. and Ly. Grey de Wilton, and Lord Belgrave (him I do know a little and like him very well). In the evening I went to

[448] Charles Arbuthnot q.v. was précis writer in the Foreign Office Sept. 1793 – Mar. 1795 when he was apptd. sec. of legation, Stockholm. He entered Parliament for East Looe on 27 Mar. 1795 having given up his F.O. salary which had disqualified him, see *Thorne*, iii, 79

[449] C. was unsuccessful on Frere's behalf in 1795 but did succeed in persuading Lord Grenville to appoint him to the post in Apr. 1799. Grenville was not pleased with the result and sent him as minister to Portugal in Oct. 1800 as a result of his inefficiency in the F.O., see *Thorne*, iii, 842

Whitehall, where I found a world of people – and then to the Abp.
of York's, where another world were just going away – and where, as
usual, I stayed supper.

*23. [March]* Monday morning – W.[illiam] L.[eigh] arrived in town
and brought me account of you all – which I had great satisfaction in
hearing detailed at full length during a long walk which we took into
the City. We agreed to meet at the House of Commons – and to dine
together if I could get away. This I could not do in any tolerable
time, as there were some Tax Bills going thro' the House, upon which
it was possible there might be a division. Division however there was
none – and I got away in time to go with Gr. Leveson to Whitehall
and catch the family – Boringdon and Morpeth at dinner. In the evg.
I met Leigh at the Play – and we supped together at the Bedford
Coffee house. W. L. brings me back into my town habits of 3 years
ago – for I have not supped at a Covent Garden Coffee house after
the Play this long time.

*24. [March]* Tuesday Frere breakfasted with me. I was at home all
the morning till it was time to go and dine with Mr. Pitt, as I had
agreed to do, previous to the House of Commons. Dundas, Elliot and
the Bp. of Lincoln[450] dined there. Pitt told me that he must answer
Fox[451] – but that after that the debate would be open, as he hoped,
for me to take part in it. Fox[452] spoke at great length, and made by
much the ablest speech that I ever heard him deliver, Pitt answered
him less at length and with less brilliancy and effect, I think, than
usual – owing, however, to a very natural and obvious cause, that it
was Fox's business to *bring forward* every topick for enquiry, and Pitt's
to *keep them back*, and to persuade the House not to enquire at all.
After Pitt, got up Sheridan – and made a most vile speech, as all his foes
and friends and he himself among the rest afterwards acknowledged.[453]
The length of the preceding speeches had occasioned me to give up
my intention of entering fully upon the subject of the debate, but
there were some little detached observations in Sheridan's speech, so
wrong and so mischievous and so tempting that it was impossible not
to feel a desire to reply to them. 'Do you intend to speak?' said I to
Dundas, next to whom I was sitting. 'No, but you do – don't you?'

[450] Sir George Pretyman Tomline 1st Bt., Pitt's former tutor and Bishop of Lincoln
1787–1820
[451] Fox's motion was for a Committee on the State of the Nation, the standard formula
by which Opposition brought into question the general policy of the administration.
In this case Fox concentrated on the administration's war policies and the Fitzwilliam
episode in Ireland
[452] 'Fox spoke ... infallible adviser' (p. 228), printed in *Marshall*, 83–84
[453] Amongst other diatribes, he poured scorn on the strength of the army and the
country's commercial resources, aguments not likely to appeal to loyalists in war time,
see, *Parl. Hist.*, xxxi, col. 1402

'Why, I did, and I should like to reply to some of Sheridan's arguments – such and such a one for instance. Is it adviseable, think you?'
'Oh yes I think so by all means. I think somebody besides Ministers
ought to speak upon this debate'. Sheridan was now just finishing.
'Well, shall I speak or no?' 'Yes, yes, get up, but I would speak shortly
too, and come at once to the two or three strong points that you mean
to take, for the House, you see, is tired and impatient, and you will
not expect a very good hearing.' There was no time for deliberation,
and so up I got, and in truth I found the House *was* impatient, and
sight of a new speaker, when they thought all was over and that they
might come to a division at once, and go to supper, did not contribute
to appease them. I was no sooner up, therefore, than I began casting
about me how to get down again decently without seeming to be
bullied, and without appearing to design to bully the House by
perseverance. And this I effected at the expence of some lungs by
travelling as rapidly as possible through the parts of Sheridan's speech,
which I wished particularly to attack, and subjoining but a few out
of the many excellent observations that at an earlier hour I should
have offered to the House.[454] N. *Bene* – not to speak again after Fox
has spoken 4 hours and Pitt 2. *N. Bene* also – not to look upon *Dundas*
as an infallible adviser. As soon as the division was over – which was,
I think, 219 to 63 – indeed I ought to say I know it was so – for I was
one of the tellers – I went out into the crowd to look for Leigh – but
he was gone home in great perplexity at having heard the Jacobins
in the Gallery *damming me for presumption* in speaking after three *great
guns* had fired. Dundas offered to carry me home and feed me by the
way, and so I went with him, his son and his nephew (the Lord
Advocate of Scotland)[455] to Somerset House where we found Lady
Jane not yet gone to bed, and supper just ready – and we supped and
talked and laughed to a late hour – the subject of our talking and
laughing being Jenkinson's marriage, which is to take place to-
morrow. I had almost forgot to say that Jenkinson was in the House

[454] The speech does seem a little disjointed in composition but contains some interesting
points as far as C. is concerned. He declared himself a 'friend' to the independence of
the Irish Parliament and on that ground felt it was inappropriate for the British
Parliament to state whether it was a good or a bad thing for the Irish to legislate further
relief to Catholics; later, he attacked Sheridan's view that places and pensions should
be taxed more heavily to support the war effort, arguing that ample rewards for present
and past services was the only way to ensure that the state could avail itself of the
talents of all its citizens rather than be forced to rely on those with 'ancestral dignity
and hereditary virtue', see *Parl. Hist.*, xxxi, cols. 1403–07. The versions in *Parl. Reg.*,
2nd series, vol. 41, 134–37, *Woodfall*, vol. 6, 350–353, and *The Senator.*, vol. 12, 782–83
are substantially the same as that above. C.'s jibe against 'ancestral dignity' was a well-
worn theme of his, see *Dixon*, 22
[455] Robert Dundas (1758–1819) q.v.

to-day, in such spirits and such fidgets that it was quite uncomfortable to sit near him.

*25. [March]* Wednesday morning I went to call on Jenkinson as I had promised last night – and to take a last view of him in his state of celibacy. This evening he and Lady Louisa are made one. I found him very busy buying white purses for which it seems the bridegroom has occasion in some part of the ceremony, though I know not what. The special licence was lying upon the table, and he was in hourly expectation of the arrival in town of the Dean of Canterbury – whom he was to take with him to Wimbledon to tie the knot of his felicity. From the Wimbledon [sic] J. and Ly. Louisa are to go immediately after the ceremony to Addiscombe, which Lord and Lady Hawkesbury have given up to them for the week. They had a prospect of being obliged to go much further for a resting-place when it was probable that the marriage would happen without Ld. H.'s consent. They were to have gone, as I told you long ago, to Charles Ellis's at Wootton, but I am not sure whether or no I mentioned to you in what a fuss Charles Ellis's cook came to me about a fortnight ago, to say that if the new-married gentleman and lady who, he understood, were expected at his master's house in the country, and whom he was ordered to go down and attend – would be so kind as to give him, through me, just two or three days' notice of their coming, that he might have everything ready for their supper upon their arrival. He is an exquisite cook, and I have no doubt the supper would have been a master-piece. I am afraid Addiscombe may not afford one so well adapted to the occasion.

I dined with Leigh at Mr. Borrowes's – where there was large Irish party, and among them some of the delegates who have come over with Addresses upon the Catholic business, and the recall of Ld. Fitzwilliam.[456] From Borrowes's I came home – and Leigh with me – who stayed with me all the evening.

*26. [March]* Thursday. Frere breakfasted with me. At home all the morning. At the House of Commons there was no business to detain me – but I had an opportunity of speaking to Mr. Pitt about Frere's business – and he assured me that he had spoken to Lord Grenville – whose answer was that another arrangement had been in train for filling Arbuthnot's place, but that if that should not be completed, which was possible, Frere should have it. Frere and Leigh dined with me, and stayed comfortably here all the evening.

*27. [March]* Friday. At home all the morning. Leigh went to

---

[456] Early in March Edward Byrne (d.1804), John Keogh (1740–1817) and John Hussey, styled Baron of Galtrim (d.1803) arrived in London as deputies of the Catholics of Dublin to press the case for Grattan's Catholic Relief Bill, see above p. 218, n. 433

Wanstead but returned time enough to dine at Mr. Frere's, where I dined also, and where L. met his old friend the Bp. of Lincoln. There were also Mr. and Mrs. Bates (the famous singer,[457] to whom I left W. L. listening with rapture and delight.) I went to Whitehall for an hour or two, then called on Leigh at his hotel, and we went together to supper with Mrs. Crewe.

*28. [March]* Saturday morning – Leigh and Frere and his father breakfasted with me, and we went together to see the Shakespear manuscripts at Mr. Ireland's in Norfolk Street, and we all agreed, I think, in believing so much as we did see to be genuine. What they prove, or whether they prove anything as to the genuineness of the new Play (Vortigson) [sic] which Mr. I. asserts to have been discovered at the same time and in the same place with these papers, but which he does not shew – is another question. Vortigson, we understand, is not to be published until it has first been produced upon the stage.[458]

I took leave of W. L. who sets out this evening for Bath – whither I have promised to follow him in about a week and to stay with you during the Easter Recess. I dined at Whitehall where was only the family. Granville Leveson leaves town to-morrow with Morpeth, and they go to Boringdon's (Saltram) for the holidays. Boringdon went the beginning of the week. He wanted me to be of the party – and I should have liked it very well – but it is rather too great a journey to undertake for a fortnight. Besides I had promised to spend the Recess at Bath – but Bath, as Boringdon argues with me, was exactly in the way to Devonshire, and would therefore be an additional reason for my taking this time for paying him the visit that I had long owed him. But [459] the chief reason of all, and one which will prevent perhaps for a long time to come my discharging this debt to Boringdon, is one which I cannot state to him. I mean, the residence of my mother at Exeter and at Plymouth – between which places she divides her time. At the latter place Mr. Hunn resides constantly and from either of them the distance of Saltram is so inconsiderable that not only she would expect me to come over frequently to see her (which I should willingly do if it could be done quietly and without much observation) but I would not answer for it that she, or he, or both of them would

[457] Jonah Bates (1741–99), musician and conductor; Sarah Bates (d.1811), a specialist in sacred music

[458] William Henry Ireland (1777–1835) forged manuscripts of, or about, Shakespeare in 1794–95, using as guides the Elizabethan documents in the lawyer's chambers where he worked. One of his Shakespeare forgeries was the play *Vortigern and Rowena*, which was first produced (but unsuccessfully) by Sheridan at Drury Lane in 1796. Ireland subsequently admitted to fraud

[459] 'But the chief ... a fellow' (p. 231), printed in *NER*, 533–34

not come some fine day to visit me at Saltram, and that, you know, under all circumstances, would be rather inconvenient and distressing.

My poor mother is now at Exeter. She is well, and I think she seems to write in tolerable spirits. Mr. Hunn is at Plymouth. They maintain no sort of intercourse with each other, nor have they done for these two years past. Even when they are in the same street (or nearly so as I believe they were situated last summer at Plymouth) she never sees him but by accident, and he passes her window daily – nay passes *her* in the public walks without taking any notice. He is a scoundrel. Good God, that she could ever link herself to such a fellow!

*29. [March]* Sunday morning I went to Wanstead – stayed there all night, and till evening of

*30. [March]* Monday. During this visit I perceived plainly in little bits and scraps of conversation with different members of the family, that it would have been taken kindly, and indeed would not have been much more than was expected of me, if I had proposed to spend the short Recess of Easter at Wanstead, instead of going to a distance, to which in truth it was but little proportioned – and *that* – for the sake of being with you, with whom I am to be all the summer. And when I recollected the kindness and attention which I had experienced at Wanstead, just this time twelvemonth, when after my illness I most wanted to be treated kindly, I could not but feel in some degree the justice of the expectation which they had entertained of having me there now, and the propriety of my fulfilling that expectation. And I resolved therefore in my own mind, though I did not communicate my resolution at that moment to them, that I would set about obtaining a release from my engagement to Bath, and return to them as soon as the House should adjourn for the holydays. I was indeed fettered with other promises and engagements besides that to you. I had written to the Dean to say that I would see him at Christ Church in the course of the week – and I had promised Edward Legge to be with him on Friday at his new living at Witney, which lies exactly in the way from Oxford to Bath. But these I could put off without much difficulty, or I could even keep these engagements in either case – by going to Oxford a day or two sooner than I had intended and still returning to Wanstead by the end of the week – or, as there was just a chance of your not seeing the matter, that I should state to you as occasioning the alteration of my plans, exactly in the light that I did, and not immediately releasing me from my engagement to Bath – I might go to Legge's and there wait your answer, in which case I should be able to return to Wanstead, if your answer allowed it, in good time – or should be so far on my way to Bath, if you rather wish me to come there. On this plan I determined after some deliberation.

Monday night I returned to town in time to go and hear the end of the debate in the House of Lords upon Lord Guildford's motion on the State of the Nation. Ireland of course made a prominent feature in the debate – but Lord Fitzwm. not being yet arrived, as they had hoped he might be, there was but little to be made of that topick. Upon every other topick the Lords as well as the House of Commons had so often lately given their opinion that there was nothing new to be expected.

*31.* [*March*] Tuesday I received a letter from Jenkinson at Addiscombe putting me in mind of my promise to come and see him – and fixing to-day for my coming. But the state of preparation and uncertainty in which I was about going out of town, prevented me from complying immediately with his desire – thinking that I should find a better opportunity when my plans were more determined.

There was a House of Commons to-day, but no other than common business except indeed a speech of Mr. Halhed in support of Mr. Brothers's prophetical character, prefacing a motion for his books to lie on the table – altogether one of the most extraordinary performances that was ever heard in Parliament – perfectly sober, accurate and unanswerable in argument, supposing the premises to be sound and true – but in those premises, to be sure, perfectly mad, inasmuch as they went to prove Brothers not so.[460] When the House was up I knew not where to get a dinner, till Wallace told me of a turtle that was to be dressed this day at the Piazza Coffee house in Covent Garden – and persuaded me to go with him in search of it. We dined there accordingly, but alas for turtle – it turned out to be a mistake. In the evening I went to Whitehall – and afterwards supped with Mrs. Crewe.

*1st April* Wednesday – I wrote to you at Bath to get released from my engagement, on the plea of the shortness of the Recess, not thinking it right at this time to state my feelings about Wanstead. Still however I was in doubt about my visit to Oxford and to Legge – whether to wait in town till your answer came – but that would not be till Friday at soonest, and then I should be too late to see the Dean who was to leave Oxford by that day, and hardly in time for Legge, with whom I had promised to be before that day – and yet to go so far for so few days and to come back again (if it should turn out as I hoped it would that you agreed with me about Bath) seemed foolish. However, all my things were packed up, the chaise at the door and Fleming ready, and so in I got and drove away. Passing through Oxford Street in my way out of town, and yet but half reconciled to the idea of going to Oxford at all, it struck me that I had not seen Frere for a long time, and that I would just call as I went by his door. I did so and found

[460] As Halhed's motion was not seconded, it was not put

him confined with the remains of a fever which had been upon him for some days – and in so moving a plight, as joined with my former irresolution about going out of town, determined me to send Fleming and my chaise back again, to stay with Frere this day, and put off till to-morrow my journey to Oxford, or my decision whether to go there or no. I wrote to the Dean not to expect me at all – giving sundry good reason for my not being able to leave town – and to Edwd. Legge, to say that I would let him know by another letter whether he was to expect me or no. I stayed with Frere all day – dined – and read all the evening to him, and left him so well that he promised to come to me tomorrow.

2. *[April]* Thursday – Frere came according to his promise, to breakfast with me, and found me again unresolved whether to go out of town or no. The chaise was again at the door, and Fleming again ready for the expedition. The folly of going to Witney the day before I might expect to receive your answer from Bath, which might make it unnecessary for me to go out of town at all, was obvious, – but then my engagement to Ed. Legge – and the chaise ready. 'Well Ed. Legge will not expect me until he hears from me again – and as for the chaise, I am ashamed to send it away indeed – but if you will come with me to Wanstead, Frere, and dine there, it will do you a great deal of good, and it shall decide me not to go to-day to Witney'. Frere agreed, and we set off for Wanstead, where we arrived at two o'clock to the great surprise of the good family who had given me up for gone. We spent a very comfortable day and returned to town at night.

3. *[April]* Friday morning came, your letter from Bath – which set me quite at ease about all my plans, by shewing that you had taken my reasons for staying in town so well that I had nothing to do but to follow my own feelings upon the subject – and to write to you, which I did, to explain more fully the *real* reasons of my wishing to release myself from my engagement to you, that I might spend the Recess at Wanstead. I wrote also to Edwd. Legge to whom my journey to Bath being put off was a sufficient reason for deferring my visit to Witney. I wrote to Wanstead to say that I would be with them to-morrow and stay till the meeting of the House of Coms. on Thursday – to Jenkinson to offer myself to him for the middle of next week, if there should be no business in Parlt. (which was probable) for the two or three first days of the meeting – and to Lord Gower to propose coming to Wimbledon at the end of next week, if they should not be returned to town sooner. Frere came to tell me that a brother of his in Wales being very ill, he was obliged to set out this very night in the mail coach to see him. Good Friday is properly a sober day fit for retirement, and, having a great many little odd things of one kind or other to do and to meditate, I stayed at home and alone all day.

*4th. [April]* Saturday morning I went to Wanstead and spent Sunday 5th, Monday 6th, Tuesday 7th and Wednesday 8th there, in a very quiet, comfortable and satisfactory manner, without any bustle or interruption, except that on Tuesday a large party (Mr. and Mrs. Foster, later of Bordeaux, and their family)[461] came to dine with Hetty, and I had the satisfaction of finding myself of some use in doing the honours of the table.

*9th. [April]* Thursday I returned to town and found letters from Ld. Gower desiring me to come to Wimbledon on Saturday, and from Jenkinson, saying that they should have left Addiscombe by this time, and gone to Lady Bristol's at Wimbledon – and that they should be in town the beginning of next week, at their house in Jermyn Street. So I shall see them at Wimbledon on Saturday.

I went down to the House of Commons where there [were] but few people and but little business. I found nobody whom I knew to give me a dinner, or to go and dine with me, so I made a virtue of necessity, dined alone and went early to the Play so as to see it all, which I have not done before I know not when – and from the Play came quietly home, supping at Carey Street in my way.

*10th. [April]* Friday – I employed part of the morning in walking about to see what was doing, and the rest in reading Lord Fitzwilliam's letters to Lord Carlisle in justification of his own conduct, and in abuse of the conduct of Mr. Pitt.[462] A[463] more idle, intemperate publication, or one that more effectually defeats its own purpose I believe it would not be easy to name. It is plain from his own account that he went to Ireland with strict injunctions from the Cabinet of this country to keep off the discussion of the Catholic question for the present.[464] The merits of that question are nothing to the purpose. It is very possible to think with Lord F. that the complete removal of all the remaining restrictions on the Irish Catholics would be a wise and proper measure. I am myself inclined to be of that opinion. But wise

---

[461] Unidentified

[462] Earl Fitzwilliam wrote two letters to Lord Carlisle, but intended for wider circulation, justifying his conduct as Lord Lieutenant of Ireland. The first of 6 Mar. 1795 was pub. in Dublin on 1 Apr. and appeared in London on 10 Apr. with the title *First Letter. A Letter from Earl Fitzwilliam ... to the Earl of Carlisle*. The second letter of 23 Mar. was pub. in Dublin on 30 Mar. with the title *A Letter from a venerated Nobleman ... to the Earl of Carlisle* and in London on 4 Apr. with the title *Second letter. A Letter from Earl Fitzwilliam ... to the Earl of Carlisle*, see R.B. McDowell (ed.), *The Correspondence of Edmund Burke*, (Cambridge, vols. 1–, 1958–) vol. viii (1969), 172, n. 5; 209, n. 2

[463] 'A more idle ... who please' (p. 235), printed in *Marshall*, 99–100

[464] Fitzwilliam's argument as expressed in his first letter to Lord Carlisle was that the cabinet had left a decision on the subject of Catholic relief 'to my judgement and discretion', see E.A. Smith, *Whig principles and party politics: Earl Fitzwilliam and the Whig party 1748–1833*, (Manchester, 1975), 202

or unwise in itself, there are a thousand reasons for wishing to avoid the discussion of it in times of ferment and danger. And he acted most imprudently therefore if he was misled, and most mischievously if he resolved of his own accord to hasten, or not to do all in his power to prevent its being now brought forward. He pretends he *could not* prevent it. The truth or falsehood of this assertion can only be proved by subsequent events. If the Viceroy who succeeds him can prevent it, nobody will easily believe that he, with all his popularity, with all his influence over the minds of Grattan and those concerned in his Administration, themselves the leaders of the question – was unable to do so – and if, either in pursuance of his own private opinions, or influenced by those whom his situation entitled him to guide, he refused to exert the utmost of his ability to perform what he had it in his instructions, and what it was obviously for the peace of the two countries to do – in suppressing for the time a matter so full of danger and inflammation – he abused his trust most grossly, and it was a duty of Govt. here, both from wisdom and from necessity, to recall him. As to the dismissals from office,[465] of which he talks so much, they make but a small part of the question, but what little they do make, is against him. It appears by his own acknowledgement that his whole administration was one continued *job*, covered with the thin pretence of punishing jobbers. To get rid of the Beresfords was his pretext – to bring in the Ponsonbys[466] his object. As for the publick good, let those believe him to have cared about that, who please.

Among others I called this morning on Mrs. Crewe, and found that she was going to Hampstead, where I left word that I would come to dinner. I then went in search of Wallace to propose to him to carry me there. Accordingly we met at the House of Commons – where there being no business to detain us, we set off in his carriage for Hampstead – dined very pleasantly at Mrs. Crewe's little villa, which has been much improved since last year, and returned after dinner to town. I supped with the Markhams.

*11th. [April]* Saturday morning I went to Wimbledon according to my engagement with Ld Gower and Ly. Suth[erlan]d. My first business on my arrival at Wimbledon was to pay my respects at the other side of the Common to Jenkinson and Lady Louisa, who were settled

---

[465] Fitzwilliam's argument as expressed particularly strongly in his second letter to Lord Carlisle was that it was his dismissal of John Beresford, the 1st commr, of the Irish Revenue Board and an ardent supporter of Pitt's policies in Ireland, together with his associates which was the real reason for his recall, not his policy on Catholic relief, see E.A. Smith loc. cit., 202–03

[466] The Ponsonby family headed the Irish branch of the whig party. Fitzwilliam had proposed that his kinsman, George Ponsonby q.v., should be appointed Irish Attorney General

at Lady Bristol's till Monday, when they take possession of their house in Jermyn Street. I found them both as well as could be expected.

At Lord Gower's I found the Chief Baron and Ly. Louisa Mcdonald. They stayed there, this day, and Sunday the 12th and 13th. Monday morning I returned to town.

On Monday there was a House of Commons but nothing particular in it. I dined at Whitehall, where were Lord and Lady Worcester, Lord Thurlow and the Duke of Bridgewater. The two last in high spirits at having this day carried through the House of Lords their final resolution in favour of Mr. Hastings, whose champion Lord Thurlow has been throughout, and has now brought him safely, as it appears, to the door of an acquittal. The formal verdict indeed is not yet pronounced in Westminster Hall, but there is every reason to believe that it will be comfortable to the separate Resolutions which have been moved by Lord T. relative to the several Charges, and carried in the House by a decisive majority. The guilt or innocence of Mr. Hastings is a subject upon which, not having come early to the consideration of it, and not having all the information necessary on the momentous and complicated points contained in it, I have never ventured to make up my opinion – but whatever the truth of the Charges alledged against him may be, one thing is clear, as to the mode in which the trial upon them has been conducted – which is, that the protraction of it to so enormous a length has been a cruel oppression upon the individual and a disgrace to the national justice; and be the final sentence fair or unfair, be it to acquit or to condemn, one cannot but rejoice at this circumstance, that some sentence is at length about to be pronounced. Where the blame of the protracted length of the trial ought to fall, it is perhaps not so difficult to determine. The Lords certainly might have prevented it at least by a diligent discharge of their judicial duty. By sitting from day to day they might have compressed into two years, I believe into one, what has now lasted seven, and they ought to have done so.

In the evening I went to White's and then home.

*14. [April]* Tuesday morning I went to call at Lambeth and met C. Moore and the Archbishop in a carriage on my way. I mentioned how often I had called to see C. M. without success. The Abp. said it was C. M.'s fault that he would be denied to everybody, but engaged that if I would come to-morrow he *should* see me. At the house of Commons there was business of one kind or another, which kept us sitting till about 8 o'clock. I then dined upstairs with three or four stragglers that I found there – and went in the evening to the Abp. of York's, where I supped.

*15. [April]* Wednesday I fulfilled my engagement of yesterday by going to Lambeth and found C. M. at home. He is certainly very unwell, reduced, languid and low-spirited – but without any visible cause of complaint – no loss of appetite – no want of sleep – nothing but a feverishness which perhaps is more a consequence than a cause of his general langour and melancholy. He is advised to try what change of air and dissipation of spirit will do for him, and he is going in a day or two, for the sake of the former, to Weymouth, where Woodcock has offered to accompany him. But for the dissipation, I am afraid that is not to be procured easily at Weymouth at this season of the year – and as to spirits I know nothing that his companion is less qualified to inspire, since, with the best disposition in the world, Woodcock has less of chearfulness in him than almost any of his acquaintance that C. M. could have picked out. I fear they will be a very gloomy pair, but I trust to the physical effects of sea-bathing and sea air for Charles Moore, and to the assurances which he says he receives every day from his physician that there is nothing serious that ails him. Poor fellow! It is really a very distressing thing to see him so unaccountably broken. I should apprehend that there was something on his mind, but that I know from the Archbishop that they have discussed together subjects which were most likely to weigh upon him, and that the discussion ended to their mutual satisfaction.

I dined at the Abp. of York's, and stayed there the whole evening, and supped there.

Frere is still out of town with his brother in Wales but writes that his brother is recovering.

Gr. Leveson, Morpeth, and Boringdon are just returned from Devonshire. John Sneyd comes to town to spend three weeks or a month to-day or to-morrow, and what is no small pleasure to me, Charles Ellis is to be in town on Friday for the rest of the year, and Ly. Malmesbury, who is nearly recovered of a very severe illness, will soon follow.

*16. [April]* Thursday morning I called on John Sneyd, found him, and walked about with him the whole morning – amongst the mob that were assembled to see the Princess of Wales go to Court.[467] We *blackguarded*, among the blackguards, to get a good place to see her, but in vain – for lo! when the coach came by we were on the wrong side of the way.

I dined at John Ellis's (Charles's elder brother) with Wallace – in the evening went to the Play, and from the Play to sup with Mrs. Crewe, where J. Sneyd and Arbuthnot came also.

---

[467] The marriage of the Prince of Wales and Princess Caroline had taken place in the Chapel Royal on 8 Apr., the Princess having arrived in England on the 5th. This is presumably a reference to the Princess's first visit to the weekly Thursday levee in the Queen's Drawing Room

*17. [April]* Friday morning I received from Bath the first intelligence of Fanny's acceptance of Col. Spencer (quod faustum felique sit!)[468] I called on Bess Canning and Bess Patrick, who are in town for this week at Mr. Johnson's – to give them tickets for themselves and Harry &c. for Mrs. Crewe's masquerade. I went to the House of Commons, which was not up till about 8 o'clock. I dined upstairs – and then came home to dress. Wallace and Leveson and I met at Lady Louisa Jenkinson's, where we supped very pleasantly – put on our dominos and went together to Mrs. Crewe's. I had never in my life been at a masquerade, publick or private, and was therefore all delight and admiration. Tish at her first Ball at Bath was nothing to me in point of friskiness. From Mrs. Crewe's, where I stayed till the company began to thin, Wallace seduced me to the Publick Masquerade at the Haymarket, which I found at least as dull and disgusting as the other had been pleasant and lively. I stayed however some time to see the humours of it – but when at about 1/2 past 4 o'clock the gentlemen began to get quarrelsome and the ladies drunk and sick, I whipped my domino into my pocket and walked home to the Temple to my bed.

*18. [April]* Saturday I was not long up before Charles Ellis came to me. I ordered my outer door to be shut, for we had to talk of many subjects, and our talk lasted the whole morning.

I dined at Lord Carnarvon's. There was Bobus Smith and Beauclerk, the Duke of Somerset and his tutor, and several others. The Opera – and from the Opera to supper with Charles Ellis – Lady Malmesbury is come to town, but is not yet well enough to go out much – nor settled enough to receive one constantly at home. Ld. M. had let his own house for this year, not expecting to want it. In Mrs. Robinson's house at Privy Garden there is not room for Ld. and Ly. M., so they are for the present at an hotel, till Mrs. R. goes out of town, which she will soon do, and then Ly. M. adjourns to Privy Garden, where she will be established.

*19. [April]* Sunday Lord Gower had asked me to Wimbledon to-day where Gr. Leveson and Morpeth are going. But I was engaged to dine with the Bootles, and therefore could not be of the party. I dined at the Bootles with a large party of all sorts and sizes, some of whom I knew. In the evening I called at Whitehall, where I found

---

[468] Frances Canning's engagement to her sister-in-law Jane's brother, Brent, subsequently Sir Brent Spencer (c. 1760–1828) who was promoted to brevet lt.-col in 1794, see *Thorne*, v, 229. C. regarded Spencer as a blackguard as a result of the financial terms he insisted on as part of the match and his own claim to £4000 prize money for his efforts in the West Indies campaign, Canning MSS, (13), C. to Rev. William Leigh, 8, 22 June 1795

that Lord Stafford was ill, and so I went away without going in at all, and supped at the Abp. of York's.

*20. [April]* Monday I was at home all the morning till it was time to go down to the House of Commons where there was no business to keep me long. I dined at Charles Ellis's, Geo. Ellis, Boringdon, Leveson and Morpeth. After dinner I went with C. and Geo. Ellis to a children's Play at Mrs. Robinson's in Privy Garden, in which Lady Malmesbury's children, boys and girls, acted principal parts. After the Play we supped – Mrs R., Ld. and Ly. My., the Ellises and Lord Pembroke; and sat till a late hour very pleasantly.

*21. [April]* Tuesday morning J. Sneyd called on me early, and insisted upon taking me a round of visits, which consumed the whole morning. At the House of Coms. Mr. Halhed was making a second motion upon the subject of Mr. Brothers, but having heard his first I did not think it necessary to stay this out – thinking it pleasanter to go away to dinner with Charles Ellis – to meet Lord St. Helens. You of course know all about him, a diplomatick character, and one who has represented this country and done it well in half the Courts of Europe, last in Spain. I had never been in company with him before, and had a curiosity to see and become acquainted with him. He is an able and well-informed man, and as we were only four (Ch. and Geo. Ellis, Ld. St. H. and myself) we had an opportunity of talking a good deal at our ease, and I derived much instruction from his conversation. His manners are cold – but perfectly gentlemanlike.[469]

In the evening I went to the Play in pursuance of a promise made when I was last at Wanstead to meet Hetty there whenever she should make her first appearance. Our meeting was of little consequence to either of us, further than the keeping of my promise – as her box was crammed so full with the family and her attendant Wanstead beaux, that I could hardly get a shake of the hand through the crowd from her. It was pleasant to see her looking so well and in such spirits.

From the Play I went to sup with Lady M[almesbur]y at her hotel, and Charles Ellis came there to meet me.

*22. [April]* Wednesday I was busy all the morning. No House of Commons to attend, being a day of Canals and other private business. I dined with Jenkinson and Ly. Louisa. There were Lady Jane Dundas, Fred. Hervey, Wallace and Boringdon. They are established very handsomely, and the dinner too was very pleasant. But I do not know why – I have my doubts whether they will be a constant and

---

[469] Alleyne Fitzherbert, 1st Baron St. Helen's had been a diplomat since 1777. His last mission was not in fact to Spain but to the United Provinces where he had been ambassador from Apr. 1794 to c. 15 Jan. 1795 when he left the Hague on the approach of the French army

comfortable house. I cannot explain what or where the cause of this suspicion is, but somehow or other I cannot help apprehending that we shall not find Jenkinson's house altogether such as before his marriage we used to determine it should be. It is not fair to judge from the first year indeed, and indeed there is as yet nothing from which to judge otherwise than favourably. She is delightful. He has all the disposition in the world to do everything that is pleasant to his friends – but he does not go about it in quite the right way. I suppose there is something in the novelty of his situation to be sure. The cares of a married man seem to have come upon him at once. But after all, it will all be right, I am persuaded. One must give a man some time to recover himself.

In the evening I went to Whitehall. Lord Stafford is got well again. From Whitehall to White's for half an hour, and then to sup with Mrs. Crewe, where Windham came, whom I have not met this long time except in the House of Commons. We had a coze after Mrs. Crewe's own heart.

*23. [April]* Thursday morning I went down early to Westminister Hall, being the day of Judgement there upon Hastings's trial. The Hall was crowded beyond all example in every part, and made altogether one of the greatest spectacles that can be imagined. The only part of it that was not well filled was that which ought to have been the best attended, that is, the peers, who were only 29 or 30 in number. I mean those who were robed to give their votes. Plenty of them were there as spectators. The questions upon which the vote of guilty or not guilty was to be pronounced were 16. The first round was the most aweful and impressive ceremony possible, and was heard with the most profound and reverent attention, but as soon as one had heard all the peers once or twice, so as to become acquainted with their sentiments and their manner of delivering them, the awe and reverence was pretty much worn off and there was no refuge left from the tiresomeness of the 16 repetitions, but in *quizzing* their several Lordships, which helped away the morning not unentertainingly. When the last vote of acquittal was pronounced there was a general silence in expectation of Hastings's saying something – and a foolish rumour had gone abroad that whatever he might say Fox was determined to answer. This I presume the Lords would never have permitted. And Hastings was too wise to give any provocation of the kind. He simply bowed and retired, which was, to my mind, in much better taste than if he had made the longest and most eloquent address that could be devised. When all was over I congratulated my friend the Archbishop of York, who next to Hastings himself was, I believe, the person in the Hall most interested in the verdict. His son, you know, was in Mr. H.'s employment in India, made a considerable fortune, and has been on the trial one of the most material witnesses in his favour.[470] All this ought perhaps in delicacy to have prevented the Abp. from taking so active a part as he has done throughout the trial, and from giving his vote upon it at all. But he thought otherwise.

In my way from Westmr. Hall I called upon Goddard, whom I have not seen above once or twice the whole winter. He has been very unwell and has thoughts of going abroad soon to recruit his health in hopes of being able upon his return home to assume a more important and more lucarative but more laborious post in Ld. Grenville's Office. From what he tells me of the arrangements about to be made in that Office, I am almost afraid that Frere's succession to Arbuthnot is not likely to be effected. I find, however, that Mr. Pitt has done *his* part by speaking to Lord Grenville, as he promised me, for so Ld. G. told Goddard. I should have been very angry if the failure (should it fail) had originated with *him*. House – nothing particular. I dined at C. Ellis's, with Geo. Ellis, Sneyd, E. Legge and Gr. Leveson. A very pleasant dinner and a long one. Late in the evening I went for half an hour to Lady Guildford's (the first assembly I believe that I have visited this year) and then home.

*24. [April]* Friday I was at home all the morning. In the House of Coms. there was nothing to do – but a notice was given there by Ld. Milton[471] (Ld. Fitzwm.'s Secretary in Ireland) and in the H. of Lds. by Ld. F. himself, of their intention to bring the Irish business forward in some shape or other for discussion.

I dined with Garthshore (Dundas's private secretary and the Dean's great friend). There were Sneyd, Boringdon, H. Legge, the Lawyer – and Mr. Monck, husband of Ly. Eliz. Monck (which said Ly. Elizth. is a dear friend of Boringdon – and Leveson and Morpeth – and is, as they all assure me, very pretty and very pleasing, and a person with whom I ought to be acquainted).[472] In the evg. I went to Whitehall, and from Whitehall home.

*25. [April]* Saturday – at home all the morning. I dined at Whitehall – the family and Boringdon. Went to the Opera – from the Opera to Lady Malmesbury's at her hotel, and then home.

*26. [April]* Sunday morning I devoted to paying a multitude of visits which has been long accumulating upon my hands. I dined at

[470] William Markham (1760–1815), e. s. of William, archbishop of York q.v. and private sec. to Warren Hastings and, later, Resident of Benares
[471] Hon. George Damer, 2nd Earl of Dorchester, styled Visct. Milton 1792–98. M.P. Malton 1792–98; chief sec. to Ld. Lt. [I], 1794–95
[472] Henry Monck, an Irishman, had m. Lady Elizabeth Araminta Gore, 2nd da. of the 2nd Earl of Arran

Ryder's with Gr. Leveson, Wallace, Ld. Malden,[473] Mr. Smyth (of
the Treasury) and Mr. Robt. Smith, head of the banking house[474] –
a great personal friend of Mr. Pitt. In the evening I went to Whitehall
and then with Sneyd to supper at Mrs. Crewe's. Sneyd has brought
with him to town a book of drawings illustrative of the Bath Guide,
incomparably good. They were exhibited to-night for publick entertainment at Whitehall – and everybody agreed that he must publish
them.[475] He must bring them with him to Ashborne the first time he
comes there.

*27. [April]* Monday – at home all the morning till it was time to go
to the House. In my way down called on C. Ellis – and took him to
call on Ly. Sutherland. Some day to be fixed immediately for our
going to Wimbledon. In the House of Coms. the King's Message
relative to the P. of Wales's Establishment and to his encumbrances,
was delivered. It excited a good deal of murmuring, and produced a
motion for a Call of the House – which is appointed for this day
fortnight.[476]

I dined with Newbolt and his wife and met there Sir Digby and
Lady Mackworth.[477] You may remember my having mentioned them
to you before as a Mr. and Mrs. Mackworth, living at Oxford. Their
history is rather interesting. He was the second son of Sir Herbert
Mackworth, and by him intended and proclaimed the heir to his
fortune, in exclusion of the elder brother, who was little better than
an idiot. Sir Herbert, however, died some years ago without executing
the instrument necessary for leaving the estate to this, his second son –
and the eldest of course succeeded to it. Mackworth then married,
and having four or five children was left completely destitute, with
only a small annuity to subsist him and his family – and came to
Oxford at rather an advanced period of life to qualify himself for

[473] George Capel Coningsby, 5th Earl of Essex, styled Visct. Malden 1757–99. M.P.
New Radnor Boroughs 1794–99

[474] Robert Smith, 1st Baron Carrington. M.P. Nottingham 1779–97

[475] There were at least two guides to Bath in circulation at this time: *The Stranger's
Assistant and Guide to Bath*, (Bath, 1773 and reissued in 1793 and 1795); and a new
edition of Christopher Anstey's *The New Bath Guide*, pub. in London in 1794

[476] The Prince's income was £73,000 but his debts had grown since the last settlement
by Parliament in 1787 to £630,000. The government proposed that the income should
be raised to £138,000 but that £38,000 should be set aside annually to pay off the
debt. The opposition in Parliament to such generous terms was so great that Pitt was
forced to modify them in June by raising the proportion of income to pay off the debt
to £78,000 p.a., see A. Aspinall, *The Correspondence of George Prince of Wales*, (London,
8 vols., 1963–71), iii, 4–5. C.'s subsequent circumspection on this issue may have been
due to the fact that he had been favourably received by the Prince on their first meeting
in Sept. 1790, see *Marshall*, 27

[477] Sir Digby Mackworth 3rd Bt. who m. 1788, Jane, only da. and h. of Rev. Matthew
Deere

taking Orders, and to live cheaply there till he should be able to enter upon the profession. Last year his elder brother (who had never been upon good terms with him) died suddenly, leaving no children – but bequeathing by a Will of five lines long the whole of his property, real and personal, amounting to many thousands a year, to a young wife whom he had lately married, and to her disposal for ever. Mackworth succeeded to a barren title, which only made his former poverty more conspicuous and more distressing. The character of his late brother, and the circumstances of the Will give room to hope that something might be tried to set it aside, as having been fraudulently obtained. How this may turn out if they should go to law is very doubtful, but there has been a compromise offered to them by the Dowager Ly. Mackworth and her friends of about £800 a year, I think, and a sum in ready money, and they are now consulting with their Counsel whether or no it will be adviseable to accept it. I trust their Counsel will determine what is most for their advantage. He is a very good sort of man, and his wife, Ly. M. a very charming, pretty and clever woman.[478] They are great friends of Newbolt's. It was at their house at Oxford, during the Encaenia, that N. and his Julia first met and became enamoured of each other.

In the evg. I went to Ly. Malmesbury's and supped with her and Ch. Ellis.

*28. [April]* Tuesday – at home all the morning. House of Coms. – nothing but ordinary business. I dined with Charles Ellis. Nobody but Geo. Ellis and Gr. Leveson – a very, very comfortable dinner – from which I went in good time to sup with the Markhams.

*29. [April]* Wednesday morning. Messrs. Wathen and Phipps, the oculists came, in consequence of a note from me, to advise upon the subject of my styes. They can cure them, they say, with great certainty, by an ointment, of which they applied a small portion to each, and taught me how to do so every morning. But then this cure is slow, and the application is exceedingly painful, so that they shall not be surprized, if, after having gone on with it for some time, I shall resolve upon having that on the right eye, which is large, and will stand a long siege before it surrender, cut out – which can be done safely, in a moment, and for ever. That on the left, which is hardly perceptible, will yield in a much shorter time, for the ointment.

I did not go out the whole day except just walking down to the House to assure myself that there was no business there, and back again – but was very long all the morning – dined by myself – and returned to my occupations after dinner. At night I went to P. Patrick's to sup with the Irish Club, to which I have been a great truant, not

---

[478] It appears that the offer was accepted

having attended it once, I think, since my coming to town. I played my rubber at whist, and talked Irish politicks till 1/2 pt. 12.

*30. [April]* Thursday at home all the morning. In the House of Coms. nothing. In the H. of Lds. Ld. Fitzm.'s business was to have come on (Ld. Guildford has undertaken to move it) – but it is put off till next week on account of the D. of Portland's illness. He is not very dangerously indisposed, I believe, but will be about again in a day or two.

I dined with William Spencer and his wife. Wm. Spencer is a son of Ld. Charles Spencer's – brother of the D. of Marlborough. He was at Christ Church for about half a year in my time, and lived very much with Wallace and Jenkinson and Henry Spencer and myself. Since that he has spent most of his time abroad – in a state of dreadful ill health, during which he has married a very pretty foreign wife, a German I think, and is now returned to live, upon God knows what means, in England. He is a clever and well-informed man, but of the strangest and wildest disposition imaginable.[479] Wallace and Sneyd dined there. In the evening I went to Whitehall, and from thence came home, supping at Carey Street in my way.

*May 1st.* Friday morning – whether it was the German cookery of Spencer's dinner, or the execrableness of the port, of which we drank a good deal after dinner, I know not – but I found myself so very unwell that I would have given a great deal to stay at home all day. At the House of Commons there was nothing to call for my attendance. But I had promised to attend a Committee upstairs appointed to enquire into the abuses of the Post Office, in which, the friends of Govt. neglecting to attend, questions were carried every day against them. I went there for a few hours and wrangled a point or two about a *cheese* that was stated to have come in a frank to one of the Clerks of the Post Office.[480]

I dined at Whitehall – nobody but the family. Soon after dinner I came directly home.

*2ᵈ [May]* Saturday morning – I called in Downing Street, wanting to speak to Mr. Pitt upon two or three matters that are coming before the House of Commons – particularly to know what he means to do about the Prince of Wales's debts – but Mr. Pitt was gone into the country. Being once out in the morning, the day was consumed I am afraid rather idly – so that not returning home till it was time to dress

---

[479] William Robert Spencer (1769–1834) who m. 1791, Susan, wid. of Count Spreti and da. of Count Jenison Walworth. Lord Henry Spencer, s. of the 4th Duke of Marlborough was a Christ Church contemporary of C.'s and had been a member of the Debating Club

[480] A select committee set up to enquire into abuses with regard to franking in public offices. There is no record of C.'s participation on 1 May

for dinner, I had no opportunity of knowing till then that W[illiam] L[eigh] was come to town – and no time to go in search of him. He left word however that he would breakfast with me to-morrow. I dined at Charles Ellis's. There was a large party consisting of Lord and Lady Malmesbury, Ld. St. Helens, Mrs. Robinson, Elliot, Geo. Ellis and Mundy (of Shipley). In the evening I went to the Opera, and from the Opera came home.

*3ᵈ [May]* Sunday morning W. L. came to breakfast with me, and we were together the whole morning walking ourselves off our legs, and talking over Ashborne Hall and its inhabitants, and Fan particularly, who alas! is not to be one of its inhabitants much longer. Wherever she goes, God grant that she meet with those who know as well how to value her worth, and who will study as much to promote her happiness, as those whom she leaves behind her. It was no common engagement that should have obliged me to leave Leigh, when our walk was over, to find his dinner where he could. But I had promised weeks ago to dine this day with Boringdon, to be made acquainted with his friend Lady Elizth. Monck, of whom he has talked so much to me, and whom, when I know her, I am to like of all things. The party were Morpeth, Leveson, C. Greville and Lady Charlotte, Lord Grandison, a stupidish old fellow[481], I think, and the said Ly. Elizabeth, with her husband, Mr. Monk, who seems but a dolt. Lady Elizth. is very pretty and very pleasing, and if her mind keeps the promise of her countenance, very quick and intelligent. In the evg. Charles Ellis called at Boringdon's in his way from I know not what place, where he had dined, to be *chaperoned* to Whitehall. We went there, and found all the world – old and young. The old were at their cassino. The young agreed to play at *jeu de violon* – the setting a person something to perform, which he is to find out by musick. J. Sneyd and Ed. Legge performed admirably. It came to my turn – but there were strangers come into the room, before whom I was not disposed to exhibit – so when I was turned into the passage to wait till my task should be settled and I called in to perform it – I made a sign to C. Ellis to meet me by another door – and in the midst of the consultation we got into his carriage and went off to supper with Lady Malmesbury.

*4th. [May]* Monday morning Leigh called – and we settled to meet at dinner at Clive's – if I could get away from the House of Coms. – failing that – to meet at the Play. In the House of Coms. Mr. Barham[482] made a motion for papers relative to Sir C. Grey and Sir. J. Jervis's conduct in the West Indies. The papers were granted, and it was

[481] George Bussy Villiers, 4th Earl of Jersey and 8th Viscount Grandison (I). He was approaching his 60th birthday
[482] Joseph Foster Barham (1759–1832). M.P. Stockbridge 1793–99

announced that some specifick motion would be founded upon them some future day. The conversation upon this subject lasted so long that I found it quite out of the question that I should be able to get to Clive's before dinner was quite over. Therefore I thought it better to secure something to eat by going with Morpeth and Granville Leveson to Boringdon's – where we had been asked to dine, and where we knew therefore we should find food and company – and we arrived there just as dinner was over. We found Sneyd, Legge and a large party besides – got our dinner at a little table in the adjoining room, and joined them at their claret immediately. At about 1/2 pt. 9 however I left them to their claret and went to Drury Lane to look for Leigh, whom I did not find there, and not finding him I came home.

*5. [May]* Tuesday morning Frere called on me just returned to town. W. L. called to renew our engagement for dining at Clive's for to-day, and with some persuasion I prevailed upon him to find good reasons for putting off his return to Bath a day longer, and meeting Frere here at a comfortable little dinner to-morrow.

There was no business at the House that required attendance. I was at home all the morning. We dined at Clive's, W. L. and I, with nobody but the Clives themselves – and sat with them till it was time to go and sup with Mrs. Crewe.

*6. [May]* Wednesday Frere breakfasted with me and stayed all the morning, and indeed all the day. W. L. called in once in the course of his flying visits in the morning, and made us accompany him to look at his new phaeton – and returned to dinner at six o'clock. They did not leave me much sooner than it was time for them to go home to bed. To-morrow morning W. L. is to set off in his new phaeton for Bath.

*7th. [May]* Thursday Frere breakfasted with me. At home all the morning. I was engaged to dine with the Birches[483], and really intended to fulfil my engagement, and to bind myself thereto the more closely, had covenanted with Edw. Legge who was engaged there also, that neither of us would be *off* without giving the other due notice. But then here came unexpectedly a ticket from Willy for the Hackney Play, in which he acts a principal character, and this is the night that his mother and sister are to be there, and so it would be in the highest degree neglectful in me if I were not to go there. And to dine at Birch's, and get to Hackney in time for the Play, is impossible. In this dilemma I sent my excuse to Birch, in direct violation I am ashamed to say of my compact with Legge, from whom I must expect a tempest of reproach. Having to get an early dinner before I set out

[483] Unidentified

for Hackney, I thought I could not do better than take this opportunity of dining at the Law Club at the Crown and Anchor – where to my shame and to my cost too, I had not dined once this year. To my shame – not so much – because it is really incompatible with House of Commons hours – but to my cost most certainly, inasmuch as there is a rule of the Club which imposes a fine of 6s. pr. week upon every member who shall miss a whole week without dining there one day, during term time – and here are one two, three, or perhaps four terms, of three and four weeks each, during which I have been incurring the forfeiture. I find, however, that I shall not be liable to the like forfeiture any more. Some friends of mine in the Club have proposed and carried an amendment to the rules by which parliamentary attendance is in future to be an exemption from the fine – an exemption which I could not have proposed myself, as I am the only person of the Club in Parliament, but which is certainly no more than fair, considering that fines ought to fall on *wilful* omission only, and my omissions arise from the necessity of attending elsewhere.

After dinner I set off for Hackney. The Play was the Merchant of Venice. Willy enacted Bassanio, and really did it in a manner that surprized and pleased me exceedingly. Hetty was there in an extacy at the applause which her son gained, and little Bess clapping with all her might. I returned to town when the Play was done, and brought Harry with me.

*8th.* [*May*] Friday I was at home all the morning, very busy, and among other business, writing an answer to a letter from Mr. Milner, the poor Yorkshire clergyman, with whom my mother's two boys were, who had taken it into his head that I could get him a living by applying to the Chancellor in his favour – a mistake which I lost no time in correcting.

I went down to the House of Commons, and finding nothing to detain me there, adjournd to the House of Lords, where all our House was crowded under the Throne to hear the debate upon the Duke of Norfolk's motion respecting Ld. Fitzwilliam's recall.

Before I left the House of Coms. I got a quarter of an hour's conversation with Pitt upstairs in the Speaker's room (a little room by the side of the Gallery where one retires when one has anything to discuss privately, during the House of Coms.' debates), upon the subject of the Prince's Establishmt. He seems not so much attached to any plan of his own, as willing to collect the sense of people in the House, and to adopt whatever shall seem most universally approved. He feels it to be a business the[484] most ungracious and unpleasant that ever a Minister had to bring forward, and feels it the more as he

---

[484] '... the most ungracious ... at once' (p. 248), printed in *Marshall*, 87–88

knows that the unpopularity necessarily attached to it will fall upon
him as fully as if the debts had been contracted with his approbation,
while the Prince, on the other hand, will be no less angry with him
for expressing his disapprobation of them and for not proposing to
pay them at once. We talked of Frere's business, which from his
account of Lord Grenville's answers, I am afraid is not very likely to
succeed. He told me à propos of the debate of to-night in the House
of Lords that he had a letter this morning from Lord Camden,[485]
written just as the debate in the Irish House of Commons upon Mr.
Grattan's Catholick Bill was beginning, and that he thought it not
improbable that before the Lords' debate was over to-night, an express
might arrive with the news of the Bill being *thrown out*. It would be
curious enough if its arrival should interrupt Lord Fitzwilliam in the
midst of a speech in which he was proving how *impossible* it was to *keep
back* the Catholick Bill in the Irish H. of Coms. I stayed in the House
of Lords till 11 o'clock at night, when the heat of the House and the
dulness of the debate becoming oppressive, and having heard Ld. F.'s
defence of himself, which was as weak in speaking as in writing, and
Ld. Westmorland's panegyric on his own Administration,[486] which
was by much the most absurd and ludicrous composition and exhi-
bition that I ever witnessed – and having had no dinner, I gladly
acceded to Charles Ellis's proposal of going home with him. We did
so, dined or supped, and sat tête-à-tête till past 4 in the morning. The
division in the H. of Lds. was 100 to 25.

*9th. [May]* Saturday morning Frere breakfasted with me. The news
is arrived concerning the fate of the Catholick question in Ireland. It
has been thrown out in the House of Comms. after a debate of 16
hours by a majority of 155 to 84 – a pretty plain proof that Lord
Fitzwilliam must have been either grossly misled or inclined grossly
to mislead – when he pronounced it to be impossible to prevent the
House of Coms. from passing it.

I was at home all the morning till dinner time. I dined at Charles
Ellis's – with Lady Malmesbury and Miss Cozens[487] (who you know
is governess to Ly. M.'s children – but of a higher species than
governesses usually are, and treated with perfect familiarity and
equality) – Ld. St. Helens, John Ellis, Geo. Ellis, J. Sneyd and Dr.
Warton.[488] Dr W. is the most delightful old man that I ever saw. He

[485] The 2nd Earl, had succ. Earl Fitzwilliam as Ld. Lieut. of Ireland in Mar. 1795
[486] The 10th Earl of Westmorland was Earl Fitzwilliam's predecessor as Ld. Lieut. of
Ireland, 1790–94
[487] Unidentified
[488] The Rev. Dr. Joseph Warton (1722–1800), 2nd master at Winchester, 1755 and
head-master 1766–93. A friend of Dr. Johnson, he is known principally for his *Essays*
on Pope pub. in 1756 and 1782

was Master of Winchester School for I know not how long – till about
two years ago when he retired: a first-rate scholar both in ancient and
modern literature – a writer of great taste – he has been known to all
persons of literary eminence, and admired by all who knew him, for
these many many years – having lived in the world, but with a perfect
*Parson-Adams like* simplicity and ignorance of all worldly matters, and
is now at the age of upwards of 70 years, in as full possession of all his
faculties – with a mind as vigorous, and spirits as lively as if he were
only five and twenty. This was not quite the first of my acquaintance
with him. Two years ago, or thereabouts, when I passed through
Winchester in my way to Portsmouth (whither I went to take care of
Holland before he set out on his travels) Sturges, who had been
Warton's scholar, and who was then at his father's house in Winchester, took me to the school, and introduced me to the old man, and
I had just enough conversation with him to wish of all things that we
might be better acquainted. His acquaintance with Ch. Ellis is from
having met him in Hampshire at Ld. Malmesbury's, and at his
brother's (John Ellis). Ld. M. was his scholar formerly, and retains
the highest veneration and love for him. We made up to each other
very kindly – and his conversation upon a variety of subjects was
wonderfully pleasant and interesting. He is now quite an idle man,
comparatively with his former laborious employment – lives quietly
greater part of the year at his parsonage at Wickham in Hampshire,[489]
but comes up to town for a month or six weeks in the spring to amuse
himself and pick up books and news, and see what is going on. His
present *business* is an edition of Pope's Works, which he is preparing
for publication, and which will, I have no doubt be a most useful and
entertaining book, as it is also one much wanted, as there is at present
no sensible edition of Pope extant.[490] Dryden is still in a worse plight,
and I wanted Warton to promise that he would undertake him as
soon as he had done with his successor and rival. But he tells me that
somebody else (Malone, I think)[491] has it in contemplation. I hope to
see a great deal of Warton while he is in town, and I have engaged
that if ever anything calls me into Hampshire again I will not fail to
take Wickham in my way.

In the evening I went to the Archbishop of York's and supped
there.

*10. [May]* Sunday. Frere breakfasted with me. I dined at Charles
Ellis's, with Sneyd, Ed. Legge, Geo. Ellis, Lord Sackville, his brother

[489] He was rector of Wickham, 1783–1800
[490] He published an edition in 1797
[491] Edmund Malone (1741–1812), critic and author, who published an edition of
Dryden's works in 1800

Geo. Germaine,[492] and Ld. Villars.[493] These three last are *hunting* connexions of Charles, and *for* hunters, very remarkably gentlemanlike and pleasant. Ld. V. is the son of the famous or rather infamous Ly. Jersey. The conversation did not take exactly the same turn as yesterday's. But I like variety and can accommodate myself to it, and we did very well. In the evening I went to the Archbp. of York's and supped there – as did the Dean of Christ Church, who is come to town for his annual visit, occasioned by his attending at Westminster School to elect the boys on the Foundation to Christ Church. He is to call on me some morning.

*11. [May]* Monday I was at home all the morning till it was time to go down to the House of Coms., and on going down there I found that the Speaker was so ill as to be hardly able to take the Chair, and we adjourned therefore till Thursday to give him time to recover. I dined at Whitehall where Ed. Legge dined, and Ld. Gower and Ly. Sutherland. They settled that we should come to Wimbledon (Leveson, Legge &c.) on Sunday, and that I should bring Charles Ellis with me.

I had promised Boringdon and Leveson that I would become better acquainted with their friend Lady Elizth. Monk. She is at home every evening, and they are in constant habit of going to sit with her. This evening, finding Leveson bound that way, I agreed to accompany him. We found nobody but Boringdon and Morpeth with Ly. Elizth., and during the hour or two that we staid, I thought she seemed as pleasant and cultivated and intelligent as I had conceived her to be the first day of my seeing her. She is moreover very good-natured, and I mean to go to her again. From Ly. Elizth.'s I went to Privy Garden to sup with Ly. Malmesbury, where I found Charles and Geo. Ellis, and where Leveson followed me.

*12. [May]* Tuesday – at home all the morning. No House of Coms. I dined at Mr. Rose's (of the Treasury) where were Wallace, Robt. Dundas, W. Dundas and his brother the Lord Advocate of Scotland, Ld. Dalkeith,[494] and a large party of young members – a dinner – rattling and tumultuous but not at all unpleasant. The Opera, and then home.

*13. [May]* Wednesday. At home all the morng. No House. I dined at Charles Ellis's, with Ly. Malmesbury, Sir R. and Ly. Payne, Dr. Warton, Leveson, Geo. Ellis and Miss Carter. This last is a very

---

[492] Hon. George Germaine (1770–1836)

[493] George Child-Villiers, styled Viscount Villiers 1773–1805, when he succ. as 5th Earl of Jersey. His mother was believed to be one of the mistresses of the Prince of Wales

[494] Charles William Henry Montagu Scott, styled Earl of Dalkeith 1772–1807, subsequently the 4th Duke of Buccleuch. M.P. Marlborough 1793–96

pleasant, clever, entertaining and good-natured elderly lady – a sister,
I believe, or some near relation of the learned Miss Carter, who
translated Epictetus, and though not so learned, yet as ingenious as
her sister or anyone else can possibly be.[495] She is a great friend of the
Malmesburys, the Paynes, and a neighbour (in Hampshire) of the
M[almesbur]ys and of Dr. Warton, a valuable addition to society. I
wonder how it happens that I have never met her before. In the
evening I was obliged for the sake of keeping a promise which I had
made to the Markhams, to go to their sister, Mrs. Law's assembly,
the first assembly I think at which I have been this year – and likely
enough to be the last.[496] After staying there a proper time I went to
Privy Garden to supper. J. Sneyd and Geo. Ellis came there too – but
Charles is very ill with a violent cold, and is therefore ordered to stay
at home.

*14. [May]* Thursday. Frere breakfasted with me. At home all the
morning till it was time to go down to the House. In my way down
called on Ld. G. and Ly. Sutherland to excuse myself from coming to
Wimbledon on Saturday. The day proposed was Sunday but they
have altered it to Saturday, and on Saturday I am engaged and
cannot go.

At the House of Coms. the Speaker being sufficiently recovered,
the Prince of Wales's business came on. Pitt's plan is simply this – not
to give one farthing for the payment of the debts in *addition* to the sum
voted for his Establishment, but to vote first for his Establishment
exactly the same sum, neither more nor less, that would have been
voted had there been no debts in the case, as necessary to support *a*
Prince of Wales – and then out of that sum to set apart a certain
portion (together wth. the whole of the Duchy of Cornwall) for the
gradual liquidation of the debts, and for the payment of interest upon
them till they shall be altogether discharged – and further so to tie up
the remainder of the sum voted for the Establishment, that the P.
shall have no power to apply it to other purposes than those for which
Parlt. intends it – and to guard by every possible restriction against
his incurring any debts in future. The question of to-night was the
first point only – viz. the amount of the sum proper to be voted for
the Establishment of the Prince of Wales, or of *a* Prince of W.,
independently of any consideration of his debts. The amount proposed
by Pitt was £125,000 besides the revenues of the Duchy of Cornwall,
which are about £13,000 more, making in all about £138,000 pr. an.

---

[495] Elizabeth Carter (1717–1806), a distinguished linguist and writer. Her translation
of *Epictetus* was published in 1758. The Miss Carter that C. met was presumably a sister
[496] C. had forgotten that he spent half an hour at Lady Guildford's assembly on 23
April 1795, see p. 241

And this was carried after a tedious debate, on a proposition of Mr. Grey's for substituting £100,000 instead of £125,000, and after three divisions – of 260 to 99, 249 to 99, and 241 to 100. The debate lasted till 12. I dined upstairs in the course of it, and as soon as it was over, being excessively tired, I was glad to get home as fast as possible. There is no point upon which I am more determined, than that I will take no part whatever in any of the debates upon this subject. Pitt[497] has got into a scrape, not indeed of his own making – for there was no way of avoiding the business on his part – but by determining at once to hear, nor say a syllable in any shape upon the subject of the debts at all, and that mode of conduct the clamour out of doors would hardly have permitted. Short of this measure there is nothing left but different modifications of which he must adopt the best, or the worst, as the torrent of popular inclination out of doors, and of country gentlemen's fancies within may carry him. All modes that have been or can be proposed in so disgraceful and calamitous a business are bad, and so I shall content myself with my assistance to Pitt as far as attending and voting with him, whichever way he may be obliged to go – but as for the reasoning of the matter, there are country gentlemen enough ready to do it. The plan that most restricts the Prince, and which, while it enables him to discharge the claims of creditors, most plainly manifests the indignation of the H. of Commons, at his having any such claims to discharge, will most meet my approbation.

  *15. [May]* Friday at home and busy all the morning. House of Commons. Nothing particular. I dined at Mrs. Crewe's with Dr. Burney,[498] Roger Wilbraham[499] (an old Cheshire friend of Crewe's – in Parliament, and a strenuous Foxite, and a great quiz), Mr. R. Crewe,[500] Mr. Davenport[501](a Cheshire squire, a brother-in-law of J. Sneyd) and J. Sneyd himself. From Mrs. Crewe's I went in the evening with Sneyd to Charles Ellis's, who is still confined with his cold – and there we found a very pleasant supper, with very pleasant people – Lady Malmesbury, Miss Carter, Dr. Warton, Geo. Ellis, Leveson and Ed. Legge – and we stayed with him, as you may suppose, somewhat later than befits an invalid. I like Dr. Warton more and more, and Miss Carter too improves every day upon acquaintance.

  *16. [May]* Saturday. Frere breakfasted with me. At home greatest part of the morning. I called on Ch. Ellis however, and found him much recovered, so much so as to be able to go out. I dined with

[497]'Pitt has ... my approbation', printed in *Marshall*, 88
[498]There were two Dr. Charles Burneys in 1795: one, the musician and author, (1726–1814); the other, his son, the classical scholar, (1757–1817)
[499]Roger Wilbraham (1743–1829). M.P. Bodmin 1790–96
[500]Richard Crewe, bro. of John, 1st Baron Crewe q.v.
[501]Davies Davenport (1757–1837) of Capesthorne Hall, Cheshire

Jenkinson and Lady Louisa to meet the Dean of Christ Church. There was only Leveson besides. Ch. Ellis was to have come, I thought, and so did he, for the Dean, for whom the party was made, had asked him in Jenkinson's name, but Jenkinson, who called in the morning upon him, did not repeat the invitation. What can be the matter with Jenkinson that he is so little comfortable with all his old friends, in comparison with what we expected from him? It was to be a constant house – diners – suppers and the Lord knows what – but here is no such thing, and yet *she* seems to wish it too, and they might have about them certainly (though I say it who am one of them) the pleasantest set of young men in London – and yet there is *something* I know not what in the way. Well, time will explain I suppose. In the meantime marriage does give men odd turns, to be sure. In the evening the Opera – and after the Opera, to supper at Lady Malmesbury's. The Ellises – Leveson – Ed. Legge, Sneyd, &c.

*17. [May]* Sunday morning was occupied in receiving and paying visits in various parts of the town. I dined at Ch. Ellis's – Geo. Ellis, Boringdon, Leveson, Digby, Legge, Sneyd. In the evening I went to Whitehall, and afterwards to sup and to meet the Dean at supper, with the Markhams.

*18. [May]* Monday – Frere breakfasted with me. At home all the morning. In the House of Commons I expected nothing to come on, or at least nothing that would threaten a division, or require attendance: and I had fixed this day for Goddard to dine with me tête-à-tête, and talk over all his plans previous to his going out of town for some months, for the recovery of his health. Unluckily a motion of Genl. McLeod's[502] about I know not what army arrangements came on – and the House was so thin that it was hardly fair to go away, lest we should be beaten on a division. I was obliged to stay therefore till the debate finished and the House divided – 67 to 22, and then got home to my chambers just as Goddard, exhausted with long waiting, had fallen to, and was rapidly demolishing the dinner. His health has been very uncertain and uncomfortable, insomuch that he hardly feels himself equal to the fatigues of his present situation, much less to the undertaking a higher and more active and responsible one, such as the Under-Secretaryship of State, which Lord Grenville would no doubt give him whenever he makes the projected new arrangements in the Office, in return for his long services. Goddard is now going to Buxton and Matlock for a few months. He is then to go abroad, and I hope will so far re-establish himself as to return to reap the fruits of his labours in a place of honour and emolument. I learned from him that Arbuthnot's place, which I wanted for Frere,

[502] Norman MacLeod q.v.

is given to a brother of Lord Mornington's,[503] in exchange for the appointment of Chargé d'Affaires, which he leaves, and in which Arbuthnot succeeds him, at Stockholm. I wish Frere could have had it.

At night I walked with Goddard to the other end of the town and went to sup with Mrs. Crewe.

*19. [May]* Tuesday. At home all the morning. In the House of Coms. Jekyll made his long promised and often delayed motion about Ld. Fitzwilliam's recall – a subject so flat and stale now, that it commanded but little attention, and in Jekyll's hands was not much more acceptable to the Party for whose service it was intended, than to those against whom he directed it. Jekyll made a long speech, at least it threatened to be very long, – and relying upon this circumstance and upon another no less comfortable – viz – that Mr. Silvester Douglas, whom I saw taking notes, and who being Ld. Westmorland's last Secretary in Ireland, was of course bound to undertake the defence of his administration – would answer Jekyll – I readily agreed with Charles Ellis that we might safely and properly go and get our dinner at Sir R. Payne's, and return to the best part of the debate (if it had any good part at all) and to the division. We went accordingly, dined very comfortably at Sir Ralph's, with Ly. Malmesbury, Dr. Warton, Geo. Ellis and King, and returned to the House time enough to hear that Fox had spoken, which was provoking enough in our absence – and to find, what was still more provoking, that Silvester Douglas yet had to speak. And so he did. The debate lasted till 12. The old topics were gone over and over. The division, 188 to 49. Charles and I supped with Ly. Malmesbury.

*20. [May]* Wednesday[504] morning I called on Mr. Pitt by appointment, and talked over with him Wilberforce's motion for peace, which is to come on to-morrow, and to which it was agreed between us that I should move the previous question (if determined to be moved). The Emperor has agreed to accept the loan offered him by this country of £4,800,000, and has actually opened the campaign by a victory over the French near Mentz.[505] Si sic omnia. I dined to-day with Mr. Maxwell in Camomile Street with a party, none of whom I knew. After dinner I returned quietly home.

*21. [May]* Thursday. Frere breakfasted with me. At[506] 1 o'clock I went to a Council at Mr. Pitt's, on Wilberforce's motion, where I met

---

[503] Hon. Henry Wellesley, 1st Baron Cowley, who was apptd. précis-writer in the F.O. in 1795

[504] 'Wednesday morning ... near Mentz', printed in *NER*, 534

[505] For the details of the Anglo-Austrian subsidy treaty of 1794 see n. 398. For Mentz read Mayence

[506] 'At 1 o'clock ... the nation' (p. 255), printed in *NER*, 534

the usual people – Dundas, Windham, Atty. and Sol. Genl., Master
of the Rolls, Sr. Wm. Scott, Serjt. Adair, Jenkinson, Anstruther, &c.
Previous Question to be moved upon it (no mention by whom). From
Mr. Pitt's I came home to dress and get a bit of dinner, and then
sallied forth by water (a way that I find very quick and convenient
for going between the Temple and the House in fine weather) being
very pleasant and not more than 10 minute's voyage – and arriving at
the House of Commons about 5 minutes pt. 4, found not Wilberforce
speaking, but the House up for want of a sufficient number of members
to enable the Speaker to take the Chair. What a shame! – a pretty
way of attending to the business of the nation. What to do for the rest
of the day – dressed – and having dined at a little after 4 o'clock, I
called at Leveson's and found Charles Ellis there, with whom, not
knowing what better to do with myself, I agreed, not indeed to dine
again, for that exceeded all power of stomach, but to meet him at
dinner at Lady Malmesbury's. I did so. There was only he and Geo.
Ellis – Oh yes – and a Dutch Admiral of the name of Zinckel. In the
evening I called at the Archbishop of York's – and found nobody at
home but the Abp. himself – so having sat with him a quarter of an
hour I made my retreat. I called in at White's and found nobody that
I liked. I called at Mrs. Crewe's, and found her not at home. It was
a day of disappointments – and to add to my ill luck I found that I
had a violent inflammation coming on in one of my eyes. I returned
for consolation to Privy Garden – supped – and went home to bed.

*22.* *[May]* Friday morning. The inflammation in my eye was so
bad that I took a dose of salts on my own advice, and sent for Wathen
the oculist to know what further methods he would have me pursue.
So bad and so painful was the inflammation that I would [have] given
something to have been able to stay at home all day – but I had
engaged to dine with the Clives – an engagement of my own making
and the day of my own appointment – and to have sent an excuse
however true or however good might have looked a flight – so with
my bad eye I went to them. I did not go to the House of Commons
however in my way. Lord Sheffield dined there, and Mrs. Clive's
great friend Ly. Margaret Perceval.[507] In my way home I called at
Whitehall and found Lord and Lady Stafford alone, and sat with
them some time, but I did not then know that I ought to have wished
them joy.[508]

*23.* *[May]* Saturday morning. I found my eye by no means the
better for having been so little nursed yesterday, and I would [have]

---

[507] Lady Margaret Perceval, 6th da. of the 2nd Earl of Egmont
[508] Their daughter was soon to be married to the Hon. Dudley Ryder, 1st Earl of
Harrowby

given more than yesterday to have been able to nurse it to-day. But to-day, for my thorough plague and destruction I had fixed with Borrowes, at his earnest request for dining with him at his little villa at Banstead, and had agreed to carry Harry and Willy with me, and to take Epsom races in our way. Epsom Races – a dinner at Banstead – sixteen miles from town – a broiling hot day! Three in the chaise! And a painful encreasing inflammation in my eye! Oh! Oh! But to have disappointed Borrowes would have been to mortify him beyond bearing, and to injure myself irreparably in his good opinion, so it must be endured. Luckily my post horses were not obtained till it was late, and so when we got to Epsom the Race was over, but then we had to walk and gawk about the course and the booths, and then to go four miles further to dinner. A little, little room in a little, little house, the sun full upon it – smoking victuals – the company fresh, or rather foul from the Race Course, and after a whole morning's exercise – wine – nob and nobs! My eye all the time burning and torturing. Oh! how I rejoiced when eight or nine o'clock came, and I found myself in the cool of the evening returning to town with no other hazard than that of being robbed on the road or overturned by a drunken postboy. By about 12 o'clock I found myself safe landed at my chambers, and to console myself for the sensible mischief that I had done to my eye, and for the fatigue of the day altogether, I had the consciousness of having satisfied Borrowes – and the hope that he would not speedily find another Race-day on which to plan for himself the like satisfaction.

I must not omit to say that before I set out this morning I had received two pieces of intelligence – by one of which I found that I ought to have offered my congratulations at Whitehall last night and by the other that there was reason, though I did not know it nor did he at that time, for offering my condolence to the Abp. of York the night before. David Markham,[509] the poor Archb[isho]p's favourite son, and the favourite, I believe, of everybody that was acquainted with him, is dead. He was killed in a skirmishing battle at St. Domingo. The news arrived yesterday – and was known to the Duke of York at the moment, I believe, certainly within a very few moments after the Archbishop had been with him soliciting promotion for his son. It is a dreadful stroke for the old man and I fear will weigh more heavily upon him than his age and his infirmities can well bear.

The other piece of news was brought to me this morning by Edward Legge, who had heard it yesterday with as much surprize as it occasioned me on his telling it – Lady Susan Leveson is to be married

[509] David Markham (1766–1795)

to Mr. Ryder.[510] Had I been to guess among the men who frequent
Whitehall, which had made his address and been received, I scarce
know one that I should not have pitched upon before Ryder. I never
saw the smallest symptom of attachment on his side, or of preference
on hers towards him. So far from it, that, as there are many little
peculiarities in his manners that do not quite hit my fancy, so I
have often and often indulged myself in remarking pretty freely and
ludicrously upon them, not only before, but to Lady Susan, as well
as to other persons of the family; an indulgence from which I should
cautiously have refrained had I had the smallest suspicion of any such
connexion being likely to take place between them. Edward Legge
recollects a thousand instances in which he has been equally unlucky.
And as for J. Sneyd, in whose opinion Ryder stands very low, and
who is usually unreserved in the delivery of his opinion, into what
scrapes he must have got himself.

24. [May] Sunday morning – I again found the inflammation in
my eye much encreased and encreasing, and again wished most
heartily that I could have stayed at home all day to nurse it – but
again I had an engagement which I could not possibly put off –
having refused more than once this winter to dine at Lord Sheffield's,
who makes great shew of good-nature and attention to me, as being
an old friend of my father's, and might be apt to construe as a slight
so frequent a refusal of his invitations. I carried my eye to Mr. Wathen
in the morning to be dressed for the day, and I went, as I was obliged
to do, in great pain to dinner at Lord Sheffield's. There was a very
large party, all of them, except Boringdon, strangers to me – even the
mistress of the house, Lady Sheffield, whom he has lately married –
a sister of T. Pelham's. There is Miss Holroyd, his eldest daughter,
with his fortune and title entailed upon her – and then she may be, I
should think – for such an ugly, shrill unpleasant piece of goods I have
seldom seen or heard.

In the evening I went to Lady Malmesbury's – where I supped –
with Charles and Geo. Ellis, and with Sneyd, who, to my great sorrow,
and that of all who know him, goes out of town to-morrow.

25. [May] Monday morning. The inflammation in my eye was, as
might be expected, considerably worse. It was such a comfort to me
to reflect that I had no engagements to-day, but such as I could and
would put off and stay quietly within doors, sopping and bathing and
cooling my inflammation. I wrote to Frere to state my case, and desire
him to come and console me, but he was out of town, I suppose at his

[510] Lady Susan Leveson Gower, 6th da. of the 1st Mq. of Stafford who. m. 30 July
1795, Hon. Dudley Ryder, 1st Earl of Harrowby

friend, Mr. Orde's,[511] in Hampshire. Charles Ellis, however, came to me in the morning and stayed with me all day till it was time for him to go and dine at his brother's, where I was to have dined also – and from whence, after dinner he returned to me, bringing George Ellis with him, and they supped and stayed with me till it was time for me to go to bed.

*26. [May]* Tuesday I found my eyes better, and continued my regimen and confinement to make them quite well. I was at home all , day, and all day in the receipt of visitors – Charles Ellis and I know not who else in the morning – in the evening Charles and Geo. Ellis and Newbolt, who stayed and supped with me.

*27. [May]* Wednesday morning I perceived the benefit of my two days' nursing and confinement by finding my eyes so much better as to be able to go to the House of Commons – where Wilberforce's motion for peace, which failed on Thursday last for want of a House, was to come on, to which I intended to move the Previous Question, at least to take my chance if no Minister interfered with me. I stayed at home and dined before I went down to the House. Wilberforce[512] made a long speech and not a bad one, but one by far the most *answerable* that I almost ever heard. He was seconded by Mr. Duncombe, the other member for Yorkshire.[513] Whilst he was speaking I intimated to Mr. Pitt, behind whom I was sitting, my intention of moving the Previous question, which he very much approved and encouraged. 'Windham seems preparing himself to rise', said I. 'Need I mind that?' 'Oh, no, no – get up and take your chance of catching the Speaker's eye' – I did so. Windham however did rise at the same time, and seemed earnestly bent upon speaking, and the Speaker seldom fails to point to a Minister who wishes it. Windham therefore began, and I of course gave up all thoughts of speaking for a time – till, finding him take the subject in a way that did not appear to me, and I was pretty sure could not appear to Pitt or to anybody who had entered into the matter of the consultation in Downing Street on Thursday last, the proper way of treating it, and finding also that some points were omitted which it was very material to state – I took occasion to ask Pitt aside, whether or no there would be any harm in saying a few words after Windham by way of seconding the motion for the Previous Question, and just touching upon such and such topics which he seemed to have forgotten. 'None in the world – I wish very much that you would do so'. This I determined to do. We were

[511] Probably Thomas Orde, 1st Baron Bolton q.v. who lived at Hackwood Park, nr. Basingstoke, Hants.
[512] 'Wilberforce made ... the other' (p. 259), printed in *Marshall*, 85–86
[513] Henry Duncombe (1728–1818). M.P. Yorkshire 1780–96

now, as it appeared, near the end of Windham's speech, and I was
ready to start up after him, and tag my appendix to his motion –
when something said across the House to him by Opposition, set him
suddenly on fire, hurried him on into a declamation of an hour long,
and into a violent personal attack upon Fox, the consequence of which
was that he had no sooner sat down than Fox rose to answer him.[514]
I rose too, but seeing Fox up, immediately gave way, knowing that
there is nothing so ungraceful, or which the House take[s] so ill and
so deservedly, as a young man contending for precedence with an old
one. Here then was an end of the debate, as far as young speakers
were concerned, for after Fox on one side none but a Minister can
decently follow on the other.[515] The debate indeed lasted but a little
while – the division came on, I think, by 11 – the numbers were 86
to 201 – the strongest minority I believe that has yet appeared against
the War, but not so strong as we had been taught to apprehend it
would be.

After the debate I went home to a comfortable supper at Charles
Ellis's with Morpeth and Leveson and Boringdon, who had been
under the Gallery during the debate – and very, very pleasant the
supper after a debate always is.

*28. [May]* Thursday. I was at home all the morning till it was time
to go down to the House of Commons. In my way down I called on
Jenkinson, whom I found in all the bustle of preparation for setting
out to join his Regiment. He is ordered instantly to Brighthelmstone
to keep the peace at the execution of two soldiers of the Oxfordshire
Militia, who are to be shot for rioting and pulling down mills, &c. –
and whom it is feared there may be some attempt to rescue on the part
of the rest of the militia that were concerned in the same transaction.
Jenkinson puts on a most formidable appearance of resolution, and
Lady Louisa bears the idea of his danger from balls or brickbats as
courageously as can be expected.

In the House of Commons there was a little debate upon the
Austrian Loan: in truth a very little. The spirit of debating seems
quite at an end for the Session. Wilberforce's motion was considered
as the parting struggle, and though Opposition must say something
upon all measures relating to the War, and must even divide for form's
sake, it is indeed little more than form, as the debate of to-day lasted
no longer than till between 7 and 8 o'clock – and the division was
only 77 to 43 – scarcely more than 100 members in the House. After

[514] Windham's decision to direct his attention to the Opposition in general and Fox
in particular was no doubt in retaliation for their attacks on him during the debate on
Grey's similar motion for a negociated peace of 26 Jan. 1795
[515] It was Pitt who wound up the debate

the division I dined upstairs with Dundas and Mornington. In the evening I called at Whitehall and was proceeding into the Drawing Room when I met Granville at the door, who told me that I should find there all the two families of Harrowby and Stafford assembled – as assemblage more formidable than I chose to encounter. I therefore turned my steps to Privy Garden, where I supped, in less aweful company, with Lady M[almesbur]y, Charles and Geo. Ellis.

*29.* [*May*] Friday. At home all the morning. Dined at Boringdon's, with Leveson, Morpeth, Ed. Legge, Charles and Geo. Ellis. In the evening I accompanied Boringdon and Leveson to their friend Lady E. Monck's, where Morpeth came also. She is very pleasant and very clever indeed, and I like her more and more every time I see her. In my way home I called on Mrs. Crewe, and supped with her.

*30.* [*May*] Saturday. At home all the morning. I dined at John Ellis['s], with Charles and George [Ellis] and Capt. Parker,[516] Mrs. Ellis's brother, just made an Admiral among 20 or 30 others, whose promotion is expected to be announced in this night's Gazette. I went to the Opera, and meeting Windham there, persuaded him to go with me to sup at Mrs. Crewe's, which he did – and with nobody besides but Elliot, we had a very pleasant supper.

*31.* [*May*] Sunday morning was spent as usual in receiving and paying visits. Among the former was Mr. Borrowes and Sir Brooke Boothby. Among[517] those upon whom I called were Sheridan and his new wife,[518] whom I saw last night at the Opera for the first time – and he introduced me to her. She is not very pretty, I think – but wilder and more strange in her air, dress, and manners, than anything human, or at least anything female that I ever saw. I am told indeed that she is nothing to what she was on the first night of her appearance, and I daresay in proportion as she humanizes more and more, she will be more pleasing, for there is something interesting and animated in her countenance, and her friskiness and vivacity if [they] were not carried to such an excess as to look like impudence, would have an air of innocence not unpleasing. I did not improve my acquaintance this morning for they were not at home when I called. Another visit which it was rather painful to pay was to the Markhams. I went there indeed rather to enquire after them, than with any expectation of being let in. But hearing that they were to leave town for Bishopthorpe next day, and that the Archbishop was able and inclined to see anybody that came, I went in and sat with him some time. He seems

[516] Christopher Parker (d.1804), e. s. of Sir Peter Parker 1st Bt, was apptd. vice-admiral of the blue, 1795. His sister, Antoinetta, was the w. of John Ellis q.v.

[517] 'Among the ... not unpleasing', printed in *NER*, 534–35

[518] Hester Jane (c. 1771–1817), e. da. of Newton Ogle, Dean of Winchester

to have borne the shock of his son's death with more fortitude than could well have been expected from his age, and from the excess of his affection for David, and of the pride which he took in him. The girls, indeed, appeared to look forward with no small apprehension to their father's first arrival at Bishopthorpe, where it was planned that David should come to them. They judge, however, and I think rightly, that it will be better to get him settled there during the first tumult of his grief than to let it subside in town, to be renewed again on his getting down to the country. They all go to-morrow.

I dined at Charles Ellis's with a large and pleasant party, consisting of the Malmesburys, Ld. St. Helens, Sir B. Boothby, Dr. Warton, Miss Carter, Elliot, Leveson, Legge and George Ellis. In the evening I went with Leveson and Charles to Whitehall and had some conversation with Ly. Susan for the first time since her marriage with R[yder] has been settled. I returned home with Charles – supped tête-à-tête and sat for ever.

*June 1st.* Monday I was at home all the morning and eat a bit of dinner by myself before I went down to the House of Commons.

The Prince's[519] debts were the subject of this day's discussion, and as it is a discussion in which I take no part, and feel no interest, I consider the House on such a day only as a spectacle, and cast about me to make it as pleasant and entertaining as I can. This I have usually found it best to do, by getting with the young ones, Ch. Ellis, Leveson and Morpeth under the gallery or in some quiet unostensible part of the House, and *quizzing* the debate, and the several speakers in it – an amusement, which passes the time very pleasantly, as the speakers upon this subject are those whom one does not see every day, and are most of them, not as is usual in common questions, one of this side, and the other of that, but each of a particular opinion of his own, which he has formed and digested in his closet, and brings forth most gravely for public approbation, but is surprized to find not a soul came into it.

This produced the pleasantest confusion imaginable – and this, with the comments which naturally suggest themselves upon it, and the laughing which is apt to arise from them – has generally so completely drawn off our attention from the exact state of the question before the House, that when a division comes, and they come pretty frequently upon this business, we find ourselves reduced to the necessity of watching to see who goes out, and who stays in, and to vote most profligately and unconstitutionally rather by example than from any very studied conviction. This was the case with us in the several

[519] 'The Prince's ... his debts etc.' (p. 262), printed in *NER*, 535. For the case of the Prince of Wales' debts see above p. 242, n. 476

divisions to-day – one of which was 256 to 52, another 242 to 46[520] – larger majorities – or at least smaller minorities than there have yet been upon any question relating to the Prince – owing to a message which Anstruther[521] brought down to the House from him to-day, and which I will answer for it, he was not without much difficulty persuaded to send – stating his perfect readiness to acquiesce in any measures that the House of Commons should think proper for the arrangement of his establishment, discharge of his debts etc. The debate was over about 11. Meeting Pitt in the lobby in our way out, he took me home with him to supper. Dundas, Ryder and Mornington came also, and I was not sorry to have an opportunity of indemnifying myself for my scanty and solitary dinner by a good supper and a pleasant sitting after it.

  *2ᵈ·* *[June]* Tuesday – at home all the morning till it was time to go down to the House. Mr. Barham made his promised motion upon the subject of Sir C. Grey and Sir J. Jervis. You may remember my telling you early in the year all that I had heard and all that I thought of their conduct in the West Indies[522] – particularly of the Proclamations by which they called upon the inhabitants to pay a contribution (fixed by them, Sir C. G. and Sir. J. J. according to their own estimate) in lieu of a general confiscation. They urge in their defence. and I believe truly, that the Proclamation, though issued, was never acted upon, orders having come out from Government for its annulment before they had carried it, in any degree, into execution – an accident, which may and must save them from legal inquiry, though it does not much diminish their moral culpability. Had the proceedings against them in Parliament, however, been taken up by any person of great talents or great consequence – had the West Indians themselves been agreed upon their mode of conducting them – and had Mr. Barham himself or any other person moved for an *enquiry* into Sir C. Grey and Sir. J. Jervis's conduct, instead of moving as he did to-night for Resolutions to disavow the Proclamation in question, I believe the enquiry would have been carried – for Grey and all his friends, who boasted so loudly of Sir C. G.'s innocence, and are always crying out against Previous Questions, and such other means as it is customary to adopt to screen the conduct of individuals or of Government in particular instances, from investigations, must necessarily have joined with the West Indians in such a motion, and they would then very probably have

---

[520] 266 to 52 and 252 to 46 are the figures given in *Parl. Hist.*, xxxii, col. 101. The former division figures are confirmed, and the latter modified to 253 to 46 by the *The Commons' Journal*, vol. 50, 560, 566

[521] Sir John Anstruther q.v.

[522] C. conveyed his views most forcibly in this journal on 27, 28 Nov. 1794, see above, pp. 156–7

outnumbered those whom the desire of Government not to betray the actual state of the Wt. India islands, or whom a general dislike of all investigations into the particular conduct of commanders, that are acknowledged *in the main* to have done great service to the country (and there are very many who argue thus) would have influenced to vote against the enquiry. But as it was managed now, the whole business might as well have been let alone. By moving the disavowal of the Proclamation, Mr. Barham furnished a ready answer that the Proclamation having never been acted upon, it was annulled and virtually disavowed already, and that any further proceeding upon it was therefore unnecessary, and being unnecessary was, as all such retrospective proceedings are, unless when warranted by strong necessity, dangerous. Grey and the Opposition were able to get off triumphantly, for as they were not dared to investigation, they could say safely, that if they had been dared to it, they would have agreed to it. Government was relieved from a dilemma to which it would have been reduced by a motion for *enquiry* – the dilemma of either *resisting* an *enquiry*, when called for by *both* parties concerned, by the accused as well as the accusers – or if they had acceded to it, of seeming to be less tender of commanders, who happened not to be their political friends (for Sir C. Grey and Sir J. Jervis are not so) than of those who had *Party* as well as merit to screen them – at the same time that the services of those commanders were acknowledgedly such as to entitle them to at least equal protection. This last consideration would, I am apt to believe, have led Government to oppose even the enquiry, had it been proposed – but not being proposed, they had no difficulty in their conduct – for *not* to disavow what they had already disavowed, was all that they had to do – and this was natural and simple enough. To Barham's motion, therefore, all parties, even the West Indians themselves, expected the Previous Question to be moved, and were ready to acquiesce in it by way of hushing the business for ever, and under a tacit sort of acknowledgement that men who had done such eminent service as the commanders of the W.I. expedition, though they might have made some faux pas in their civil administration, had some claim that their military glory should cover their political error – especially as their error had been intentional only, and not carried into complete or mischievous effect. Upon these grounds I was myself satisfied of the propriety of getting rid of Barham's motion by a Previous Question, or question of adjournment, or some such usual way – and went down prepared to vote for it. But when I came to the House I found the matter somewhat changed. Dundas, who never does things by halves, and who, having planned the Wt. Indian expedition himself, and chosen the conductors of it, feels this as *his* question, and Sir C. G. and Sir J. J. as *his* commanders –

though he had said last night at supper that a Previous Question or
Q. of adjournmt. would content him, brought with him to-day a
couple of panegyrical Resolutions, to be moved after Barham's motion
was got rid of, the purport of which was that nothing in the said
Proclamation attached blame to the two 'gallant officers' – and repeating to them, upon this occasion, the thanks already voted them by
the House of Commons. This, I confess, struck me as too much. To
shuffle the faulty part of their conduct out of sight, and shade it with
their laurels might be proper and fair enough, but to praise them for
it, and so to take it in fact upon ourselves seemed quite unnecessary –
and for these Resolutions, therefore, I could by no means think of
voting. I staid the debate out, from curiosity, dining upstairs with Ch.
Ellis, who being a West Indian, came down to vote against Sir C.
Grey and Sir J. Jervis in any or every shape in which their conduct
should be canvassed, and was delighted to hear from me that though
I should certainly have given my vote for hushing up the matter of
the Proclamation in oblivion, I should certainly not go so far contrary
to *his* opinions and interests as to blazen it as wise and meritorious.
The debate lasted pretty late – and when the division came at about
1/2 past 1, I took up my hat and went my way home.[523] It was the
thinnest House that I have seen this Session. I believe most people
staid away from feeling much as I did about the question – that
though candour and good-nature and political convenience were
against a *condemnation* of Sir C. G. and Sir J. J. for the Proclamation,
yet the devil himself could not be expected to be *so* candid and *so*
good-natured as to find in it matter for the praise and for the virtual
adoption of the House of Commons. 'You white-wash rather violently', said I to Dundas. He laughed with hardened assurance, but did
not gainsay me.

*3ᵈ· [ June]* Wednesday. Frere breakfasted with me. At home greater
part of the morning. In my way down to the House I called on
William Barnard and his wife &c &c at their lodgings in Bond Street.
At the House of Commons was the 2ᵈ· reading of the Austrian Loan
Bill – the principle of which has been so often discussed and decided,
that little was said upon it by anybody. That little was said by Fox,
and answered by Pitt. There was a division (for Opposition are
pledged to divide upon it). The numbers were 65 to 30,[524] and the
House was up early enough for Morpeth and Leveson and myself to
get in good time to dinner at Whitehall. Boringdon dined there too.
In the evening I was obliged to return home early to receive the Irish
Club, who this evening did my chambers the honour of supping there.

[523] Barham's motion was defeated 67 to 17
[524] 60 to 35 are the numbers given in *Parl. Hist.*, xxxii, col. 43

Not above 4 or 5 came – and we passed an Attic evening – and separated at 12.

*4. [June]* Thursday Frere breakfasted with me, and after breakfast, being the King's birthday, we sallied forth to the other end of the town, and walked the streets amidst the crowds of gazers and pickpockets all the morning: an amusement in which I much delight, but which was not this year enlivened by so pleasant an incident as that of the overturn which Sturges and I witnessed last year, and which I related to you for your recreation.

I dined with Mr. and Mrs. Crewe. There were Elliot, R. Crewe, T. Tyrwhitt,[525] the Prince's little Secretary, a great quiz – and Richardson,[526] who was an excellent person to taste his oddity, and with whom I assisted very willingly in bringing him out for the entertainment of the company. In the evening I walked about with Richardson, looking at the illuminations, got wet through, and came home to dry myself in bed.

*5 [June]* Friday. I was at home all the morning, and eat my bit of dinner before going down to the House.

The Prince's debts were again under discussion, and again I took my post as usual under the Gallery with Ch. Ellis, Granville-Leveson, and Morpeth, where we amused ourselves and our neighbours with a running commentary on the dull text of the debate; and this by the way was somewhat livelier than usual – being diversified by a speech from Sheridan, the strangest and most incongruous and unconstruable that ever fell from the mouth of man – toading, republican, full of economy and of generosity, and in short a medley of sentiments irreconcilable in themselves, but which it was business to court the Prince and keep well with the people by endeavouring to reconcile. We divided two or three times – with as much knowledge of the subject of our discussions as usual in these debates (the numbers 148 to 93, and 153 to 29), and at past 1 we all went to supper at Charles Ellis's, which was not so dull.

*6th. [June]* Saturday Frere breakfasted with me. At home all the morning. I dined at Charles Ellis's with Lady Malmesbury, Lord and Lady Hampden (whom I never saw before and do not much like upon this first sight of them. She seems rather affected, though clever, and he a great puppy and a great fool) – Sir Ralph and Lady Payne, Miss Carter and Leveson. In the evening I went to the Opera and afterwards to supper at Lady Malmesbury['s] with Lord M., Ch. and Geo. Ellis and Lord Pembroke.

*7th [June]* Sunday morning is my morning for visits. Among those

---

[525] Thomas Tyrwhitt (1762–1833); priv. sec. to the Prince of Wales, Mar. 1795
[526] Probably Joseph Richardson q.v.

of this day was one to Sir Brooke Boothby which I paid in company with Charles Ellis. We found him in little lodgings, I think in Half Moon Street. I dined with the Master of the Rolls and Lady Arden. There was nobody but Wallace and Richard Ryder,[527] younger brother of Ryder – at the Bar, and lately come into the House of Commons. He is certainly very sensible and though not prepossessing in his manners, may I believe upon further acquaintance prove a pleasant man. He certainly has not the affectation of his elder brother. With him I went to Whitehall in the evening. From Whitehall I went to sup with Mrs. Crewe where I found Elliot and your friend Miss Hayman.[528]

*8th.* [June] Monday. I was at home all the morning, and dined tête-à-tête with Charles Ellis in my way to the House of Commons. The Prince's Bill came on again – and again we found less amusement in attending to its progress through the House than in laughing at the debate and the debaters – meaning by *we*, as before – Charles and Morpeth and Leveson and myself. We had plenty of divisions – I think six – in the course of the evening, and divided upon them all *in confidence*, that is, without the remotest idea of the point upon which we were voting. How profligate! But then the points to be sure were chiefly of one complexion – the rejection of new and fanciful amendments, and the confirmation of the plan as proposed by Pitt, and modified in the former debates by Fox and others. I need not add that we were pretty constantly in the majority. The debate was over about 11, and Charles and I went to supper at Lady Malmesbury's, where Geo. Ellis met us, and two or three other persons dropped in.

*9.* [June] Tuesday morning, I should gladly have stayed at home, finding the inflammation in my eye returning upon me – and what is singularly provoking, in my *other* eye – not that where it had tortured me before. But I was engaged, and could not help keeping my engagement, having broken a similar one twice last year, and once already this – to a breakfast at Mrs. Lloyd's at Kensington. She is housekeeper to the Palace or some such thing, and gives two of these fetes every year, and asks all the world to them.[529] I meet her often at dinner at Whitehall – and having been always invited, have shamefully neglected to attend her at Kensington partly from laziness, and partly from not always knowing know to get there. To-day I made Charles

[527] Hon. Richard Ryder (1766–1832). M.P. Tiverton 26 Feb. 1795–1830. His elder brother was Hon. Dudley Ryder, the 1st Earl of Harrowby q.v.

[528] Probably the Miss Hayman who was governess to Princess Charlotte from 1797 and subsequently keeper of the Princess of Wales' Privy Purse until she resigned in disgust in 1814, see D.M. Stuart, *Daughter of England*, (London, 1951), 11

[529] See above, p. 32 and n. 36, p. 117

Ellis drive me in his curricle. We returned to town just time enough to call at the House of Commons, and to find the House up for want of 40 members, which, if we had arrived 5 minutes sooner (for it was but so much after 4) we should have prevented – 38 there were already. We dined (that is Charles and I) with Newbolt and his wife – nobody else except Sturges. I stayed with N. and Mrs. N., as did Sturges, the whole evening and then returned together to the Temple – my eye much inflamed.

   *10. [June]* Wednesday morning I found my eye so bad that there was nothing left for it but to stay at home all day, and to send for the oculists to administer to it. They came – and recommended blooding with leeches, which operation I shall perform to-morrow or to-night if Norris comes in time. Frere breakfasted with me and stay'd dinner, and all day. In the evening I sent a note to Charles Ellis at the House of Commons, informing him of my confinement. He came himself in answer to it, and sat with me till it was time for him and Frere to leave me to repose.

   A note from Lady Sutherland to take leave on going out of town. Lord Gower's eyes very bad indeed. They are going to Cheltenham for the waters.

   Little Charles Reddish came to me this morning by appointment, to hear a long lecture from me upon a subject that had given me some alarm and uneasiness on his account. It appears that he has long cherished a violent passion for the stage, and a prepossession that he should made a considerable figure and fortune in that way. He had actually gone so far as to intimate to his aunt a determination to obtain my consent and his mother's to trying, or if he failed in obtaining them, to make the trial without. His aunt, after concealing the matter from me for some time, thought it now too serious to be withholden from my knowledge any longer. I wrote to her fully upon the subject, and desired her to send him to talk to me upon it. He came, and I represented the matter to him in such a light as I flatter myself has shewn him the folly of his notions about it – and obtained from him a solemn promise that he would think of it no more, but concenter [sic] all his thoughts and exertions in his present situation with the grocer.

   *11. [June]* Frere breakfasted with me, but could not as yesterday indulge me by staying with me all day. In the morning came Norris with three leeches, whom he introduced to me, and whose endeavours to reduce the inflammation in my eye were continued for some time, and attended with considerable success. During the remainder of the day I was in the receipt of numerous visitors. I dined indeed alone, but with Charles Ellis, Leveson and several more in the morning – with Bobus and other nearer neighbours in the evening I contrived to pass the day much to my satisfaction without much recourse to reading or writing, both [of] which were strictly forbidden me.

*12. 13th. 14th. [June]* Friday, Saturday and Sunday. The inflammation of my eye continued getting better and I continued to nurse it at home with all proper attention – and to receive a sufficient number of visitors morning and evening to prevent me from throwing myself back in my recovery by too intense application. On Friday, independent of visits, I had Charles and Geo. Ellis, Sturges and Frere to dine with me. On Saturday Frere alone, and on Sunday I was so well by dinner time as to be allowed to go and dine with Ly. Malmesbury who, like me, has been confined for this week past, but with a worst complaint, a fever, and is not yet like me quite recovered. She was well enough however to have Charles and me to dinner. We stayed with her all the evening, and in the evening her friend Lady Palmerston joined us and stayed supper. The Palmerstons[530] are persons whom most people know, and whom everybody ought to know – for they are very pleasant, good sort of people, and keep a constant house in London, and at their place in Hampshire – not to mention Sheen, where they have a very pretty villa – and at all these places they are glad to see one – and from what little I have yet seen of her, and at different times of him, I shall be glad enough to go there.

*15th [June]* Monday morning I was so well as to sally forth early and taste the fresh air (of the Strand and Piccadilly) after my confinement. In the House of Coms. there was that everlasting Prince's Bill again,upon one clause of which (for allowing the Princess £5,000 a year pin-money, or some such matter), Morpeth made a little speech and acquitted himself very creditably. After hearing Morpeth, and dividing with him (for nothing goes without a division) I thought I had had enough of this business for some time, and that I might properly and safely go as far as Privy Garden to dinner, at Lady Malmesbury's, resolving to return to the House of Coms. in the ev^g·· and leaving word with the doorkeeper to send to me upon any division. Ld. and Ly. Palmerston, Ld. St. Helens, Sir B. Boothby, Elliot, Miss Whitworth[531] and Mrs. Galley[532] (Ld. St. Helen's sister) – Charles and myself formed a party rather larger than a sick person should in prudence have entertained. But Ly. M. is much better, and we are not very noisy. I improved my acquaintance with Ly. Palmerston, and we are to dine at Sheen on Saturday. In the evening Charles and I went down to the House, joined Leveson and Morpeth under the

[530] 'The Palmerstons ... go there', printed in *NER*, 535

[531] Probably Mary Whitworth, 3rd da. of Sir Charles Whitworth, and the sister of the 1st Earl Whitworth

[532] Selina, da. of William Fitzherbert of Tissington Hall, Derbys. who m. Henry Galley (afterwards Galley Knight) of Langold Park, Yorks.

Gallery, and amused ourselves as well as we could, and divided with great perseverance throughout the debate[533] – the last, I hope, that we shall have upon this tiresome business. After the debate I met Windham looking as if he had nothing to do, and as if he would be glad of anybody that would help him to do it – and so I proposed going to sup at Mrs. Crewe's. He agreed – and we set out accordingly – and should have had a very pleasant supper, if we had not found, upon our arrival in Grosvr. St., that Mrs. Crewe was at Hampstead.

*16 [June]* Tuesday morning. I called on Mr. Pitt by appointment, for the purpose of talking over with him the state of things political, and parliamentary, previous to the end of the Session and to my going out of town. The [534] conversation began with my lamenting the few opportunities that there had been for speaking in the course of the Session – and observing how strange it was that a period so important and so interesting, and during which so many questions of great magnitude[535] had gone through the House, should have produced so little discussion – hardly one debate except that on the first night of the Session – which had lasted beyond 11 or 12 o'clock, and none in which without obtruding myself too forwardly on the House, I could find a fair occasion for exerting myself to the degree and in the manner that I was anxious to do. In answer to this Mr. Pitt agreed with me as to the fact of the Session having been one that afforded few opportunities and assured me that he had often and much lamented it on my account, knowing as he did as well the anxiety which I had to distinguish myself, and the readiness in which I had been for any occasion that might occur on every question that [had] been discussed during the year. The reason of this dearth of opportunities was obviously this – that at the time when so great a question as the War is depending, no other question of whatever importance is likely to take the smallest hold on the minds of men – and I must have observed there that many things had passed through Parliament this Session almost without notice, which, in quieter seasons, and when the attention of the public was not engrossed by a single object, would have given rise to many discussions – at the same time, too, that the War thus occupies *all* the attention of the House, there are sufficient reasons

[533] On the Prince of Wales' Annuity Bill

[534] 'The conversation ... answered me' (p. 276), printed in *Marshall*, 101–110

[535] In the course of the fifth session of the 1790 Parliament the Commons had debated, *inter alia*, the continuation of the suspension of Habeas Corpus; the negotiating a peace with France; the Anglo-Austrian subsidy treaty; the recalling of Earl Fitzwilliam from Ireland; the conduct of Sir Charles Grey and Sir John Jervis in the West Indies; the Establishment of the Prince of Wales; the abolition of the slave trade; and the dispensing with the services of ministers. C. had spoken twice: on 30 Dec. 1794 in seconding the Address; and on 24 March 1795 in defence of the general conduct of ministers during Fox's censure motion

why that attention is itself very small and very difficult to be engaged. The subject has been so often and so amply treated in every possible point of view for these three years past that there can be nothing new to be said upon the principle of it. And as to the conduct of it, in all or any of its parts, that indeed furnished Opposition with many topicks of attack – but it could furnish to a person on the side of Government no means of defence – except to Ministers themselves, who knowing all the motives, and being responsible for all the effects of whatever was done, were *alone* competent to give the reasons for any attempt that might have been undertaken, and to make the excuses for any failure that may have been incurred – and from Ministers *alone* does the House expect, or is it willing to hear anything upon the subject. Under these circumstances he would fairly say that though he was solicitous in a very great degree for my success and for my seizing every opportunity to promote it in the House of Commons, he should yet, if I had asked his advice at the beginning of the Session, have advised me rather to hold back than to press too eagerly forward in the discussions that were to take place in the course of it – and he would confess that glad as he always [was] when I did find an opportunity of exerting myself, he had yet been more pleased and satisfied with seeing me give way at times, when he well knew I was perfectly prepared and exceedingly anxious to take part in the debate – than he should have been at my making more frequent and continued efforts to bring myself into notice – I had done enough already to establish my character &c. – and I might be well contented for the future to let things take their course secure of improving every opportunity that came in my way, but not going out of my way to seek them. He had indeed wished very much that I could have moved the previous question the other night on Wilberforce's motion, when Windham came before me – though Windham having spoken, it would undoubtedly have been wrong in me to rise after him. But even if I had spoken on that day, or if I had taken part in any other general debate on the war during the Session, he desired me to recollect how very little *new* there was to be advanced beyond what I had already had an opportunity of stating fully, and with all possible advantage and credit &c. &c. on the first day of the Session.[536] And on this score indeed he had to congratulate himself for having afforded me so early and so good an opportunity by requesting of me as he had done to second the Address. I was to recollect too how much *better off* I had been than any other person on the Government side of the House, excepting those whose situations exposed them to the *necessity*, as he should say, as I perhaps should call it, gave them the privilege of

---

[536] On 30 Dec. 1794 in the debate on the Address, see above, pp. 176–6

explaining and defending from *facts* within their knowledge and on their responsibility, all the errors imputed to Administration. For with the exception of them only, the Ministers themselves – who was there of us, beside myself, that had ever delivered their sentiments at length on the state of the War and of the country during the Session – no young man certainly. If *his* opinion or that of those with whom he acted and communicated, were of any weight or importance in my mind, he could with truth and pleasure assure me that his and their opinion of me, and of the service of which I had been to the common cause &c. &c. was &c. &c. and their *reliance* upon my exertions, should those exertions have been called forth, no less firm and satisfied than if there had really been occasion for them to be displayed in their fullest extent.

From this conversation turned upon more general topicks relating to Parliament. And I took occasion to express a wish that he could point out to me any particular subject or suite and set of subjects, which he apprehended were likely to come before the House of Commons – that I might make myself master of them, and obtain as it were a sort of right and property in them – a circumstance which I thought would put me upon surer and higher ground in the House than the merely taking part in the general subjects of war and peace, whereon people were already wearied with discussions, so as (according to his observation) to be unwilling to hear any more upon them except from Ministers themselves, and from them only in the way of *information* rather than of reasoning and persuasion. There was a difficulty, I said, and awkwardness in my present situation in the House of Commons, owing to my having no peculiar line or province that I should call or think my own – so that I was of necessity reduced to speak only upon such topicks as were *everybody's* property, and those were of course of such importance as to call up either Pitt himself or Windham or Dundas – and after a Cabinet Minister had spoken – there was an appearance of arrogance very unpleasant to one's own feelings, and very disgusting to the House in all probability in a young man's presuming to follow them. It was very well for the first Session or two, to speak with no other view than to establish the character of a speaker, but having once done that it appeared to be of more consequence to one's stand and consideration in the House and in the country to choose proper times than to display one's talents for speaking. He acknowledged the truth of the remark that I had made, and saw and felt with me the awkwardness of the situation – but where was the remedy? To foretel[l] exactly what subjects might be brought before Parliament was out of his power. There was one remedy indeed in his power, and which he should be happy to apply if I approved it. It was office. But upon this point he did not know what might be my opinions or inclinations. I had but to make him acquainted with them, and I might depend upon his desire to meet them as fully as he could do, and as I could wish. This, I said, was a subject upon which it became me rather to hear his opinions than to dictate to him my own. He said – no – He wished exceedingly to be made fully acquainted with all that I thought and felt about it. He was exceedingly glad that such an opportunity as this had presented itself to us, and he begged that I would speak to him without hesitation or reserve.

Upon this adjuration, I said, I would explain myself to him as fully and fairly as he required. I certainly would not deny that official employment was an object of my ambition, provided it was accompanied with such circumstances as would alone make it worth my acceptance or justify me in my own eyes or in the eyes of the world for accepting it. By this I meant not to arrogate an immediate claim to very high offices – but simply to state that not having an independent fortune, and being bound therefore by the common course of things and the established opinion of the world, to pursue a profession – I could not creditably leave that profession for an office of mere income and idleness – but must have such a one as by giving me immediate and ostensible employment, would evince that if I received publick money I meant to do publick duty – would prove at once my inclination to acquire knowledge and afford me such opportunities for doing so as would entitle me, in due time and gradation to an advancement to higher trusts and more responsible and important stations. I wished before I proceeded to know whether he approved of my way of judging of the matter. He expressed his warmest concurrence in everything that I had said, and signified his desire to hear further.

There was one other point, I said, on which I wished to be understood by him and to know whether he agreed with me. It was this – that *if at all* I should wish to have an office, as *soon* as possible – if possible, before the next Session of Parliament – and that not as I was sure he would do me the justice to believe, from any sordid motive, and any eagerness to begin receiving the emolument – but for these two reasons – first – that as it was with a view to my stand and situation in the House of Com^s· chiefly that I was desirous of official employment at all I should wish not to go through a *third* Session on the same footing on which I had stood during the first two. I did not like (after a certain reputation once gained) to be still considered as a young man, candidate for a place, and endeavouring to speak his way into it. The second reason regarded my profession of the Law. I was now of that standing at Lincoln's Inn that I could in point of time, and ought therefore to be called to the Bar in one or two Terms. Now I did not mean to say that the eyes of all mankind were fixed on me, to enquire what I was doing, and why I was not even in Westminster Hall. But he would easily understand that a person coming from a publick school and as large College as Eton, and Christ Church, must have many contemporaries, many a year above, or a year below him in age, who knew exactly his standing and progress from their own, and in whose eyes a man owed himself some justification for inaction. He would not be surprized that I should prefer having this justification plain and understood without my explaining it. It was obviously much more pleasant to plead the possession of an employment which occupied one's time, than the expectancy of one. And further it would, I thought, be a much more creditable thing to abstain from BEGINNING the practice of a profession, on account of official employment than to have begun, and then to abandon it – and still further – it would at any time hereafter, when the changes and chances of political life might throw one back upon the profession be much more to one's credit and comfort to have to *begin* with it, and thereby mark effectually one's intention and determination than to have to take it up, where one had left it off a few years ago – in which there would be nothing marked or decided and respectable – but an appearance on the contrary of fickleness and indecision.

In this way of thinking Pitt completely agreed with me – and to this, and all that I had said besides, he answered – that nothing could be more proper or suitable to his own opinions than the view that I had taken of the subject, and that nothing, that it was in his power should be wanting to carry my wishes into effect, as nearly as could be in the very manner, and he hoped too by the time that I had mentioned. It remained only to consider what offices there were of such a description as would answer my purpose. Was there any particular situation that had occurred to me – or any sort of employment upon which I had fixed my choice more than on another? He should be happy to hear my election – and he would tell me fairly how far he thought it judicious and feasible. I answered that upon that part of the subject indeed I must speak ignorantly and at hazard – but that if I were to say what office of all others it was, that I had the greatest desire to fill – not immediately indeed, but at the distance of some little time, and when I might have prepared myself for it in some degree by official habits and application – it was that of Secretary in Ireland.[537] I am afraid that he would think I looked very high, to have that even at a distance in my contemplation. I requested him to

[537] The official title of the post was Chief Secretary to the Lord Lieutenant which carried a salary of £4,000 p.a. C.'s preference for this post is interesting because of his Irish lineage which was often thought of as a disqualification. It is also ironic that while he did not succeed in this ambition, the politician who did, in 1798, was his future rival, Lord Castlereagh

tell me if he thought so – but I would confess that, why it was I knew not, but I certainly did not feel as if I should shrink from the duties of that place, whatever they might be – always understanding to be sure, a previous acquaintance with the forms and conduct of business, to be acquired by practice here, as by practice alone it can be acquired. He would not suppose, I trusted, that I had any intention of pressing him for anything like a *promise* of this situation – in the way of which I could understand there must be many obstacles; and there might be many more which escaped my observation. I only meant, in compliance with his desire, to explain distinctly which way my wishes pointed – that if they were in any way wrong, I might by his advice and assistance give them another and more suitable direction – but that if he saw nothing in them improper and extravagant, I might learn from him what probability there was of their ever being accomplished, and might in the meantime prepare myself in the way that he should suggest for the time, when their accomplishment might arrive. His answer was – that in the object to which my wishes pointed, he saw nothing either improper or extravagant – that of my ability &c. for executing the office he entertained no doubt – that I had justly and fairly observed that a *promise*, in the case of a place, so lately new-filled as this was by Pelham,[538] and in the filling of which so many interests and so many inclinations were to be consulted, was more than he could rationally undertake to give – but that he would say at once, he saw no insurmountable obstacle in the way of the accomplishment at some time hence. In the meanwhile it would certainly be expedient, both with a view to that object, and on the other grounds before stated that I should have some office here more immediately. Was there any one that I could point out to him, as more desirable, or more easy to be obtained than another? for he waited my designation – and would do his best to follow it.

He lamented indeed that the number of efficient working offices, except those of the very first rank was so small as to make the selection of such a one as I described out of very few indeed – the Under-Secretaryships of State and the two Commissionerships of the India Board (which last he had got erected but a few years ago) comprized nearly the whole. I mentioned one of the Under-Secretaryships of State in the Duke of Portland's Department,[539] which was now vacant and had been so ever since the death of Mr. Broderick at the beginning of the year.[540] I knew indeed that these offices had not of late years

---

[538] Hon. Thomas Pelham q.v., had been appointed in March 1795
[539] The Home Office
[540] Thomas Broderick (1756–95), the 2nd s. of the 3rd Visct. Midleton. Under-sec. in the Home Office, 1794–95

been considered as Parliamentary ones, having been filled chiefly by
private men, but I considered that as no objection, or at least as one
of no great weight, and the business of the Secretary of State's Office
was I thought such as would at once open to me great opportunities
of general information, and assign to me also, in some measure, in the
House of Commons, that sort of province which I have described as
so desirable. There was indeed one point, respecting this situation, as
connected with the D. of P. – which I felt it necessary to mention. It
was this – that I·should wish it to be understood that I accepted the
office, through *him* (Pitt) not from any want of respect and high
estimation for the D. of P. – but because there had [been] between us
in former times some negociations,[541] which the *then* difference of our
political sentiments had broken off – and which, though they had left
on my mind the strongest feelings of gratitude and good opinion
towards the D. for the kindness which he at that time intended me,
and which I was under the necessity of declining, occasioned me at
the same time to feel a sort of delicacy about anything that might look
like an advance on my part towards a renewal of intercourse – an
appearance which would be at once impertinent and fallacious –
impertinent as it was not my business to make any such advance –
and fallacious as my political conduct, though now the same with his
Grace's, was by no means either regulated by his at present, or likely
to be so hereafter. Upon this ground, Pitt said, I might depend upon
it I had nothing to apprehend. He would take all possible care not to
compromise me in any thing that he said upon the subject – but to
make the recommendation of me to the place wholly his own act with
the Duke of Portland. How the Duke might be situated indeed with
regard to that place – he did not exactly know. He had heard that it
was promised – he was not at liberty to say to whom – but to a person
whose convenience it did not suit to accept it immediately; but for
whom it was to be kept open till his other avocations would permit
of his accepting it. He would enquire into the truth of this report –
and would let me know the result of his enquiry before I left town. If
the Duke had no such promise upon his hands, he would instantly
recommend me to him for the place (which was exclusively in the
Duke's gift) and had no doubt of the business being concluded at
once. If there were this impediment in the way, he should then
think it improper to intrude his recommendation between the Duke's
promise, and the execution of it – and would therefore, in that case,
turn his thoughts to other situations, one of which he would endeavour

[541] In March 1793 the Duke of Portland had offered to bring him into Parliament. C.
had declined because Portland's party contained members who supported radical
parliamentary reform, see *Thorne*, iii, 380

to find for me that should answer the description which I had given to him of my wishes, and the purposes to which I desired to apply it – and this he hoped to be able to do within the time that I had specified.[542] We parted after a conversation which lasted through his breakfast, and a considerable time after it – in which we seemed to understand each other as completely as it was possible to do so – and from which I came away very much satisfied with the opportunity that I had had of opening my mind fully to Pitt, and with the manner in which he had received and answered me.

In the House of Commons this day came on the India Budget – that is to say Dundas's account of the flourishing state of the affairs of the East India Company, which he gives once a year to a thin House – nobody presuming to contradict, and very few to understand him. The House was to-day so thin, that I felt quite ashamed of getting up in the middle of Dundas's speech, and walking out to dinner – but I thought his nerves were as little likely to be shocked by such an appearance of inattention on the part of a friend, as anybody's that I knew; and I was engaged to dine with Beauclerk, to whom I have been engaged five or six times this winter, and have never gone – and so I sneaked away the first favourable opportunity, and found at Beauclerk's Morpeth, Leveson, Boringdon, Digby and Bobus Smith (for Beauclerk was of Eton, as well as of Christ Church, and knows the people therefore) – and dined very comfortably, and know after all as much of India affairs as any of those whom I left listening to Dundas, – as much as Windham for instance, next whom I had been sitting in the House of Coms., and whom I left, not listening, indeed, but sleeping very soundly – for he had dined. From after dinner I walked about the streets with Bobus talking over my conversation of this morning – till about 11 o'clock when I went to supper with Ly. Malmesbury – and met there Charles and George Ellis.

*17th.* [*June*] Wednesday. Frere breakfasted with me. At home all the morning. I went to Harry Canning to dine at his uncle Paul's new house at Blackheath, with him and his new wife, who seems a very pleasing good sort of woman.[543] I returned to town late in the ev$^{g.}$ and finding the House of Commons up, came straight down.

*18.* [*June*] Thursday at home all the morning. In the House nothing particular. I dined at Charles Ellis's, with a large party of mixed people – Boringdon, Leveson, Morpeth, Digby, Sturges and Newbolt

---

[542] Pitt was unable to place C. in the Home Office but in January 1796 persuaded Lord Grenville to agree his appointment as under-sec. of state in the Foreign Office
[543] Paul Patrick q.v. His wife has not been identified

and finally Frere – whom I have introduced to Ch. Ellis, and wish them to know each other well, and C. Ellis has shewn his disposition to do so by making this party of some of our best young ones, for him immediately. Frere was not quite at ease – as, though he had seen most of them individually, I believe, he had never encountered so many all together before. But I hope he will get on, for the usage of the world, and the behaviour requisite for mixed society, is all that he wants, and without that even all that he has will lose great part of its value, or at least of its currency. Sturges and I went with Newbolt home, and finding Mrs. N. stayed and supped there.

*19. [June]* Friday. Busy, one way or another, all the morning. In the House of Coms. nothing but a report that we are to be prorogued in about a week. I dined at Charles Ellis's, with a party as large, but not of the same kind as that of yesterday – Lady Malmesbury, Ld. and Ly. Palmerston, Miss Carter, Miss Whitworth, Elliot, Geo. Ellis, Leveson. Ly. M., Elliot and I stayed all the evening and supped.

*20. [June]* Saturday – At home till two o'clock – when I went to Lady Malmesbury – and with her, Charles and Geo. Ellis, and Elliot set off for Ld. Palmerston's at Sheen – a fine rambling old house, more like a family seat in a distant county than a villa near London. There were besides our party – Lady Stawell, Miss Carter, Miss Whitworth – and we dined and supped &c. very pleasantly and returned after supper to town.

*21. [June]* Sunday. All the morning called upon and calling. I dined with Boringdon. There were Leveson, Mr. Monk (Ly. Elizth.'s husband) and Geo. Robinson, a young man about town, pleasant and rather clever.[544] In the evening I went to Whitehall, and then to sup with Lady Malmesbury for the last time this year. She leaves town to-morrow. I think, however, I shall see her in Hampshire, for she makes me promise to take her in my way into the country. Charles and Geo. Ellis go out of town also to-morrow – but Charles promises to return in about a week for a day or two, and I shall return from Wanstead, whither I meditate going in a day or two – to meet him.

*22. [June]* Monday. Frere breakfasted with me. At home all the morning. Went with Sir Ralph and Lady Payne to dine at Mrs. Crewe's Hampstead villa. There we met the Duchess of Leinster and Mr. Ogilvie with Miss Ogilvie and her destined husband, a Mr. Lock[545] – and Lady Clermont was there too, and a hundred more – a noisy, jolly sort of dinner, like an ordinary. In the evening I returned

[544] Unidentified
[545] The Duchess of Leinster, the w. of the 1st Duke had, following the latter's death, m. William Ogilvie. Their da., Cecilia Margaret Ogilvie, m. 12 July 1795 Charles Lock, 2nd s. of William Lock of Norbury Park, Surrey

to town with the Paynes – went by myself to the Play – and from thence came home.

*23. [June]* Tuesday. Busy at home or abroad all the morning. I dined with Mr. Pitt. By the way it is a bad style – that into which Pitt has fallen this year – of not giving dinners. This is the second time since my coming to town that I have dined with him, and I can hear of nobody else that has done so oftener. It is a very great remissness on his part, especially as his dinners are always good, and now and then pleasant. There were to-day – the Attorney and Solicitor-General, Sr. Wm. Scott, Mr. W. Grant, Wm. Dundas, Mornington, Smyth, Wallace and Windham – and as Dr. Johnson used to express himself, 'We talked great talk'. In the evening I went to the Opera, and from the Opera came home.

*24. [June]* Wednesday morning I went[546] by an appointment which I made yesterday to call on Mr. Pitt – and to learn from him the result of his enquiries respecting the Under-Secretaryship in the Home Office. He has made enquiry, he says, and finds that the case is, as he had before heard it stated, and as he stated it to me, that the Duke of P[ortland] has promised the office to a person who cannot at present conveniently enter upon it, but for whom the Duke wished to keep it open, till he can. Under these circumstances he (Pitt) could not properly interfere with the Duke's wishes by any suggestion or recommendation. The matter therefore must rest for the present, where we left it at the end of our last conference. He would keep in his mind everything that had passed between us upon the subject of office – he would do his best to find or make some arrangement that should answer my wishes, and meet the description that I had given of what would be most likely to do so – and he hoped to be able to do this within the time that we had agreed to be the most desireable. When anything occurred he would let me know. Meantime I might depend upon him. And thus we made our adieus for the Session.

Nothing in the House of Commons.

I dined with Wallace at the Piazza and went with him to the Play. From the Play I came home, supping at Carey Street in my way.

*25. [June]* Thursday – at home all the morning till about 3 o'clock, when I called by appointment on Sir Ralph Payne – that I might go with him to call upon the Chancellor. I find from Sir Ralph that Ld. Loughborough has taken it into his head that I am offended with something that he has said or done, or that I am disposed to offend him – but why he has taken this into his head I cannot conceive. I think on the contrary that he has been remarkably civil to me, and I have done all proper things, at least I imagine so, towards him – going

---

[546] 'I went ... last conference', printed in *NER*, 536

to his Levée early in the year, and – nothing else indeed, but there is nothing else left to do. Calling in a morning upon a man in such high and constant employment is a very idle business. It has indeed happened once or twice perhaps that I have been engaged, when he has asked me to dinner, or have been prevented by the House of Commons from going to him. But whatever the cause of his error, it is fit that the error should be removed, and so I went to call upon him. We did not find him at home indeed; but the civility is done, and now he may ask me to dinner again, when he pleases. Having made up by differences with the Chancellor in the morning, it was my fate to have a falling-out with the ex-Chancellor in the evening. I dined at Whitehall, where were Boringdon, Morpeth, Ed. Legge, Granville of course, and Lord Thurlow[547] – who did not dine there indeed, but came in from the House of Lords immediately after dinner. He came in seemingly in a great fluster and out of humour at something that had happened elsewhere – and as he took his wine, he declaimed with great vehemence upon sundry subjects – and among others upon the gross absurdity of all those who are advocates for the abolition of the slave trade. Nothing was more remote from my intention than getting into a dispute with Lord Thurlow; it is never pleasant, as a young man to oppose one's self to a man of his station, age and character, and in addition to that, he was apparently in a temper now to be no very delectable opponent. But one or two propositions that he laid down and enforced with extraordinary vehemence, were of such a nature, to my apprehension so absurd, that I could not help modestly and humbly interfering with a question of, *do you really think, my Lord?* – or some such quiet form of inter-rogatory, to which I got such a reply as put me to the necessity of rejoining – and from this arose a controversy carried on wholly between us two, without a word of assistance or contradiction from any other person, till I know not what hour, ten or eleven at night. I believe the particular proposition upon which the dispute began was this – that the Abolitionists were either *insincere* or *damned absurd* in not *beginning* with the abolition of slavery *in the Islands* instead of stopping the importation, and that if they could not do all, they ought not to attempt doing anything. My objections to this proposition were, 1st – that when one cannot do *all* that one wishes in a good work, I do not see why one is to sit quiet and do nothing. 2$^{dly.}$ that being able to accomplish a part only at a time, it is natural to begin with that part which is easiest to accomplish – and that it would be pride and folly in the extreme, to insist upon setting out in every undertaking (of the

---

[547] Lord Chancellor from 1778, with a break in 1783, until sacked by Pitt in 1792 for intriguing against ministers

end of which one thinks proper and beneficial to be accomplished at all) with the most difficult part of it – determining to risque the success even of what one might do if one chose it, upon the success of what, after all, one may find it impossible to do. 3$^{\text{dly.}}$ that though all parts of the slavery are, God knows, bad enough, yet I cannot help thinking that the reducing to that state those who are not yet in it, and tearing from their country fresh victims with all the feelings of home and connexions lost about them – is of the two more barbarous than continuing those who are already so in their present state – or the breeding up those who are born on the spot, as slaves, who, having never known another state, are not aware of the comparison, nor subject to the regrets which the others feel; and 4thly, that if even all these arguments were false, yet all that is proved against the Abolitionists is that they may have misjudged the way of attaining their object – not that they are insincere in their attempts to attain it, and 5thly, 6thly, in short our arguments grew out of one another to the length and extent that I have mentioned; and I felt sure then that I was on right ground. I found afterwards all the hearers (except Ld. Stafford, whose opinion I have not heard) of my way of thinking upon the point in question – even Granville Leveson, though he is upon the whole question against me – being an anti-Abolitionist. I cannot describe to you how strange and difficult and delicate I felt the situation in which I was involved during this dispute. My antagonist spared no strength and kept no management in his language, but used to the utmost all the advantages that his age &c gave him over me. I would not for the world have [been] betrayed into any heat or intemperance, which would have been highly unbecoming, and besides very distressing to Lord Stafford, who seemed to enjoy the debate beyond measure, listening with infinite eagerness, and turning from one to the other, as we spoke by turns, with unceasing curiosity and interest. But then I was just as little disposed on the other hand to be beaten and routed without resistance – so that, in presence of Morpeth, Boringdon, Leveson, Legge, not to mention Ld. Stafford himself – I managed therefore as well as I could to keep my temper without acquiescing, and to fight manfully without violence, and they tell me that I managed this very happily, and as Boringdon said next day, play'd the 'Humble deferent *young man*' with success.

From this contest I went to sup with Mrs. Crewe.

*26. [June]* Friday. At home all the morning. In the House nothing. I dined at Boringdon's – Mr. and Ly. Elizth. Monk, Ch. and Ly. Charlotte Greville, Ed. Legge, Leveson, Morpeth. A very pleasant dinner during which the battle of yesterday was talked over, and Ed. Legge expressed great indignation at the manner in which Ld. T.[hurlow] had received a little observation of his, and dismissed instead of deigning to answer it. I had forgot when I said that none of the by-sitters interfered: for Legge did once, in answer to some objection of Ld. T.'s to the plans which had been proposed for the abolition, say what was perfectly true, 'But, my Lord, in the *last Bill*,[548] I think there was nothing liable to this objection', and then went on to prove that there was not. Now this Ld. T. could not have *refuted* – so instead of giving himself any trouble in trying to do it, he simply looked round full in Legge's face and said, in the surliest and most contemptuous tone possible. '*Bill*, here's no *Bill* in question, that I know of' and did not condescend to take the smallest further notice of *Legge* or his observation. Legge, you may be sure, did not condescend to offer another. I had not observed this circumstance at the time of its happening, being wholly occupied with my own share in the combat, but I found it had not escaped Leveson, Boringdon and Morpeth, and they even prepared to plague Legge with a 'Bill! Here's no Bill', in answer to everything that he uttered.

In the evening I went to the Play and thence home – supping at Carey Street in my way.

*27th [June]* – Saturday – Parliament was prorogued – the Speech indicates an intention of prosecuting the War with vigour and determination, at least for another campaign. News arrived just in time for the Speech, of Lord Bridport's having beaten the French fleet, and taken three ships of the line.[549] There was a violent report to-day of a Dissolution. I heard it from so many and seemingly so good authorities, that I was tempted for a time to believe it probable, and actually betted half-a-crown upon it with Lady Stafford, who would not believe a word of the matter. At the House I met Pitt, and said to him in such a tone that he might take me in jest or in earnest, and give me a serious answer or not, as he thought fit – 'So you are going to send us off to our constituents in a great hurry'. 'No, no, we must not send you yet, not "unannointed, unanealed" ', was the reply – by which I conjecture that there will be no dissolution till Peace is at least in prospect, if not in hand. I sent Lady Stafford her half-crown. I dined at White's with Boringdon. We had planned a tête-à-tête to talk over a thousand matters previous to our both going out of town. But our plan was marred by Lord Douglas[550], who, calling in at White's and hearing that we were to dine there, proposed joining our party, and there was no refusing it. Lord Douglas is a mighty good

---

[548] Presumably Wilberforce's bill debated on 26 Feb. 1795

[549] The 1st Baron, and subsequently the 1st Visct. Bridport is sometimes confused with his brother, Lord Hood. An admiral of the blue in 1795, he achieved a victory over the French fleet off Port l'Orient on 23 June

[550] Alexander Hamilton, styled Mq. of Douglas and Clydesdale 1767–1806 and succ. subsequently as the 7th Duke of Brandon

sort of man for ought that I know but I would as lief he had bestowed himself elsewhere. In the evening the Opera and afterwards to supper with Mrs. Crewe.

I intended going to Wanstead to-morrow but Charles Ellis comes to town for that day, and I must dine with him.

*28 [June]* Sunday Frere breakfasted with me. Called on people, and was called upon, all the morning. Charles Ellis came to town according to his engagement. I dined with him according to mine, and having full powers of invitation for whom I pleased, I made Granville Leveson dine with us. They too are of dispositions not unlike each other, and formed I think to be exceedingly good friends, and I am fond of having them together. There are some people who mix so well that a trio is no more than a tête-à-tête, not indeed upon all subjects but upon many. There are others, who, though very good friends, A with B, B with C, and C again with A, will yet no do at all when they are all three together. I could name a hundred instances where the coming in of a person, the intimate friend of both parties when apart, is yet a clog and damp to their intercourse when together. We three did so well together that we did not stir from table till Leveson was obliged to leave us at half past 11, and when he was gone Charles and I went on so well without him that we did not separate till a late hour in the night, or rather the morning.

*29th [June]* Monday I should certainly have gone to Wanstead but that Lady Stafford pressed me very much to dine once more at Whitehall before I went out of town, and held out the meeting Lord Thurlow as an inducement. I could not refuse without seeming to decline meeting him after our dispute. I had besides another inducement to remain in town this day, which was an invitation to sup with Lady Elizth. Monck. I was with Charles Ellis the whole morning, whom I found in a great fuss about the Dissolution, the report of which is renewed with as much assurance as ever, but I give no credit to it.

I called on King the Under-Secretary in the Duke of Portland's Department; and talking with him about my plans and about the vacant Under-Secretaryship in his Office he seemed to think that Pitt might be mistaken as to his opinion of that vacancy being filled. He promised to enquire and to let me know. Charles goes out of town to-day, first to Dr. King's (John King's brother – and formerly Charles's tutor – the tutor to whom he sent the £5,000) at Woodstock – from whence he promises to be ready to come to meet me at Belmont[551] whenever I give him due notice of my setting out for that place. I dined

---

[551] Belmont, near Southampton in Hants., was the home at this time of Lord Malmesbury

at Whitehall. There were Boringdon, Morpeth and Lord Thurlow, the same party as on the day of our discussion, with the exception of Edw. Legge, but the day passed off in perfect serenity. This day there was a great meeting of people in St. George's Fields upon the subject of a petition for Parliamentary Reform, change of Ministry, &c. &c.[552] Boringdon had been there and gave us an account of what passed. Nothing very formidable. Very little mention among them of the *scarcity*, which after all is the most dangerous and most deplorable evil under which we labour at present, and may, if not timely provided against, produce very calamitous consequences. The members of the Privy Council are meeting about it every day.[553]

In the evening Boringdon, Morpeth, Leveson and I walked about the streets mingling with the crowds that came from St. George's Fields, and hearing their reflections. No tumult. We went to the Play, and from the Play to Ly. Elizth. Monck's, where we found her sister, Ly. Anne Hatton[554] (whom I do not much admire at first sight), Mr. Monck and Geo. Robinson. We supped very pleasantly, and so ends my London winter, for to-morrow I leave town for Wanstead.

The whole talk of to-day is about Lord Fitzwilliam's duel with Mr. Beresford. The quarrel, it seems, was made up at the intervention of the police officers – a mode of reconciliation which I do not exactly comprehend, as I cannot conceive that any arguments could be suggested by Townshend and McManus which had not occurred to themselves before, and if there were no new arguments suggested, I do not see why their determination to fight should yield altogether to the accident of their not being able to fight at the particular moment or on that particular spot. But so it was, 'And so', as Lord Fitzwilliam said on leaving the ground, 'here is, I thank God, the last act of my Irish Administration'.[555]

*30th.* [*June*] Tuesday morning. I left town and arrived to dinner at Wanstead, where I found Jane Linley on a visit, and where I staid quietly, with the interruption of two days only – till Sunday July 12th. During the whole of this time we were very snug and pleasant –

[552] The London Corresponding Society convened a meeting at St. George's Fields, Middlesex on 29 June 1795

[553] The 'scarcity' was of food due to poor harvests in 1792 and 1794 and to an exceptionally severe winter, 1794–95, which depleted stocks further

[554] Lady Anne Jane Gore, e. da. of the 2nd Earl of Arran had m. 1783, Henry Hatton of Clonard, Co. Wexford

[555] John Beresford q.v. demanded satisfaction of Fitzwilliam as a result of the latter's allegations of his being guilty of malversation. They met in a field near Paddington on Sunday 28 June but a duel was forestalled by a magistrate arresting Fitzwilliam just before he intended to turn and fire, see E.A. Smith, *Whig principles and party politics: Earl Fitzwilliam and the Whig party 1748–1833*, (Manchester, 1975), 210–12, Townshend and McManus appear to have been the constables who accompanied the magistrate

walked in mornings, read aloud in the evenings – and had no political differences – insomuch that I really thought Hetty had come to her senses, and seen that a woman has no business at all with politicks, or that if she thinks at all about them, it should be at least in a *feminine* manner, as wishing for the peace and prosperity of her country – and for the success and credit of those of her family (if she has any) who are engaged in the practical part of politicks. So much delighted was I with this apparent change in her system of thinking, that I actually formed a plan which I confided to little Bessy and Bess Patrick of taking a lodging, or small house somewhere in their neighbourhood whenever I should be much engaged in business as to render my stay in or about town necessary during the whole year, to which I might come down as often as I had a day to spare, or of an evening, to return the next morning, whereby I should keep up with the family a more constant intercourse than I have hitherto had it in my power to do – should be a sort of comfort to them perhaps – and should find in their society a pleasant relaxation from the fatigues of publick employment. I commissioned the two Besses to look out for some such place, and to let me know if they have heard of it. But alas! these pretty schemes were all routed and put to flight by a violent altercation which arose, I scarcely know how, between me and Hetty on the very last day of my stay at Wanstead, in which it appeared that her political prejudices and personal hatred of all those with whom I am connected and partiallity to all who hate me, were not done away but had been smothered only with great difficulty and much secret struggle till now, and were ready to blaze out with redoubled vehemence on any accidental occasion. I am grieved at it. But I will not live where I can have no confidence. I should feel very little relief from the fatigues of business and of Parliament, in going among a society where I could not unbosom my thoughts with pleasure or with safety, where I must either sit wrapped up in my own contemplations, force the conversation upon indifferent subjects, or run the risque of having to dispute upon every proposition that I might happen to throw out relative that what had been passing [sic] in the world – where anything that happened to have gone amiss would be received with triumph, and anything successful, however deeply even my personal interest might be involved in it, heard with distrust and grudging and despondency. I am truly grieved for Bessy's sake, whom I love and admire exceedingly, and who has a heart and an understanding and above all a sweetness of temper that cannot fail to be loved and admired by all who know her. It vexes me that I can have so little of her society. It vexes me for her sake that she should be breeding up in a school where it does not seem to be understood that a female politician is at best like 'a dog walking on his hind legs', as Dr. Johnson very wisely

says – a thing out of place and nature, and if a bitter partizan as well
as a politician – becomes a plague to herself and to all about her,
forfeits the happiness which she might enjoy in the society of her
natural friends and connections for a foolish ambition of being admired
by men who are too wise to have any sort of respect for them in reality,
and who, if they do pretend to admire, do so only the more effectually
to conceal their contempt. To this general rule there are certainly
exceptions, but few of women, bred up among politicians, married
early in life to men of great eminence and abilities, or called forth by
circumstances of uncommon exigency and importance. But for women
in private life the rule is at least the safest that they can follow. I regret
it the more, as from *Harry*'s being about to leave them, they will be
deprived of one chearing source of variety and entertainment which
his weekly visit used to afford them. He, you know, is going to
Hamburgh to be in a counting-house there for a year or two, and
will return, I have no doubt, much improved and enlightened and
enlivened by his absence from Broad Street, which at least is a negative
point that he will gain whatever positive advantages he may gain
also. He is very worthy and well-intentioned, and of sufficient strength
and cultivation of mind, but he wants to be roused and put upon his
mettle, and with his mother on one side of him, and his uncle on the
other, he might drawl on for ages without any quickening impulse of
spirit and exertion.

I have said that I passed two days in town during this fortnight.
They were Monday the 6th and Tuesday the 7th. I had several little
affairs of divers kinds to transact. I came up to town for that purpose
on Monday, and having done so much as I could do that day, I called
and offered myself to dine at Whitehall. Granville had left town for
Plymouth, where his Militia is quartered, the day before. I dined
there with the Chief Baron and Lady Louisa. In the evening I went
to the Play. There were Mr. R[yder], Lady Susan *Ryder* and Ly.
Georgina.[556] From the Play I went home to supper with Abbot, whom
I met there – the lawyer that was – the Clerk of the Court of King's
Bench, and now within these three weeks come into Parliament for I
forget what Cornish borough.[557]

*7th.* [*July*] Tuesday. I proceeded in transacting my business, and
calling – some calls. Among others I left my name at Ly. Susan
Ryder's. I dined with Mr. Borrowes – a large Irish and City party.
In the evening, walking from the City towards the Playhouse, I met
Newbolt in a great fuss, going to a newspaper office to have an article
inserted, purporting that 'he was called to the Bar'. The reason of his

[556] Lady Georgiana Augusta Leveson Gower, Lady Susan's sister
[557] Charles Abbot, 1st Baron Colchester, was returned for Helston on 19 June 1795

anxiety to make this known to the world is as follows. The Chancellor asked him the other day if he could get himself called to the Bar this Term. Newbolt answered 'No, not having kept all his Terms' – for he did not at that time see the drift of the question. The Chancellor, it seems, has a Commissionership of Bankrupts to give away, which he can give only to a barrister. He certainly meant this for Newbolt. N. has since got himself called to the Bar, but the Chancellor does not know it. The advertisement put into the newspaper, which his Lordship reads, will inform him of this particular, and get Newbolt, I hope, made Commissioner of Bankrupts.[558] I went with him upon the business, and afterwards seeing a debate advertised for the 'Ciceronian School' or some such seminary of eloquence upon the question of 'whether the people who met in St. George's Fields deserved well of their country', we went, as we often used to do in our early Temple life, to hear the debate, though we did not, as we then used to do, take a part in it. From this Ciceronian School I went to the Play, where the first person that caught my eye stuck up in a front row of the front boxes, was Mrs. Crewe. I had no notion of her being in town, nor she of me. I joined her party, which consisted of Miss Hayman, and a pleasant Frenchman, a M. Du Pont[559], emigré and friend of Burke – went home with her to supper – heard from M. Du Pont a great many interesting anecdotes of the Revolution, among others a history of Mad. Tallien[560], which some day or other I will tell you – took leave of Mrs. Crewe and Miss Hayman, and for the second time closed my London winter, for on

*8th [July]* Wednesday morning I finished all the business that I had come to town to do, and indeed one piece of business more than I had expected, for a man came to me this morning with a bill for £10, drawn upon me by *Saml. Reddish* at Botany Bay. It was accompanied by a letter from him describing his situation there as by no means uncomfortable. He has ground to cultivate, a hut to live in, and two convict servants to assist him in the cultivation. He has no promotion in the army yet, indeed, being nothing better than a *supernumerary sergeant*. If I can get him a commission presently he will be a man of the first rank and fashion at Sidney Cove.

I called on my aunt and grandmother at Somers Town and took leave of them for the summer. My poor old grandmother is dropping gradually into the grave. No disease or complaint but universal decay

---

[558] It would appear that Newbolt was not made a commr. of Bankrupts as he is still recorded as sec. of the Comm. of Peace in *The Royal Kalendar* for 1795

[559] Pierre-Gaëton Dupont (c. 1759–1817), a *conseiller* of the Parlement of Paris and the translator of Burke's *Reflections* into French

[560] Jeanne-Marie-Ignac-Theresa Cabarrus (1773–1835), da. of a Spanish financier who m. (2) in 1794, Jean-Lambert Tallien q.v.

of body and mind. I returned to Wanstead to dinner. Jane Linley is no longer here. I took her to town with me on Monday. But her place is supplied by Mr. Walker[561], the philosopher, who is reading a course of lectures to the neighbourhood, and makes this house his home during the intervals of his lectures (except that he does not sleep here) and Hetty seems to think her victuals and drink very well repaid by a little extra philosophy and plenty of republican politicks.

I stayed at Wanstead, as I said before, the remainder of the week till Sunday 12th – walking, reading and amusing ourselves very pleasantly. I must not omit the mention of one of our amusements, which was the making a copy of vile doggrel verses upon a grand breakfast that Mr. Bowles,[562] Hetty's great neighbour, had given at the instigation of his sister Lady Rushout,[563] to all the fine people of London, and from which all the Wanstead nobility and gentry were excluded. This whole family were in general wrath and indignation, and I know what might have been the consequence if their passions had not found vent in rhyme.

*12th [July]* Sunday morning I took my leave of Wanstead to proceed on my route towards Ashborne – my final destination for the summer – my way lying first by Eton – where I am to take Stratty, put him to school and enter him for the foundation – thence to Clandon Park in Surrey – a house which the Archbishop of Canterbury has taken, where I am to stay some days with Charles Moore – then to Belmont in Hampshire, where I am to spend a week or ten days with the Malmesburys – then to Oxford – where Frere is to meet me – and from whence I proceed uninterruptedly to Ashborne.

I should have gone to Eton this day but that I had received a card from the Chancellor to dine with him at Hampstead. You remember the scrape in which I was with him, and of which Sir Ralph Payne informed me.[564] A refusal might have confirmed him in the idea that I meant to slight him. I therefore put off my journey one day – sent to Sir Ralph and Lady Payne to beg that they would take me to Hampstead and bring me back – and accompanied them there to dinner at 5 o'clock. There was a large party – lawyers chiefly – Masters in Chancery – and among them Newbolt and his wife. The Chancellor and I were very *gracious* to each other – and so I flatter myself all is well. I returned to town with Sir R. and Ly. Payne, and came immediately home to prepare for setting out next morn[g.]

*13th. [July]* Monday morning at 12 o'clock my chaise, new-lined

[561] Probably Adam Walker (?1731–1821), an author and inventor who taught physics at Eton and Winchester, see *Hinde*, 27
[562] George Bowles (1732–1817) of Wanstead Grove, Essex
[563] Rebecca Bowles (d.1818) who m. 8 June 1766, John Rushout, 1st Baron Northwick
[564] See above pp. 278–9

and new-painted and new-hung, and altogether so smart that you will scarce know it again, came to the door. I fetched little Stratty from his uncle's in the City – set off – and arrived at Eton, at the Provost, Dr. Davies's[565] house, just in time for dinner. Dr. Davies, you know, was Head Master when I was at Eton. We were always very good friends, and since I left Eton, and since he became Provost, he has always been pressing me to give him a day at Eton. Upon hearing of my intention to come with Stratty, he wrote to me to insist upon my making his house my inn, and expecting me yesterday, had made a party to meet me at dinner. I was sorry to find this, as it looked strange and unkind to have disappointed him. To-day we were alone. After dinner I took Stratty to my old dame, Mrs. Hannington's and committed him to her care. The Provost then ordered his chariot and insisted upon taking me up to the Terrace.[566] Nothing in the world makes this good man so happy as a word from the King and Queen to himself or to anybody that is with him. The K. and Q. were walking in full Terrace. 'Stand this way, this way', says Dr. D. 'Here they'll see and speak to you immediately'. 'Probably not', said I, 'for I do not go to Court, and it is likely that they may not know me'. 'I'll warrant you – know you – that he shall – here's Lord Courtown (and so he was) – stand by him – there, between him and me – they know you, I warrant'. And so indeed he took pretty good care that they should, for no sooner were they come up and had begun addressing themselves to Ld. Courtown and to himself, than the Provost, without waiting for any further provocation than a look from the King – 'Mr. C., Sir. Mr. C. – come to Eton to bring a little cousin, Sir – always happy to see a scholar that does us so much credit in the world, Sir' – and on he was going while I looked as foolish as might be. The K. and Q. very good-naturedly did not laugh, but went through their string of questions and compliments – routed up the old story of the Microcosm, and hoped my little cousin would follow my steps both at Eton and *Christchurch* and *elsewhere*. 'If Hetty heard this', thought I.

The King enquired also after Bobus and after Frere – their professions, diligence &c. I wish he had asked after Easley Smith also – it might possibly have been of some service to him that the King should know he was in the army. But he did not ask, and I had not the Provost's easy manner of introduction, by which I could begin, 'Mr. Easley Smith, Sir – Mr. Easley Smith' and so go through his history without solicitation. As soon as the Provost was satisfied with the King's having spoken to us, in the face of the world, he would

[565] Jonathan Davies (1736–1809). Provost of Eton 1791-d.
[566] At Windsor

have consented to return to Eton, had we not seized upon the Bishop of Salisbury,[567] who took us to see his fat son,[568] my contemporary at Eton and at Christ Church ('There's a difference between a Bishop and a Dean' &c.) – now grown thin in person, but large in pluralities, and with the addition of a wife. After this visit we returned to the Lodge. I drank tea with the Provost, and prosed over old Eton stories till 10 o'clock, when I was obliged to go and sup with my old tutor, now Head Master, Dr. Heath, and his wife.

*14. [July]* Tuesday morning. After breakfasting with the Provost, I proceeded to introduce Stratty to Dr. Langford[569] the Master of the Lower School, and Mr. Briggs[570] his tutor – and finding it to be the unanimous opinion as well of them as of the Provost, Dr. Heath, and all whom I consulted upon the subject, that he was yet too young to go upon the foundation, and that a year passed as an Oppidan would be of great advantage to him – I wrote to Hetty to state the arguments and desire her decision upon them. I then took leave of the Provost and of little Stratty, and set out for Clandon.

I never was more shocked, surprized and afflicted than by a paragraph which I accidentally saw in the newspaper of this morning, announcing the sudden death of poor Henry Spencer at Berlin.[571] Such a loss – and so unexpected – I know not what to believe or how to reconcile myself to the possibility of its being true, till on my arrival at Clandon I found the news too fatally confirmed. The family were at dinner. The Archbishop absent. I enquired of Ch. Moore the cause of his absence. He had received an express the day before from Berlin, and was gone to break the dreadful intelligence to the Duke and Duchess of Marlborough, and to support them under the distress which it must occasion to them. Poor Spencer! He was one of those whom I have known and loved best! He had talents as powerful and as various as almost any man of his age, that I ever knew! His judgement and his taste in matters of feeling or of morals, as well as of literature, were almost intuitively quick, and almost unequalled for delicacy and correctness, and accompanied with a playfulness of ridicule which no man ever possessed in greater abundance, or displayed with less offence. The qualities of his heart were equally estimable – a temper even and mild to a remarkable degree – as being joined with a spirit of uncommon erectness and energy, and affections which, though not perhaps easily won, were warm and constant

---

[567] Dr. John Douglas (1721–1807). Bishop of Salisbury, 1791-d.

[568] Rev. William Douglas (c. 1769–1819) who m. Anne, da. of Baron de Brackel of Yverdun, Switzerland. In 1795 he was vicar of Gillingham and Dorset

[569] William Langford (c. 1744–1814). Lower Master at Eton 1775–1803

[570] Thomas Briggs (1767–1831). Assistant master at Eton 1792–1802

[571] He d. at his post of envoy extraordinary to Prussia 3 July 1795

towards all, who had obtained a place in them. To his family he was not only the pride and boast and distinguishing ornament, in the eyes of the world – but he was, as I have heard and as I have in some times had opportunities of observing – the bond of their union, the centre of their affections at home, 'the hoop of gold' that bound them together. His father[572] placed in him great part of his pleasure and all his pride. His mother, capricious, overbearing and intractable to everyone else, to him alone was all that a mother should be. And his sisters, amidst a thousand domestic vexations and perplexities, found in him, and in him only, a certain consolation and protection and repose. His publick character I of course know only from the opinions of others whose situation enabled them to form an estimate of it – but collecting their opinions and comparing them, I find, not that sort of qualified commendation which a young man's exertions obtain, as being *for a young* man eminent or extraordinary, but praise so plain, so ample and so uniform, as could be earned only by the performance of essential good services to the country, not by the promise of them – such as proves that even now he had no superior in the profession to which he belonged, and that had he lived to acquire experience in proportion to his other merits, he would not long have had many equals. What he was as a friend, I know from what I feel in the loss of him. It is true, and perhaps it is a consolatory truth, that we had been so separated from each other for some years, as in some degree to make one less sensible of that loss which, however it operates upon my feelings, occasions no immediate and perceptible void to me in the habits of daily life and of social intercourse or conversation. But I should hate myself if, from such accidental circumstances, I could reconcile myself the sooner to a misfortune essentially so severe, or if because our communication had been by the course of events suspended for a time, not broken off, I were capable of forgetting how delightful it had formerly been, or of ceasing to think how anxiously I had looked forward to the moment when, such interruptions being at an end, our intercourse might and would have been renewed with encreased delight, and to our reciprocal satisfaction and advantage.

I stayed at Clandon till Saturday the 19th. The Archbp. returned from his melancholy duty on Thursday. The cause of Spencer's death, it seems was a cold caught in an open carriage at night – a fever or ague followed, and I am afraid his complaint was either ill-understood or improperly treated. There was no company there during my stay,

---

[572] The 4th Duke of Marlborough, by all accounts an overbearing recluse, quarrelled with his brother, Charles, in 1790 on the marriage of the latter's son to his own daughter; and in 1792 cut relations with his eldest son and heir on the grounds of the latter's extravagance and indolence

except Lord and Lady Bulkeley, who came on Thursday, and who seem very good sort of people. Charles Moore is infinitely better – I trust recovering certainly and completely.

*19th.* [*July*] Saturday. I took leave of Clandon, and arrived at Belmont to dinner. I found there Lord and Lady M[almesbury], their two daughters and Miss Cozens, and Charles Ellis. Ed. Legge had been here for a day or two, but was gone before my arrival. This continued to be the party till Monday the 27th – when Mrs. Robinson arrived, and with her the two boys from Eton, and on Tuesday the 28th came Geo. Ellis. The time during my stay at Belmont I passed very quietly, very uniformly and very much to my liking – walking, riding, reading and writing occupied the morning. We dined at 4. In the evening, beautiful weather – walking and trap-ball on the lawn with the children – and when the evening shut in, billiards, all together – reading, talking and the game of 20 questions, which I brought here, and with which everybody is beyond measure entertained. One day indeed (Tuesday the 21st) we all went to dine with Dr. Warton at his parsonage at Wickham, a village about ten miles from Belmont on the Portsmouth Road. One or two days – but not much oftener, there was company from the neighbourhood to dine at Belmont – the parson of the parish on a Sunday always. One day (Saturday the 25) we all went to Portsmouth or rather to Gosport to see sights and ships – went on board the *Commerce de Marseilles*, the largest ship in the French navy, when taken at Toulon – and the *Tigre* – a 74 – one of Ld. Bridport's three prizes. The dockyard we saw too and all the rarities of the parts – then dined at the inn at Gosport and returned home in the evening.

Excepting these we had no changes or breaks in our quiet manner (Oh! yes, once, one fine evening Charles and I and Lady Malmesbury went in her phaeton to a cricket match on the Downs) – but the time flows tranquilly for near a fortnight. I meant not to have staid so long. One great cause of my prolonging my stay at Belmont beyond the week, which I had already destined for the visit, was that Frere wrote to me to say that he was prevented by his sister's illness from leaving town, and could not meet me at Oxford before Friday or Saturday. That I might give him the meeting on the first of these days I determined to leave Belmont on Thursday the 30th. On that day Lady Malmesbury, George and Charles Ellis set off on a visit to Miss Carter in the Isle of Wight. I was invited too, and had partly promised to go with them – but Ashborne had much stronger calls on my inclination – and so I sent our apologies. They set out early in the morning. The boys and Mrs. Robinson went with them to see Portsmouth. My chaise was at the door, but Lord Malmesbury now left alone, begged me so earnestly and so pleasantly to put off my going till evening, that had he asked even a longer time I could hardly have refused him. As it was I agreed to stay without much hesitation. We passed the whole day tête-à-tête – and had of course much conversation upon many subjects – among others, what naturally interested me most, and what I was much pleased to find so interesting to him, as to induce him to begin upon it and pursue it with great curiosity and kindness – was my own political plans and destination: upon which subject, having lived for 31 years in the political world, and seen the changes and chances of it, with an eye of no common observation, he is the man of all others perhaps best calculated to assist one with sober, useful advice, and he appeared not only willing but anxious to afford me all such assistance. I talked over with him the Under-Secretaryships, the Irish Secretaryship &c. Indeed the Irish Secretaryship he was himself the first to mention, as what he thought most likely to suit me – or *that* perhaps I might not have mentioned to him. (By the bye I have had a letter from King since my coming to Belmont, in which he tells me that upon enquiry he finds the vacant Under-Secyship. in the Home Office to be engaged precisely as Pitt had described it). In short we went over every circumstance connected with my plans and prospects, and Lord M. has wasted a great deal of useless breath, and bound himself by many vain asseverations, if he does not in fact mean to be a very active and a very pleasant friend to me in the pursuit of them. We dined together at an early hour – with the children, and in the evening, having sent Fleming on with the chaise to Alresford, Lord Malmesbury rode with me that stage, and we parted with expressions of desire to meet again, and with a promise on my part that, if we did not meet before, I would certainly pass my Christmas at Belmont.

I got to Popham Lane on Thursday night.

*31st. [July]* Friday I got to Oxford by dinnertime. Frere does not come till to-morrow. Nobody at Oxford except Dawkins at All Souls. Legge was to have been there but has left a note informing me that he has been obliged to go to Sandwell[573]. I dined and supped with Dawkins at All Souls.

*1st August.* Saturday morning I passed in a visit to Sir Digby and Lady Mackworth, whom you have often heard me mention as living at Oxford – on Augustus Legge, whom I now discovered to be here, attending an election of Fellows at the College – of which he is a Fellow – Merton; and on Bartlam,[574] whose name you will find in my former journals from Oxford, who is standing for a Fellowship of that College. Frere arrived at 5 o'clock. We dined and supped at the inn.

[573] Sandwell Park, Worcs., one of the seats of the Earl of Dartmouth
[574] John Bartlam q.v.

Dawkins dined with us and he and Bartlam supped with us. I had a letter from Ed. Legge this morning, desiring me and Frere to take Sandwell in our way to Ashborne. Frere agrees to do so.

*2ᵈ· [August]* Sunday morning. After breakfasting with Dawkins at All Souls, we set out on our journey, meaning to reach Sandwell in the evening. No occurrence on the road except that we overtook Anstruther, the Counsel M.P. &c. – and dined with him at Stratford – and at night, arriving at Birmingham so late that it was impossible to think of going on to Sandwell, we supped with Anstruther and slept at Birmingham.

*3ᵈ· [August]* Monday we reached Sandwell soon after breakfast, found there nobody but Ld. and Ly. Dartmouth, Ly. Charlotte and Mr. Duncombe, to whom she is going to be married – and Ed. Legge. We passed a quiet day.

*4. [August]* Tuesday. Leaving Sandwell early after breakfast and meeting no obstacle but fat Mr. Birch,[575] who stopped us for five minutes on the road, I need not tell you that we arrived to dinner at Ashborne.

[575] Unidentified

# INDEX

Page references are listed under the names and titles of persons as referred to in the text. In order to save space, references on consecutive pages have been hyphenated rather than listed separately. ? before a reference indicates an uncertain identification.

Grey, General Sir Charles, 1st Earl Grey: conduct in the West Indies, 156–7, 245, 262–4; patronage of, 205, 212

Grey, Charles, 2nd Earl Grey: his 'incivility' during C.'s maiden speech, 58; C. attacks his retirement, (1794), 104; his conduct in debate, 47–8, 55–8, 65, 79, 84, 103–4, 139, 180, 186, 191–96, 202 (his peace motion, 1795), 252, 262–3 (on Sir Charles Grey's conduct in the West Indies); mentioned, 95–6

Grey, Sir Henry George (1766–1845), 89, 94–5

Grey de Wilton, 1st Baron and later 1st Earl of Wilton, 227

Grey de Wilton, Lady, 227

Grose, Sir Nash (1740–1814), 122

Guilford, 2nd Earl of, 232

Guilford, Anne, Countess of, 241

Guilford, 5th Earl, see North, Hon. Frederick

Halhed, Nathaniel Brassey (1751–1830), M.P., 207 and n., 214, 232, 239

Hamilton, Lady, 108

Hamilton, Lord Archibald (1770–1827), M.P., 6, 108

Hamilton, Sir Charles 2nd Bt., M.P., 177

Hamilton, 10th Duke of, see Douglas, Mq. of

Hampden, 2nd Visct., 265

Hampden, Catherine, Viscountess, 265

Hannington, Mrs, Dame at Eton, 137 and n. 295, 288

Hardy, Thomas (1752–1832), 8, 155

Hare, James (1747–1804), M.P., 198

Harrison, John (1738–1811), M.P., 77

Hastings, Warren (1732–1818); trial of mentioned, 66, 76–7, 92, 95, 100, 105–6, 110, 113, 117, 119, 122, 124, 126–7, 129, 236, 240

Hatsell, John (1743–1820), clerk of House of Commons, 61

Hatton, Lady Anne, 283

Hawkesbury, 1st Baron and later 1st Earl of Liverpool: resistance and surrender to R. B. Jenkinson's marriage to Lady Theodosia Louisa Hervey, 165–7, 170, 174, 178–9, 191, 200, 210, 216–7, 224, 229; mentioned, 91–2, 96

Hawkesbury, Lady Catherine, 91, 96, 216, 229

Heath, Rev. Dr. George (1745–1822), Headmaster at Eton, 41, 135–6, 289

Henley, 1st Baron, see Eden, Sir Morton

Hervey, Frederick William, see Bristol, 5th Earl and later 1st Mq. of

Hervey, Lady Theodosia Louisa: betrothal and marriage to R. B. Jenkinson, 164–7, 169–70, 179, 183, 190, 200, 229, 236, 239–40, 253, 259; mentioned, 42, 54, 72, 76, 100, 154, 157, 238

Hickel, Karl Anton (1745–98), artist, 10, 113, 120

Higginson, Mr ?William, merchant, 43 and n., 127, 204, 221, 223

Hinchcliffe, Henry (c. 1768–1848), 145

Hobart, Hon. George Vere (1761–1802), 45

Hobart, Lord, later 4th Earl of Buckinghamshire, 39, 44–5, 47, 53, 56, 61, 87

Hobart, Lady Margaretta, 39, 45, 53

Holland, 3rd Baron, 6, 66, 68, 94, 139, 150, 182, 249

Holroyd, Miss, da. of 1st Baron Sheffield, 257

Home Office: use of spies by, 154–5; patronage of, 275, 278; personnel of 274–6, 278, 282, 292

Hood, Admiral Sir Samuel, later 1st Visct. Hood, 38

Hopkins, Richard (c. 1728–99), M.P., 159

Hotham, Miss, 30

Howe, Admiral Richard, 1st Earl Howe, 32, 34–6, 121

Howe, Mrs Caroline, sister of Earl Howe, 76, 108, 116–7, 126, 141–2

Hunn, Mrs Mary Anne, née Costello, C.'s mother: relations with C., 4, 11, 33, 61, 119–21, 128, 230–1; her eye ointment, Collysium, 33 and n. 40, 140; mentioned, 3, 36

Hunn, Richard, C.'s step-father, 4, 231

Hunn, William, C.'s step-brother, 101, 152

Huskisson, William (1770–1830), M.P., 104, 158, 190

Ireland, William Henry (1777–1835), author and forger, 230 and n. 458

Irish Club, see under Clubs